Hollywood Death and Scandal Sites

For Barb,
who's put up with me for 25 years.
And for Abby, Teddy and Colin,
who are still learning how.

And to my friends,
Carolyn, Jody, Dick, Tony and Judy,
Tom and Mary, Park and Carol,
Liz, and Mitch (thanks for the apartment during all
my L.A. trips), who have listened to my stories for years
and still pretend they're paying attention.

And to Lew Goldstein,
who used to wash my car.

Hollywood Death and Scandal Sites

*Sixteen Driving Tours with Directions
and the Full Story, from Tallulah
Bankhead to River Phoenix*

by
E.J. FLEMING

McFarland & Company, Inc., Publishers
Jefferson, North Carolina, and London

Library of Congress Cataloguing-in-Publication Data

Fleming, E.J., 1954–
Hollywood death and scandal sites: sixteen driving tours
with directions and the full story, from Tallulah Bankhead to
River Phoenix / by E.J. Fleming.
p.   cm.
Includes bibliographical references and index.
ISBN 0-7864-0160-5 (softcover : 50# alkaline paper) ∞
1. Motion picture actors and actresses—California—Los Angeles—Death.
2. Motion picture actors and actresses—California—Los Angeles—Biography.
3. Los Angeles (Calif.)—Guidebooks.   I. Title.
PN1998.2.F558   2000
791.43'028'092279494—dc21   99-56773

British Library Cataloguing-in-Publication data are available

Manufactured in the United States of America

*McFarland & Company, Inc., Publishers
Box 611, Jefferson, North Carolina 28640
www.mcfarlandpub.com*

Contents

Introduction   1

Tour 1—Old Hollywoodland   5
Tour 2—Hollywood Central   35
Tour 3—Hollywood Hills   45
Tour 4—The Sunset Strip   56
Tour 5—West Hollywood   62
Tour 6—Hancock Park   70
Tour 7—Beverly Hills, Coldwater Canyon   79
Tour 8—Beverly Hills, Benedict Canyon   93
Tour 9—Beverly Hills Flats, South of Sunset   121
Tour 10—Bel Air   145
Tour 11—Westwood and Century City   155
Tour 12—Brentwood   168
Tour 13—Pacific Palisades, Santa Monica and Malibu   183
Tour 14—San Fernando Valley   202
Tour 15—Far San Fernando Valley   221
Tour 16—Locations Off Maps   224

Bibliography   255
Index   263

"I hated Hollywood."
—Grace Kelly

"Hollywood will pay you ten thousand for a kiss,
and fifty cents for your soul…"
—Marilyn Monroe

Cecil B. DeMille telegram to Jesse Lasky, 1913:
Flagstaff no good. STOP. Want to rent barn in
place called Hollywood. STOP. $75.00 a month. STOP Cecil

Lasky telegram reply to DeMille, 1913:
OK on month to month only. STOP.
Don't make any long commitments. STOP. Jesse

Introduction

Nobody is sure why death and scandal are such fascinating topics. They are even more fascinating when someone famous is involved. Nowhere is there a bigger concentration of famous someones than in Hollywood. It is the perfect backdrop, with sun, beautiful women, incredible mansions, and too many Rolls-Royces to count—all in a place created by an industry based on fantasy. With the movie industry's dark history noted for all kinds of excess—from obscene wealth to sex—stories of Hollywood death and scandal are even more interesting.

The movies weren't born in Hollywood, but in Princeton, New Jersey, in 1889 when Thomas Edison unveiled his Kinetoscope, which let people watch 15-second "motion pictures" for a penny. The 50-foot-long films moved over rollers exposed to an electric light through a revolving shutter. In 1893 Edison built the world's first self-contained movie studio, a small cabin named "Black Maria" for its black tin walls. That same year he released the ten-second feature *The Sneeze*, which showed a friend sneezing. The film debuted on April 14, 1894, at the Holland Brothers Kinetoscope Parlor at 1155 Broadway in New York City, an old shoe store housing ten of Edison's machines. For 25 cents—an hour's wage—five separate shows were available, none longer than 16 seconds.

The Kinetoscope's downfall was that only one person at a time could look through the eyepiece, which limited ticket sales, so engineer Thomas Armat developed the "Vitascope," which revolutionized the movies by projecting a series of stills onto a wall fast enough to simulate movement. Now moviemakers could connect separate scenes into a full-length movie, and parlor owners could fill row after row of chairs. Absolutely anything and everything was put on film, and by 1897, 10,000 Vitascope parlors were packing in eager viewers.

The movie industry was off and running. The first permanent theater was Thomas Lally's Electric Theater in Los Angeles, which opened in 1902, and three years later rival John Harris offered lavish seats and piano accompaniment in his "nickelodeon." The debut attraction was Edwin S. Porter's 1903 saga *The Great Train Robbery*, which netted Harris $22.50. Within a month his take was $1,000 a week. The same movie ran continually from sunrise until midnight. During 1908 over 10 million Americans saw nickelodeon movies, and by 1910 the nickelodeon network was replaced by 10,000 full-fledged movie theaters.

The real relationship between the movies and Hollywood began in 1906 when several filmmakers—led by D.W. Griffith's Biograph Films and the Nestor Film Company—came from New York to California for winter filming. The area offered excellent topography for outdoor scenes and cheap real estate. Although Los Angeles was already an oil boomtown, movie demand pushed real estate prices up from $700 an acre in 1910 to $10,000 an acre in 1915.

When the studios came in 1906 Beverly Hills was still just a stark wasteland of bean fields, orange groves, and empty canyons named Morocco Junction. After several years of drilling failed oil wells, Burton Green's Rodeo Water and Land Company borrowed the name of his Beverly Farms, Massachusetts, hometown and laid out a hotel and housing project to recoup some of his losses. When his homesites didn't sell, Green made maps showing the locations of the movie stars' homes to attract star struck buyers. It was the birth of the "star map." Slowly the houses began selling, and early in 1911 Green finished his crown jewel—the Beverly Hills Hotel, sitting in pink splendor amid the bean fields, without a house in view for miles. The popular new hotel (with the only bar in town) fueled rapid growth in Beverly Hills, but it still boasted a population of only 550 in 1913.

In 1913 the Centaur Film Company was the first studio to relocate totally to Hollywood, paying $40 a month to rent the dilapidated Blondeau Tavern Barbershop at Sunset and Gower, using the nearby fields to make movies. Soon after, Cecil B. DeMille ventured west after scouting Arizona sites for locations. Visitors to the Hollywood Bowl Museum can tour the barn DeMille rented during that trip, which was also used for years on the set of the television show *Bonanza*. It was originally part of a farm on a corner at Selma and Vine and was eventually used as the set for hundreds of movies. DeMille began filming his first Hollywood movie on December 29, 1913—the silent classic *Squaw Man*, one of 300 movies made during 1914. DeMille used local stage actors alongside real cowboys and Indians, and after costs of just $12,000 *Squaw Man* grossed $225,000.

Huge profits like that fueled a wild race to Hollywood. Adolph Zukor's Famous Players Studio and lead actress Mary Pickford arrived in 1914, as did Mack Sennett's Keystone Studio and Hal Roach's Roach Studios. Thomas Ince and a host of others soon followed. But the conservative locals didn't warm to the outsiders. While DeMille filmed *Squaw Man* he was shot at twice by angry residents, and the first negative of the film was sabotaged, forcing him to sleep in the film lab to protect the only other copy. Hotels boasted signs ordering "No dogs! No Jews! No Actors!" Even the word "movies" was a slur, DeMille telling his first Hollywood neighbors "those 'movies' are crazy" so they would rent him a house. When no one in Hollywood would sell Carl Laemmle land for a studio in 1915, he went to the barren San Fernando Valley and registered a 250-acre lot as a municipality. Named Universal City, it was designed solely as a studio for moviemaking.

By 1919 Beverly Hills had begun a transformation from bucolic outpost into hot property when the "King and Queen of the Movies" moved in. Newlyweds Douglas Fairbanks and Mary Pickford bought a 20-year-old hunting lodge high up a dirt road in the San Ysidro Canyon and enlarged the small cabin into a palace boasting 50 opulent rooms and the biggest "pool" in the United States—30,000 square feet and bordered on two sides by a sandy beach. The fawning press dubbed the chateau "Pickfair."

People began flocking to the area, even though from Hollywood to the ocean Sunset Boulevard was only a rutted dirt road. By the early 1920s Beverly Hills had replaced Hollywood as the residence of choice for the movie elite. Pickfair and the surrounding streets became the focus of fan interest from around the world. "Flickers" (so named because the images flickered on screen, later shortened to "flicks") were the fifth largest industry in the United States by 1917, and while a typical family earned less than $1,000 a year, producers and stars earned $10,000 a week. Such incredible cash attracted enormous greed, unspeakable evil and spellbinding scandal.

Most early industry scandals were drug-related since drugs were abundant, cheap and the long-term effects still unknown. Heroin, cocaine and morphine were easy to find; the better-known drug dealers had offices close by the studios, ensuring that fixes were never far away. Dealers had names like "Captain Spaulding" and "Mr. Fix-it" and dealt through a network of low-level studio couriers. The most famous dealer—"The Count"—put heroin inside peanut shells to be sold by the bag. Stars used drugs to cure the hangovers caused by their preferred drinks—"bathtub gin" or fruit punches laced with 200-proof alcohol.

The first casualty was violet-eyed Olive Thomas, a dazzling beauty discovered when she was 14. By 17 "Ollie" was a world-famous Zeigfeld Follies star and the first "Vargas Girl." Married to Mary Pickford's little brother Jack, she was dubbed by artist Alberto Vargas "The Most Beautiful Woman in the World." Thomas was also the first star earning more fame by death than life. During her September 1920 honeymoon she was found dead in the Royal Suite at Paris' Hotel Crillon, lying nude atop some of her 150 furs. Despondent over her and Jack's cocaine addictions, she had taken a mouthful of mercury. Adding to her despair, Jack had infected her with syphilis, then considered untreatable. Jack himself overdosed just three years later.

Even virginal Mary Pickford was touched by scandal, when rumors swirled that her world-famous 1921 wedding to Douglas Fairbanks was preceded by an affair. At the time, adultery would have ended the careers of even these two enormous stars.

Within a year the "King of Comedy" Roscoe Arbuckle was tarnished by a widely reported scandal. "Fatty" skyrocketed from a $3-a-week extra in 1913 to a $3 million-a-year ($150 million today) star in 1921. When a young actress died at his 1921 Labor Day party—a year to the day that Olive Thomas died—he was unfairly charged with manslaughter. He was acquitted after three publicity-driven trials, but studio heads pulled his films from theaters, ending his career. He was reduced to working as an assistant using the name "Will B. Good" and died broke at 42.

Within a week of the 1922 Arbuckle verdict the fatal shooting of director William Desmond Taylor rocked the industry. Taylor was linked to child star Mary Miles Minter. Her image as "the next Mary Pickford" was destroyed when the 17-year-old's monogrammed panties and graphic love letters to Taylor were found in the 50-year-old homosexual's home.

A month after the Taylor murder, the world's most popular male star was quietly hospitalized for a fatal morphine addiction. Dashing Wally Reid starred in 100 movies, and from his 1910 debut until his 1923 death made more movies and more money than any star of his time. One debutante fan traded a $25,000 emerald necklace just to peek into his dressing room. Fans were stunned when Reid died in a private sanitarium, but the trade had known about his little secret for years.

He began using drugs after suffering a neck injury in a 1920 movie and was long rumored to be a hopeless addict. In March 1922 Reid collapsed on a movie set and crumbled to the floor in tears. He was quietly taken away in a private ambulance and died an agonizing death all alone in a padded cell at the Banksia Place Sanitarium several months later. It was rumored that his wife Dorothy Dandridge let doctors put the unfortunate man "to sleep." When Reid died the California Board of Pharmacy announced that it had 500 movie people on its drug addict rolls.

The reeling business was further shaken by the 1924 death of director Thomas Ince, carried off William Randolph Hearst's yacht *Oneida* after a Labor Day cruise in San Diego. Whether you believe the Hearst press or the shipboard witnesses, Ince either died at home from indigestion or was shot to death by Hearst. Crew members confirmed that the insanely jealous Hearst shot Ince after finding Ince having sex with *his* mistress, actress Marion Davies. San Diego papers screamed "Producer Shot on Yacht!!!" but copies of those early editions soon vanished forever.

At the same time, Barbara LaMarr—

"The Girl Who Was Too Beautiful"—was being killed by drugs. A 1924 overdose publicized her problem, and a 1926 arrest while carrying 40 cubes of morphine confirmed that it would kill her. Prosecutors realized she wouldn't survive jail and let her go home to die, which she did soon after. Louis B. Mayer described LaMarr as the most beautiful woman in the world, and later paid her homage by giving Czech starlet Hedwig Kiesler the name Hedy Lamarr.

Within a year of LaMarr's death over 30 major stars and Hollywood notables were dead of drug overdoses. Shell-shocked industry heads and fans alike were stunned by the endless carnage and scandal. The studios enacted morals clauses and developed a conduct code, but they couldn't stop the death. Fed by the excesses of the business, it has continued to this day. Whether it is Arbuckle, Monroe, Barr or Doherty, Hollywood still generates an uproar. Despite carefully constructed images, the stars, studios and ever-present "fixers" can't stop the continuing litany of scandal.

That's how this book came about. There are countless tour guides, maps, and tapes showing where stars lived, worked, or played. Some show how they died, some where they're buried. Most are redundant and almost none are very well researched. A good number are downright fiction. Until now no guide has presented the tour highlights—or lowlights—showing where all this mayhem actually happened.

It is admittedly more interesting to see where Marilyn Monroe died, where Bugsy was shot, or O.J.'s mansion than to see the gates at Barbra's house. That is why this guide is available, so enjoy and don't feel guilty. Your friends may tease you for buying such a morbid book but pretty soon their curiosity may also be piqued.

The tours are designed to be continuous with as little backtracking as possible.

Each can be traveled by finding a starting point on a local map and following the directions from there. *The Thomas Guides* are a good bet for maps and can be found in most bookstores. Before you set off it is important to keep several things in mind.

Most importantly, a majority of the locations on the tours are *private property*. It is usually okay to take pictures, but *do not* approach any homes or residents. Respect the owner's right to privacy and remember to follow cemetery rules about pictures. Basically, have fun but don't bother the locals.

Touring is more fun if you are organized. Have maps and information handy and bring plenty of film. It also helps to list pictures *as* they're taken so you know which house is which when you're looking at 150 pictures a month later. Drive carefully and *wear your seat belt*. Pay attention to roadway and traffic conditions. Most streets are well-traveled and busy, so stay alert. Every attempt has been made to verify directions and availability, but road repairs or unforeseen conditions may force you to detour—more reason to have maps for help.

It is easier to anticipate specific stops if you remember that houses are numbered sequentially. The "spread" between houses is usually the same—for example 804...806... 808, 701...703...705, 12000...12004... 12008, and so on. Note the spread on each street and it is easy to plan stops. To take pictures, pull safely off the roadway as far as conditions allow. Never take pictures from a moving car or from the roadway! A careful stop allows you to read the stories, and you'll take better shots. Don't be embarrassed taking pictures—being a tourist is socially acceptable here, and the only people around will likely be gardeners, nannies and other tourists. You won't see them again, so why be embarrassed? Enjoy your tour—when you're done, you will have seen a true history of the *real* Hollywood and the movies!

Tour 1:
Old Hollywoodland

Begin Tour 1 at 6000 Santa Monica Boulevard, just east of the Hollywood (101) Freeway, between Rossmore and Western Avenues:

The oldest of the movieland cemeteries, Hollywood Memorial Park is guaranteed to put you in the mood for the rest of the tours. Opened in 1899, Hollywood Memorial was the cemetery of choice for movieland until Forest Lawn became popular in the 1930s. Dozens of famous names throughout, but begin at the Santa Monica Boulevard gate. Enter and drive past the fountain to the first street. Go left on Maple and within 50 feet on the left next to the road by the bushes is the grave of Carl "Alfalfa" Switzer, the former *Our Gang* child star who was shot to death in a 1959 argument about a borrowed dog. Continue through Woodland Avenue to Midland Avenue, left on Midland as it curves to the right. Just off the roadway on the right side you can find director John Huston (*The Maltese Falcon* [1941], *The Red Badge of Courage* [1951], and *Chinatown* [1974]) in Lot 8, and actor Adolphe Menjou (*The Front Page* [1931], *The Three Musketeers* [1921], and *A Star Is Born* [1937]) in Lot 11. The Huston stone was imported from his native Ireland. Around the corner on your left on Lakeview is Griffith J. Griffith, who donated all of the acreage which became Griffith Park to the city of Los Angeles. Griffith tried to shoot his first wife to death, but only shot her through the eyes.

Continue around to the right on Lakeview and notice the double crypt next to the road, the grave of Cecil B. DeMille. Walk past DeMille down toward the water—beneath the two tall evergreens and the large urn is actress Janet Gaynor, winner of the first Academy Award in 1928, and her husband, movie costume designer Gilbert Adrian. Gaynor, who starred in dozens of films including *Seventh Heaven* (1927) and *Street Angel* (1928), was killed in a San Francisco cab crash that also injured actress Mary (*Peter Pan*) Martin. Gaynor is interred next to her husband, the bisexual Gilbert Adrian, born Adolph Greenburg in Waterbury, Connecticut. Adrian was discovered by Irving Thalberg designing women's clothing in a Paris boutique, and hired him to create costumes for Valentino. He became chief costume designer for MGM, a post he held from 1928 through 1942, responsible for groundbreaking wardrobes for Valentino, Marlene Dietrich, Greta Garbo, and Joan Crawford. Macy's sold over 100,000 copies of the Adrian dress Crawford wore in *Letty Lynton* (1932), and when Dietrich began dressing like a man in Adrian-designed clothes, the world was stunned. The brilliant Adrian also designed each and every costume worn by the "Munchkins" in *The Wizard of Oz* (1939), personally selecting every color, pattern, material, button and bow.

Just below the Gaynor-Adrian grave,

Top: The shooting death of Carl "Alfalfa" Switzer was the result of an argument over a lost dog, but it is not known if it is the same dog on this headstone. *Bottom:* The impressive crypt of MGM studio head Cecil B. DeMille.

notice the decorated grave on the right near the pond. This is the reputed grave site of "The Woman in Black," actress Ditra Flame, who for 30 years stood vigil over Rudolph Valentino's grave on the anniversary of his death, dressed in black veiled mourning clothes and quietly reciting Valentino's poems to anyone listening. Next to her on the right is a headstone for Jayne Mansfield, though she isn't buried here.

Walk along the water about 50 feet to the right (as you stand facing up the hill toward DeMille) of Mansfield and you will find Virginia Rappe, whose simple grave (lot 257) is marked with a small evergreen. Rappe was a party girl whose mysterious death during a Roscoe Arbuckle hotel party ruined him. When she died, rumors swirled that Arbuckle had smothered her with his 300 pound body and had violated her with a champagne bottle, but more than likely her death from peritonitis was the result of a botched abortion. Next to her is the grave of her boyfriend Henry Lehrmann, a minor silent film director dubbed "Pathé" by other studio workers for his annoying habit of describing himself as a famous French director. He was actually a streetcar conductor from Vienna. Mack Sennett nicknamed Lehrmann

"Suicide" after he watched Lehrmann release a lion into a crowd of extras to film their reactions. The bizarre Lehrman worshiped Rappe's memory for the rest of his life, visiting her grave every Sunday and buying the plot next to her. He was also a prominent witness for the prosecution, although he knew almost nothing about the weekend party.

Continue around and notice the large mausoleum down by the lake with the name "Douras" over the entrance. It is the family crypt for Marion (Douras) Davies, lifelong mistress of publisher William Randolph Hearst. Buried with her is Arthur (*Dagwood*) Lake, who was married to Marion's favorite niece, actress Patricia Lake. Rumors persist that Lake was actually the illegitimate daughter of Davies and Hearst. They supported her for her whole life, she lived with Marion, and was left half of Marion's estate. Lake told friends that Hearst told her that she was, indeed, his daughter. At the back corner of the Douras tomb is Hannah Chaplin, mother of legend Charlie (Lot 260). Soon after he brought her here from England, she fell ill and died.

Just in front of the Douras crypt is the memorial bench of Tyrone Power, star of *The*

B-movie actress Virginia Rappe's death at a party hosted by "Fatty" Arbuckle destroyed his career.

Top: Buried with actress Marion (Douras) Davies in the family crypt are her parents, nephew Arthur "Dagwood" Lake, and his wife Patricia Lake. It has long been rumored that Lake was the illegitimate child of Davies and her lover, William Randolph Hearst. In front of the Douras crypt is Tyrone Power's headstone. *Bottom:* The grave site of Charlie Chaplin's mother, who died in a sanitarium shortly after he brought her from England to the United States.

Mark of Zorro (1940), *The Sun Also Rises* (1957), and *Witness for the Prosecution* (1957). He suffered a fatal heart attack while filming a swordfight in *Solomon and Sheba* (1959), only 44 at the time of his death.

Continue around the pond to the Cathedral Mausoleum. On the lawn in front are singer Nelson Eddy (Lot 89) and Columbia Studios founder Harry Cohn (Lot 86), who chose the same tomb as DeMille's to annoy his rival. He also placed it on a raised platform to make it look bigger than DeMille's. Cohn was called "White Fang" and "a man you stand in line to hate." It was said he physically or verbally raped every female employee he ever had. His studio office door had no handles and was operated from a button at his desk: nobody entered or left unless he allowed it. When he was sued by actor Charles Vidor for abusive treatment, the judge ruled in Cohn's favor, saying that abuse was the nature of the profession and Cohn's abuse was indiscriminate and habitual. When Cohn was told that his favorite starlet Kim Novak was having an affair with Sammy Davis, Jr., he apparently had a heart attack that led to his death. One wag credited the large crowd at his funeral to people "making sure he was dead," and one mourner was quoted as saying "this is what you get when you give people what they want." To the right of the Cathedral Mausoleum is the fabulous grave of Douglas Fairbanks, who has his own reflecting pond.

Inside the Cathedral Mausoleum, in the second hall on your right is William Cunningham Deane-Tanner, better known as William Desmond Taylor. His unsolved 1922 murder helped bring about the downfall of several major stars amid a scandal of sex, drugs, and the movies. In the alcove directly across from Taylor are Horace and Daeida Wilcox, who originally laid out their "Hollywood" community to be a devoutly Christian community, giving land free to any Protestant churches that asked them for some.

Further down, in the Alcove of Remembrance (niche 5, tier 1, corr. C) is actor

Peter Lorre, star of the Bogart movies *The Maltese Falcon, Casablanca,* and *They Drive by Night.* Straight across the main lobby in crypt 1205—which will always have fresh flowers adorning the face—is Rudolph Valentino. For years after his death, "The Lady in Black" visited the crypt on the anniversary of his death, threw away any flowers there and replaced them with her own red roses. She would then spend hours reciting poems by Valentino. Valentino's vault is directly above that of June Mathis, a silent movie casting director responsible for discovering the former New York cabaret dancer and bringing him to Hollywood.

Across from Valentino near the entrance is actor Peter Finch (*Network* [1976]) in crypt 1224. In the next alcove by the window near the bottom is Barbara "The Girl Who Was Too Beautiful" LaMarr, who died in 1926 at 30 from anorexia, alcoholism and drug abuse. Eleanor Powell is in the main foyer, her remains inside the replica of a book with her name on the binding (niche 432, tier 3, Foyer E/W). In the area outside and behind the Cathedral Mausoleum you can find Woody Herman (crypt 6680, Unit 10).

Douglas Fairbanks, Sr.'s memorial is just to the right of the Cathedral Mausoleum. Continue on Maple Avenue past Fairbanks to Woodland. Just up on the right side of Woodland you can find Theodore Roberts, one of Hollywood's first character actors. Roberts arrived in Hollywood in 1915 and starred in hundreds of silent movies, usually cast as the tall mustachioed sheriff or bartender. Continue on Maple to the next cross-street, Pineland, go left and just past the middle of the block on your left next to the road is Bugs Bunny voice wizard Mel Blanc. His marker reads "That's All Folks." Across the street along the row of palm trees is actor Paul Muni, star of *Scarface* (1933). It is hard to find, but look between the second and third palm trees and a little south.

Mobster Bugsy Siegel is interred in an upper crypt back in the right corner of the Beth Olam Mausoleum, behind a simple

The grave site of screen legend and Hollywood pioneer Douglas Fairbanks, Sr.

marker that says "In Loving Memory from the Family."

The Abbey of the Psalms is next to the Beth Olam. Enter through the older main entrance in the middle back of the building. Just inside the last alcove on the left is character actor Louise Calhern on the wall in the main aisle (niche 308, tier 3). Nearby is actor James Cruze (niche 211, tier 2). At the rear in the last alcove on the left is Renee Adoree (crypt 219). Born Jeanne de la Fonte, the daughter of circus performers, Adoree was a French actress who starred in King Vidor's *The Big Parade* (1925) and dozens of

movies during a 30-year career. Just past Adoree on the same side is director Victor (*Gone with the Wind*) Fleming (crypt 2081, corr. G-2). Walk through the aisle to the next alcove toward the front of the building, and on the left is Darla (*Little Rascals*) Hood, who ended her career as the voice of Charlie the Tuna in television tuna ads (crypt 7231, corr. G-4). Across from Hood, down the small aisle going toward the front of the building, you can find director and studio head Jesse Lasky on the wall on the left (crypt 2196, corr. G-3). Lasky was an original partner with Cecil B. DeMille, responsible for films such as *Sergeant York* (1941), *Rhapsody in Blue* (1945), and *The Great Caruso* (1951). Just to the right in the alcove in front of Lasky, to the right in the nearby Sanctuary of Peace, is actor Clifton "Mr. Belvedere" Webb (crypt 2350, corr. G-5). Webb reportedly haunts this area, causing mysterious night lights and loud noises in empty hallways. He also haunts his former home in Beverly Hills. The Talmadge Sisters—Natalie, Norma and Constance—are interred in the Sanctuary of Eternal Love near the front corridor near the front door under a beautiful marble crypt and stained-glass window (corr. G-7).

If you reenter through the main door, enter the alcove on your right and take your first aisle on the right toward the front of the building. Just to your left in the large alcove, facing the front, is Charles Chaplin, Jr., author-actor-son of the legendary Charlie (crypt 1065, corr. E-2). Continue through this alcove toward the front to the last alcove, and you can find actress Joan Hackett in the far left (front) corner facing the alcove. Her amusing marker states, "Go away—I'm asleep" (crypt 2341, corr. D-3). Walk toward the exit at the end of the hall by the main

entrance, and on your left in the last alcove on the left you can find the crypt of Edward G. Robinson, Jr., son of the *Little Caesar* star and a minor actor in his own right (crypt 4386, corr. E-4).

In the columbarium, you can find actress Agnes Ayers (niche 3, tier 3, lower south wall), actress Bebe Lyons (niche 5, tier 1, corr. C), and actor Ben Lyon (niche 432, tier 3, main foyer). Bandleader Nelson Riddle's crypt is in the T-building (niche 702, tier 7, corr. T-1).

(Exit Santa Monica. Left two blocks to Gower. Right to:)

1225 Gower Street, Philip Van Zandt suicide site

On February 16, 1958, 54-year-old actor Philip Van Zandt committed suicide in his apartment here. The Amsterdam-born actor, who appeared in over 300 films from 1920 to 1957, began his career in Laurel and Hardy's *Boobs in Arms* and later joined Orson Welles' Mercury Theater. Van Zandt had a minor role in Welles' *War of the Worlds* and

Movie star Joan Hackett did not want to be bothered anymore.

starred in the classic *Citizen Kane* (1941), *Life with Father* (1947) and dozens of "Three Stooges" shorts such as *Three Arabian Nuts* and *Dopey Dicks*. Van Zandt's death was caused by a massive overdose of sleeping pills. Appropriately, his last movie appearance was in the 1957 film *The Lonely Man*.

The next cross-street (north) is Lexington, which during the early 1900s was Hollywood's Park Avenue, home to the movie elite. Cornelius Cole founded "Colgrove," now South Hollywood, in 1893, naming ten Hollywood streets for members of his family. He suffered a fatal heart attack in his mansion at 6121 Lexington in 1921. Cecil B. DeMille's first Hollywood mansion was across from Cole at 6136, where he lived before moving to a Laughlin Park estate in 1915.

(Gower to Afton. Left to:)

6230 Afton Place, Marie Prevost death site

Here at the Aftonian Apartments, 43-year-old Marie Prevost was found dead on January 23, 1937. Mack Sennett's first "Sennett Bathing Beauty" began in *Uncle Tom's Cabin* (1919) and starred in Ernst Lubitsch's *The Marriage Circle* (1924), *Three Women* (1924) and *Kiss Me Again* (1925). When her career ended with the advent of sound she drifted into "B" movies and alcoholism, dying here of acute alcohol poisoning and "extreme malnutrition." Found lying in a pile of bounced checks and an I.O.U. signed to pal Joan Crawford, she was covered with tiny bite marks from her dachshund, who had tried for two or three days to either wake her up or have lunch.

(Afton to Vine. Right to Sunset. Left to:)

Hollywood Athletic Club, 6525 Sunset Boulevard, Tyrone Power, Sr., death site

Built in 1920, the Hollywood Athletic Club was the most popular residence for male stars, a private club offering plush apart-

ments, gym facilities, and privacy. John Barrymore hosted weekly drinking parties in his ninth floor penthouse, later occupied by John Wayne. Another 1920s resident was movie leading man Ramon Novarro, but he preferred young male prostitutes over drinking pals.

Silent screen star Tyrone Power, Sr., was a longtime resident of the club. On December 30, 1931, he suffered a fatal heart attack here and died in the arms of his distraught teenaged son. Tyrone Power, Jr., went on to even greater film renown than his father.

(Sunset to:)

6665 Sunset Boulevard, Charles Crawford murder site

During the 1920s, attorney Charles Crawford was a local power broker, putting deals together between police, mobsters, studios, or anyone else willing to pay. At a time when the police and D.A.'s offices were the most corrupt in the country, Crawford brokered shady deals for corrupt local officials, becoming the wealthiest—and most feared—lawyer in L.A.

On the afternoon of May 20, 1931, he was visited at his offices by David Clark, a district attorney turned reform candidate for district court judge. Shots rang out, and Crawford and a friend—reporter Herbert Spencer—were killed. Though neither was armed, Clark was somehow acquitted, claiming self-defense. Rumors that Clark was on the take never died. His huge mansion at 162 South Detroit at Beverly Drive fueled many of the rumors. The mansion being so large that it is now a dozen apartments, Clark's critics rightly wondered how a young assistant D.A. afforded the digs.

(Sunset to Las Palmas. Right to:)

1738 North Las Palmas, Las Palmas Hotel ("Black Dahlia" home)

For over 60 years the Las Palmas Hotel on the right at Yucca has been home for thousands of souls struggling to make it in movies. In the 1940s one of the nameless tenants was 22-year-old Bostonian Beth Short. The dark-haired beauty lived anonymously, sharing a cheap apartment with friends, trying to find work and doing what was necessary to pay bills. By 1946 the work was prostitution, and Beth was a fixture at local Hollywood bars.

She lived in a succession of rundown Hollywood hotels like the Hawthorne at 1611 Orange and later at 1852 Cherokee, sneaking out when she could not afford a dollar a night rent. Short never found fame as an actress but as "The Black Dahlia" she became a household name after her dismembered and meticulously cleaned body was found in a vacant lot near Santa Monica and Crenshaw on January 15, 1947. The mutilated body had been cut in half and dumped among the winter weeds. Newspaper reporters dubbed Short the "Black Dahlia" for her black clothes and a flower tattoo on her thigh that had been sliced from the body. For months her killer, who was never found, taunted police with notes which included some of Short's personal belongings.

The **Aftonian Apartments, site of Marie Prevost's 1937 death, remain unchanged to this day.**

The Dahlia mystery may have been explained by author Jan Knowlton's 1995 book *Daddy Was the Black Dahlia Killer*. Her brutal father routinely beat his wife and children and threatened to kill them. It seems that everywhere George Knowlton lived until his 1962 death—from Boston to Los Angeles—young women died. During that time over 25 murdered woman were proven to have had contact with him, including young Beth Short. His daughter Jan remembered watching him kill "Aunt Beth" with a hammer in their Anaheim garage, memories that became the basis for her book. Knowlton frequented bars favored by Short, and her friends knew that her boyfriend "George" was a Massachusetts hunter working in a local foundry. Knowlton was from Massachusetts and always worked in foundries, and although his daughter knew details of

the murder that had been sealed in police files and known only to detectives, police have discounted her story.

Johnny Arthur was a popular vaudevillian discovered by Florenz Ziegfeld, who moved on to become a major movie star from 1920 through the 1940s. The veteran movie comic appeared in over 200 movies in the 1930s and 1940s, but by the 1950s he had no movie work and had completely disappeared from view. When old friend Don Marlowe stopped at an out of the way Los Angeles café for coffee, he was stunned to see the once-huge star washing dishes in the back. The humiliated Arthur committed suicide the next morning in his hotel room at the Las Palmas, which was costing him $5 a week.

The Las Palmas Hotel was also the set for Julia Roberts' apartment in the 1992 film

Pretty Woman. On the Las Palmas side of the building, you may recognize the fire escape climbed by Richard Gere in the romantic final scene.

(Yucca right to Cherokee, site of:)

Yucca and Cherokee, Percy Kilbride accidental death site

Percy Kilbride starred in hundreds of movies after debuting in *White Woman* (1933) and *Keeper of the Flame* (1935), but was most noted as "Pa Kettle" in the movie series about the famous Kettle family. Beginning with *The Egg and I* (1947) he reprised the role a dozen times until *Ma and Pa Kettle in Waikiki* (1955). The 76-year-old Kilbride and friend Ralf Belmont were both struck by a car at this spot returning from the market to their homes at the Lido Apartments at 6500 Yucca. Belmont died at the scene and Kilbride died several days later of severe brain injuries on December 11, 1964.

On this corner at 1749 Cherokee stood the mansion purchased by L. Frank Baum after earning millions from his children's book series about a mythical land called Oz. Baum nicknamed his estate "Ozcot," built a huge aviary for 300 birds, and lived there until his death in the home in 1919 at 63. His wife Maud lived long enough to see the popular book become a world-famous movie in 1939. Baum actually wrote 13 books about his fabled make-believe land, but only one, *The Wizard of Oz,* is remembered today. His last words were, "now we can cross the shifting sands," which probably referred to the never ending desert that surrounded his storybook world. A former apartment of Beth "Black Dahlia" Short is just up the block at 1842 Cherokee.

(Yucca to Whitley. Left up the hill to:)

Whitley Heights, Valentino, Bushman, LaMarr homes, Beulah Bondi death site

Named after H.J. Whitley, who built the 1918 hilltop tract to copy an Italian village, Whitley Heights was the "Beverly Hills of the Silent Era" and home to dozens of stars. Jean Harlow lived at the top of the hill at 2015 Whitley Avenue. Go right on Whitley Terrace around to Wedgewood Place, where Rudolph Valentino and Natacha Rambova lived at 7667 in a mansion torn down for the freeway. Just past Wedgewood, down right on Milner at the dead-end at 2047 (or 74) Watsonia Terrace is Villa Villambrosa, built for Janet Gaynor and husband Gilbert Adrian and later rented by Dame Judith Anderson. Gloria Swanson lived at 2058 while filming *Sunset Boulevard* (1950), and later William Faulkner rented the home.

Return to and continue around to the right on Whitley Terrace and you will see a lovely mansion covering the corner at 6697,

William Randolph Hearst bought this Whitley Heights mansion and rented it to director Robert Vignola. Hearst and mistress Marion Davies used the site for romantic getaways, and Marion was allowed to stay here without Hearst because Vignola was a homosexual.

which was purchased by William Randolph Hearst and loaned to director Robert Vignola. Hearst bought the house for secret meetings with his mistress Marion Davies, and thought homosexual Vignola a perfect companion for Davies. Richard Barthelmess lived next door at 6691 above the garage with the pineapple statues on top. He was visited there by actress Norma Talmadge during an affair that lasted during her ten-year marriage to an elderly Joe Schenck.

Nearby at 6672½ is the hillside home of Barbara LaMarr, who as a 14-year-old runaway from Yakima, Washington, was told by an L.A. judge that she was "too beautiful to be left alone in the city unattended." Reporter Adela Rogers St. Johns, who happened to be present, said that the teenager was so lovely she "took my breath away." She quickly began collecting—and disposing of—wealthy husbands, going though six in eight years. Her second was a handsome L.A. lawyer who married her even though he already had a wife and three children at home. When he ended up in jail for bigamy he banged his head against the bars while calling out her name, dying soon after from head injuries. When she refused a marriage proposal from MGM director Paul Bern—who later married Jean Harlow—he tried to drown himself in a toilet. She rocketed to stardom as Douglas Fairbanks' lover in *The Three Musketeers* (1921) and starred in dozens of others such as *The Prisoner of Zenda* (1922) and *Thy Name Is Woman* (1923) before a huge drug addiction led to her death in 1926. At the height of her stardom, she lived in this secluded home suspended over the hillside, complete with a tunnel from the garage directly into her bedroom to accommodate her famous and secret lovers.

Beulah Bondi (Jimmy Stewart's mom in *It's a Wonderful Life* [1946]) lived at 6660 for 40 years until her death on January 11, 1981. After her heart attack here at 93, the home was bought by Rosalind Russell. The house at 6641 was the set for the 1941 Bette Davis movie *Now, Voyager*.

At the top of Whitley Heights at 2020 Grace is the former entrance to what was once the largest mansion in Hollywood. "Topside" sat amid the tall palms, an opulent 40-room palace built by actor Francis X. Bushman that boasted the country's first

Actress Beulah Bondi died in her longtime Hollywood home, later owned by Rosalind Russell.

Top: Silent screen star Barbara LaMarr's Whitley Heights home hangs over the hillside below the garage. *Bottom:* A typical Whitley Heights street. Silent film star Richard Barthelmess lived in the house above the garage on the left.

in-ground swimming pool. Bushman kept over 300 Great Danes on the estate. The mansion was later rented by Eleanor Boardman, Blanche Sweet, and Tyrone Power. When developers leveled the site in the 1980s to make way for the condominiums now on the site, the Whitley Heights Preservation Society was formed so that no other neighborhood home would meet the same fate.

(Exit Whitley Heights via Whitley down hill to Yucca. Left to the intersection curving around at Grace/Hudson at:)

6500 Yucca Street, Lido Apartments, Victor Killian murder site

Character actor Victor Killian appeared in 150 films including *Public Menace* (1935), *The Adventures of Tom Sawyer* (1938) and *Blood and Sand* (1941). He lost an eye during a movie knife fight with John Wayne while filming *Reap the Wild Wind* (1942), but was most recently the "Fernwood Flasher" in the 1970s *Mary Hartman, Mary Hartman* television series. On the night of March 11, 1979, the 88-year old was bludgeoned to death as he sat in his favorite chair watching television. The gruesome murder remains unsolved.

Later during the same month, another elderly character actor—Charles Wagenheim—was murdered at home in a remarkably similar and also unsolved killing. What makes the Wagenheim and Killian murders more interesting is that they each occurred the day *after* each man taped a guest appearance on the television series *All in the Family*.

(Yucca to Wilcox. Right to:)

1735 Wilcox Street, Shelton Hotel, Clara Blandick and Jenny Dolly suicides

Demolished in 1987, the Shelton was a quiet home for ex-stars with small retirement apartments, and the site of several famous deaths. Eighty-one-year-old Clara

Blandick was born Clara Dickey and was best remembered as the careworn "Auntie Em" from *The Wizard of Oz* (1939), but she got her start on Broadway in 1912 and had appeared in 100 other films such as *Romance* (1930) with Greta Garbo, *Tom Sawyer* (1930) with Jackie Coogan, *Pillow of Death* (1945) with Lon Chaney, Jr., *Frontier Gal* (1945), *A Stolen Life* (1946) with Bette Davis, and *Life with Father* (1947).

After suffering from severe arthritis for years, on the morning of April 15, 1962, she had her hair done, filled her living room with mementos, put on her best dress and took a huge overdose of sleeping pills. Lying on the couch, she covered herself with a blanket, and tied a plastic bag over her head. A note found near her body said, "I am now about to make the great adventure. I cannot endure this agonizing pain any longer. It is all over my body. Neither can I face the impending blindness. I pray the Lord my soul to take. It's time for me to die. Amen." She was a week shy of her eighty-second birthday.

Other former Shelton residents were the Dolly Sisters, identical twins Yansci ("Jenny") and Riszika ("Rosie"), between 1910 and 1927 one of the most famous vaudeville acts in the United States and Europe. The pair debuted with the Ziegfeld Follies in New York and later starred in hundreds of Broadway and London musical stage productions. Even after their retirement in 1927 at the age of 35, they remained the toast of Europe, hobnobbing with royalty as the honored guests of every casino on the French Riviera. While in London traveling with her lover Gordon Selfridge, who once offered her $10 million to marry him, Jenny was horribly disfigured in a 1933 Paris car accident, scars even the best surgery couldn't help. She returned to the United States in despair and on June 1, 1941, made a noose from her drapes and hung herself in her living room. Her sister married three times, and after each divorce returned to the Shelton, where she died alone of a heart attack.

(Wilcox to Hollywood. Left to Ivar. Left to:)

1714 Ivar Street, Hotel Knickerbocker (Irene Gibbons suicide site, D.W. Griffith death site, William Frawley death site)

The once-elegant Hollywood Knickerbocker was the site of a spooky 1936 Halloween rooftop séance held by the widow of Harry Houdini, and the site of the 1944 arrest of actress Francis Farmer. The alcoholic Farmer was arrested for a trivial traffic violation, leading to years of terror in a mental health system she couldn't escape, leaving her a zombie after years of lobotomies and primitive electroshock treatments.

On November 15, 1962, 60-year-old

The Hotel Knickerbocker, last stop for such legends as D.W. Griffith, Irene Gibbons, and William "Fred Mertz" Frawley.

MGM clothing designer Irene Gibbons leapt to her death from her eleventh floor room. Earlier that day she tried slashing her wrists, but her second try was more successful, landing on the lobby roof. Her note apologized to the guests for the trouble she knew she would cause.

David Ward "D.W." Griffith suffered a fatal cerebral hemorrhage in his one-room studio on July 23, 1948. The "Father of the Movies" produced 500 films between 1909 to 1930, including *Birth of a Nation,* the 1915 Civil War epic that grossed $50 million by commanding $2 tickets ($75 today). His *Intolerance* (1916) set covered 50 acres at Sunset Boulevard and Vermont Street, including a 150-foot-tall castle featuring a dozen 50-foot-tall elephants lining a courtyard. It cost $300,000 ($4 million today) for a single scene using 16,000 extras. When he died, he had been unemployed for 20 years, spending his last years as a well-known neighborhood drunk.

The Knickerbocker was also William Frawley's home. He was a 30-year veteran when he became Fred Mertz in *I Love Lucy.* Star of approximately 100 films including *The Lemon Drop Kid* and *Miracle on 34th Street,* the famous drunk promised Lucy and Desi if he missed one taping due to drinking he could be fired. For 40 years Frawley shared a top-floor suite with his sister before moving to the nearby El Royale. In an interesting coincidence, Frawley suffered a heart attack in front of the hotel during a March 3, 1966, walk. Dragged into the lobby, he died on a lobby couch at 79.

Just east at 6249 Hollywood Boulevard once stood the Regent Tobacco Shop. On August 23, 1943, Bette Davis' husband Arthur Farnsworth collapsed while leaving the shop and died of a cerebral hemorrhage. The couple had a "classically European marriage," meaning they both fooled around at will, and their frequent and violent fights were well known. When an autopsy showed that Farnsworth died from a skull fracture that was several weeks old, rumors arose that Davis pushed him down stairs at home or that he had been beaten by an unknown lover's husband. Jack Warner and his fixers managed the Farnsworth inquest to keep Davis out of the papers.

(Ivar to Yucca. Right to Vine. Right to Hollywood. Left to Wilton. Right to Harold. Left to:)

5620 Harold Way, Bela Lugosi death site

Bela Lugosi was born in Transylvania in the Hungarian mountains, and came to the United States after the 1921 Hungarian revolution. His early movie experience was in romantic roles, but after turning down the lead in 1931's *Frankenstein* he was cast in *Dracula* the same year. Other horror roles in *Murders in the Rue Morgue* (1932) and *The Raven* (1933) typecast Lugosi, but contrary to popular rumors, he enjoyed his role as the king of horror films. When the British Film Censors prohibited importing horror films in 1937, calling *The Raven* too scary for kids, Hollywood stopped making the films and Lugosi's career ended overnight. In 1937 his only role was an extra in a "B" movie, and in 1938 he had none. Though he starred in *The Son of Frankenstein* (1939) he never regained his earlier fame, resorting to personal appearance tours and low-budget films. His final movie was the 1956 stinker *Plan 9 from Outer Space,* made for $800 and arguably the worst ever made. Produced by Ed Wood, Jr., star Tor Johnson's home was the primary set, and Tor's policeman son lent his squad car for filming. Lugosi died during filming and a taller blonde replacement was used for the rest of the movie.

A lifelong heroin problem led him into rehab over a dozen times, the last time just days before his death. In 1955 he entered Los Angeles General Hospital—accompanied by a squad of reporters—seeking a cure for his addictions. At the time he could not find an

The modest final home of movie "Dracula" Bela Lugosi.

unscarred place on his legs for the injections. He was released three months later, but within a year he was dead. The 67-year-old Count died here on August 16, 1956, suffering a heart attack sitting in his favorite chair. Lugosi was buried in his signature costume, complete with white face makeup and fangs. As the hearse bearing his body exited the funeral home leading a procession on a pre-set route, something unusual happened. While the driver held on in panic the vehicle inexplicably exited the parking lot *by itself*, jetted through oncoming traffic and turned in the wrong direction. As the other vehicles careened along trying to keep up, the car drove itself along Hollywood Boulevard past Vine before returning to the correct route. It was at that point the petrified driver was able to control the car. He pulled over, jumped out of the car and ran away. The car had retraced a route that Bela had walked every day of his life!

Lugosi lived in several homes in Hollywood during his five marriages, but after becoming a star his principal residence was a lovely mansion at 1146 North Hudson. For several years early in his career he lived quietly in a secluded Tudor duplex on Carlton Way, which according to present residents is still visited by the former resident. Present tenants believe that Lugosi is still in residence, and particularly enjoys making life miserable for any cats living there.

(Harold to St. Andrews. Left to Hollywood. Right to:)

5272 Hollywood Boulevard, Ford Sterling death site

Ford Sterling was a 15-year-old circus clown when he came to Hollywood in 1901 to work as an extra for $5 a week. He became Mack Sennett's chief comedian and leader of a squad of incompetent policemen named for Sennett's Keystone Studio. The Keystone Cops were born when Sennett, Sterling, and Mable Normand went to a 1912 Shriners Parade in downtown L.A. The cost-conscious

Sennett used the parade as a free backdrop for a comedy, buying a baby doll in a nearby store and telling Normandie to "find the baby's father from the marchers." When one of the Shriners stepped out to help Normand, Sterling stepped in to argue with the unnerved marcher. Unexpectedly, local police arrived and chased Sterling and Normand down the street—all captured on film.

Sennett's seven bumbling cops featured two famous 300-pounders: Sterling and Roscoe "Fatty" Arbuckle. But Sterling's face was the most famous, featuring a tiny cap, overdone eyebrows and a huge well-trimmed goatee. In addition to 100 *Keystone Cops* comedies, he also worked with Laurel and Hardy and Buster Keaton. He married fellow silent star Teddy Sampson, and on October 13, 1939, Sterling suffered a fatal heart attack in his home at 54.

Several other original "Cops" also died in Hollywood, coincidentally on the same street. Charlie Murray was a stuntman known for his athletic pratfalls. Recognized by his trademark handlebar mustache, Murray died at his home at 449 North Highland (at Rosewood, south of Melrose Avenue) on July 29, 1941, from lung cancer. Fellow member Charlie Chase became a regular at 14, found by Sennett working as a laborer at the studio. Chase became a major star, second only to Sterling in popularity. He died at home at 2157 North Highland (at Milner north of Hollywood Boulevard) on June 20, 1940, also from lung cancer.

(Hollywood to Normandie. Left to:)

1731 North Normandie, Albert Dekker "accidental" death site

Possibly the most notorious—and certainly the strangest—of accidental deaths was that of Albert Dekker, who was found dead in his apartment bathroom here on May 5, 1968. The 61-year-old Dekker had a long Broadway and screen career, usually cast as an evil villain in films such as *Dr. Cyclops* (1941) and his last film, *The Wild Bunch* (1969).

He was found kneeling naked in his tub, hanging from the curtain rod, his arm and leg bound with ropes and a loosely fitted noose looped around his neck. There were hypodermic syringes piercing his arms and legs and sexual domination phrases written on his chest in bright red lipstick. He was also wearing the most dainty lady's silk lingerie. The bindings were all connected to a rope held in his hand, and since there was no sign of forced entry and doors were bolted from the inside, investigators believed that the once-regal actor died accidentally during a private sex romp.

(Normandie to Franklin. Left three blocks to gates into:)

Laughlin Park Estates, Cecil B. DeMille death, Chaplin and Fields homes

The private neighborhood behind the gates was a popular residential area for early stars, and very exclusive. The most famous estate is at the top of the hill and includes houses at 2010 and 2000 DeMille Drive. While living at 2000, Cecil B. DeMille purchased 2010 from Charlie Chaplin and connected the two with a long arboretum. He used 2010 as his office and guest quarters, although the leaded-glass front door to the house featured an engraving—still visible today—of Chaplin's "Little Tramp" character.

DeMille teamed up with fellow New Yorker Jesse Lasky in 1913 to form the Jesse L. Lasky Feature Play Company, and was the second studio to relocate in California. DeMille was the first moviemaker to become a "director," stalking his movie sets in jodhpurs, hip boots and a riding whip as he screamed directions into a megaphone. He cracked his whip whenever he became annoyed about anything on his sets. He was a stern and unyielding taskmaster; during filming off the Mexican coast, DeMille

The Laughlin Park home of Charlie Chaplin was later purchased by Cecil B. DeMille and added to his own mansion next door.

jumped into shark-infested waters to encourage his cast to do the same. While personally lighting a hundred exploding pots aboard a ship set, several exploded, throwing the unconscious director into the Pacific Ocean. He would tolerate nothing less from his actors, belittling them publicly for the slightest sign of weakness. DeMille suffered a fatal heart attack inside his home here on January 21, 1959, dead at 78. His last words were "nothing matters."

Across the street at 2015 is the pink stucco mansion of W.C. Fields, who once said, "I'm free of prejudice. I hate everybody equally." His lifelong mistress Carlotta Monti supported the view when she said, "They have said that he was crotchety, castigating, had a jaundiced eye, was larcenous, suspicious, shifty, erratic, cheap, and mercenary. I can only confirm those." After fellow comedian Ed Wynn received more laughs than Fields while the two appeared in a vaudeville show, Fields didn't speak to him for over five years.

Fields was a very popular vaudevillian performer and reputed to be the finest juggler in the world. He made a hilarious debut in *The Pool Shark* (1915), but didn't return to the movies for ten more years. His films *The Dentist* (1932), *The Barber Shop* (1933), *The Pharmacist* (1933), and *The Fatal Glass of Beer* (1933) became instant hits, and brought Fields instant acclaim as a comic genius. Annoyed at child co-star Baby LeRoy during filming, he filled the youngster's bottle with gin, and as he watched the toddler pass out on the floor, harrumphed, "That kid's no trouper." As his two bottle a day scotch habit ruined his appearance—his bulbous red nose was not movie makeup—Fields managed several hits in the 1940s like *My Little Chickadee* and *The Bank Dick*, but by 1946 was dead from alcoholism. He died in a local sanitarium on Christmas Eve, the day he hated most.

During life, Fields didn't believe in owning real estate, renting this home for years until the owner tried to raise his rent $25 a year, at which point the frugal comic moved out. Below the DeMille and Fields

homes was the residence of DeMille's daughter Katharine and son-in-law Anthony Quinn. Visiting his grandparents on March 16, 1941, Quinn's 3-year-old son Christopher wandered over to Fields' estate and accidentally drowned in the reflecting pond in front of the mansion as he tried to retrieve a model boat the comic left floating in the water. Though professing a keen hatred of children, the death had an enormous impact on a distraught Fields, who immediately threw the boat in the furnace and had the fountain filled in. The estate was most recently the home of Lily Tomlin. Laughlin Park is a gated private community, with the gates usually, but not always, down.

(Franklin to Los Feliz. Right and immediately on your right notice the house surrounded by trees on the corner at:)

5470 Los Feliz Boulevard, Clifford Clinton bombing site

The house behind the shrubs at the corner was the site of a mob hit during the 1930s that severely hurt the mob's influence in Los Angeles. At that time the entire city was controlled by the mob, chock full of brothels, illegal bookmakers and unauthorized casino ships filling every harbor from Los Angeles to San Diego. The police department was overseen by mobsters and, the D.A.'s office was the most corrupt in the country. In 1941 Raymond Chandler said "law is where you buy it in this town." In 1935 restaurateur Clifford Clinton publicly took on the mob and their puppet mayor Frank Shaw, who for years had used city coffers as a private bank account, skimming millions for the mob. His mob pals tried to kill Clinton in his home here, violating the mob rule that "we only kill our own" for the first time.

On the night of October 27, 1937, a huge explosion rocked the house but Clinton and his family survived. He became an instant hero and his battle with the mob a local cause célèbre. The publicity led to

Once owned by Walt Disney, this Silverlake home was the site of one of the most famous murders in L.A. history: the Manson Family's killings of Leno and Rosemary LaBianca.

Shaw's expulsion as mayor. After he was thrown out, nearly 40 police officials took early retirement, and all of them moved to Mexico. Neighbors Basil and Ouida Rathbone watched it from their home at 5254 Los Feliz, later owned by fighter Jack Dempsey.

(Continue on Los Feliz past Vermont to Griffith Park Boulevard. Right to Rowena. Left a block to Waverly. Left to:)

3311 Waverly Drive, LaBianca murder site

In a once-elegant neighborhood that has seen better times, this home was once owned by Walt Disney. Originally numbered 3301, in 1969 it was the home of Leno LaBianca, who had moved in as a child 40 years earlier. On the night of August 10 Leno and wife Rosemary were stabbed to death by members of the Manson "Family" inside the house. Charlie Manson's direct involvement—he entered the home and tied up the pair so followers could butcher the helpless couple—earned a death sentence, later commuted to a life term when the Supreme Court outlawed the death penalty.

(Continue on Waverly to Hyperion/ Glendale. Right to Griffith Park Boulevard. Left a block to Angus Street. Left a short distance to Micheltorena, and right to:)

1923 Micheltorena Drive, Antonio Moreno–Daisy Danziger home

The once-impressive house at 1923 Micheltorena was built in 1923 by silent screen star Antonio Moreno as a wedding present for his actress-wife Daisy Canfield Danziger. "Crest Mount" was the couple's home until February 18, 1933, when Danziger separated from Moreno and filed for divorce. Danziger's actions fueled ongoing rumors that the Latin actor's marriage to the beautiful oil heiress was a sham, a publicity stunt to hide Moreno's much-rumored homosexuality.

The rumors swelled when just ten days later Danziger was killed in a mysterious auto accident when her car flew 250 feet over a cliff off of Mulholland Drive near Laurel Canyon Drive. It has been rumored that Danziger's ashes are interred here at Crest

Mount, and there does appear to be a grave site of sorts behind the home. Moreno is buried at Forest Lawn in Glendale.

(Continue on Micheltorena to Sunset Boulevard. Right to Vermont Avenue. Right a short distance to Franklin. Left on Franklin past Western a block or two to Van Ness. Right across Foothill straight up the hill onto Briarcliff. Right winding up the hill until it meets Verde Oak. Just below the road at the intersection is:)

5608 Briarcliff Road, Will and Ariel Durant death site

Writer Will Durant married Ariel when he was just 18 and she 15—she roller skated from her home to the church! Durant and his wife eventually authored the renowned *Story of Civilization* series, *The History of Philosophy* and won a Pulitzer Prize for their *Rousseau and the Revolution.* The couple came to Hollywood in the early 1920s along with the huge European "salon" crowd relocating to the Los Angeles area. The 86-year-old Durant suffered a fatal heart attack in the couple's longtime home here in June 1981. Ariel died just a few months later, also from a heart attack, on October 25, 1981.

(Continue on Briarcliff to Live Oak Road. Left on Live Oak to:)

2177 Live Oak Road, Cary Grant–Randolph Scott love-nest

Although some contemporary writers dispute the fact, it is fairly clear that Cary Grant was homosexual. In 1932 he moved from New York to Hollywood along with then-lover Jack Orry-Kelly, but fell in love at first sight with handsome Randolph Scott. The twosome immediately moved in together, sharing a series of Hollywood apartments and then this home while their studio told the public they were just pals. They were photographed all over town together, attending

Philosopher-writer Will Durant and his wife Ariel both died at this Hollywood Hills home.

movie premieres and having dinners, and according to writer William J. Mann, described in the papers as "Hollywood's twosome" and a "happy couple." The more famous they became, the louder the whispers however, and soon they were forced by Paramount to spend time with women, but still one scribe wrote that the couple "was carrying this buddy business too far."

In 1934, Grant married young actress Virginia Cherrill (best known as Charlie Chaplin's co-star in his classic *City Lights*), who seemed oblivious to the obvious signs of his homosexuality. When the newlyweds moved into the La Ronda Apartments at 1400 Hayvenhurst in Hollywood, Scott took the apartment next door. The *Hollywood Reporter* noted that "The Cary Grants and Randolph Scott have moved, but not apart." Not surprisingly, Cherrill moved out after three months, and Scott moved back in. Their relationship lasted for years, as Grant married a succession of short-term wives and Scott married women but wouldn't live with them.

(Reverse on Live Oak to Briarcliff to Foothill. Right to Canyon. Left to:)

1937 Canyon Drive, murderer Charles Rathbun home

On November 16, 1995, gorgeous blonde Linda Sobek left her Hermosa Beach home to meet a photographer named "Chuck" for a photo shoot. "Chuck" turned out to be Charles Rathbun, a photographer specializing in automobile pictures. The 27-year-old Sobek, a former Oakland Raiders cheerleader, was an aspiring actress who had just received her big "break"—a role on television's *Married ... with Children*. When she didn't return that evening and missed her costume fitting for the *Children* role, friends knew something was wrong.

After a worker found her modeling photos and pages torn from her appointment book in a dumpster in the Angeles National Forest northeast of Burbank, the missing-persons search became a body search. With almost 1,000 square miles of rugged peaks and hidden valleys, the forest is a popular dumping spot for garbage of all kinds, including bodies, among them the still-missing body of "Billionaire Boys Club" victim Ron Levin. Police might never have found Sobek's had they not discovered a lending receipt for a new Lexus sport utility vehicle near the pictures in the dumpster. It was made out to Charles Rathbun, who told police that he had indeed met with Sobek that day for an *Auto Week* photo shoot.

Several days after Sobek disappeared, Rathbun, knowing that he had become the sole suspect, holed up in his home here getting drunk and contemplating suicide. When his lawyer and a friend came here with the police, Rathbun emerged waving a .45 pistol, which discharged and wounded his former girlfriend. Quickly arrested, Rathbun later admitted to killing Sobek, but claimed she died accidentally when he ran her down with the borrowed Lexus, panicked and hid the body. After taking police to the secluded burial site, Rathbun was charged and convicted of murder when a coroner stated that Sobek's body had no injuries consistent with being hit by a car. She had apparently been asphyxiated by the 6'3" Rathbun and buried in a shallow grave.

He was given a life sentence after his 1996 trial, during which it was found that Rathbun had a rape conviction in Ohio, and was also a prime suspect in the 1993 murder of another blonde model, Kim Pandelios, who was discovered in a shallow grave very close to Sobek's. She also left home the day she disappeared to meet a photographer at a Denny's restaurant near the freeway.

(Canyon to Franklin. Right to Tamarind. Right to the middle of the block on the right:)

1950 Tamarind Drive, Tamarind Place Apartments, Kenneth Bianchi home

Half of the "Hillside Stranglers"—the other being cousin Angelo Buono—Kenneth

Bianchi lived in the Tamarind Apartments during a four-month 1978 crime spree that took the lives of ten young women. The bodies of the raped and strangled victims were all found lying on hillsides near the freeways, and the pair taunted police by leaving several bodies in Elysian Park next to the police academy, and one body was laid out pointing directly at police headquarters. After Bianchi's arrest for a Washington double murder, police noticed his address here was also the home of prostitute Kimberly Martin, the ninth Hillside victim. They also found that Bianchi had lived on the same Glendale block as two other victims. He confessed to the Hillside murders to escape the death penalty and soon gave up his accomplice Buono. The victims were abducted and taken to Buono's home in Glendale where they were tortured, raped and killed.

Incredibly, the pair once had attempted to abduct the lovely daughter of actor Peter Lorre, 27-year-old Catherine. When the duo, disguised as policemen, discovered that their intended victim was the daughter of a celebrity they let her go, fearing publicity. She survived to testify at Buono's trial.

(Reverse on Tamarind and notice the large building on the south side of Franklin, site of:)

5930 Franklin Avenue, Chateau Elysee Apartments

As you reverse on Tamarind, notice the lovely chateau-like building across Franklin. One of the most beautiful buildings in Hollywood, and now the "Celebrity Center" headquarters of a science fiction–based pseudo-religious organization, the Chateau Elysee Apartments were built on the site of producer Thomas Ince's home. Construction was begun by publisher William Randolph Hearst shortly after Ince turned up dead aboard Hearst's yacht in 1924. The building was gifted to Ince's widow Elinor, who owned the apartments until her death.

It has long been rumored that Hearst shot Ince after interrupting a deck-side tryst with Marion Davies, who was Hearst's mistress but who carried on a long affair with Ince. The gift of the Chateau Elysee turned a quiet Hollywood rumor into a full-fledged movieland legend. During the 1930s, loving couples such as Cary Grant and Randolph Scott, Gloria Swanson and Joseph Kennedy, Sr., and Clark Gable and Carole Lombard all shared lovenests at the Elysee. Other former residents included George Burns and Gracie Allen, Ginger Rogers, Edward G. Robinson, and Errol Flynn. From 1951 to 1973 the building was a retirement home called Fifield Manor.

(Tamarind to Franklin. Right to Argyle, adjacent to:)

1844 Vine Street, Cudahy Mansion site, Lou Tellegan suicide

A casualty of the wrecker's ball when the freeway was built was a 50-room Italian chateau that once stood at the spot under the bridge, built by Elizabeth Cudahy, the widow of the founder of the meatpacking dynasty who threw lavish parties to hobnob with movie stars. A famous eccentric, the slightly skewed Cudahy appeared at every party as Queen Nefertiti in full Egyptian garb. She became totally unhinged after her son John killed himself at his 7269 Hollywood Boulevard mansion, and after the suicide she never left the house, staying behind drawn velvet curtains for over 20 years.

A frequent guest at the legendary Saturday evening parties was Lou Tellegan, an elegant and sophisticated Greek actor married to opera diva Geraldine Ferrar. He starred in early classics *Queen Elizabeth* (1912), *The Long Trail* (1917), *Flame of the Desert* (1919) and *Single Wives* (1924). During a November 1, 1934, party, he committed a bizarre hari kari in one of the bathrooms. Applying white face makeup and leaving dozens of old press clippings on the sink, Telegan stabbed himself in the heart with a pair of gold sewing scissors.

In what may have been the first example

World-renowned tennis star Bill Tilden died penniless in his apartment here, after several sex scandals involving young boys left him a social outcast.

of "spin control," writer Anita Loos offered a more romantic description of the death in her autobiography *A Girl Like Me*. Loos described a severely depressed Tellegan shooting himself in the head in a suite at the Knickerbocker Hotel. According to Loos, he was clutching in his cold hand a gossip column describing him as a has-been.

(Franklin at Argyle. Right to:)

2025 Argyle Avenue, Bravo Apartments, Bill Tilden death site

William "Big Bill" Tilden, one of the greatest tennis players of the century, won three 1920s Wimbledon titles, the U.S. men's title seven of eight years from 1920 to 1928, and led the United States to nine straight Davis Cup titles. He was adored by the media and a favored guest at Hollywood parties. A frequent visitor to Pickfair, he played with Errol Flynn and Spencer Tracy at Chaplin's house and with Garbo and Hepburn at Clifton Webb's. Personal demons destroyed his life, though.

Unknown to his fans, Tilden was raised by an unstable mother who kept him at home with her until 18, dressed in girl's clothes and called "June." He was allowed no contact with other children, especially girls, whom he was told carried frightful venereal diseases. His pedophilic tendencies probably aren't surprising, but his 1942 arrest for homosexual acts with a young boy left him an outcast. Arrested again for violating parole, he was so universally hated that his alma mater, Pennsylvania University, removed him from the alumni lists. Tilden suffering a fatal heart attack here on June 14, 1953, leaving a $9 "estate."

(Across the street on Argyle notice:)

2026 Argyle Avenue, DeMille Manor, Beatrice DeMille death site

Across the street at 2026 is the building purchased by Cecil B. DeMille for his mother Beatrice, and was the site of her

Cecil B. DeMille built this Hollywood apartment building for his mother, where she died in 1923.

October 8, 1923, death. Her doting son visited daily during her last year while he filmed *The Ten Commandments* (1924). Her death the day shooting ended was an eerie forerunner to his own death, which occurred the day shooting ended on his second version of the same movie.

(Argyle to the crest of the hill. Right on Holly Mont [depending upon the map you have, it is either spelled Hollymont, Hollymount, or Holly Mont] to:)

6215 and 6221 Holly Mont Drive, haunted houses

The two houses at 6215 and 6221 have reportedly been haunted for years, with countless examples of furniture chasing people around rooms and books flying off shelves. When a local bishop came to perform an exorcism his ceremonial hat vanished and a scepter filled with holy water exploded. His hat was later found in a locked third floor attic. The hauntings may be related to the secret tunnel hidden behind a bookshelf recently discovered in one of the two houses that connects several of the hillside homes. Deep in the tunnel a makeshift grave was found, saying simply "Regina, 1922." It just may be that "Regina," whoever she was, is still in residence.

(Holly Mont to Vista del Mar. Right to:)

Corner of Vista del Mar and Dix avenues, Harry Greenberg murder site

Ben "Bugsy" Siegel was the first of the New York mobsters to set up camp in L.A., arriving in 1935 and soon becoming a Hollywood fixture hanging with stars such as Clark Gable, George Raft and Gary Cooper. In his spare time he directed mob inroads into the movie business and the gambling wires servicing local bookies. As handsome as some of his Hollywood pals, he was also a cold-blooded killer, one of the mob's private death squad, known as Murder, Inc. His friends dubbed him "Bugs" because of his

The Hollymount Castle, one of two haunted houses on the steeet.

terrible temper, but anyone who used the term in front of the mobster risked death. It was Siegel who once said of the mob, "we only kill each other."

In 1939 Siegel's former personal enforcer Harry Greenberg sought Bugsy's help with New York gang bosses that he had double-crossed. Greenberg became understandably concerned when his partner—Abe "Kid Twist" Reles—was thrown out of an eleventh-floor Coney Island hotel window while under police protection. Reles and Greenberg had become government "snitches," and when Abe's testimony sent a dozen mobsters to the electric chair the mob understandably wanted Greenberg also. Old friend Siegel offered "Greenie" protection, renting him a small bungalow at 1804 Vista del Mar Avenue, on the south side of Franklin where the apartment building now stands. Bugsy's "help" involved tipping the bosses to Greenie's hideout, and helping them plan his murder.

On the evening of September 22, 1939,

as Greenberg got out of his car at this corner he was ambushed by three men and shot 24 times. Six bullets were fired by best old pal Bugsy, who left a lavish party at his Bel Air estate to participate in the killing. After the hit, he returned to the party. He was indicted for the murder, but when witnesses began dying charges were dropped. A month later "Whitey" Krakower, one of the three triggermen, began bragging about the killing, which annoyed his employers. Siegel again volunteered to clean up the situation, and personally shot Krakower to death back in New York. That killing is a testimony to the true Siegel, since Whitey was his wife Esther's little brother. In the 1993 hit movie *Bugsy*, Elliott Gould played the hapless Harry Greenberg.

(Reverse on Vista del Mar up the hill to Scenic. Left around the corner onto Primrose. Straight to Alcyona. Right to El Contento. Right to intersection with El Contento, Quebec and Creston, and

notice the lovely house sitting on the corner facing at:)

6301 Quebec Drive, *Double Indemnity* movie site

This home receives an honorary place in this listing, since it was the setting for the 1944 Billy Wilder classic *Double Indemnity*. In the movie, Fred MacMurray and Barbara Stanwyck plotted her husband's murder so the pair can collect on a large insurance policy.

(Right and around to the left on Creston to Vasanta. Right down the hill onto Temple Hill. Charlie Chaplin's first Hollywood home—a lovely Moorish mansion—is nearby at 6147 Temple Hill. Continue to Scenic. Left to Beachwood. Left to Graciosa. Right to Cheremoya. Right to:)

2261 Cheremoya Drive, Ray Raymond murder site

On April 16, 1927, former Vitagraph child star Paul Kelly severely beat fellow actor Ray Raymond at his home here. Raymond died several days later at home from the battering. In an example of a classic love triangle, Kelly was having an affair with Raymond's wife, actress Dorothy MacKaye. Kelly and MacKaye bribed their doctor to alter Raymond's death certificate and arranged for a hasty cremation. They were thwarted when local police spoke with a maid who mentioned the fight, and minutes before the cremation was to begin police saw the body of an obviously pummeled Raymond, and an investigation led to the doctor, Kelly and Mackaye. They were each sent to prison, but the lovebirds were wed after their respective releases.

In a wonderful example of Hollywood's short memory, Kelly later starred in *Call Out the Marines* (1942), *Flying Tigers* (1942), and *Deadline for Murder* (1946). His most interesting postmurder casting may have been his starring role in 1946's *The Glass Alibi*.

(Reverse to Beachwood. Right to just past Winans. On the right behind the large parking gates is:)

Film set of 1944's *Double Indemnity*, starring Fred MacMurray and Barbara Stanwyck.

The Cheremoya Drive bungalow where Paul Kelly beat fellow actor Ray Raymond to death in 1927.

2428 Beachwood Drive, Peg Entwhistle last home

Lillian Millicent Entwhistle's sad death has become the ultimate symbol of the price of fame in Hollywood. With several Broadway roles to her credit, Entwhistle's only Hollywood success had been a small role in RKO's *Thirteen Women* in 1932. The broke former stage star lived for a short time at the Hollywood Studio Club for women (6129 Carlos) because phone service was free with the rent. Forced to move from there, "Peg" moved in with an uncle here, convinced that she was a has-been at 24.

On the night of September 18, 1932, Peg slowly walked through the cool evening up Beachwood toward the "Hollywood" sign on the hillside above. Constructed in 1923, it was aglow with the blaze of 5,000 lights promoting a housing development in the hills above Beachwood. She somehow climbed to the top of the "H" and silently dove to her death. Her broken body was discovered by hikers the next morning, crumpled in the scrub brush 100 feet below the glowing sign. A suicide note was found in her pocket, telling her uncle "I am afraid I am a coward. I am sorry for everything. If I could have done this long ago I could have saved a lot of pain." In a poignant irony, her death was unnecessary—unbeknownst to her she had been selected for a part in a movie to begin filming the next week. The letter arrived the day of her funeral.

(Beachwood to:)

2470½ Beachwood Drive, Larry Edmunds suicide site

A small garage-guesthouse at the rear of 2470 was once the home of bookshop owner and Hollywood gigolo Larry Edmunds. The bookstore bearing his name still sits at 6644 Hollywood Boulevard. From the cramped bookstore Edmunds became friendly with the Hollywood elite of the 1920s and 1930s, having close friendships with W.C. Fields, the Barrymores, Basil Rathbone, writer Peter Viertel, and virtually every starlet in Hollywood.

Lovely Peg Entwhistle left here on a cool summer night in 1932 and committed suicide by jumping off the Hollywood sign up the street, becoming one of the most famous actresses in Hollywood history for all the wrong reasons.

Edmunds had a voracious sexual appetite—allegedly for both sexes—bedding a literal "Who's Who" that included Mary Astor, Marlene Dietrich, Paulette Goddard, and dozens of others. By the 1940s Edmunds' star began to fade and he drifted into alcoholism and mental illness. In February 1941 his body was found in the kitchen, with his head lodged inside the gas stove. His suicide note explained that when he found himself cutting off the heads of the little men that were crawling through the walls to kill him, he realized he was seriously disturbed and had to kill himself. Love notes and mementos from friends of both sexes filled the house.

(Beachwood to Glen Green. Right to:)

2552 Glen Green Drive, Peter Duel death site

The 31-year-old actor began his career in movies such as *Missing in Action* (1961)

and *The Hell with Heroes* (1968) but was remembered for the 1970s television series *Gidget* and *Alias Smith and Jones.* On December 31, 1971, he sat naked beneath his Christmas tree here and put a bullet through his head. Whether it was an accident or suicide was unclear but in either case it was successful.

(Reverse to Beachwood. Right to Belden and Westshire. The streets above were part of a development begun in 1923 named "Hollywoodland." The entrance to the development was marked by the stone gateposts standing at this spot, which were originally designed to hold gatemen for security. The first home built was the "Hollywoodland Sales Office," the blue building across the street at 2690-2700. Right on Westshire. Left on Woodhaven and see the large home on right:)

The one-time home of Clark Gable and Carole Lombard is allegedly haunted by an unnamed former owner.

2720 Woodhaven Drive, Clark Gable–Carole Lombard haunted home

The lovely castle house here was built in 1920 by theater magnate Alexander Pantages as a wedding present for his daughter. When she tired of the stairways the home was sold to director Rex Ingram and moviestar wife Alice Terry, who lived here for years. Newlyweds Clark Gable and Carole Lombard rented the house for several years before moving to their San Fernando Valley ranch.

It is not known if they witnessed anything like the ghostly hauntings reported in the house over the years. A former resident refuses to leave, as subsequent tenants view objects moving around by themselves, lights blinking on and off in empty rooms, and doors locking by themselves. The tower library is a favorite setting for the shadowy hijinks, and a spectral woman is often seen walking through the empty hallways of the spooky home.

(Woodhaven to Beachwood. Right to:)

2946 Beachwood Drive, Spring Byington death site

Spring Byington was a Broadway star turned movie actress who starred in 100 films, usually cast in mother-in-law or grandmother roles in movies such as *Little Women* (1933) with Katharine Hepburn, *Way Down East* (1935), *Mutiny on the Bounty* (1935), and *The Devil and Miss Jones* (1941). She was nominated for an Oscar for her supporting role in 1938's *You Can't Take It with You.* Byington suffered a fatal heart attack in her home on September 9, 1971, at 77.

(For a wonderful, uncluttered view of the Hollywood sign, reverse on Beachwood to Ledgewood. Turn right to Deronda and proceed right up the hill and you will find several spots with gorgeous views for your "Hollywood" sign picture. Reverse to Beachwood. Right to Belden. Right to Flagmoor. Short

The impressive former home of director George Wolf, allegedly still visited by Wolf's spirit.

left to Durand. Right and see another good view of the sign. Below the sign is:)

Castillo del Lago, Bugsy Siegel speakeasy, Madonna stalker shooting site

The multilevel mansion hugging the hillside below the Hollywood sign was built for oil entrepreneur Patrick Longdon in 1926 and contained 20,000 square feet over nine levels, 12,000 of that in staircases and towers. A week after completion Longdon's wife died in her brand new bedroom and he moved out. For six years in the 1930s it was used as a speakeasy and brothel by Bugsy Siegel, and after sitting abandoned through the 1950s and 1960s, it was renovated and purchased in 1992 by pop singer Madonna. She painted the house in orange and white stripes, later relenting to local complaints and repainting the mansion the present color.

Late on May 29, 1995, her guards shot intruder Robert Hoskins after he climbed the fence surrounding the estate. Yelling that he was married to the singer and that he had come to pick her up, or cut her throat, he was shot three times. He was convicted and given 10 years on trespass and stalking charges.

(Durand to:)

2869 Durand Drive, "Wolf's Lair"

This fairy tale castle was built in 1925 by studio art director turned developer George Wolf and included a heart-shaped pool, a tiny turret for his beloved pet monkey, and priceless Tiffany windows throughout. Later owned by Doris Day and Efrem Zimbalist, Jr., it is supposedly still haunted by the original owner, who died while seated at his kitchen table.

Tour 2:
Hollywood Central

Begin Tour 2 at the Hollywood Roosevelt Hotel at 7000 Hollywood Boulevard. This area of Hollywood Boulevard is the center of classic old Hollywood, and it is worth stopping and seeing Grauman's Chinese Theatre and the famous Forecourt of the Stars, the Max Factor Museum, and the interesting sidewalk "Walk of Fame."

7000 Hollywood Boulevard, Hollywood Roosevelt Hotel

The Hollywood Roosevelt was built in 1927 by a group led by Louis B. Mayer and Douglas Fairbanks and Mary Pickford. Site of the first Academy Awards in 1928, it was also the set for the 1950s television series *This Is Your Life*. It seems that ghostly residents are also checking in and out.

Marilyn Monroe hangs around a basement corridor near a full length mirror that was once in her studio dressing room, and Montgomery Clift won't leave the favorite suite where he stayed when filming. He still moves towels around, makes noise, and leaves phones off the hook in Room 928 when nobody's checked in there. Footsteps are heard in empty halls outside the room, where Clift always studied his lines while pacing the hallway.

(Hollywood to Sycamore. Right/north to the second apartment south of Franklin:)

1776 North Sycamore Avenue, Bobby Fuller death site

Bobby Fuller was an unknown bar musician when his "Bobby Fuller Four" band recorded the 1965 hit "I Fought the Law." Following up with "Love's Made a Fool of You" the next year, he became world famous. On July 18, 1966, Fuller's body was found curled in the fetal position in front of the apartment he shared with his mother here. His death was caused by a large "ingestion of gasoline," a particularly gruesome death. The death was rumored to have been drug-related, but police never determined how or why Fuller was killed, and the murder remains unsolved.

(Sycamore to Franklin, right to Orchid. Left to Bonita Terrace. Right to Pinehurst. Left to:)

2035 Pinehurst Drive, Wilfred Buckland murder-suicide site

The first studio set designer and the father of Hollywood studio art, Buckland developed interior klieg lighting, which allowed for the use of indoor sets. He worked for the original Lasky Players, with Cecil B. DeMille on *Squaw Man* (1915) and later with Marshall Liesen on *Robin Hood* (1922). For the Liesen classic he built the largest set in history, a mammoth castle covering 40 acres.

Singer Bobby Fuller was found dead on the sidewalk in front of his mother's apartment here, the victim of a gruesome murder.

He shared this home with actress wife Vida Buckland and their son Bill. After Vida's cancer death here on July 18, 1946, Buckland shot his unstable 36-year-old son as he slept and turned the gun on himself. His note said simply, "I'm taking Bill with me." Schooled at Exeter and Princeton, young Bill developed severe mental illness during college, and Buckland thought his son wouldn't survive if he outlived his father.

Next door at 2029 struggling writer Edgar Rice Burroughs wrote a children's book about a jungle man named "Tarzan" in 1933. Just up the street at 2042 songwriter Carrie Jacobs-Bond wrote the immortal tunes "I Love You Truly" and "The End of a Perfect Day." She called her home "The End of the Road," a lovely mansion and gardens she built in 1917 that still stands today.

(Reverse to Franklin. Right to:)

7001 Franklin Avenue, Magic Castle haunted house

This Renaissance mansion was built in 1925 for Janet Gaynor and her husband Gilbert Adrian. Now the Magic Castle, it is the longtime home of a club devoted to magic. With a secret membership list joined by invitation only, former members include Cary Grant and Steve Martin. The downstairs pub is haunted by longtime bartender Loren, who is repeatedly seen, by employees and guests, standing behind his old bar cleaning glasses. Above the Magic Castle covering the top of the hill is the gorgeous Bernhiemer Mansion, an incredible Oriental mansion built in 1911 by two wealthy antique dealers, the brothers Bernhiemer, who collected Oriental art and antiques. Their palace is an exact replica of a 14th century palace still standing in Japan. The brothers imported 500 native craftsmen—stonecutters, wood carvers, painters, and gardeners—to

The former home of Janet Gaynor, now the site of a private club devoted to magic (and allegedly haunted by a former bartender).

create the incredible palace and grounds, which they named "The Yamashiro." It is now the Yamashiro Restaurant, once a private club for the movie industry and a popular movie set.

(Franklin a block west to:)

7047 Franklin Avenue, Janis Joplin overdose death site

Formerly named the Landmark Hotel, on the night of October 3, 1970, 27-year-old singer Janis Joplin was staying in Room 105, the first room to the right of the entrance facing the parking lot. After spending the evening drinking at Barney's Beanerie at nearby 8447 Santa Monica—where James Dean also had his last meal the night before his fatal car accident—Joplin returned to her room and took a massive dose of pure heroin. She then went to the lobby for cigarettes, walked back to her room and collapsed face down on the floor. She struck the floor so hard that her nose and

facial bones were shattered, and she was found the next day by hotel maids.

(Franklin to Outpost. Right to La Presa.
  Right to:)

7050 La Presa Drive, Marie Wilson death site

Buxom blonde actress Marie Wilson grew up in Hollywood dreaming of becoming a star and was signed to a Warner Bros. contract at the age of 15. She debuted in *Stars Over Broadway* (1935) and appeared in small roles in movies such as *Satan Met a Lady* (1936), *China Clipper* (1937), *Boy Meets Girl* (1938), and *Rookies on Parade* (1941). By 1942 Wilson was well-known and typecast as the typical "dumb blonde" roles when Ken Murray hired her to appear on his weekly television *Blackouts* program performing a satirical striptease act. Incredibly, the act ran for over 2,330 shows, the most popular segment on the show.

Wilson is best remembered for her role

Singer Janis Joplin's overdose death occurred in a first-floor room just to the right of the entrance to this Hollywood motel.

as Irma in the late 1940s to early 1950s movie serial *My Friend Irma* with Dean Martin and Jerry Lewis. It was a role she had performed on radio for ten years before MGM brought it to the movies. She also starred in *A Girl in Every Port* (1952), *Never Wave at a WAC* (1953), *The Story of Mankind* (1957), and her final film, *Mr. Hobbs Takes a Vacation* (1962). On November 23, 1972, Wilson died in her Hollywood home after a long battle with cancer at the age of 56.

(Reverse to Outpost. Right up hill to Senalda. Right to:)

7141 Senalda Drive, Paul Douglas death site

Burly Paul Douglas played football for the first professional football team in Philadelphia, the old Frankfort Yellow Jackets, and after retiring in 1930 became one of the country's top sports announcers, broadcasting over 1,000 baseball games for NBC and CBS. His voice was recognized all over the country, and he was soon working in radio announcing *The Jack Benny Show, Easy*

Aces, Burns and Allen, and *Jack Armstrong, All American Boy.* In his off hours he appeared in Broadway plays, starring in one of the most successful plays in history, Garson Kanin's *Born Yesterday.* Moving to Hollywood, the husky tough guy debuted in *A Letter to Three Wives* (1948), which made him a star, and he appeared in dozens of movies including *It Happens Every Spring* (1949), *Love That Brute* (1950), *Angels in the Outfield* (1951), *High and Dry* (1954), and *This Could Be the Night* (1957).

Douglas' final film role was in the 1959 hit *The Mating Game,* and he had signed to star in Billy Wilder's movie classic *The Apartment* when he suffered a fatal heart attack at his Hollywood Hills home just a month before filming was to begin. The 52-year-old actor died getting out of bed on September 12, 1959, with his wife, actress Jan Sterling, at his side.

(Reverse to Outpost. Right down the hill past the last home of singer Russ Columbo at 1940 Outpost Circle—later owned by actor Alan Ladd—to Hillside. Right to El Cerrito. Left to:)

1780 El Cerrito Place, Bobby Stanciu shooting site

On April 11, 1960, young actor Bobby Stanciu died in this apartment in an unsolved and suspicious shooting. He allegedly killed himself playing Russian roulette in the apartment he shared with actress Beverly Aadland.

Aadland was Errol Flynn's final teenage lover after a lifetime of underage paramours. She brought the brooding Flynn happiness during the last year of his life, after he first seduced her at 15. The 60-year-old Flynn suffered a heart attack on October 14, 1959, just minutes after young Aadland had given him a final kiss. His final screen effort was *Cuban Rebel Girls* (1960), starring as a Cuban freedom fighter with Aadland as his lover. He had frittered away $8,000,000 in earnings, leaving Aadland penniless.

(El Cerrito to Hollywood Boulevard. Right on Hollywood Boulevard to Fuller. Right to:)

1734 North Fuller, Kate Charleson suicide site

Lovely Kate Charleson was the younger sister of actress Leslie Charleson—Dr. Monica Quartermaine on the soap *General Hospital*—playing small parts except for one feature role as Debra Winger's best friend in the 1983 film hit *Terms of Endearment*. Despondent that her career never reached beyond that role, the 43-year-old actress committed suicide by looping a rope over a light fixture in the bedroom of her Hollywood apartment (#107 on the first floor) and hanging herself on October 12, 1996. According to reports, after Kate called older sister Leslie and told her she was about to kill herself, Leslie called the police and frantically raced here to stop the suicide. But when they arrived the young woman was found hanging from the light fixture.

In addition to career disappointments, Kate had a history of drug abuse and drinking problems, and just before her death she had begun using heroin. When her drug problems caused her to lose her home and a long-term lesbian relationship, she killed herself.

(Fuller to Franklin. Left to Camino Palmiero. Right to:)

1822 Camino Palmiero, Ozzie Nelson haunted death site

The home of the Ozzie and Harriet Nelson family was the only house they ever owned, purchased in 1941 and their home for 40 years. Oswald P. Nelson was the youngest Eagle Scout ever at 13, a three-sport athlete at Rutgers University, and he earned a law degree in 1930. With no Depression-era jobs available, he formed a band and toured the United States with singer and later wife Harriet Hilliard.

After numerous guest appearances, they were given their own radio show, which became hugely popular, and Ozzie earned movie roles in films such as *The Big Street* (1942), *Hi Good Lookin'* (1944) and *People Are Funny* (1946). It was the couple's long-running *Adventures of Ozzie and Harriet* television show that led to superstardom. The set was an *exact* replica of this home, down to pictures and furniture, changing little during the show's 22-year run. The house was also the site of Ozzie's death from liver cancer on June 3, 1975, at the age of 69.

Subsequent owners feel the ghost of Ozzie opening and closing doors and turning faucets and lights on and off in empty rooms. According to Laurie Jacobson's *Hollywood Haunted*, one owner felt "something—or someone—unseen getting 'fresh' with her. At night while she was asleep, her covers would be pulled back, and she would feel someone kissing her neck and breasts. Each time, when she awoke the covers were down, but no one was there."

At the corner you can see the mansion on your right at 7357 Franklin, once the home of Al Jolson and Ruby Keeler. The

The lovely former home of Ozzie and Harriet Nelson and their television family is allegedly still visited by Ozzie's ghost.

home on the left at 1800 Camino Palmiero belonged to Samuel Goldwyn.

(Camino Palmiero to Franklin. Right around to left at Waddles Garden Park to Hollywood. Right to Curson. Right to:)

1825 Curson Avenue, Charles Laughton death site

During a distinguished 40-year career Charles Laughton starred in classics such as *The Devil and the Deep* (1932), *Mutiny on the Bounty* (1935), *The Barretts of Wimpole Street* (1934), *Les Misérables* (1935), and *The Hunchback of Notre Dame* (1939), winning a 1933 Academy Award for *The Private Life of Henry VII*. He and wife Elsa Lanchester ran a respected acting school here, but while his professional credits are impressive, his personal life was bizarre.

The only woman Laughton ever made love to was wife Elsa, whom he married in 1927 after a sexless two-year courtship. Three years later Elsa witnessed a fight between Laughton and a homosexual youth, which forced Laughton to admit his homosexuality. Elsa replied, "It's perfectly all right. It doesn't matter. I understand." She also went immediately deaf and remained so for three months. The couple somehow remained married for over 30 years. Longtime drinker Laughton succumbed to liver cancer on December 15, 1962, sitting in his beloved schoolroom here when he died at 63.

(Reverse to Hollywood. Right to Stanley. Right to:)

1712 and 1717 North Stanley Avenue, Tallulah Bankhead home, Orson Welles death site

In 1931, the home at 1712 Stanley was rented by Tallulah Bankhead from William Haines while she filmed *Tarnished Lady, The Cheat,* and *The Devil and the Deep.* Bankhead was the leader of Hollywood's 1930s "café society" and an avowed bisexual. The serious cocaine addict particularly enjoyed stealing lovers from personal rivals. Friends knew when she had indulged because she always stripped naked after imbibing, saying, "Cocaine isn't habit forming darling. I've been taking it all my life." If a cocaine-addled Bankhead thought a party needed a lift, she performed naked cartwheels to get things going. One of her sexual romps with a famous blonde starlet was interrupted by Mickey Rooney when he entered the crowded bathroom during a party here. In her memoirs Bankhead describes entertaining guests here and clearly seeing a ghostly horse trot by the front window. Neighbors later confirmed they saw the same sight many times.

The mansion across the street at 1717 North Stanley was the last home of writer-director Orson Welles. It was there on October 10, 1985, that the 70-year-old writer and producer of the radio classic *War of the Worlds* and the movie blockbuster *Citizen Kane* (1939) died of a heart attack.

(Reverse and note brick mansion on right at corner:)

7655 Hollywood Boulevard, Peter Lorre death site

Hungarian actor Peter Lorre (born Lazlo Lowenstein) studied psychology under Sigmund Freud and Alfred Adler before joining the stage and movies. Typecast as the sinister villain with his deep set eyes, round face, and menacing whisper, he debuted in the Fritz Lang classic thriller *M* (1931), starred in the 1930s *Mr. Moto* movies and played the psychopath in dozens of films such as *Mad Love* (1934) and *Crime and Punishment* (1935). He is perhaps best known for roles in the Bogart classics *Maltese Falcon* (1941), *Casablanca* (1942) and *Strange Cargo* (1940). His career skidded by the 1960s, his final appearances being in the 1964 comedies *Muscle Beach Party* and *The Patsy*. At the age of 59, Lorre suffered a stroke and a heart attack and died in this large mansion on March 23, 1964. His eulogy was given by another sinister villain, best pal Vincent Price.

West on Hollywood Boulevard past Fairfax at 7940, actor Harris Glenn Milstead

The home and death site of *Casablanca* and *Maltese Falcon* star Peter Lorre.

had a fatal heart attack while visiting friends at the Plaza Suites Apartments. Better-known as his transvestite alterego "Divine," he was a Broadway veteran best remembered for his role in *Hairspray* (1983). At the time of his March 7, 1988, death, he was 42.

In the 1920s, a palatial estate stood nearby at 7269 Hollywood Boulevard, at the time the grandest—and saddest—home in Hollywood, haunted by the ghost of actor John Cudahy, who committed suicide there in 1922. Sole heir to the Cudahy meatpack-ing fortune, he splattered his brains and blood over the living room walls with a shot-gun. No amount of paint could conceal the stains, and no wallpaper stayed in place on the spot. Red blotches soon reemerged and paper simply fell off the wall. Norma Tal-madge so hated the home that she got a di-vorce from her producer-husband Joe Schenck rather than live there after he bought the house in 1924. It was then bought by Emil Jannings, a major silent star of such hits as *Loves of Pharaoh* (1922), *Peter the Great* (1923), *The Way of the Flesh* (1927), and *Sins of the Fathers* (1929). He bought the house in 1928, although his manager and his wife both begged him not to buy the man-sion. Within a year his career inexplicably stalled, and he ended up in bankruptcy by 1930. Returning to his native Germany, Jan-nings became a propaganda filmmaker for Adolf Hitler and Joseph Goebbels. After the war, his ties to the Nazi party made him persona non grata in movies across the world, and he died broke and forgotten in Germany in 1950. Before songman Irving Berlin moved into the old mansion in 1930 he and his wife had the house exorcised by a Catholic priest. Gossip queen Louella Par-sons called it "the Jinx Mansion" and wouldn't even enter the grounds. When no one could be found to buy the house at any price after the Berlins moved out in 1933, it was torn down.

(Stanley to Hollywood. Right to Court-ney. Right to Courtney Terrace. Right to cul-de-sac at:)

1803 Courtney Terrace, Franchot Tone–Barbara Payton–Tom Neal triangle, Tone beating site

One-time professional boxer Tom Neal appeared in over 180 films, including *Flying Tigers* (1942) with John Wayne, and was a moody tough guy off the screen as well as on. In the 1950s he had a tempestuous affair with Barbara Payton, a gorgeous B-movie actress later jailed for prostitution. At the same time, she was having an affair with Franchot Tone, the former husband of Joan Crawford who starred in *Jigsaw* (1949) and *Man on the Eiffel Tower* (1950).

After private detectives confirmed the affair to Neal, on September 13, 1951, he waited for the couple to leave Payton's apart-ment here and savagely attacked both. The defenseless Tone was beaten senseless, suffering a broken nose, fractured jaw, and a brain concussion that caused stroke-like effects to his face that remained the rest of his life. Payton received a broken nose. An unrepentant Neal was later imprisoned for murdering his wife in Palm Springs in 1965.

After the beating, Payton and Tone married, but it lasted less than two months, after which Payton tried to commit suicide here with an overdose of pills. By the 1960s Payton was homeless, at one point arrested for sleeping on a bench at the nearby corner of Sunset and Stanley.

(Reverse to Hollywood. Left to Curson. Right to end of first block at Hawthorne, site of:)

7560 Hawthorne Avenue and Curson Avenue, Hugh Grant arrest site

At about 1:30 A.M. on June 27, 1995, vice cops watched a BMW pull to the curb at Sunset and Courtney, a few blocks from here. In a scene repeated thousands of times every day, 23-year-old hooker Stella Marie Thompson—known to cops as "Divine Brown"—got in the car. Cops followed as the car parked in front of 7560 Hawthorne and as soon as the couple inside began engaging in a "sex act" they were arrested.

Police charging the pair with "lewd conduct" were shocked to discover Stella's "date" was British heartthrob Hugh Grant, Oxford-educated star of *Four Weddings and a Funeral* (1994), *The Englishman Who Went Up a Hill but Came Down a Mountain* and *Nine Months* (both 1995). He posted bond and retreated to England and his understandably upset girlfriend of seven years, supermodel Elizabeth Hurley. A day later Divine sold her story to the tabloid press for $160,000, telling the touching story "Hugh's Hooker: My Story."

(Curson to Sunset. Left to Gardner. Right to the second apartment on the left. Directly across from the fire station:)

1438 North Gardner Street, Ron Marquette suicide site

British model Ronald Anthony Margau had a promising career after appearing in the 1993 HBO *Red Shoe Diaries* cable series and in the 1994 television series *Malibu 2000* under the name Ron Marquette. It is

still a mystery why the apparently happy 30-year-old committed suicide in his ground-floor apartment here.

On the morning of September 27, 1994, Marquette called girlfriend Dee Dee Pfeiffer, whom he had met while the two filmed the movie *Past Tense*. Younger sister of Michelle, Dee Dee had just earned a role in the television series *Cybill*. When she arrived at the apartment Marquette walked out of a bedroom and without saying a word put a pistol in his mouth and pulled the trigger. He left no note and no explanation explaining why he wanted his girlfriend there. Remarkably, Pfeiffer managed to get through taping a *Cybill* pilot just days after the suicide.

(Gardner to DeLongpre. Right to Ogden. Right to the second bungalow on the right:)

1408 North Ogden Drive, Charles Chaplin, Jr., death site

Charles Chaplin, Jr., 42-year-old son of "The Tramp" and author of *My Father Charlie Chaplin*, died here on March 20,

Young actor Ron Marquette inexplicably killed himself in front of girlfriend Dee Dee Pfeiffer in his apartment in this building.

1968, the result of a massive pulmonary embolism. He had fallen and broken his ankle, but not knowing the extent of the injury left it untreated for a month, which led to a fatal blood clot.

At the time of his death his mother Lita Grey Chaplin was living nearby at 1440 Gardner, and a block south at 1344 Ogden is the first home of Lucille Ball, purchased for her family by the young starlet and where she lived until her marriage to Desi Arnaz.

(Ogden to Sunset. Right a block to Genesee. Right to the middle of the block on the left:)

1428 North Genesee Street, *Nightmare on Elm Street* movie house

This familiar looking house was the set of the home terrorized in the 1980s and 1990s *Nightmare on Elm Street* movie series.

(Genesee to Santa Monica. Right four blocks to Hayworth. Right to near the end of the block on the left:)

1263 Hayworth Avenue, Theresa Saldana attack site

Now called the Sunset Bermuda Apartments, for twenty years they had the romantic name Bermuda Dunes. On the morning of March 15, 1982, actress Theresa Saldana was attacked by a deranged fan on the sidewalk in front of the building. Obsessed with Saldana after seeing her in the 1981 film *Raging Bull,* Scotsman Arthur Jackson tracked her here and stabbed her two dozen times before a water deliveryman intervened. Jackson was on a "divine mission" to deliver the 27-year-old Saldana to heaven, where he would join her after being executed for her murder.

The vicious attack left the knife blade bent in half, but two weeks later Saldana appeared in court covered in bandages to testify against Jackson. He was just days away from a 1991 parole when Saldana presented threatening letters that he sent her from jail. Four years were added to his sentence, and after his June 19, 1996, release from prison the by-then 60-year-old killer was extradited to England to stand trial for a 1967 murder. The Saldana attack publicized the "stalker" problem for the first time and led to new protection laws. During the 1990s Saldana co-starred in television's *The Commish.*

(Leaving the Saldana site, if you can easily cross Fountain, do so and continue north of Hayworth to the end of the block on the left side [if northbound]. If Fountain is too busy to easily and safely cross, turn right on Fountain to Fairfax. Left to Sunset. Left to Hayworth. Left to first apartment building on the right [if southbound]:)

1443 Hayworth Avenue, F. Scott Fitzgerald death site

Writer F. Scott Fitzgerald (*The Great Gatsby, Tender Is the Night, The Last Tycoon*) lived at 1403 North Laurel, but his columnist girlfriend Sheilah Graham put him up at her first floor apartment here at the Hayworth Chateau Apartments after a heart attack left him unable to climb to his own third-floor apartment. In November 1940 Fitzgerald suffered another near-fatal attack walking to the nearby Schwab's Drugstore for cigarettes. A month later during the evening of December 21, 1940, "Scottie" suffered a massive, fatal heart attack while reading *The Princetonian* next to the fireplace in Graham's apartment.

Tour 3:
Hollywood Hills

Begin Tour 3 at Barham Boulevard just east of the Hollywood (101) Freeway just north of Hollywood. Barham east to Lake Hollywood. Right to:

3090 Lake Hollywood Drive, Ruth Ettig shooting site

In 1920, singer Ruth Ettig was discovered by mobster Moe "The Gimp" Snyder performing in vaudeville, and within weeks he became her business manager and by 1922 her husband. The first job he got her was singing at the secret casino hidden in Bugsy Siegel's Castillo del Lago mansion. With mob help Ettig became the most popular torch singer of the day. Ettig divorced the obsessive Snyder in 1937 and took up with her pianist Myrl Alderman, moving to L.A. to escape Snyder's stalking.

On October 15, 1938, Snyder kidnapped Alderman at gunpoint from his NBC studio and drove him to the couple's Hollywood Hills home. He shot Alderman twice and was arrested as he chased Ettig through the house. Snyder was convicted of attempted murder, but lawyer Jerry Giesler managed an acquittal on the kidnapping charges, convincing a jury that since Alderman was going home anyway, Snyder didn't really kidnap him. Ettig's bizarre life story was told in the 1955 Cagney classic *Love Me or Leave Me*.

(Reverse to Barham. Right to Craig. Left to Floyd. Left to:)

3341 Floyd Terrace, Iris Adrian death site

During the 1930s and 1940s Iris Adrian appeared in 150 movies, usually playing some version of the brassy blonde gum-chewing gangster's moll or wise-cracking barfly. She began as a Ziegfeld dancer after being discovered in a 1929 Hollywood beauty contest, and made her screen debut in 1935's *Rumba*. She later starred in several Laurel and Hardy comedies and in films such as *Road to Zanzibar* (1941) with Bing Crosby and Bob Hope, *His Butler's Sister* (1943) with Deanna Durbin, and the 1945 thriller *The Woman in the Window* with Edward G. Robinson. Her final film roles were in the 1960s, in *The Odd Couple* and Disney comedies *The Love Bug*, *The Apple Dumpling Gang*, and *Herbie Goes Bananas*. She died of heart ailments in her home on September 17, 1994, at 81.

(Floyd to Blair. Left to Barham. Right over Freeway to Cahuenga. Right to Oakshire. Left one block to Oak Glen. Right to:)

3365 Oak Glen Drive, Harry Langdon death site

Harry Langdon was a leading silent film comedian in the early days of Hollywood, rivaling Chaplin in popularity and earnings. The Iowa-born Langdon began his vaudeville career as a 12-year-old ventriloquist who could play any musical instrument by ear. He perfected a facial expression that was born during his very first theater performance, when extreme stage fright caused a look that left the audience in stitches. After a ten-year vaudeville career, the by-then world-famous Langdon received a $1 million a year contract from Mack Sennett in 1925 to appear in Sennett comedies. His fat jowls, wide eyes and bewildered look enthralled audiences the world over in movies such as *Tramp, Tramp, Tramp* (1926), *Long Pants* (1927), *Three's a Crowd* (1927), and *The Chaser* (1928).

On the verge of worldwide stardom in 1927, the petulant actor decided that only *he* could direct his own movies. He quit working for Sennett and began producing his own movies, but the quality was far below studio level, and the public ignored his work. Within four years he was broke after four multimillion dollar divorces, forgotten by his fans, and as Mack Sennett observed, "the most tragic human figure I have ever come across." He died in obscurity at 60 in his small home here on December 23, 1944. Langdon was not the first, nor will he be the last, actor undone by a huge ego.

(Oak Glen to:)

3429 Oak Glen Drive, John Matuszak death site

It was here that former Oakland Raiders football star turned sometime actor John Matuszak died of an apparent drug overdose in 1989. "Tooz" was only 31 when he died.

(Oak Glen to Oakley and onto Multiview. Right to:)

3502 Multiview Drive, Shannon "Savannah" Wilsey suicide site

In 1987 Texas teenager Shannon Wilsey came to L.A. to live with her father, but by 1992 she was starring in porn movies using the name "Savannah." Her porn films *Ecstasy* and *New Wave Hookers* are cult favorites. A girlfriend of MTV comic Pauly Shore, Wilsey was hurt when she slammed her Corvette into a tree in 1994, severely slashing her face. Overwhelmed by a battle with drugs and depressed from the accident, she shot herself in the head with a rifle inside her garage on July 11, 1994. She was only 22.

Her mother later filed a lawsuit blaming rocker Greg Allman for the death, alleging that after befriending the 16-year-old at a mall, he gave her gifts, took her on the road with his band and introduced her to drugs.

(Reverse to Broadlawn. Left to Cahuenga. Right to Woodrow Wilson/Mulholland. Hard right on Woodrow Wilson to:)

6969 Woodrow Wilson Drive, Frank Christi murder site

A type-cast "bad guy," Christi starred in dozens of 1960s and 1970s TV shows like *Charlie's Angels* and *The Rockford Files*. His final movie role was in *The Godfather* (1972). On July 9, 1982, the 52-year-old was murdered in a hail of gunfire in his driveway. Neighbors heard the frightened Christi begging for his life before he was shot over a dozen times. He apparently made the mistake of dating the girlfriend of a local hood, who allegedly hired three ex-cons to kill the actor. When the three blabbed to prison pals boasting of the killing, indictments were returned in 1992, but all three men have been on the lam since.

At nearby 6233 Mulholland Drive writer Aldous Huxley died of cancer at 70 in a home borrowed from Virginia Pfeiffer. Nobody noticed because of a more famous murder in Dallas on the same date: November 22, 1963.

(Woodrow Wilson to:)

7357 Woodrow Wilson Drive, Aleta Alexander suicide site

Aleta Alexander was a prominent Broadway star when she came to Hollywood in the early 1930s to try her luck in the movies. Although she had a few minor roles, her success didn't approach that of her stage work, and by the summer of 1935 she was suffering from severe depression. When she also discovered that her husband of only four months, actor Ross Alexander, was cheating on her, the despondent star killed herself with a hunting rifle on the front lawn of their Hollywood Hills home. She was only 28 years old.

A little over a year later her former husband, overwhelmed by the guilt over his wife's suicide, climbed into the hayloft of a San Fernando Valley barn and shot himself with the same rifle. The barn, located at 17221 Ventura Boulevard, was on a farm the couple had purchased as a weekend retreat.

(Woodrow Wilson to Soper. Left to Palo Vista. Right to:)

7422 Palo Vista Drive, Dick Sargent death site

Dick Sargent debuted in *Prisoner of War* (1954) with Ronald Reagan and appeared in 100 films, but is best known as the second "Darren" in television's *Bewitched* from 1968 to 1973. Early in his career, he was forced to keep his homosexuality hidden with a phony marriage and appearances with buxom young actresses staged by his studios. Sargent went public at 1991's "National Coming Out Day" and became a vocal gay activist. He lost a long fight with prostate cancer and died here on July 8, 1994, at 64.

(Reverse to Woodrow Wilson. Past the intersection at Mulholland, the site of:)

Woodrow Wilson—Mulholland Drive shoulder, Carl Chessman abductions

During the 1940s the shoulder just ahead on Mulholland was a "lovers' lane" with its panoramic view of L.A. Small-time bandit Carl Chessman kidnapped several women from the spot during a month-long robbery and rape spree during the summer of 1948 that eventually landed him on death row. Nicknamed the "Red Light Bandit" because he used a red police spotlight on his getaway car, Chessman was put to death after 13 years on death row although none of his victims was killed. Directly above the spot is the magnificent mansion built by Rudy Vallee, later occupied by actress Ann Harding, and most recently by Arsenio Hall.

(Woodrow Wilson to Seattle. Right to:)

2840 Seattle Drive, Anthony Perkins death site

The only son of stage and movie star Osgood Perkins, Anthony Perkins spent his childhood almost entirely with his mother, Janet, due to the long and frequent absences of his father. After several years of New England summer stock work, Perkins made his debut in the 1953 film *The Actress* with Spencer Tracy. After several other small roles and after losing the lead in 1954's *East of Eden* to James Dean, Perkins was tapped to star in the 1960 Hitchcock classic *Psycho*. In a striking coincidence, Perkins' *Psycho* character was also obsessed with his mother.

Perkins had his first real relationship with a woman at the age of 39, and although he married at 41 and fathered two sons, rumors persisted that the handsome actor was indeed gay. When he became ill in 1990, a positive test result for the AIDS virus was leaked to the tabloid press, and Perkins learned the results reading in a supermarket checkout line. After battling the dread disease for several years, Perkins died of complications of the virus in his Hollywood Hills home here on September 12, 1992, at the age of 60.

(Reverse to Woodrow Wilson. Right on Woodrow Wilson to:)

7708 Woodrow Wilson Drive, real *Ghostbusters* house

Comedian Dan Ackroyd allegedly received the inspiration for the 1988 movie *Ghostbusters* while he lived in this home for several years. According to reports, the home was plagued with lights that worked by themselves, doors that locked themselves, and strange night noises. It may not be a surprise, since earlier residents of the house include Mamas and the Papas lead singer Cass Elliot, who died in London of a heart attack caused by obesity in 1974, and actress Natalie Wood, who drowned in a mysterious boating accident off Catalina Island in 1981.

(Woodrow Wilson to:)

7917 Woodrow Wilson Drive, John Cassavetes death site

Not visible from the road, the house at 7917 was shared by actor-filmmaker John Cassavetes and his actress wife Gena Rowlands. Cassavetes debuted in *Taxi* (1953), and followed up with the imaginative *Shadows* (1959), a film with no script, improvised dialogue and no clear direction. The creative work was a huge critical success, allowing Cassavetes to direct other films such as *Too Late for Blues* (1961) and *A Child Is Waiting* (1962), while starring in movies including *The Dirty Dozen* (1967), *Rosemary's Baby* (1968), and *The Fury* (1978). His other independent movies were commercial successes as well. *Faces* (1968) earned three Oscar nominations, *Husbands* (1970) won critical acclaim, and *A Woman Under the Influence* (1974) earned Rowlands an Oscar nomination for Best Actress. All of Cassavetes' movies had one thing in common: they were shot like home movies, with friends starring and his home the set. After battling health problems Cassavetes suffered a fatal heart attack in the home on February 3, 1989, at 59.

(Woodrow Wilson to:)

7944 Woodrow Wilson Drive, Gia Scala suicide site

According to Louis B. Mayer, British actress Gia Scala "looked like Ingrid Bergman, Grace Kelly, and five sexy Italian actresses below the neck." Born Giovanna Scoglio, she debuted in *All That Heaven Knows* (1955) and followed up in films such as *Price of Fear* (1956) and *Guns of Navarone* (1961). Her promising career was a memory when she overdosed here on April 30, 1972, at 38. A year earlier she had tried suicide in London by jumping off a bridge but was pulled from the Thames River by a passing cabby.

(Woodrow Wilson to Woodstock. Left to:)

2500 Woodstock Road, Naturalist Church murders site

In 1982, two members of the eccentric Naturalist Church were found slain inside the church's compound hidden in the Hollywood Hills. Though rumored relationships with the drug trade were suspected, nothing was ever proven and no one ever charged in the shotgun slayings.

(Reverse to Woodrow Wilson. Left to:)

8000 Woodrow Wilson Drive, Inger Stevens death site

Swedish actress Inger Stevens took an overdose of barbiturates here on April 30, 1970. The 35-year-old beauty had starred as television's *The Farmer's Daughter*, and in the movies *Hang 'Em High* (1968) and *A Guide for the Married Man* (1967). It was never determined whether the strange death was a suicide, an accident or something more sinister.

(Woodrow Wilson to intersection with Woodrow Wilson, Mulholland, and Laurel Canyon. Right on Laurel

Canyon half a mile down the hill just past the intersection with Dona Doratea Drive to:)

3110 Laurel Canyon Drive, Ramon Novarro murder site

Ramon Novarro was one of the "Big Three" Latin Lovers of the 1920s along with pals Antonio Moreno and Rudolph Valentino. His films included *The Prisoner of Zenda* (1922), *Where the Pavement Ends* (1923), and *Ben-Hur* (1926), and though he was described as "too beautiful to be taken seriously," he received 10,000 fan letters a week from fans who were unaware that he was an alcoholic with an appetite for young male prostitutes.

Leaving films in 1935, he lived in seclusion in a house decorated by fellow homosexual William Haines entirely in black fur and silver wallpaper. Guests were allowed to enter only if they were wearing black, white or silver. On October 31, 1968, the 63-year-old was beaten to death by two young brothers he had met earlier at a Hollywood gay bar. They were caught when police checked phone records and found that the pair made long distance calls to girlfriends back in Indiana *while* they were beating the helpless Novarro. A famous but unproven story was that Novarro was found with an Art Deco dildo stuffed down his throat. The trinket was a gift from best friend and one-time lover Rudolph Valentino. Novarro's Spanish-style mansion was redone in 1991.

(Reverse to Mulholland. Right to Mulholland Terrace. Right to:)

8115 Mulholland Terrace, Rick James assault site

In 1981, Rick James was at the top of the music world with the huge dance hit "Super Freak." He soon began a ten-year-long addiction to crack cocaine which ended when he was arrested in 1991 with his girlfriend Tanya Anne Hijazi and charged with

bringing a woman to their rented home here and holding her hostage for several days. She was allegedly threatened with death if she tried to leave or told anyone of an ordeal during which she reportedly was burned with a cocaine pipe and forced to perform oral sex on Hijazi. Although cleared of those charges, the pair was later convicted of assaulting a young woman in a West Hollywood hotel—now called the Argyle Club. Hijazi served 15 months in jail, and James received a ten-year sentence. The now-clean singer was released from jail in 1997.

(Reverse to Laurel Canyon. Right to:)

2600 Laurel Canyon Drive, Sam Rummel murder site

In the early morning hours of December 11, 1950, celebrity lawyer and "Mouthpiece of the Mob" Samuel Rummel was blasted by several shotguns as he walked into his Laurel Canyon home. His only client at the time was mobster Mickey Cohen, then on trial for several federal weapons charges and fighting an ugly turf war with Mafia lord Jack Dragna. Rummel was a casualty of one or the other of these little disagreements.

On the right side of Laurel Canyon you will pass Laurel Canyon Park, a popular spot for hikers and dog walkers. On April 2, 1989, 36-year-old actor David Rappaport committed suicide there by shooting himself in the chest with a .357 magnum pistol. A British stage star, Rappaport was a tiny 3'11" but became a huge star when he came to the United States to star in the 1985 television series *The Wizard*. He also had an ongoing television role on *L.A. Law* in the late 1980s, but for some reason he sat under some bushes in the middle of the park with his beloved dog and shot himself. It was his second suicide attempt.

(Laurel Canyon to the intersection with Lookout Mountain, and on the hillside to your left note the site of:)

2398 Laurel Canyon Drive, alleged Houdini estate ruins

Escape artist Harry Houdini also appeared in several forgettable movies such as *The Master Mystery* (1918), *The Grim Game* (1919), and *Terror Island* (1920). According to legend, the huge estate that once covered the hillside on the left side of Laurel Canyon at Lookout Mountain belonged to Houdini during his Hollywood period, but according to biographers his only West Coast home was a rented bungalow near Paramount Studios. As of 1997 the servants' quarters at the top of the hill were all that remained of the stately Mediterranean villa built in 1915, among four dozen Laurel Canyon homes that fell victim to a 1959 fire. The maze of rambling paths, arches, fences, and Oriental monuments covering the hillside below the site are a haunting reminder of a grander time, perhaps the basis for the Houdini rumors that have swirled around the site since the early 1960s.

Houdini's interest in the occult might explain 50 years of ghostly noises and nightly visitors at the site. The abandoned property lay unwanted for almost 20 years until it was purchased by a Georgia man in 1996. Even *that* purchase is shrouded in mystery: the buyer claims he was persuaded to purchase the weed-choked lot by an old man he met while visiting the property. The elderly gentleman wore a silk suit and laid out playing cards revealing numbers that were to be his purchase price. Perhaps it was Houdini's ghost?

Houdini died—appropriately—on Halloween night, 1926. There is a similar location at 2450 Canyon incorrectly attributed as Houdini's. For several decades after his 1926 death, Houdini's widow lived just up the street at 2435 Laurel Canyon Boulevard, where she often entertained the psychics who visited the area. If you wish to visit the ruins, turn left at the intersection onto Willow Glen and park carefully on the right. The site is on the right or southeast corner of the Laurel Canyon and Lookout Mountain.

(Right from Laurel Canyon onto Lookout Mountain. A short distance on the right to the small bungalow with three large windows across the front at:)

8227 Lookout Mountain Drive, Bessie Love haunted house

On the right side just in from Laurel Canyon notice the tiny bungalow with three large windows across the front, nestled among the

The ruins of Laurel Canyon mansion reputedly rented by Harry Houdini still cover the hillside below the site.

Bessie Love's canyon cottage was built on the site of an 1800s double killing, which might explain the hauntings that continue to this day.

trees and plants, the former home of silent screen actress Bessie Love. The gorgeous and talented Love debuted in 1914 and starred in the first movie musical, 1926's *The Broadway Melody.* Love bought this secluded bungalow in 1918 in an area then called "Bungalowland," popular for the quiet country atmosphere sought by stars such as John Gilbert, Charlie Chaplin and Fatty Arbuckle. Locals told Love that the site was haunted by two men murdered by highwayman Tiburico Vasquez in the 1830s, and after five years of terrifying night voices and ghostly apparitions Love left and never returned. Residents have reported similar happenings as recently as 1997.

Just past the Bessie Love home at 8305 Lookout Mountain is a home that was originally built in 1914 as part of a three-bungalow brothel that was frequented by the movie people relaxing in the canyon. The main house featured a large bed that could be rolled into a compartment hidden in the wall at the head of the bed—with its occu-

pants still onboard—if the police should arrive unannounced.

(Lookout Mountain to just before stop sign at Wonderland. Notice the three-story house near the power lines on the right:)

8421 Lookout Mountain Drive, Roscoe "Fatty" Arbuckle home

The home clinging to the hillside above the street was a weekend retreat for Roscoe "Fatty" Arbuckle during the 1920s. Arbuckle weighed 16 pounds at birth, and by the time he began his movie career was over 300 pounds. The rotund comic starred in hundreds of silent film comedies between 1909 and 1920, and after splitting from then-partner Buster Keaton, he became the highest paid comedy star of silent films, earning a $3 million contract in 1920 for only three films. His career crashed in 1925 amid unfounded allegations that he killed a young girl during

Roscoe Arbuckle's unusual Laurel Canyon hideaway.

enter the home on July 1, 1981, and either watched or assisted in the brutal and gruesome torture murders of four residents. The victims were all friends of Holmes'. Charged but subsequently acquitted, he died of AIDS on March 13, 1988, probably not shocking since he reportedly had video sex with over 14,000 women.

(Continue up the hill on Wonderland and carefully reverse to Skyline. Right to Sunset Crest. Right to:)

2111 Sunset Crest Drive, Robert Bloch death site

Robert Bloch was a prolific pulp fiction writer of over 400 stories and books, 25 novels and hundreds of movie and television scripts. His most famous work was a little-known 1940s horror novel titled *Psycho* that Alfred Hitchcock made into a classic film. Bloch died of heart failure in his home on September 23, 1994, at 77.

(Reverse to Laurel Canyon. Right to Kirkwood. Right to Ridpath [at Mannix]. Right to:)

8443 Ridpath Drive, Lila Leeds– Robert Mitchum drug bust site

Robert Mitchum's life story is the stuff of action movies: His railroad worker father was killed in an accident when he was two, and as a young man he rode the rails with hobo pals. At 15 he spent a summer on a Georgia chain gang for being a "dangerous and suspicious character with no means of support," and after walking away from his work detail one hot afternoon escaped to California to

a July Fourth party he hosted in his San Francisco hotel suite. He was acquitted after three trials, but he was finished in movies and died a penniless broken man on June 29, 1933, at 46 in New York.

(Lookout Mountain to Wonderland. Right past the school to:)

8763 Wonderland Park Drive, John Holmes "Wonderland murders" site

After starring in an estimated 2,250 porn films, years of drug abuse left John Holmes impotent, and by the 1980s his only source of income was from delivering drugs for a dealer living here. He arranged for a competitor to live on the beach, surf, and soak up the sun.

He married in 1940 and took a wartime job as a metal-worker at Lockheed Airport in Burbank, and played local theater roles on the week-ends. His movie debut was in *Hoppy Serves a Writ* (1942), replacing an actor who had been killed in an on-set acci-dent—when Mitchum was handed his wardrobe, the dead actor's blood and brains were still staining the hat and shirt. During the next year he had small roles in 18 movies including *Border Patrol, Gung Ho,* and *Thirty Seconds Over Tokyo.* By 1948 Mitchum was a household name, while his friend Lila Leeds was a strug-gling actress doing "B" movies to survive. When police raided Leeds' canyon home here on September 1, 1948, they re-portedly found three mari-juana cigarettes, at the time a huge scandal. The couple were branded as "dope fiends" and were denounced in the press. Mitchum was so cer-tain the arrest would end his career that he wrote "former actor" on the police booking sheet that asked for his occupation.

The much-publicized 1949 trials led to jail terms for both, equally well-publicized as photographers were allowed to freely follow each around their respective prisons. Pic-tures of Mitchum ran in every fan magazine, and after his release the unrepentant Mit-chum told the press that "prison was just like Palm Springs, but without the riff-raff." While Mitchum went on to a huge career with over 150 starring roles, Leeds was com-pletely ruined, and she disappeared without a trace. Mitchum died at his Palm Springs home in early 1998.

The former drug house and site of the gruesome "Wonderland Park Murders," where three people were beaten to death in the second-floor living room.

(Reverse to Laurel Canyon. Right to the intersection with Mount Olympus. Carefully reverse direction at the light and immediately bear right onto the access road running parallel to Laurel Canyon. The third house on the right is:)

1826 Laurel Canyon Boulevard, Gary Cooper–Lupe Velez love-nest

When young Montanan Gary Cooper came to Hollywood and became a star, his parents followed soon afterward. He pur-chased a bungalow for them at 529 Cahu-enga Boulevard in Hollywood, coincidentally on the same block as his *Wolf Song* (1929) co-star Lupe Velez, who lived at 565. Cooper and Velez carried on a heated yearlong affair, even though both of his parents fiercely objected to the relationship with the much older and clearly volatile starlet. When his parents began making nightly strolls past her house to see if their wayward son was inside, she sold the home and purchased an out-of-the-way canyon bungalow. In the 1920s and '30s, sleepy Laurel Canyon was a weekend getaway spot where movie stars could escape their fans. Laurel Canyon Boulevard was a narrow, winding two lane blacktop snaking through the mountains. Cooper took up residence here at 1826, and he and Velez made their home here for over a year.

Like all of Velez' affairs, the Cooper tryst was all-consuming until it burned out in a year or so. Her temper didn't help—the tempestuous "Mexican Spitfire" routinely beat him black and blue, and on more than one occasion he showed up for work with black eyes. When he broke the relationship off, she took a shot at him with her pistol as he drove away from this house. When the affair ended, Cooper was an emotional and physical wreck and had withered to less than 130 pounds. He was so unable to function that MGM was forced to send him to Europe for four months to recuperate. Velez left Laurel Canyon and soon married *Tarzan* star Johnny Weissmuller and moved into the Beverly Hills mansion where she would commit suicide just a few years later.

(Continue on the narrow access road to the end near the Laurel Canyon Country Store. Bear left to the light at Laurel Canyon. Left heading south on Laurel Canyon to Hollywood Boulevard. Right up the hill winding around to:)

8545 Hollywood Boulevard, Sidney Toler death site

Sidney Toler appeared in dozens of Broadway plays between 1919 and 1930 and authored over 70 others, including *The Belle of Richmond, Ritzy, The Golden Age,* and *The Man They Left Behind.* He arrived in Hollywood in 1930 to star in movies such as Greta Garbo's *Madame X* (1929), Katharine Hepburn's *Spitfire* (1934), *Here Comes the Groom* (1934), and *Double Wedding* (1937). Toler is best remembered for his portrayal of Charlie Chan in 25 movies after taking over the role following the death of the original Chan, Warner Oland. Some of the more memorable Charlie Chan roles included those in *King of Chinatown* (1939), *Charlie Chan in Treasure Island* (1939), *Charlie Chan in the City of Darkness* (1941), *Charlie Chan's Murder Cruise* (1940), and *Charlie Chan at the Wax Museum* (1940).

Suffering late in life from intestinal cancer, he nonetheless filmed the final two Charlie Chan films so ill that he could not walk. All of his scenes were filmed either standing still or sitting. He finally succumbed to the disease at his Hollywood Hills home on February 13, 1947.

(Hollywood Boulevard to:)

8825 Hollywood Boulevard, Lenny Bruce death site

The house hanging above the street was the last home of comic Lenny Bruce and the site of the 41-year-old's fatal drug overdose on August 2, 1966. At 19 and after two unsatisfying years in the navy, Bruce earned a dishonorable discharge by pretending to have become a homosexual during his tour of duty aboard ship. He began his comedy career as a stage emcee in smoky burlesque houses in New York, quickly becoming involved with the jazz and drug scenes popular in the 1950s. His first marriage—to a stripper named Honey—ended when he informed police about her drug use, and she was jailed for two years. Their bizarre relationship somehow carried on until his death. His reputation for onstage lunacy—he once emceed a show standing naked on stage—made him a legend, and his routines clearly were designed to shock even the toughest audience.

By the late 1950s, Bruce was a hopeless drug abuser, hooked on over a dozen different drugs. His arms were a mass of scars, and his mind was slowly turning to mush. By 1966 he was a total burnout, and while sitting naked on the toilet he shot himself up with a huge dose of heroin and fell instantly dead on the floor with the needle still stuck in his arm. It may have been on purpose, since he was in poor health, bankrupt, had no work, and had received a foreclosure notice on the home that morning. He had tried to flush it down the toilet just before his death.

Tour 4:
The Sunset Strip

Begin Tour 4 at Chateau Marmont Hotel, 8221 Sunset Boulevard, located in the heart of Hollywood near La Cienega Boulevard, the site of:

Chateau Marmont Hotel Bungalow 3, John Belushi death site

On March 5, 1982, a lethal "speedball" of cocaine and heroin killed *Saturday Night Live* star John Belushi in this bungalow. Although a lifelong drug abuser, Belushi still was able to turn his *SNL* popularity into roles in movies such as *Animal House* (1979), *Blues Brothers* (1981), and *Neighbors* (1977). His drug problems were totally out of control when the 33-year-old comic died. Because he was deathly afraid of needles, groupie friend Cathy Smith gave him the fatal shot inside his rented bungalow. She spent 18 months in jail for a manslaughter conviction after an investigation was started when she told *The National Enquirer* that "I killed John Belushi. I didn't mean to—but I was responsible for his death." In the interview, given to the tabloid just 12 days after Belushi's death, she also admitted to supplying the heroin used in the "speedball" as well as injecting him with the drugs.

(Sunset to Alta Loma. Left to:)

1200 Alta Loma Drive, Sunset Marquis Hotel, Van Heflin death site

Oklahoman Van Heflin was discovered by Katharine Hepburn doing a local 1936

play and cast in her *A Woman Rebels* (1936). One of the great character actors of all time, he starred in *Johnny Eager* (1940), *Sante Fe Trail* (1940), *Possessed* (1947), *East Side/West Side* (1948), *Shane* (1953), and *The Greatest Story Ever Told* (1965). The 60-year-old Heflin made his last appearance in *Airport* (1970), completed just weeks before he suffered a fatal heart attack during his daily swim in the hotel pool here on July 23, 1971.

(Alta Loma to Halloway. Right to:)

8563 Halloway Drive, Sal Mineo murder site

Handsome teen heartthrob Sal Mineo starred in *The Rose Tatoo* (1951), *West Side Story* (1952) and *Rebel Without a Cause* (1955) alongside his friend and alleged lover James Dean. By the early 1970s however, Mineo's once-promising career was on the skids and he was relegated to roles like a nameless monkey in 1972's *Planet of the Apes*. The 37-year-old Mineo was rehearsing a Hollywood stage production of *P.S. Your Cat Is Dead* when he was murdered here on February 12, 1976. He was stabbed in the heart during a robbery as he walked from his parked car into his rented apartment here, bleeding to death on the floor of the carport. Two years later ex-con Lionel R. Williams was charged and convicted of the murder after he bragged about the crime to cellmates in a Michigan jail while incarcerated on other charges.

(Reverse to Alta Loma. Left to Sunset. Left to:)

8439 Sunset Boulevard, House of Francis brothel

The most famous brothel in the United States, Madame Lee Francis' "House" here was the whorehouse of the rich and famous during the wild 1930s and 1940s. Regulars Errol Flynn and John Gilbert routinely made pal Irving Thalberg wait in the lobby reading *The Los Angeles Times* while they cavorted upstairs. Customer service was stressed; Lee once had the entire staff color all their hair blonde to satisfy one VIP client. Studios regularly used the House to entertain foreign distributors and stars, and each of them had a charge account at the shop.

One evening in the summer of 1930 as a drunken Spencer Tracy left the brothel he became so belligerent that he was "restrained with handcuffs and leg straps" by police before being carted off to jail. Lee Francis' career as the grand Hollywood madam came to an end when she was arrested on January 16, 1940. The resulting conviction and 90-day jail term ended a 30-year career providing entertainment to a galaxy of movie stars.

(Sunset to Sunset Plaza. Right to:)

1293 Sunset Plaza Drive, Danny Arnold death site

For over 30 years Danny Arnold was an outspoken advocate of quality television and movies with a reputation for battling studios over quality issues. From the 1950s through the 1990s Arnold produced award-winning television programs such as *Bewitched*, *My World and Welcome to It*, and *Barney Miller*. He won Emmys for writing for *My World and Welcome to It* (1970) and *Barney Miller* (1982) and in 1985 was awarded the Writers

Guild of America lifetime achievement award. He began his career in movies with roles in *Scared Stiff* (1953) and *Sailor Beware* (1955) with Dean Martin and Jerry Lewis, then co-wrote *The Caddy* (1956) for the duo. In the 1950s Arnold gave up movie work to concentrate on television. He died at his home on August 19, 1995, from heart failure at 70.

(Sunset Plaza past the former home of James Dean [1541] to Evanview. Left to the modern home at:)

8850 Evanview Drive, Judy Garland "attempted" suicide site

Singer Judy Garland is best remembered as Dorothy in *The Wizard of Oz* (1939), but the talented star fought a lifelong battle with depression and was placed in sanitariums a dozen times and made almost that many suicide attempts. Her problems were a work issue as well, and after 15 years of attitude and tardiness troubles, MGM head Louis B. Mayer fired her on June 17, 1950, at the young age of 28.

Three days later the fragile Garland got up from a meeting at her rented home here, went into her bathroom, broke the mirror and sliced her own throat. Husband Vincente Minnelli and her publicist saved her life, and with studio help, the suicide attempt was kept out of the papers. She recuperated at another rented house at 10000 Sunset. On June 27, 1969, in London, she was found dead on a toilet at 47 from an overdose of barbiturates.

(Continue on Evanview to:)

8860 Evanview Drive, Carl Wilson death site

In 1961, Carl Wilson started a garage band in Hawthorne, an L.A. suburb near the beach, with his brothers Brian and Dennis, their cousin Mike Love, and close pal Alan Jardine. Brother Dennis decided the band should use a surfing theme for their music, and the Beach Boys legend was born. Although the band's stage fright limited their debut New Year's Eve 1961 performance to three songs, the audience loved them and they almost immediately became universally recognized for their hits such as "I Get Around," "Good Vibrations," "Little Deuce Coupe," and "Help Me Rhonda." Brother Dennis drowned in a 1983 accident in Marina del Ray, and other brother Brian has been plagued with personal problems, but the music has lived on. On February 7, 1998, Carl lost a year-long battle with lung cancer and died at his home here with his family at his side.

(Reverse to Sunset Plaza. The lovely three-level hacienda just up the block catty-corner on Sunset Plaza is:)

1618 Sunset Plaza Drive, Jack Albertson death site

Jack Albertson had hundreds of movie and television roles from *Miracle on 34th Street* (1947) to *The Shaggy Dog* (1958) during a 50-year career, but is most remembered as the "Man" in the 1970s television series "Chico and the Man" alongside ill-fated costar Freddie Prinze. After later roles in *The Poseidon Adventure* (1972) and *Dead and Buried* (1981), Albertson died at his home here on November 25, 1981, at 74 from cancer.

(Reverse on Sunset Plaza to Sunset. Right to Horn. Right to:)

1210 Horn Avenue, Humphrey Bogart–Mayo Methot home

Humphrey Bogart and his third wife Mayo Methot lived in a grand mansion that stood at Horn and Shoreham during the 1940s (now the site of the Shoreham Towers). French actress Methot was a vicious drunk with a terrible temper once described as a "blend of Zelda Fitzgerald and Tugboat

Annie." Their 1938 wedding set the tone for their marriage when a drunken Bogie stalked out of the reception after a fight with Methot and spent the night drinking with friends. The only things the two had in common were sex and alcohol—he once said, "The whole world is three drinks behind; everybody should take three drinks, and we'd all be fine."

Known in the press as the "Battling Bogarts,'" their seven-year marriage featured drunken brawls, assaults and studio cover-ups. Their friends named the house "Sluggy Hollow," and he named their sailboat *The Sluggy*. Direct phone lines linked studio publicity and fire departments that responded to the battles, and a carpenter was on call 24 hours a day to repair damage done to the house. A dozen extra doors were kept in the garage at all times, replaced at a rate of two a month after Methot would blast them with her .45 pistol. During one altercation near their beloved yacht, Methot threw Bogart off a dock in front of a large group of friends. During a family Thanksgiving, she hit him over the head with the turkey. When an enraged Methot threw a full drink at Bogart, the glass whistling past his head, he calmly turned to a witness and said, "It's a good thing she's a lousy shot."

Peter Lorre once invited the couple to his nearby Hollywood Boulevard home after betting friends that he could have them fighting within five minutes. When they arrived he simply said, "General McArthur" and walked away. In less than a minute Methot was biting Bogart and he had thrown his drink at her! When she thought Bogart was sleeping with Ingrid Bergman during the 1942 filming of *Casablanca*, she stabbed him in the back with a kitchen knife. After taking ten stitches, Bogart reportedly told the attending physician, "Ain't she a pistol?" In 1944 Bogart left Methot for 20-year-old actress Lauren "Betty" Bacall, who would become his fourth and final wife in 1945. A washed-up Methot was found dead in an Oregon motel room in 1949.

(Horn to Shoreham to:)

8787 Shoreham Drive, Shoreham Towers, Diane Linkletter suicide site, Alexander Godunov death site

Diane Linkletter, youngest daughter of writer and television star Art, had an LSD flashback and leapt from her sixth floor window on October 4, 1969. A friend of the 21-year-old allegedly tried to grab her but told police that he could only grab her belt, and she fell to her death. Interestingly, the "friend"—Edward Durston—was also with model Carol Wayne when she died during a Mexican getaway with him in 1985. Buxom Wayne was best known as the *Tonight Show* "Tea Time Matinee Lady," and was found floating in the surf near the couple's hotel. Durston had disappeared, and though no alcohol or drugs were found, Wayne somehow had drowned in only a foot of water. Charges were never filed since police were never able to track Durston down for questioning.

Longtime Towers resident Miriam Hopkins rented an apartment previously occupied by actor Ronald Colman and swore to everyone that the rooms were haunted by Colman's ghost, telling them she spoke with his spirit repeatedly.

Another former resident was ballet and movie star Alexander Godunov, who died here on May 18, 1995, at 45. The Russian dancer defected during a 1979 Bolshoi Ballet tour and after quitting ballet in 1982 turned to movies. He debuted in *The Money Pit* (1984) and starred as an Amish farmer in *Witness* (1985) and a psychotic killer in *Die Hard* (1988). He died in his apartment of acute alcoholism.

Nearby at the bottom of the hill at 8814 Sunset, where the Book Soup Bookstore and Book Soup Bistro now stand, was the site of the Utter-McKinley Mortuary, recognized by a clock with no hands hanging over the front door. It was from there that actor John Barrymore's body was swiped by drinking buddies and taken to Errol Flynn's house, where it was placed in a chair in the den to await Flynn's return from a night of partying. A drunken Flynn almost had a heart attack when he walked past his departed friend's body in his den. The office building across Sunset was the headquarters of Carolco Pictures, headed by Jose Menendez at the time of his murder.

(Shoreham to Sunset. Right to:)

8860 Sunset Boulevard, Viper Room, River Phoenix death site

In the 1940s this bar was called the "Melody Room" and was a favorite hangout of Bugsy Siegel. In 1993 it was owned by Johnny Depp, and was a favored hangout of the young Hollywood party set. On Halloween night, 1993, actor River Phoenix took a fatal drug overdose inside and died on the sidewalk by the front door. The 23-year-old had starred in *Stand by Me* (1986), *Sneakers* (1987), *Indiana Jones and the Last Crusade* (1988), and received an Oscar nomination for *Running on Empty* at 17. Although he was a vocal vegetarian, Phoenix had no qualms about drugs. While visiting here he injected himself with a fatal "speedball" of heroin and cocaine and like his hero John Belushi, was killed by it. He collapsed in convulsions and after being carried outside he died by the front door. The apparently very self-aware star told a doorman, "I'm gonna die, dude" as he was carried past. Appropriately, "viper" was 1920s slang for an opium addict.

(Sunset to:)

9049 Sunset Boulevard, Mickey Cohen ambush site

During a long-running 1940s gangland war with mobster Jack Dragna there were several attempts on gangster Mickey Cohen's life. One occurred in front of this club—then called "Sherri's"—on the night of July 18, 1949. As Cohen and some friends exited the popular nightspot a car drove by and sprayed the Cohen party and the front of the building with gunfire. Cohen suffered a minor shoulder wound but two bodyguards were killed and syndicated columnist Florabelle Muir was wounded as she purchased a paper at a nearby stand. She was hit in the arm by a ricocheting bullet, and Cohen took her to the hospital himself. He also escaped a later bombing of his Brentwood home.

(Sunset to Doheny. Right to St. Ives and notice the house catty-corner on your right at:)

9191 St. Ives Drive, Spencer Tracy death site

This small house was one of three guest houses built for director George Cukor's estate above here at 9166 Cordell. His three haciendas were the sites of hundreds of star trysts. For 15 years actor Spencer Tracy lived in this one while his family lived in a nearby home, his wife Louise raising their children while he carried on a 30-year affair with actress Katharine Hepburn.

Young Spencer Tracy was thrown out of several dozen Milwaukee grammar and elementary schools before befriending a young Pat O'Brien during high school. He and O'Brien moved on to Broadway and eventually Hollywood. He debuted alongside another young actor—Humphrey Bogart—in 1930s *Up the River,* followed up in films like *Me and My Gal* (1932) and *Fury* (1936), and earned back-to-back Oscars for *Captains Courageous* (1937) and *Boys Town* (1938). Tracy and Hepburn met in 1941 filming *Woman of the Year* and began an affair that would last until his death, although he never divorced the long-suffering Louise. The pair starred together in nine films such as *Adam's Rib* (1949) and *Pat and Mike* (1952). Tracy's screen successes and kindly image belied a dreary personality, however.

He was not a very nice man, haunted by severe depression and obsessed with death. He was a well-known ugly drunk with a hair-trigger temper who routinely attacked photographers and smashed their cameras. MGM employed a full-time ambulance crew whose only job was to pick up Tracy when local bars called. Drunk or sober he swore a blue streak, angering fellow star Loretta Young, who carried a "cuss jar" and charged anyone swearing in her presence 25 cents. Tracy once asked her what it would cost to say "damn," and when she responded "a quarter," he flipped a bill into her jar and said, "Here's $20 Loretta. Go fuck yourself."

On the morning of June 10, 1967, just after Tracy completed filming *Guess Who's Coming to Dinner* (1967), Hepburn heard a thud in the kitchen here where Tracy was making tea and found him dead on the floor. Studio publicists told the press that Tracy was alone when he died, and was found by his loving wife Louise. When Louise finally met Hepburn face-to-face, she allegedly replied, "I thought you were a myth."

Tracy's landlord Cukor died in his beloved Cordell mansion on January 23, 1983. He was a groundbreaking director of hits such as *Tarnished Lady* with Jean Harlow (1931), *A Bill of Divorcement* (1932), *Dinner at Eight* with Greta Garbo (1934), *Little Women* with Katharine Hepburn (1935), and *David Copperfield* (1935). His estate was headquarters for the homosexual crowd; his fabled Sunday pool parties were always standing-room-only.

(Doheny to Oriole. Right around to Thrasher. Left to:)

9061 Thrasher Avenue, Moe Howard death site

This was the last home of the most famous of "The Three Stooges," the trio's ersatz leader Moe Howard. Brooklyn-born Moses Horwitz worked at the Vitagraph Studios, earning roles in comedy short features. In 1922 Moe and brother Shemp joined Ted Healy and Larry Fine as "Ted Healy's Stooges." After a 1933 pay dispute, the brothers and Fine quit and were signed by Columbia Pictures, where they worked for 25 years. When Shemp left the group at that time he was replaced by younger brother

Jerry, known as "Curly." Through 30 years of various "Stooge" partnerships Moe remained the leader of the group.

When siblings Shemp and Jerry died, Moe retired here, making college and personal appearances around the country. When close friend Fine died on January 24, 1975, a heartbroken Moe lost interest in life and quietly died of cancer only four months later on May 4, 1975. Helen, Moe's wife of 50 years, died a few months later in the house they had shared for so many years.

(Reverse on Thrasher and Oriole to Doheny. Right to:)

1654 North Doheny Drive, House of Alex, Shannen Doherty home

This was the one-time home of famous Hollywood Madam Alex Adams. In 1971 Alex purchased an escort service, paying $5,000 for six aging call girls and a customer list of exactly six elderly men. By the early 1980s her service was the best known in L.A., employing 250 beautiful women of all sizes and shapes and serving a 7,000-person client list. Some of her hookers made over $10,000 weekly, but on March 10, 1988, she was arrested and after being sentenced to probation she "retired." A young Heidi Fleiss was reportedly "sold" to Alex by a boyfriend to settle a $450 gambling debt, but later swiped Alex's customer list and opened her own stable. A routine police investigation of a December 13, 1992, jewelry theft from this house led to Fleiss' own arrest as the second Beverly Hills madam. Madam Alex used a rented house at 8973

Lloyd Place in Hollywood to store her inventory of drug paraphernalia for her girls. She died in 1995 at a small West Hollywood bungalow.

In 1992, the Doheny house was rented by high-strung television actress Shannen Doherty, who was later evicted for nonpayment of rent and sued by the owner for $25,000 in damages to the house.

(Doheny to Swallow. Left to:)

9255 Swallow Drive, Vincent Price death site

Horror film star Vincent Price died from lung cancer in this home on October 25, 1993, at 82. The typecast villain's career began in 1928 and included horror classics such as *House of Wax* (1953), *The Pit and the Pendulum* (1961), and *The Raven* (1962) but he also starred in nonhorror movies including *The Song of Bernadette* (1952). Price's health began to decline in 1990 when his beloved wife of 20 years died here of cancer while he was filming *Edward Scissorhands* (1991). He was so heartbroken after her death that he never made another movie.

(Reverse to Doheny and Sunset and notice the large building at 9255 Sunset, the Sierra Towers.)

Dragnet star Jack Webb died in his home there on December 23, 1992, after a long battle with cancer. Another resident was Vickie Morgan, whose rent was paid by Alfred Bloomingdale.

Tour 5:
West Hollywood

Begin Tour 5 at the flower-decked Tudor apartment, the third
on the left or east side of Sweetzer, south of Beverly at:

120 North Sweetzer Avenue, Rebecca Schaeffer murder site

On July 18, 1989, actress Rebecca Schaeffer was shot in the chest with a .357 magnum pistol as she answered the front door to her apartment building here. The 21-year-old star of television's *My Sister Sam* came out only because her intercom was broken. Killer Robert John Bardo was obsessed with Schaeffer: he saved tapes of her performances and a scrapbook of articles about Schaeffer, turning from obsessed to deadly when she sent him a signed photo. Unknown to her, Bardo's letters had become stranger and stranger but were thrown out by her studio agent so she wouldn't worry. The day before the shooting Bardo tried to enter the *Sam* set, and, incredibly, was driven to his motel by a studio guard and told to go home to Arizona. The next morning, he appeared on Schaeffer's doorstep and killed her.

He was arrested in Arizona and quickly convicted after freely confessing to the killing. The easy conviction was won by young Assistant District Attorney Marcia Clark, who later tried a less successful case against O.J. Simpson. Bardo easily obtained Schaeffer's address from the motor vehicle office, but following her murder California passed an antistalking law and a series of rules regulating the release of personal in-

formation. The L.A.P.D.'s Threat Management Unit (TMU), an elite group formed to monitor and track stalkers, was also founded after Schaeffer's death, and has saved several lives in the short time since the tragic death.

(Sweetzer north to Beverly. Right on
Beverly to Fairfax. Left on Fairfax to
theater across the street from Fairfax
High School, site of:)

611 North Fairfax Avenue, "Silent Movie" Theater Murder

This modest theater was opened in 1942 by silent film collector John Hampton, offering only movies from the early silent era. With seating for only 250 it was a reminder of the movie houses of the early 1900s. When Hampton fell ill in the early 1970s the theater was closed but reopened in 1991 when Laurence Austin—who claimed to be the son of silent star William Austin—purchased the theater. Hampton's widow, by now in her 80s, still took tickets at the door, and the viewings played to good crowds three nights a week.

The tranquility of this small slice of movie history was shattered in early January 1997 when Austin was killed during an alleged robbery. A teenaged concession worker was wounded and the 74-year-old Austin

My Sister Sam star Rebecca Schaeffer was gunned down at the front door of this apartment building when she answered the knock of an obsessed fan.

was shot several times and died in the lobby of his beloved theater. Police later arrested theater film projectionist James Van Sickle, charging that he hired a 19-year-old associate to kill Austin. The motive was money—Austin had recently named Van Sickle the sole heir to his $1 million estate.

(Fairfax to Melrose. Left on Melrose, five blocks to Kilkea. Right to the intersection with Waring and the two-story apartment on the corner to your right at:)

754 Kilkea Drive, Frank Sinatra–Joe DiMaggio "Wrong Door Raid" site

Just days after he divorced Marilyn Monroe, Joe DiMaggio and Frank Sinatra were dining at the Villa Capri when they were told Monroe was enjoying a romantic evening with another woman in an apartment here. Trying to confront Monroe and her lesbian lover, Joe, Frank and some pals kicked in the front door to this apartment late on the night of November 5, 1954. They

scared elderly spinster Florence Kotz almost to death by knocking on the wrong door; Marilyn was in a second floor apartment with an entrance at 8122 Waring (under the balcony on your right on the Waring side; Kotz' door is on your right on Kilkea).

Kotz quickly filed a $200,000 lawsuit resulting from the botched "Wrong Door Raid," awarded $7,500 and a new door. Writer James Bacon described her testimony—delivered in the finest "Edith Bunker" style—as the funniest witness statement ever given in an L.A. courtroom. Kotz' door is on the Kilkea side of the house, with the Waring entrance below the balcony on the Waring side of the house.

Just three blocks away at 740 Kings Road was the Hollywood home of writer Aldous Huxley, where wife Maria suffered a fatal heart attack the day after the couple moved in on February 13, 1955. Huxley later died in the house.

(Kilkea to Willoughby. Left to Harper. Right across Santa Monica to:)

The site of the comical "Wrong-Door Raid," where Frank Sinatra and Joe DiMaggio broke into the wrong apartment in a futile search for Marilyn Monroe.

1309 Harper Avenue, Marilyn Monroe suicide attempt site

Marilyn Monroe was living here with drama coach Natasha Lytess when she got her first studio contract with Columbia in February 1948. She was fired six months later, allegedly because she refused Harry Cohn's demand for the sex he required of all Columbia extras. Later that day Monroe tried to kill herself by swallowing over 50 sleeping pills here but was found by Lytess and taken to the hospital.

The following summer, desperate for rent money, Monroe posed for friend Tom Kelley at his photo studio at 736 Seward in Hollywood. Standing on a ladder from ten feet above her, Kelly shot a nude Monroe lying on a red velvet carpet for which Monroe was paid $50. He himself sold the worldwide rights to the photo to a Chicago printer for $300. Over 50 million copies of the resulting calendar were sold.

This entire block is full of gorgeous vintage apartment buildings, worth the walk just to see them all.

(Harper to DeLongpre. Left to Sweetzer. Left to:)

1302 North Sweetzer Avenue, Harvey Glatman victim home

Harvey Glatman was a psychotic momma's boy haunted by extreme sexual frustrations, which he tried to resolve by kidnapping several young women between July and October 1957 and photographing their torture-murders. He was eventually caught at home surrounded by a house full of evidence and later executed in the gas chamber at San Quentin. His first victim, young Judy Ann Dull, lived here and his home was at 1011 Norton in L.A.

(Sweetzer to:)

1227½ North Sweetzer Avenue, Karyn Kupcinet murder site

On November 25, 1963, the 22-year-old daughter of syndicated Chicago columnist Irv Kupcinet was strangled in her apartment here. Aspiring actress Karyn Kupcinet's nude body was found on her living room couch by actor Mark Goddard and his wife, close friends of the young woman. The unsolved murder became even more mysterious when her fingerprints were discovered on threatening love letters that had been sent to actor Andrew Prine, Kupcinet's former lover. It was later publicized that she had also been arrested for shoplifting. Her unsolved murder went largely unnoticed since it occurred just two days after the assassination of President John F. Kennedy.

(Sweetzer to Santa Monica. Right to Kings. Right to:)

1221 North Kings Road, Jack Cassidy fire death site

Television star Jack Cassidy lived in the top floor (center) penthouse here after his divorce from actress Shirley Jones. His careless late-night smoking apparently ignited a sofa while he slept on December 12, 1976, but the fire burned so hot that police were unable to identify the charred body found amid the rubble. Since his beloved Porsche was missing, friends and family hoped Cassidy was away at the time, but the borrowed car was returned the next day and the body was confirmed to be his. He died shortly after completing *The Eiger Sanction* (1977) with Clint Eastwood. The father of singer-actors David and Shaun, he was only 49 when he died.

A few blocks south at 1015 Kings Road author Theodore Dreiser (*The Titan, The Genius, An American Tragedy)* lived with his longtime companion Helen Richardson. For their entire 30 year relationship, Dreiser would leave Richardson—even for weeks or months at a time—when he discovered a woman who caught his eye, but always returned to his surprisingly willing friend. When he died at his Kings Road home of kidney failure on December 28, 1945, at 74, Charlie Chaplin led the procession at his well-attended funeral. Dreiser called himself "the loneliest man in the world," but never married Richardson until he was on his deathbed.

(Kings to Fountain. Left to:)

Actor Jack Cassidy was burned to death in a 1976 fire in his penthouse apartment on the top floor (middle) of this apartment building.

8495 Fountain Avenue, Dorothy Dandridge death site

The most brilliant black entertainer of the 1940s and 1950s debuted in the Marx Brothers comedy *A Day at the Races* (1937). The first black woman nominated for an Oscar, Dandridge later starred in *Porgy and Bess* (1959) but was victimized by a tortured private life climaxed when an oil-well Ponzi scheme bankrupted her in 1963. She was down to her last three dollars when she died in her second floor apartment here on September 8, 1965, at 42. Dandridge's death was apparently caused by a combination of several problems, including an overdose of Tofranil—accidental or otherwise—and an undiagnosed embolism resulting from a broken foot.

(Fountain to La Cienega. Left to Willoughby. Left to Alfred. Right to:)

843 North Alfred Street, Agnes Ayers death site

Lovely Agnes Ayers was a Jesse Lasky and Vitagraph silent screen star who earned superstardom before the age of 19. Debuting in 1915's *His New Job,* she starred in dozens of films such as *The Sheik* (1921), *The Ten Commandments* (1923), *The Son of the Sheik* (1926), and *Small Town Girl* (1936) and was also the one-time lover of director Jean Renoir. By the age of 42, though, she was just another movie has-been when she succumbed at home on Christmas Day 1940 of a cerebral hemorrhage.

(Alfred to Melrose Place. Right to La Cienega. Left to Melrose. Right to Westbourne. Left to:)

532 Westbourne Avenue, Florence Lawrence suicide site

Florence Lawrence was a D.W. Griffith protégé who starred in Vitagraph's *Romeo and Juliet* (1909) and the lead in the first movie serial, the *Jonesy Pictures* (1909 to 1912). Making at least two films a week, she became the first "Biograph Girl," the first film star identified in the movie's credits *by name*, and the basis for the first-ever publicity stunt. Studio head Carl Laemmle planted a story in the press that she had been killed in a streetcar accident so that he could steal her from Biograph for his IMP Studio. The stories ignited a firestorm of fan grief, only to have her reappear several days later, very much alive, as *his* first "IMP Girl."

She was severely burned during the filming of *Pawns of Destiny* (1915), leaving her with awful facial scars. After a screen absence of five years, Lawrence tried an unsuccessful comeback and was relegated to obscurity as the wife of a Hollywood used car salesman. On December 27, 1938, the 52-year-old ate a mixture of ant paste and cough syrup, dying a gruesome death in her small Hollywood home.

(Westbourne to circle at Rosewood. Right to San Vicente. Right to Rangely—note that the street is after the large street sign, not before. Left to:)

8723 Rangely Drive, Dominique Dunne murder site

The 23-year-old daughter of writers Dominic Dunne and Ellen Griffin Dunne and younger sister of actor Griffin starred in *Poltergeist* (1982) and had taped an episode of television's *Hill Street Blues* a week before her death. Dunne was strangled during an October 30, 1982, beating by her ex-boyfriend John Sweeney, the head chef at the trendy Ma Maison restaurant. Just a month earlier, Sweeney had tried to strangle Dunne during a dinner out and she had immediately broken off the relationship and changed the locks on her house. When she refused his continued appeals to reunite, the attack ensued.

After being attacked in the driveway of her home here Dunne never regained consciousness and died on November 4.

Aspiring actress Dominique Dunne, daughter of writer Dominic, was strangled in the driveway of her home here by her obsessed ex-boyfriend in 1982.

Ex-boyfriend Sweeney was convicted of involuntary manslaughter when a jury was not allowed to hear about his previous girlfriend, who endured ten separate beatings that resulted in several broken noses and a collapsed lung. Sentenced to 62 years for the Dunne killing, he was released in 1986 after less than four years in jail.

(Rangely to Robertson. Left to Alden. Right to La Peer. Right to:)

138 North La Peer Drive, Marilyn Maxwell death site

Iowa-born Marilyn Maxwell began as a chorus singer in regional theater and became a band singer, first with Buddy Rogers' band in 1937 and later the Ted Weems Orchestra. She moved on to stage roles at the Pasadena Playhouse, where she was working when she was discovered by MGM. She quickly became the top song-and-dance queen of the 1940s.

Maxwell starred in classics such as *Presenting Lilly Mars* (1943), *The Show Off* (1946), and *Ziegfeld Follies* (1944), and was also a regular in the World War II films *Salute to the Marines* (1943) with Wallace Beery, *Stand by for Action* (1942) with Robert Taylor, *Lost Harem* (1944) with Abbott and Costello, and dozens of others. At the height of her stardom, Maxwell's huge mansion at the top of 2621 Coldwater Canyon was the most popular tour bus stop in Beverly Hills. As her movie career faded, she appeared on several 1960s television series including *Bus Stop, Password, Talent Scout*, and *The Red Skelton Show*. She died in obscurity in her small Hollywood bungalow on March 20, 1972, from a heart attack brought on by pulmonary problems. She was only 59, and sadly was forgotten by her once legion of fans.

(La Peer to Beverly. Left one block past Doheny to Oakhurst. Right on Oakhurst to:)

403 Oakhurst Drive, Herbert Marshall death site

Herbert Brough Falcon Marshall arrived in Hollywood with the European and British colony during the 1920s and went on to become one of the most successful members. After starting an acting career in his native London, Marshall served with the British army in World War I, where he was wounded and lost a leg. He served alongside fellow English actor Ronald Colman in the 14th London Scots Regiment and after the war learned to walk so well with his artificial limb that few people were ever aware of his disability.

After several years on the London stage, Marshall came to Broadway, where he was discovered starring in *The High Road* and hired as a Vitagraph stock player. His first sound vehicle was *The Letter* (1929) with Jeanne Eagels, followed by roles in well-remembered movies such as *Blonde Venus* (1932) with Marlene Dietrich, *Riptide* (1934), *Angel* (1937), *A Bill of Divorcement* (1940) with Katharine Hepburn, a 1940 remake of *The Letter* with Bette Davis, *The Razor's Edge* (1946), *Duel in the Sun* (1947), and his final film, *The Third Day* (1965). Among the other women to co-star with Marshall were Dame Judith Anderson, Jennifer Jones, Greta Garbo, Norma Shearer, Constance Bennett, Barbara Stanwyck, Jean Arthur, Merle Oberon, Claudette Colbert, Joan Crawford, and Rosalind Russell. Marshall almost always appeared on-screen as the urbane, well-educated, arcane British gentleman, a role he also portrayed off-screen.

Among Marshall's five marriages were unions with actresses Edna Best, Lee Russell, and Patricia Malloray. During most of his brilliant career Marshall lived in a beautiful mansion at 714 North Foothill in the Beverly Hills "Flats," but retired to this home near the end of his life. Marshall suffered a fatal heart attack here on January 22, 1966, at the age of 75.

(Oakhurst to Santa Monica. Right to Doheny. Hard left on Carmelina past the small park and fountain to Oakhurst. Right to:)

622 Oakhurst Drive, Karl Dane mansion

Karl Dane took his screen name from his native Denmark when he arrived in the United States in 1915. Moving from vaudeville to the movies, he starred in several silent film classics such as *The Big Parade* (1925) and *Son of the Sheik* (1926) with Rudolph Valentino. The world-famous actor earned $5,000 a week, kept a household staff of 12 servants and a fleet of five Rolls-Royces. His thick Danish accent kept him out of sound movies though, and he became a pitiful victim of the new technology.

His career ending almost overnight, Dane sold his fleet of cars, fired his servants, and rented a two-room apartment at 626 South Burnside in Hancock Park. Although only a mile away, it was a continent away to Dane, who was forced to take a job as a mechanic at the dealership that had been selling him his Rolls-Royces. Drinking cost him that job, and in the ultimate irony, only two years after his last movie role Dane was operating a vending cart outside the Paramount Studio gates, selling hotdogs to movie extras. On April 15, 1934, the despondent 48-year-old shot himself in the head at his apartment. When his body went unclaimed at the morgue for two months, MGM paid for a cheap funeral at Hollywood Memorial. His home was listed as 322 Oakhurst but was renumbered in the 1930s.

(Oakhurst to Elevado. Right to Doheny. Left to Norma. Right to:)

8983 Norma Place, Alan Campbell death site

Alan Campbell was the husband and 40-year partner of eccentric writer Dorothy Parker, with whom he wrote *Tradewinds*,

A Star Is Born and many other famous screenplays. The 73-year-old Campbell died of a heart attack here on June 14, 1963. When worried neighbors asked the feisty 70-year-old Parker if she needed anything, she replied, "A new husband." Seeing their shock at her cavalier attitude, she told them, "Okay, sorry, then run to the deli and get me a corned beef on rye, and have them hold the mayo."

(Norma to:)

8967 Norma Place, Carolyn Jones death site

British actress Carolyn Jones had a 25-year career in dozens of films but is best remembered as Morticia, the eccentric wife of Gomez Addams in the 1970s television series *The Addams Family*. Jones died after a long battle with colon cancer here on August 3, 1983, at 53.

Norma Street is named for silent star Norma Talmadge, whose former studio dressing room and servants' quarters are now a two story frame apartment building just up the block.

(Reverse to Doheny. Right to Cynthia. Right to the small bungalow tucked between the two apartment buildings at:)

8962 Cynthia Street, Marina Habe last home

Aspiring actress Marina Habe shared a West Hollywood home with her parents, actress Eloise Hardt and Hungarian novelist Hans Habe. On December 15, 1968, the beautiful 17-year-old left her home in her sports car for a short drive to her boyfriend's home. She was never seen alive again. On January 1, 1969, joggers found her mutilated body amid the bushes just off Mulholland Drive at the intersection of Bowmont Drive. She had been garroted (strangled), stabbed, and her throat slashed. Habe's slaying remains unsolved.

Tour 6:
Hancock Park

Begin Tour 6 at 112 Manhattan Place, located just east of Western Avenue, between Beverly Boulevard and Third Street, in Hancock Place:

112 North Manhattan Place, Alma Rubens death site

Alma Rubens was a major silent star of films such as *Half Breed* (1916), *Restless Souls* (1918), *Under the Red Robe* (1923), and dozens of others. By the time she turned 25 Rubens had been married five times, at 18 wed for a month to elderly film star Franklyn Farnum, and later to heartthrob Ricardo Cortez.

Like many of her contemporaries she became a hopeless drug addict as her success and wealth grew, and she wasted millions of dollars from her once-huge fortune. Her drug problems eventually affected her work, and Rubens hit bottom when she lost her star role in *The Torrent* (1926) to unknown Swedish newcomer Greta Garbo. Soon afterward Louis B. Mayer unceremoniously fired Rubens, Cortez divorced her, and drugs finally and mercifully killed her.

She died in her small Hollywood home of pneumonia complicated by her drug use on January 21, 1931, at 33, after one final attempt to dry out in the California State Hospital for the Insane. Just before she died, knowing she was near death, she gave several interviews warning of the dangers of drugs. For her, however, it was too late.

(Manhatten to First Street. Right to Larchmont. Left to:)

201 South Larchmont Boulevard, Adriana Casalotti death site

In early 1936 the Disney Studios began production for what would become the cinema cartoon classic *Snow White and the Seven Dwarfs*. Eighteen-year-old actress Adriana Casalotti was chosen by Walt Disney himself from over 2,000 hopefuls who auditioned for the plum assignment providing the melodious and sweetly beguiling voice of Snow White. She was paid $900 for her work, and although she never again earned the fame she attained from that first job, Casalotti was forever known as the *real* voice of Snow White. She even decorated the front yard of her longtime Hancock Park home with a replica of the famous wishing well from the Disney classic, and it was here that she died on January 19, 1997, at the age of 80 after a long battle with cancer.

(Larchmont to Third. Right a short block to Lucerne. Left on Lucerne to:)

618 South Lucerne Boulevard, Dixie Carter–Hal Holbrook robbery site

Dixie Carter, the star of television's *Designing Women*, and husband Hal Holbrook, star of *Evening Shade*, were assaulted and robbed in their Hancock Park home on October 20, 1993. The couple was accosted as

Once a huge star but since forgotten, Alma Rubens died in this nameless Hollywood home.

they returned from a shopping trip in the driveway by two gun-toting robbers and were forced inside the home. The robbery was prevented when the couple's 24-year-old daughter snuck downstairs and saw her parents being held at gunpoint. She set off the burglar alarm and frightened the thieves away.

(Lucerne to Wilshire. Left to Lorraine.
Left to the second house in the 300
block of South Lorraine, now 357,
formerly 355, the site of:)

355 South Lorraine Boulevard, Lewis Stone death site

Character actor Lewis Stone had a 50-year Broadway and movie career, starring in over 300 films between 1915 and 1953. He debuted in *Honor's Altar* (1915) and starred in *The Northern Trail* (1921), *The Lost World* (1925), *Scaramouche* (1927), *Madame X* (1929), and co-starred with Greta Garbo in seven of her hits including *A Woman of Affairs* (1929), *Mata Hari* (1931), *Wild Orchids* (1929), and *Grand Hotel* (1932). He was

also nominated for an Academy Award for his role in *The Patriot* (1929), and starred with Jean Harlow in *Red Headed Woman* (1932) and *China Seas* (1935).

Later movie roles included *Treasure Island* (1934) and *David Copperfield* (1935), but Stone is best remembered for his portrayal of Judge Hardy in the ~~Hardy Boys~~ **Andy Hardy** movies that ran from 1938 to 1948 and starred Mickey Rooney. The series included *Judge Hardy's Children* (1938), *Love Finds Andy Hardy* (1938), *The Courtship of Andy Hardy* (1942), and *Andy Hardy's Double Trouble* (1944). Stone replaced an ill Lionel Barrymore in the Judge Hardy role. The feisty Stone once spent three months living with Native American Hopi Indians to study their secret snake-dances, and was a well-known fighter. On September 13, 1953, he suffered a fatal heart attack on the sidewalk in front of his home after collapsing while he chased some local kids who had thrown rocks and chairs into his pool. He died at the age of 73.

(Lorraine to Wilshire. Right to Rossmore.
Right to Muirfield. Left to:)

The former home of character actor Lewis Stone, who had a heart attack and died in the front yard while chasing some local kids away from his pool in 1953.

201 South Muirfield Drive, Howard Hughes home

Texan millionaire Howard Hughes was the toast of Hollywood when the 20-year-old came to L.A. in 1925 with an inheritance paying him $5,000 a day ($100,000 today). Hughes' father invented the drill bit still used today in oil fields throughout the world, but died shortly afterward when his son was only 15. Hollywood executives thought the "youthful" Hughes was a hick but he began making movies and bought RKO Studios in 1948, at the time one of the biggest movie studios in the world. Hughes lived here during his Hollywood years, through affairs with Jean Harlow, Ava Gardner, Bette Davis and Katharine Hepburn. Hepburn shared this house for a year waiting to marry Hughes, but moved out when she learned of his massive philandering.

Hughes was obsessed with movie stars, keeping a stable of young starlets hidden away in one of over 45 Hollywood apart-

ments quietly rented for them. His favorite women were routinely followed by a squad of 100 company detectives 24 hours a day, 7 days a week—Ava Gardner knew her pursuers so well that she routinely invited them in for drinks.

The magnificent Billie Dove was Hughes' first Hollywood obsession. The flawlessly beautiful Ziegfeld Follies star was introduced to Hughes by Marion Davies in 1928, and though Dove was married to director Irving Willat, Hughes fell in love with her and offered Willat $325,000 (over $3 million today) to divorce Dove. Willat demanded payment in brand new, unused $1,000 bills, which Hughes arranged, and though the Hughes-Dove affair lasted several more years, she finally tired of waiting for a wedding and moved out of this home. When Hughes tried to regain her affections by promising to set a date, she sent him a note at the church saying, "Not today dear. Not ever." He never spoke to her or ever mentioned her name again.

Billionaire Howard Hughes shared this Hancock Park mansion with a string of Hollywood beauties that included Jean Harlow, Ava Gardner, and Katharine Hepburn.

(Muirfield past former homes of Corey Haim [314] and Lynn Atkinson [324] to Fourth at:)

401 South Muirfield Drive, Nat King Cole home

In 1948 Nat King Cole bought this lovely Tudor mansion for the equivalent of $1 million as a wedding present for his wife. Neighbors in the exclusive area formed an association to prevent the sale to a black family; shots were fired at the house, fires were set, and racist signs planted in the front lawn. At a council meeting Cole was told they needed to keep "undesirables" out, to which he replied, "So do I, and if I see any I'll let you know."

In 1951, racism again haunted the family when an overzealous IRS agent named Robert A. Riddell invoked a 200-year-old law to try to quietly take ownership of the home for a trivial tax delinquency. Riddell actually tried to hastily auction the home before Cole could return from a concert tour and pay the small penalty. One of Riddell's more honest fellow agents prohibited the illegal sale. Cole lived in the home with his family until his death here on February 15, 1955.

(Muirfield past Buster Keaton's home [543] to Wilshire. Right to McCadden. Right to:)

174 North McCadden Drive, *Whatever Happened to Baby Jane?* movie site

This Hancock Park mansion was the set of the 1962 movie *Whatever Happened to Baby Jane?* starring Bette Davis and Joan Crawford. Jane (Davis) ran over sister Blanche (Crawford) just inside the driveway gate, leaving her a crippled prisoner in the house. The two temperamental stars had a similar relationship offscreen as well. In one scene Davis had to lift Crawford from a bed

When singer Nat King Cole bought this home in 1948, neighbors tried to keep him from becoming the first black resident on the street.

and place her in a wheelchair. The petulant Crawford hid 75 pounds of lead weights in a belt, and when Davis picked her up she suffered a back injury that plagued her for years. The 1991 remake starring the Redgrave sisters was filmed at 501 South Hudson near Wilshire Country Club.

(McCadden to Beverly. Left to Mansfield. Left to:)

121 South Mansfield Avenue, Margaret Dumont death site

Margaret Dumont was the foil for W.C. Fields and Groucho Marx in dozens of films, but began her career on Broadway. Dumont appeared on Broadway with George M. Cohan and toured European opera houses for several years before joining the Marx Brothers in their Broadway hit *The Cocoanuts* in 1925. She made her film debut as W.C. Field's friend Mrs. Hemoglobin in *Never Give a Sucker an Even Break* and starred in several dozen movies including *The Life of the Party* (1937), *Up in Arms* (1944), *Little Giant* (1946), and *What a Way to Go!* (1964). She is probably best-remembered as Groucho's frustrated co-star in *The Cocoanuts* (1929)—MGM's remake of their Broadway hit, *A Day at the Races* (1937), *A Night at the Opera* (1937), *Duck Soup* (1933), and *Horse Feathers* (1932).

Dumont endured Groucho's caustic insults such as "I hear they're tearing you down and putting up an office building where you're standing," and he once said that Dumont was a successful straight-man because she never understood a single joke he ever told. On March 1, 1975, Groucho asked his old friend to tape a segment for his television series *You Bet Your Life*. Just days later on March 6, she died at her Hollywood apartment here from a heart attack at the age of 75.

(Mansfield to Wilshire. Right to Burnside. Right past the Karl Dane suicide site at 626 South Burnside Avenue.

The modest final home of Marx Brothers co-star Margaret Dumont.

Burnside to Sixth. Right to Detroit. Left past the former home of killer David Clark at 162 South Detroit to First. Left to Fuller. Right to:)

137 North Fuller Avenue, Darby Crash suicide site

Jan Paul Beahm was the lead singer for California's most popular and strange punk bands of the 1970s, the Germs, calling himself "Darby Crash." According to Art Fein's *The L.A. Musical History Tour*, lead singer Crash and the band had a huge following in L.A.'s punk scene among those who enjoyed watching Crash scream obscenities and cover himself with peanut butter, broken glass or ice cream.

On a sunny Hollywood Sunday morning of December 7, 1980, Crash and girlfriend Casey wrote suicide notes and took overdoses of heroin in the guest house behind his mother's home. Crash was found dead, but Casey survived the attempt because Crash apparently deliberately underdosed his girlfriend when he prepared the shots. The suicide only briefly drew headlines, as John Lennon was murdered the next morning.

(Fuller to Beverly. Right to Highland. Left to:)

449 North Highland Avenue, Charlie Murray death site

Mack Sennett's *Keystone Cops* were born during a 1912 Los Angeles Shriners parade when Sennett, Mabel Normand, and Ford Sterling interrupted the parade to film and used the marchers and local police as the unwitting co-stars. When cops chased the stars for real, the series was born. Among the original seven cops were Sterling, Roscoe "Fatty" Arbuckle, and Murray, recognized by his trademark handlebar mustache and wide-eyed anger. The Indiana-born Murray starred in over 100 silent movies before his death at his Highland Avenue home on July 29, 1941. The lifelong smoker died of lung cancer at the age of 69.

*(Highland to Melrose. Right to
    Cahuenga. Right to:)*

565 Cahuenga Boulevard, Lupe Velez home

The lovely colonial mansion at 565 Cahuenga was the first Hollywood home of *Mexican Spitfire* movie star Lupe Velez. She was living here when she met handsome leading man Gary Cooper as the two filmed *Wolf Song* in 1928. During their tumultuous year-long affair Cooper purchased the house across the street for his parents, who strenuously objected to the relationship with the older Velez and eventually helped put an end to it.

To escape his mother's habit of walking by this house to look in the windows, Velez sold the house and moved into another home in the Hollywood Hills at 1826 Laurel Canyon. When their affair ended, Cooper

was a mental and physical wreck, losing over 25 pounds and enduring numerous Velez beatings and tantrums. When he broke off with her, Velez grabbed a pistol and took a shot at him. His studio sent him on a six-month trip to Europe before he was able to work again. The Cahuenga house was used for exterior shots of the Cunningham house on the long-running 1974–1984 television series *Happy Days*.

*(Cahuenga to Rosewood. Left to Lillian.
    Left to:)*

584 Lillian Way, Ross Columbo death site

On September 1, 1934, 26-year-old singer and actor Ross Columbo was shot to death in this bungalow. Ruggerio Eugenio di Rudolpho Columbo had a striking resemblance to Valentino and was equally vain.

When boyfriend Gary Cooper's parent's began walking by this home at night to see if their son was visiting, Lupe Velez sold the house and moved to Laurel Canyon. It was later used as the exterior for the 1970s sitcom *Happy Days*.

Singer Ross Columbo was an early rival of Bing Crosby, and was engaged to Carole Lombard when an accidental shooting at this Hollywood bungalow killed him in 1934.

The egotistical actor always carried mirrors just to admire himself and never walked past a mirror without smiling at his image. Discovered singing with Bing Crosby at the Coconut Grove, he was an international singing sensation by 20, equally popular with movie audiences, debuting in *Wolf Song* (1929) and starring in *Moulin Rouge* (1932) and *Wake up and Dream* (1933) before his death.

Columbo's best friend Lansing Brown was holding an antique pistol when it went off, firing a slug into Columbo's eye. After his death, his fiancée Carole Lombard suggested to the Columbo family that they not tell his ailing mother of the tragic death, so she was told he was on an extended European tour. She received a check and a letter from her son every week for the last ten years of her life.

Nearby at 450 North Rossmore are the El Royale Apartments, home to Harry Cohn, Fred Allen, and William Frawley, among others. A block from there, the Ravenswood Apartments at 540 was the lifetime home of Mae West, described by her nemesis W.C. Fields as "a plumber's idea of Cleopatra." Her all-white penthouse featured a life-size nude statue of herself in the foyer. She allegedly appears at séances still held there, telling the listeners that she is a member of The Crossover Club, assisting folks on to the other side.

(Lillian to Melrose. Left to Orange. Left to:)

625 North Orange Drive, Tim Hardin overdose death site

Oregon native Tim Hardin was an obscure Hollywood singer and songwriter until he penned the 1960s rock 'n' roll song "If I Were a Carpenter" for Bobby Darin. The next year Hardin released another hit, "Simple Song of Freedom," which was also performed by Darin. Hardin also wrote the Rod Stewart song "Reason to Believe," but his simple songs and laid-back personality obscured massive alcohol and heroin addictions.

In 1969, Doors lead singer Jim Morrison brought a friend along to visit Hardin at Hardin's Chateau Marmont apartment so his pal could see firsthand the evils of drugs. Hardin fled L.A. for Europe in the 1970s so he could have unhindered access to drugs and free methadone clinics, returning in the early 1980s. The 38-year-old writer was found dead in his Hollywood bungalow on December 29, 1990, dead of a drug overdose.

Tour 7:
Beverly Hills,
Coldwater Canyon

*Begin Tour 7 at 9360 Monte Leon Lane, one block north
of Sunset Boulevard on the east side of Hillcrest Road:*

9360 Monte Leon Lane, Eddie Cantor death site

Eddie Cantor was born Isidore Israel Iskowitz in Hell's Kitchen in New York City and in 1902 joined a traveling vaudeville show as a 10-year-old impressionist. By the time he entered movies in 1926, he was the most famous vaudeville performer in the United States and a Ziegfeld Follies headliner who had starred with W.C. Fields, Will Rogers, Roy Arthur, George Jessel, Eddie Buzzell, and Leila Lee.

Cantor made a silent movie version of *Kid Boots* in 1926 with Clara Bow, and among his other movies were *Palmy Days* (1932), *The Kid from Spain* (1933), *Roman Scandals* (1934), *Kid Millions* (1935), *Whoopee* (1930), *Ali Baba Goes to Town* (1937) and *Rhapsody in Blue* (1945). Most were musicals produced by Samuel Goldwyn, and all followed the same formula: Cantor singing and dancing surrounded by dozens of beautiful "Goldwyn Girls" admiring his songs and antics. The songs made his weekly radio program as popular as his movies, and his voice was recognized around the world.

Cantor was also a tireless fundraiser for a variety of charities, touring relentlessly for the USO in World War II and doing dozens of benefits every year. He allegedly coined the phrase "The March of Dimes" while fundraising for an L.A. charity, and also founded the Screen Actors Guild and the Federation of Radio Artists. Cantor's wife of fifty years—Ida, who was featured in his act—died at their home here in 1962, and Cantor suffered a fatal heart attack here on October 10, 1964, at the age of 72.

(Reverse to Hillcrest. Right to:)

809 North Hillcrest Road, Albert "Cubby" Broccoli death site

The lovely mansion at 809 Hillcrest Road was built in the 1920s for silent screen star Hobart Bosworth and purchased in the 1930s by leading man William *("The Thin Man")* Powell. The most recent resident was producer Albert R. "Cubby" Broccoli. Broccoli was born into a family of New York agronomists—his great-grandfather was said to have developed the vegetable broccoli, which earned the family their name. As a young star, Broccoli was fascinated by Hollywood, and at the age of 15 he worked for Howard Hughes as an RKO gofer. He eventually began producing films, and became friendly with stars like Errol Flynn, Clark

Singer and dancer Eddie Cantor died in this Beverly Hills home in 1964.

Gable and Humphrey Bogart, and was a fixture on the Hollywood "A" party list.

Broccoli's first solo producer effort was *The Red Beret* (1953) with Alan Ladd, and in 1960 Broccoli and partner Harry Saltzman purchased the rights to the "James Bond" character from writer Ian Fleming. Over the next 30 years they produced 17 Bond films, from *Dr. No* (1962), which introduced Sean Connery worldwide, to *Goldeneye* (1995), which starred the sixth Bond, Pierce Brosnan. The Bond films have grossed over $1 billion worldwide and have included *From Russia with Love, Goldfinger, Thunderball, You Only Live Twice, On Her Majesty's Secret Service, Diamonds Are Forever, Live and Let Die, The Man with the Golden Gun, The Spy Who Loved Me, Moonraker, For Your Eyes Only, Octopussy, A View to a Kill, The Living Daylights,* and *License to Kill.* Broccoli also produced *Chitty Chitty Bang Bang* for Disney in 1968.

He died at his longtime home here on June 27, 1996, at the age of 87. In ill health for several years, he died of heart ailments.

(Hillcrest to Doheny. Left to Loma Vista Drive. Left to Sunset. Right a short distance to Foothill Road. Right to:)

915 Foothill Road, Frank Sinatra's last home

Francis Albert Sinatra was born in Hoboken, New Jersey, on December 12, 1915, and as a young boy began singing in his firefighter father's Hoboken saloon for tips. He formed a band called the Hoboken Four, and after winning a 1937 "Major Bowes Amateur Hour," he was offered a job by bandleader Tommy Dorsey. He made his acting debut in the 1935 film *Higher and Higher* alongside Michele Morgan, and later starred in dozens of classic films including *Anchors Aweigh* (1945) with Gene Kelly, *Take Me Out to the Ballgame* (1948), *High Society* (1956) with Bing Crosby, *Pal Joey* (1957) with Rita Hayworth and Kim Novak, *Can Can* (1960), and his finest performance, an Oscar-winning role as a soldier in *From Here to Eternity* (1953).

Heartthrob Sinatra was married four

times, the first to New Jersey neighborhood girlfriend Nancy in 1939, and she bore him three children. When he fell for actress Ava Gardner in 1948, she was dating Howard Hughes but soon began an affair that was one of the hottest in Hollywood history. It became public when Frank attacked a photographer who snapped a picture of the lovers having an intimate dinner. Nancy divorced Frank, but Gardner's roving eye allegedly caused Sinatra to attempt suicide on three separate occasions. Even so, the volatile couple married in 1951, and during their short union the couple's public screaming matches were a common item in the tabloids. After divorcing Gardner, Sinatra didn't wed again until the then 49-year-old married 19-year-old actress Mia Farrow in 1966. Their May-December marriage lasted only 18 months. Sinatra married last wife Barbara in 1976. The list of Sinatra girlfriends includes Kim Novak, Lauren Bacall, Juliet Prowse, Lana Turner, Dinah Shore, and dozens of other well-known starlets.

All his life Sinatra doggedly fought rumors that his mob connections were more than just "social." Rumors began circulating early in his career that mob influence got him jobs, and he partied during one 1947 trip to Havana with mob killer Lucky Luciano, Carlo Gambino, Albert "The Executioner" Anastasia, and Meyer Lansky. Another close friend was mobster Johnny Roselli, who was found in a cement-filled 55-gallon drum in a Miami harbor in the 1960s. In 1962—then at the top of their careers—Sinatra and his "Rat Pack" pal Dean Martin spent a week performing at Chicago Mafia boss Sam Giancana's tiny bar, allegedly Sinatra's thank you for the mob's assistance in winning the John Kennedy presidential campaign. Soon afterward, the Nevada gaming commission made him sell his ownership in the Cal-Neva Lodge because of his known mob connections, and JFK immediately dropped Sinatra when a long Justice Department report detailed the extensive Sinatra-Mafia relationship. But, as with the rest of Sinatra's life, the contradic-

tion arose in 1985 when he was awarded the prestigious Medal of Freedom—the highest award given out in the United States—for his lifetime of charity work.

During the last two years of his life, Sinatra battled heart ailments and cancer of the bladder, and last appeared in public in January 1997. At around 8:00 P.M. on May 14, 1998, the "Chairman of the Board" suffered a massive fatal heart attack inside his longtime Beverly Hills home here, dying soon afterward at the age of 83.

(Foothill to Doheny. Right on Doheny to Loma Vista. Left and notice on your left the entrance to the huge estate on the left at:)

905 Loma Vista Drive, Doheny Mansion, Doheny murder-suicide site

This estate, home of the American Film Institute and the set of movies such as *Greystoke: The Legend of Tarzan, Lord of the Apes* (1987) was built in 1927 by oilman E.L. Doheny, a $4 million gift to his son Ned. On February 17, 1929, young Ned and his assistant Hugh Plunkett were found shot to death inside. Plunkett apparently murdered lover Ned and then committed suicide. While it was reported by the family to have been the result of an argument over a pay raise for Plunkett, both bodies were found in Ned's bedroom, and both of them were nude.

(Immediate rights on Loma Vista and Robert to Hillcrest. Left past the former home of Dinah Shore [1001] to:)

1012 Hillcrest Road, Morey Amsterdam death site

Morey Amsterdam was born in 1910, the son of the lead cello player in the San Francisco Symphony. Although his father wanted him to play the cello, young Amsterdam began a vaudeville and nightclub career using his cello only as a prop before

Former vaudevillian and Dick Van Dyke sidekick Morey Amsterdam—called "The Human Joke Machine"—died at his home here in 1996.

doing radio in the 1930s. He was a gag writer for such varied talents as Will Rogers, Fanny Brice, and Ronald Reagan. In 1948 he appeared on the early television show *Stop Me If You've Heard This One*, and had a two-year stint in his own *Morey Amsterdam Show*. After ten years on a variety of television quiz shows Amsterdam was cast as the wise-cracking television writer Buddy Sorrell alongside Rosemarie and Dick Van Dyke in the comedy classic *The Dick Van Dyke Show*.

Though the original show ran only from 1961 to 1968, it has never been off television, living in syndication the world over. Amsterdam died of heart ailments in his Beverly Hills home on October 28, 1996, at the age of 87. During his vaudeville career he was known as "The Human Joke Machine," and his former co-star Van Dyke said, "When Morey died, a hundred thousand jokes died with him."

(Continue past the former home of Elvis and Priscilla Presley [1174] to:)

1183 Hillcrest Road, Groucho Marx death site

Julius Marx was one of five sons, but became the most famous of all the Marx Brothers. Serious and insecure, the sullen Julius earned the nickname "Groucho" for his real personality. Groucho and his brothers left Broadway and signed a 1924 Paramount contract, releasing movie favorites such as *The Cocoanuts* (1929), *Animal Crackers* (1930), *Monkey Business* (1931), and *Horse Feathers* (1932). Later MGM released even more successful Brothers' movies, *A Night at the Opera* (1935), *A Day at the Races* (1937), *Room Service* (1938), and *A Night at Casablanca* (1946). Their last movie, *Love Happy* (1949), featured a young unknown contract player named Marilyn Monroe in a walk-on part.

Groucho's caustic wit played well on television and the movies but wore on his friends and his three wives. On August 19, 1977, the 86-year-old star lost a long fight with heart problems and died here.

(Reverse at the cul-de-sac, the last home of singer and comedian Danny Thomas [1183]. Hillcrest to Wallace Ridge. Right past the former homes of Cornel Wilde [1603], Warren Beatty [1120], Eddie Murphy and Prince [1081] to Loma Vista. Right to:)

1055 Loma Vista Drive, Barbara Stanwyck assault site

On the night of October 27, 1981, 74-year-old Barbara Stanwyck was awakened by a masked intruder inside her home here, dragged from bed and beaten bloody before she handed over her jewelry and mementos. She was left bound and gagged in a closet and wasn't found until the next morning by a family maid.

Young starlet Stanwyck's 1939 marriage to Robert Taylor was "suggested" by the studios to quell unending rumors about the sexual preferences of *both* stars. He was allegedly either bisexual or gay, and her preference for women was an open Hollywood secret. Clifton Webb called her "my favorite Hollywood lesbian," and her affairs with Marlene Dietrich and Joan Crawford were so well-reported that the crusty Stanwyck rarely denied the stories during her later years. Though Stanwyck and Taylor divorced in 1941 they remained close friends, and she was inconsolable when told of his death. She was convinced that she was in contact with Taylor's ghost, telling friends that he visited her nightly.

In her book *Haunted Houses and the Wandering Ghosts of California*, Antoinette May describes a quite testy poltergeist, or "noisy ghost," holding court at the former Taylor-Stanwyck home at 3099 Mandeville Canyon. It isn't visible from the road, but the gorgeous Mexican hacienda was used for exterior shots on the television series *Hart to Hart*. Stories describe a ghost chasing servants and throwing things. During a 1976 visit, BBC television researchers viewed an ice tray flying room to room, books and crystal falling off shelves and "chasing" people through the house, and coins mysteriously appearing in thin air and dropping to the floor in front of the startled witnesses.

(Loma Vista to:)

1141 Loma Vista, Sheldon Leonard death site

Brooklyn-born Sheldon Leonard Bershad began acting on Broadway, and went on to Hollywood in the early 1930s. He starred

Former movie star and megaproducer Sheldon Leonard lived here for 25 years before his 1997 death.

in over 140 movies, a typecast mobster or tough guy in 1940s movies such as *Guys and Dolls* and *Pocketful of Miracles* but is best-remembered for his 1946 role as crusty bartender Nick in the Frank Capra classic *It's a Wonderful Life* (1946), ringing the cash register and proclaiming, "Lookie here, I'm givin' out wings!"

After over 100 movies roles through the 1950s Leonard moved into television, first as an actor and eventually as a producer of the popular shows *The Dick Van Dyke Show*, *The Andy Griffith Show*, and *Gomer Pyle, U.S.M.C.* He also had a recurring role as Danny Thomas' agent on *The Danny Thomas Show*, and won Emmys in 1957 and 1961 for directing. He won still another Emmy for producing the kitschy 1970s hit *My World and Welcome to It*, a sitcom loosely based on the writings of James Thurber. In the 1970s Leonard produced *I Spy*, hiring comedian Bill Cosby as one of the first black leading men in television. He succumbed to heart ailments and died on January 10, 1997, at his home here at the age of 89.

(Loma Vista to Trousdale. Right to:)

350 Trousdale Place, Audrey Meadows death

Jackie Gleason thought Audrey Meadows was too pretty to play Ralph Cramden's wife, so she sent him a picture dressed in a housecoat sans makeup—Gleason hired her on the spot! Only 39 episodes of *The Honeymooners* were aired, but the television classic and the wonderful characters have enjoyed enduring popularity in the years since. When Meadows left the show she didn't need money because she was the only cast member to demand residuals if shows were rebroadcast: her foresight made her a huge fortune. She died of lung cancer on February 2, 1996, at 71, but as feisty as her alter ego Alice, she kept her terminal illness a secret until the tabloids reported it. Her sister Jayne (Mrs. Steve Allen) learned the news from a reporter.

(Trousdale to:)

370 Trousdale Place, Ross Hunter death site

Ross Hunter dedicated himself to "making all my movies beautiful," and gave 1950s movie fans a taste of the old 1930 movie glamour in his work. He went from B-movie actor to produce over 60 movies that included comedies such as *Pillow Talk* and *Back Street*, the musicals *Flower Drum Song* and *Thoroughly Modern Millie*, classic remakes of *Imitation of Life* and *Lost Horizon*, and his all-star action disaster spoof *Airport*. In 1970 *Airport* earned him his only Oscar nomination. On March 10, 1996, Hunter died of cancer at the age of 79.

(Trousdale to Loma Vista. Right to Evelyn. Right onto Alto Cedro to:)

9091 Alto Cedro Drive, Louis Malle death site

Director Louis Malle began as a cameraman for Jacques Cousteau cruising the world's oceans on the research ship *Calypso* and winning the 1956 Cannes Grand Prize for *The Silent World*. His commercial films included *The Lovers* (1958), *Pretty Baby* (1978), and *Atlantic City* (1980). Winner of every major movie award the world over, he lost a long battle with cancer on November 23, 1995, and died at home here with wife Candice Bergen at his side. He was 63.

(Alto Cedro to Hazen. Right to Bowmont. Right to:)

2220 Bowmont Drive, Joan Collins–Peter Holm residence

Star of the 1980s television hit show *Dynasty*, Joan Collins married telephone salesman Peter Holm in 1983, but their divorce a year later was even more juicy than her series. When she balked at paying him $80,000 monthly support and $2 million to settle, he threatened to take sightseers on guided tours of their bedroom, and picketed her nearby rented home at 1196 Cabrillo. The lead witness during their embarrassing court battle was a buxom blonde named Romina Danielson—called by Collins' lawyers as a witness—who graphically described a variety of sexual romps that took place with Holm here, highlighting her story with explicit accounts of one sex act performed on a flower-strewn bed. When she finished her lurid testimony, "The Passion Flower" fainted dead away on the stand. Her theatrics earned Holm a lump sum settlement of $180,000.

(Bowmont to:)

2320 Bowmont Drive, Katharine Hepburn haunted house

In 1933 young starlet Kate Hepburn came from Connecticut with her best friend and a family maid and rented this house. They were soon convinced that a small poolside apartment behind the house was haunted. One night Kate's friend Eve March watched the door latch open and close by itself, and the next day Kate and Eve both watched a ghostly man walk from the pool into the apartment, closing the door behind him. The first time Kate's younger brother Richard stayed overnight, he told Kate a young man stood over his bed all night staring down at him. He was too afraid to move until sunrise the next morning. Hepburn lived here for about five years before the house was purchased by Boris Karloff.

(Reverse on Bowmont to Cherokee. Right to El Roble. Right to:)

2126 El Roble Lane, Nick Adams death site

Nick Adams hitchhiked from Appalachia to Hollywood in 1950, and he starred in *Mr. Roberts* (1954) and *Rebel Without a Cause* (1955) before becoming Johnny Yuma on the television series *The Rebel*. On February 7, 1968, the 35-year-old was found dead in his second-floor bedroom. The cause of death was an overdose of the powerful

Former *Rebel Without a Cause* and *The Rebel* star Nick Adams' 1968 death in his home here remains unsolved to this day.

sedative paraldehyde, which would have killed him almost instantly. When nothing was found near the body to explain how Adams ingested the huge dose that killed him so quickly, rumors of murder arose. Police found his missing personal journals and all of his career memorabilia in the home of his lawyer Ervin Roeder, who was himself murdered in a mob hit less than a month later. At that funeral Roeder's girlfriend told friends she wanted to tell "the truth about Adams' death," but she was herself murdered in yet another mob hit the very next morning.

(Reverse to Cherokee. Left onto Loma Vista. Right to Carla Ridge. Right to:)

1840 Carla Ridge Drive, Irving "Swifty" Lazar death site

Irving Paul Lazar was the first super-agent, with clients including Bogart and Bacall, Cary Grant, the Gershwins, Olivier and Hemingway. Bogart dubbed him "Swifty" after Lazar got him four roles in a single afternoon to settle a bet. His Oscar-eve party, which began as an intimate 1967 dinner party for a group of friends, became the most exclusive annual event in movieland by the early 1980s. The eccentric Lazar was incredibly obsessive, never wearing the same thing twice, changing bedsheets twice every day and washing his hands anytime he touched anything. Soon after his wife Mary Van Nuys died here in 1993, the 86-year-old Lazar discontinued his daily dialysis treatments and died December 30, 1993, of liver failure.

(Carla Ridge to:)

1715 Carla Ridge Road, Walter Lantz death site

The "Woody Woodpecker" cartoon character was born when a noisy woodpecker repeatedly interrupted cartoonist Walter Lantz' 1941 honeymoon. "Woody" appeared in over 600 animated cartoons over the following 50 years. Lantz died of heart ailments at his home here on March 22, 1994, at the age of 93. The home was subsequently purchased by *Policewoman* star Angie Dickinson.

(Carla Ridge to:)

1455 Carla Ridge Road, Joanne Dru death site

Born in a tiny West Virginia coal-mining town, Joanne Dru was discovered working as a New York fashion model by director Howard Hawks and cast in his 1946 film *Abie's Irish Rose.* The gorgeous brunette then co-starred with John Wayne in western movie classics Howard Hawks' *Red River* (1948) and John Ford's cavalry picture *She Wore a Yellow Ribbon* (1949). Ford later cast Dru alongside Ben Johnson in his 1950 film *Wagonmaster,* and she also starred in *All the King's Men* with Broderick Crawford, *Thunder Bay* with Jimmy Stewart, *711 Ocean Drive, Mr. Belvedere Rings the Bell,* and *The Pride of St. Louis.* During the 1960s and 1970s Dru made numerous television guest appearances, and starred in her own series, *Guestward Ho,* in 1960.

Dru was married to actors Dick Haymes in the 1940s and John Ireland in the 1950s, and was the older sister of game-show host Peter Marshall. On September 10, 1996, she died in her home of respiratory failure after a long battle with cancer. She was 74 years old.

(Carla Ridge to Schuyler. Right to Beverly Crest. Left to:)

9402 Beverly Crest Drive, Rock Hudson death site

Romantic leading man Rock Hudson died here at his "Castle" of the AIDS virus on October 2, 1985. Although he knew for several years that he had the killer virus, he denied that he was infected until his death.

The hilltop estate of homosexual heartthrob Rock Hudson, who kept his AIDS infection a secret until his death.

In fact, he knew he had the virus for over a year when he passionately kissed actress Linda Evans during a romantic appearance on television's *Dynasty* in 1984. Just a month after Hudson's death, his live-in lover Marc Christian filed a landmark lawsuit claiming that Rock and his associates deceived him about Hudson's HIV status. He was awarded $22 million but later settled for $6.5 million.

Subsequent owner John *(Animal House)* Landis had his own legal problems stemming from the death of Vic Morrow and two child actors on the set of *Twilight Zone—The Movie*, killed when a rigged explosion sent a helicopter spinning down on top of them. Landis was later acquitted of manslaughter charges relating to the deaths.

(Beverly Crest to Lindacrest. Left to:)

1643 Lindacrest Drive, George Peppard last home

This was the last home of movie and television star George Peppard, whose career began in *The Victors* and *Breakfast at Tiffany's*. He is better known, though, for his 1970s and 1980s lead roles in the television series *Banacek* and *The A-Team*. Peppard was

married six times, twice to actress Elizabeth Ashley, and on April 18, 1994, died at 65 from pneumonia.

(Continue on Lindacrest to the corner at Readcrest Drive, and notice the house on the corner completely surrounded by a two-story hedgerow at:)

1479 Lindacrest Drive, Brandon Tartikoff death

Brandon Tartikoff joined NBC in 1976 as the director of comedy programming and led the network to dominance by developing such critically acclaimed series as *The A-Team, Hill Street Blues, Cheers, The Cosby Show, St. Elsewhere*, and *L.A. Law*. In 1991 he left NBC to take over Paramount Pictures, resigning in 1992 after a Louisiana car crash seriously injured his daughter. In 1995 Tartikoff suffered a recurrence of Hodgkin's disease that had first arisen in 1980, and on August 27, 1997, he died of the disease. At the time of his death he had founded a production company called The H. Beale Co., named after the suicidal news anchor in the movie *Network* (1976).

(Lindacrest to Coldwater. Right to:)

1700 Coldwater Canyon Drive, Bette Davis–Howard Hughes house

The home at the top of the hill behind the gates at 1700 Coldwater Canyon was shared by Bette Davis and Ham Nelson during their short marriage in the late 1930s. It was Davis who coined the nickname for the Academy Award statue when she told a reporter that the perfect buttocks of the statue reminded her of her husband Ham's. His real name: Oscar Nelson.

Davis was notoriously unfaithful to all of her husbands, but the most famous of her infidelities during the Nelson marriage was with Howard Hughes. At the time he was sharing a Hancock Park mansion with Katharine Hepburn, but he still found time to meet Davis here on a regular basis. Ham had the house bugged, and in September 1938 listened from the back of a truck parked on Coldwater to the sounds of loud love-making. He ran inside, burst in and found Davis and Hughes lying nude on a bed covered with gardenias. Ham coolly told the couple that it would cost $70,000 ($750,000 today) to keep the secret that would certainly ruin her career. Hughes calmly wrote a check as he stood nude in the bedroom, and Ham quietly divorced Davis. Every year on the anniversary of the date Hughes sent Davis a single gardenia.

In the 1940s the small gatehouse and servant's quarters just inside the left or north side of the gates (1720) was rented by Bugsy Siegel for his girlfriend Virginia Hill, although she spent a lot of time at his pal George Raft's nearby home.

(Coldwater to Heather Road. Left to:)

9624 Heather Road, Charlie Minor last home

Charlie Minor was raised in rural Georgia, but after coming to Hollywood in the 1970s became one of the best-known record and music promoters in the United States. The promotions director for A&M Records, Minor became an industry legend managing the marketing for dozens of famous bands. The flamboyant Minor was equally well-known for his lavish lifestyle and prodigious success with the ladies, once telling a pal of his past conquests, "man there've been thousands." In early 1995 one of them paid him back with a vengeance.

After trying to rid himself of girlfriend Suzette McClure, a stripper who had been stalking him for six months, Minor fled his Heather Road home here for the hoped-for security of his Malibu beachhouse at 22058 Pacific Coast Highway, behind the gates of a private Carbon Beach compound. On the morning of March 19, 1995, McClure was unable to find Minor at the Heather home and tracked him to the Malibu house. After he refused her admittance she buzzed other nearby homes until someone eventually let her in. Quietly sneaking into the home through the beachside entrance, McClure pulled out a gun and shot Minor six times, killing him instantly. She was allegedly high on crack cocaine at the time she killed the 46-year-old record mogul. When writer Ben Stein asked a former girlfriend why, of all the women Minor dated, did McClure kill him, she replied, "Maybe she was the first one who had a gun."

(Heather Road a short distance to Heather Court. Around to left to:)

1861 Heather Court, Michael Boyer suicide site

Aspiring actor Michael Boyer was the son of French-born actor Charles Boyer and his actress wife Pat Paterson. On September 23, 1965, the 21-year-old was found shot to death inside the house here. Although there were conflicting stories from witnesses, ballistics evidence that didn't match, and stories describing a love triangle involving Boyer, his girlfriend, and a male roommate, the death was ruled a suicide. Just days after

Paterson, the elder Boyer's wife of 45 years, passed away following a battle with cancer in 1978, Charles also committed suicide by shooting himself with a pistol.

Nearby, if you have time and want to continue a short distance north up Coldwater, just to the right on Cedarbrook Drive at 9560 is a lovely little house that Laurence Olivier rented from Olivia de Havilland in 1938. Although each was married to someone else at the time, Olivier shared the secret hideaway with Vivien Leigh while she filmed *Gone with the Wind* in 1938. After divorcing their respective mates, the duo were married just after filming was completed.

A short distance up Coldwater is the intersection of Coldwater and Mulholland Drive, which runs along the top of the Hollywood Hills from Hollywood all the way west almost to Malibu. Lots of interesting things seem to happen along Mulholland Drive. The Coldwater and Mulholland intersection was the site of a January 16, 1980, assault on television tough guy James Garner, who was dragged from his car and severely beaten after a minor fender bender. His assailant spent several months in jail for his temper tantrum.

Hidden from view at nearby 12900 Mulholland is a five-acre estate built for Howard Hughes that is now owned by Marlon Brando. On May 16, 1990, Brando's daughter Cheyenne's fiancé Dag Drollet was shot in the face by Brando's son Christian. He was killed by an enraged Christian because he had been beating Cheyenne. Young Brando spent five years of a ten-year sentence before a 1996 release, and the unstable Cheyenne eventually killed herself in Tahiti after several attempts.

Next door at 12850 is Jack Nicholson's estate, the site of a 1974 sexual liaison with a minor that forced director Roman Polanski to flee the United States for Europe after a conviction on statutory rape charges.

Just west at 13459 is a home rented by temperamental actress Shannen Doherty, the setting of her 1993 wedding to teenager Ashley Hamilton, son of actor George and

model Alana. Less than three months later, tabloids reported that Hamilton had left the home after a fierce argument with Doherty. Recently fired from her *Beverly Hills 90210* role, she allegedly threatened Hamilton with a gun as he was leaving.

Farther west at 14527 is the home of actor Harry Dean Stanton, where on January 20, 1996, two thieves forced their way inside, pistol-whipped the 69-year-old star and looted the home. The gunmen filled his Lexus with stereo equipment and jewelry and drove off, but a tracking device in the car led police to a Hollywood house where they were arrested.

East of the Coldwater intersection at 7740 Mulholland is Rummel Park, the site of a bizarre home designed and built by actor Errol Flynn in 1938. His "Mulholland House" was at 3100 Torreyson just below Mulholland and sported several "add-ons" personally designed by Flynn. The entryway featured a floor-to-ceiling fish tank backed by a carving of tropical sealife, but upon close scrutiny it could be seen that the fish all were endowed with oversized male genitalia. His huge mahogany liquor cabinet was fronted by an ornate hand-carved bullfighting scene: to open the cabinet the bull's testicles had to be squeezed. The cushions on several of the carved dining room chairs hid hydraulic dildos which were controlled from a panel at Flynn's chair at the head of the table. Famous voyeur Flynn also installed "bugs" in the ladies' bathrooms and peepholes in the walls, and a large mirror directly over the main guest bed. Just above was a game room surrounding a glass-bottomed card table, from which players could view the bed directly below. His huge bed was surrounded by black silk curtains decorated with golden question marks.

On May 29, 1942, the house was the site of a macabre prank when Flynn's pal John Barrymore died and several of Flynn's drinking buddies went to the mortuary, borrowed the body and sat the corpse in a chair in the study. When a drunken Flynn returned in the wee hours of the morning and saw

Barrymore in his favorite chair he ran screaming from the house! Country singer Rick Nelson was living in the mansion at the time of his 1985 death in a Texas plane crash.

(Reverse to return south on Coldwater to:)

1218 Coldwater Canyon Drive, George Raft house

George Raft and his best pal Rodolpho Guglielmi were discovered in a New York dance hall, and the two remained close friends as Rodolpho Guglielmi became Valentino. Raft's 45-year career began in 1929 in *Queen of the Night Clubs* and included classics such as *Scarface* (1932), *Johnny Angel* (1945), and *A Bullet for Joey* (1955). He acquired his on-screen gangster persona by copying his childhood pals Bugsy Siegel and "Lucky" Luciano, but he was a real-life tough guy who had learned to box as a teenaged prizefighter in his native Brooklyn. His Hollywood fights were well-publicized; a 1933 on-set fistfight with Wallace Beery put both men in the hospital, and when he filmed *Manpower* (1941) with Edward G. Robinson, the pair got into a bloody battle over Marlene Dietrich. He also beat up actor Peter Lorre during a scene from *Background to Danger* (1943) when Lorre blew smoke in his face on-camera.

Raft had very public affairs with dozens of stars including Carole Lombard, Norma Shearer Thalberg, Marlene Dietrich, and Betty Grable, and kept several hookers living here at his house at all times. Bugsy Siegel's girlfriend Virginia Hill stayed here for weeks at a time, although she lived just up the street, and according to biographers Raft bedded Hill here even while Siegel was also in residence. Had the violently unstable Siegel discovered Hill's infidelity it certainly would have meant death for the lovers. When Raft once sent Siegel a toupee as a birthday gift, Siegel stormed the home here firing a pistol into the air and threatening to kill Raft.

(Coldwater to continuation on Beverly at Coldwater Canyon Park. As you approach the park, notice the upper floors of the large orange stucco mansion on top of the hill to your right at:)

1011 (formerly 1007) Beverly Drive, William Randolph Hearst–Marion Davies death site

The 30-room mansion above the lion gates was built in 1927 for over $1 million, equal to over $40 million today. It was the last home of publisher William Randolph Hearst and his mistress Marion Davies, whose 37-year relationship lasted as long as his marriage to wife Millicent before ending when the frail 88-year-old died in his bedroom from heart ailments on August 14, 1951. The large balcony outside his death room is visible above the trees.

In 1946 Hearst and Davies left his beloved San Simeon castle and moved here to be near his doctors, and for five years an army of nurses cared for Hearst in the mansion kept at a stiflingly hot 82 degrees at all times. During his final hours a crowd of friends and family joined Marion in a macabre death watch, while Millicent stayed away. As he neared death the family convinced Marion to take a sedative for some much-needed rest, and while she was sedated Hearst died. When she awoke the next morning the house was empty except for Hearst's beloved dachshund Helena, and his body was already laid out in a San Francisco mortuary. Davies told Millicent, "You can have him now; he's dead. *I* had him when he was alive."

Within months the hopelessly alcoholic Davies married her sister's boyfriend, an alcoholic ex-sailor, in a drunken Las Vegas ceremony. So drunk that she had to be held upright by a friend, she couldn't even mumble "I do" and upon awakening the next day called her niece Patricia Lake and said, "I think I got married last night." Davies spent her last unhappy years here, succumbing to cancer on September 22, 1961, at 65.

The incredible estate has been used as the setting for numerous movies including *The Godfather* (1975) and *Billy Madison* (1996).

(Beverly to Shadow Hill. Right onto Steven and onto Laurel Way. Right to:)

1460 Laurel Way, Susan Hayward death site

Susan Hayward was born into Georgia poverty as Edith Marrener and as a child dreamed of becoming a star. David O. Selznick saw her in a local magazine ad and brought her to Hollywood to test for the Scarlett O'Hara role in *Gone with the Wind* (1939). Although she lost that role she later starred in *Beau Geste* (1939), *Reap the Wild Wind* (1942), *With a Song in My Heart* (1952), *I'll Cry Tomorrow* (1955) and dozens of other films. Nominated for five Oscars, she won for her 1956 portrayal of executed murderer Barbara Graham in *I Want to Live.* The gritty southern belle died at her home here on March 14, 1975, after a long battle with brain cancer.

Her death was one of hundreds tied to the filming of the 1956 John Wayne movie *The Conqueror,* which was inexplicably filmed in the Utah desert just upwind from the site of the 1940 atomic bomb tests at Yucca Flats, Nevada. Members of the cast and crew have been plagued by cancer deaths at a rate over *30 times* the national average— 130 of the 220 crew members have contracted cancer, killing John Wayne, Dick Powell, Agnes Moorehead, Thomas Gomez, Ted de Corsia, and Pedro Armendariz, who beat kidney cancer in the 1950s but committed suicide in 1963 when cancer of the larynx was diagnosed. Hayward, only 58 at the time of her death, was killed by cancer of the skin, breast, uterus and brain.

(Reverse on Laurel to Shadow Hill. Right to Sunnyvale Way. Right a short block to Laurel Way. Left to Laurel Lane.

Left to the lovely mansion on the right at the top of the cul-de-sac at:)

1200 Laurel Lane, Samuel Goldwyn death site

Immortal studio head Samuel ("Include Me Out!") Goldwyn was born Samuel Gelbfisz in Warsaw, changing to Sam Goldfish when he came to the United States to sell gloves in New York. He joined brother-in-law Jesse Lasky's movie business, changed his name yet again to Goldwyn, and soon headed the most successful studio in history. His Goldwyn Studios became part of Metro-Goldwyn-Mayer, which was ruled over by the despotic Goldwyn and his equally ruthless partner Louis B. Mayer. Goldwyn suffered a near-fatal stroke at his lawyer's Beverly Hills office on March 6, 1969, and retreated into seclusion in his mansion, where he died on January 31, 1974, at 94 from complications from the stroke.

(Reverse to Laurel Way. Left to Beverly. Left around the corner to the right onto Rexford and notice the mansion on your right covering the corner on your right:)

1005 North Rexford Drive, Clifton Webb haunted death site

The mansion here was built over the remains of actor Clifton Webb's home, a celebrated party spot and the site of his October 3, 1966, death from heart disease at 76. Webb starred in over 30 films including *Laura* (1944), *The Razor's Edge* (1946), *Cheaper by the Dozen* (1949), *The Titanic* (1953), *Three Coins in the Fountain* (1954), and several *Mr. Belvedere* movies. The lifelong bachelor shared the home with his adored mother, and after her death her room became a bizarre shrine in a true "Norman Bates" style. He steadfastly maintained that the home was haunted by the ghost of the previous owner, eccentric actress Grace Moore who died in a tragic plane crash at the height of her career, and his mother who visited him nightly. He often told friends that he too would haunt the house, "never leaving, even in death." He kept his promise.

Webb's ghost has been seen at parties after his death, and subsequent residents say that he still can be found standing in the library uttering his favorite phrase "well, well, well…" He was a lifelong chain-smoker, and sleeping nonsmokers are awakened covered with cigarette ashes. No cats have ever been able to live in the house, interesting since Webb absolutely abhorred cats. The ghostly appearances allegedly increase during October, the month of his death.

(Continue past the home Mickey Rooney purchased [919] after his wife was murdered in Brentwood, pass Lexington, and note the mansion on the corner on your right at:)

901 North Rexford Drive, George Gershwin death site

Prolific songwriter George Gershwin teamed with his brother Ira on the most famous songs of the 1900s, including "Swanee," "Rhapsody in Blue," "They Can't Take That Away from Me," and the musicals *Lady Be Good, Funny Face, An American in Paris,* and *Porgy and Bess.* In June 1937 George suffered a cerebral hemorrhage at the brother's nearby Rexford Drive home, and Ira borrowed this house from writers Yip Harburg and Harold Arlen for more peaceful

surroundings. Gershwin succumbed to the effects of his attack on July 11, 1937. Harburg wrote much of the music for *The Wizard of Oz* (1939) in this house, which was rented from actor Lawrence Tibbets, and several years later Bugsy Siegel rented the mansion when he arrived in Hollywood.

(Rexford to Sunset. Right to Beverly. Right to:)

911 North Beverly Drive, Edgar Allen Woolf death site

Edgar Allen Woolf was an acclaimed 1920s and 1930s screenwriter and a top MGM favorite of Irving Thalberg. He wrote the 1927 Tod Browning cult classic *Freaks,* and wrote for Jean Harlow, Joan Crawford and a host of others during his career. It was at his home here that he worked with close friend Yip Harburg and songman Harold Arlen on 1939's *The Wizard of Oz,* for which they won Academy Awards. Arlen actually wrote the movie's "Over the Rainbow" theme as he sat in his car in front of Schwab's Drugstore in Hollywood! On December 9, 1943, Woolf walked out the front door of this mansion to take his dog for a walk, but as he descended the front steps he tripped over the dog's leash and fell. He hit his head on the steps and was killed instantly from skull fractures and brain injuries. The former Broadway playwright was only 57 when he died. The home was subsequently owned by noted television director Stan Freeburg.

Tour 8:
Beverly Hills,
Benedict Canyon

Begin Tour 8 at the intersection of Beverly and Lexington Drives,
and you can see on the northwest corner of the intersection a
lovely white mansion fronted by a series of columns, the site of:

1001 Beverly Drive, Jack Haley death site

John Joseph Haley had a long list of movie credits, but as Jack Haley he is forever immortalized as "The Tin Man" from *The Wizard of Oz* (1939). Haley only got the role when the original star, Buddy Ebsen, developed a severe allergic reaction to the silver painted makeup. When he could no longer tolerate the paint, Haley was given the role. Ebsen would become famous as Uncle Jed in the campy 1960s comedy series *The Beverly Hillbillies.*

The deeply religious Haley was once honored by the Pope for his work with the Catholic Church, and on June 6, 1979, the 80-year-old Haley suffered a fatal heart attack at his longtime home here. His close friend Ray Bolger eulogized Haley by saying, "Jack, it's going to be very lonesome on the Yellow Brick Road."

(From the Beverly-Lexington intersection, left on Lexington to the intersection at Crescent. The large white mansion on your left at the corner on Lexington is:)

1700 Lexington Drive, Marion Davies mansion

William Randolph Hearst bought this Beverly Hills mansion for mistress Marion Davies in 1924 for her family. "Daisy" to her friends, Marion lived here, at a 100-room Santa Monica beachhouse or at the incredible Hearst Castle in San Simeon along the California coast. This Lexington House was site of hundreds of Hollywood parties, but the most infamous took place on September 8, 1926.

The party was to have been a double wedding—director King Vidor and actress Eleanor Boardman were set to wed, as were their old friends John Gilbert and the sultry Greta Garbo. Gilbert was obsessed with the eccentric and openly bisexual Garbo, and their bizarre relationship totally consumed him. Just two weeks earlier Garbo inexplicably told the smitten suitor she would marry him, and a double wedding was planned with Vidor and Boardman. As the wedding morning dragged on it was apparent Garbo was leaving him at the altar for the fourth time, and a depressed Gilbert retreated into one of the bathrooms. Louis B. Mayer slapped the weeping star on the back and

93

Top: Last home of "The Tin Man," Jack Haley, who died here in 1979. *Bottom:* Marion Davies' "Lexington House" was bought by William Randolph Hearst for Marion's family, who lived here until the late 1960s.

laughed, "What's the matter with you, Gilbert? Don't marry her. Just fuck her and forget about her!" Gilbert replied by flooring Mayer with one punch, who screamed, "You're finished Gilbert! I'll destroy you if it costs me a million dollars!" Gilbert's raging alcoholism and squeaky voice made that an easy job for Mayer, who blackballed him from the studio by giving him terrible roles in stinkers such as *The Show* and *Desert Nights,* and deliberately recording Gilbert's voice at even higher-pitched tones that made audiences laugh out loud. Gilbert was washed up and dead within four years. Marion's extended family lived in this house until the late 1960s.

(Left on Crescent and as you descend the hill, notice on your right the Beverly Hills Hotel property. The small buildings visible behind the main building are the hotel's world famous bungalows. Pull to right and see:)

9641 Sunset Boulevard, Beverly Hills Hotel, Jesse Lasky death, Peter Finch death, Walter Huston death

The Beverly Hills Hotel was built in 1912 for $500,000 by developer Burton Green to help promote the sale of his nearby residential lots, squatting in pink splendor in the middle of endless miles of barren lima bean fields. The area wouldn't become Beverly Hills for another two years, when the population reached 3,000. When the hotel opened, the nearest "movie star" lived ten miles away in Hollywood, avoiding the coyote and rattlesnake-infested hills above the hotel for almost ten years, when Douglas Fairbanks and Mary Pickford moved in. For 80 years the hotel has hosted celebrity functions,

affairs, scandals, and on several occasions, deaths.

In 1958, screen pioneer Jesse Lasky, who with partners Cecil B. DeMille and Samuel Goldwyn began filming silent movies in Los Angeles in 1912 and actually founded the movie industry, died in the hotel lobby of a heart attack as he drank with friends. After leaving the Jesse Lasky Feature Films Company and Paramount Pictures, both of which he once owned, Lasky produced his own films, which included *Sergeant York* (1941), *Rhapsody in Blue* (1945), and *The Great Caruso* (1951).

On April 8, 1950, Walter Huston, patriarch of the famous stage and screen family, suffered a fatal heart attack during his

Now one of the most famous hotels in the world, when the Beverly Hills Hotel was built in 1910 there was nothing but bean fields for miles around.

sixty-sixth birthday party at the hotel. Huston's vaudeville career lasted almost 20 years in the United States and his native Canada before he earned Broadway success in the mid–1920s in plays such as *The Fountain, Elmer the Great, North Star,* and *And Then There Were None.* The movie *Treasure of the Sierra Madre,* directed by his son John Huston, earned Walter an Academy Award for Best Supporting Actor in 1948. Other movie roles included *The Virginian* (1927), *Dodsworth* (1936), and his final film, *The Furies* (1950), which was completed just two weeks before his death.

Sixty-one-year-old Peter Finch starred in films such as *The Power and the Glory* (1945) and *Far from the Madding Crowd* (1967), but he is best-remembered for his final role in *Network* (1977) as a crazed news commentator who coined the phrase "I'm mad as hell and I'm not going to take it anymore!" The role earned him an Oscar, but it was awarded posthumously because as he waited to tape a television promo on January 14, 1977, he had a heart attack and died by the lobby phones outside the Polo Lounge.

In 1986 the hotel was purchased by Ivan Boesky from his father-in-law for $10 million, and sold later that same year to Marvin Davis for $136 million. In 1992 it was purchased by the Sultan of Brunei for $187 million, though he had never seen it nor had ever set foot in L.A. After his plan to turn it into his personal residence was turned down by city council, a three-year $150 million renovation was begun. Each of the Sultan's rooms cost $1.75 million, but one can still get a room for $350 a night and hang around the Polo Lounge with the stars.

The hotel's most famous—or infamous—sites are the lavish bungalows that line the Crescent Drive side of the hotel. A favorite trysting place for movie colony lovers, there are 12 freestanding units and several multiunit suites, each with a fascinating history. Six units are visible from Crescent, behind and north of the Crescent wing of the hotel. Bungalow 5, the first unit

adjacent the hotel, is the biggest bungalow with four bedrooms and the only one with its own pool. It was shared by Elizabeth Taylor and Richard Burton and was the site of many of the couple's famous loud fights. They had a standing order for two bottles of vodka with their room service breakfasts, and another two with lunch. It was also used by Marilyn Monroe and Yves Montand during filming of *Let's Make Love,* while each's soon-to-be ex-partner was also in residence. Heiress Barbara Hutton only stayed in Number 6 which is also Liza Minnelli's favorite. Number 7 was Marilyn Monroe's personal residence. Former Drexel Burnham kingpin-turned-ex-con Michael Milken hosted notorious Thursday night "no-wives" parties in Number 8, which was also home to Eddie Fisher, and Saudi arms dealer Adnan Khashoggi prefers Number 9. Elizabeth Taylor and her family lived in Number 10 when her father Frances ran the hotel's upscale art gallery during the 1930s and 1940s. Directly behind Number 10 is Number 11, which was reserved for Marlene Dietrich, who had a huge eight-foot-square bed installed specially for it. John Lennon and Yoko Ono also shared Number 11 for a short time.

Howard Hughes spent years living in Number 4 with a succession of beauties including Jean Harlow, Jean Peters, and Terry Moore. He had room service meals left by the door in the branches of a nearby tree, and for almost three years during the early 1950s he kept a brand new Cadillac convertible parked just outside Number 5 on Crescent Drive, even though it was never driven. It was ignored by police, although all four tires eventually went flat and bushes grew from inside the car.

(Reverse back up the hill on Crescent to Lexington. Left to Oxford. Left to:)

916 Oxford Way, Dinah Shore death site

Tennessee-born Frances Shore took the name "Dinah" from the song she sang during her first New York audition in 1940, and soon went from radio work to stardom, fronting for several of the big bands of Xavier Cugat and Eddie Cantor. In 1950 she became the first woman to host her own television program, the 15-minute *Dinah Shore Show* that began during television's infancy. She improved the talk-show genre during a 40-year career that earned her ten Emmys, but after a short bout with cancer she died in her home here on February 24, 1994, at 76.

(Oxford to Hartford. Right across Lexington a short distance to Pamela. Right to end of cul-de-sac at:)

1004 Pamela Drive, Buster Keaton home, Pamela Mason death site

Joseph Frank Keaton earned the name "Buster" after a family friend watched the 6-month-old child tumble down a flight of boardinghouse stairs and escape unscathed. Joining his parent's act at three, his life was on stage; during 15 years he went to school just once, for one day. In 1917 he joined Roscoe

"Fatty" Arbuckle in comedy two-reel classics like *The Butcher Boy* (1917), *His Wedding Night* (1917), *Good Night, Nurse* (1918), and *The Cook* (1918). He later produced the solo efforts *The Boat* (1921), *The Paleface* (1922), *The Electric House* (1923), *Sherlock, Jr.* (1924), *The General* (1926), and *Steamboat Bill, Jr.* (1928).

Never using stuntmen, he fractured a leg during *The Electric House* (1922) and was blown off a moving train by a water tank in *Sherlock,* only later learning that he had broken his neck. His most famous stunt—staring deadpan as a hinged three-story housefront falls around him as he stands in a window gap—left only a half an inch of clearance around his unprotected body.

In 1925 he built a 30-room Italian villa at the end of the flower-lined drive here that contained ten acres of gardens featuring remote-controlled streams stocked with trout. The front was accented by a 60-step marble stairway flanked by statues that led to a 50-foot Romanesque marble pool lined with hand-painted tiles. He hired his landscaper away from Pope Pius XII. Over $20,000 ($400,000 today) was spent to move a line of

This secluded mansion was built by Buster Keaton and Natalie Talmadge. Keaton later lost his beloved home when the unhappy couple divorced.

trees from the front to the back—they now frame the long driveway. In order to make grand entrances like his movie swashbuckler friends, Keaton rigged the living room drapes so he could swing down from the second floor balcony.

The gorgeous estate was also the backdrop for Keaton's bizarre marriage to actress Natalie Talmadge, whose mother and sisters moved in after the wedding, and who inexplicably convinced Natalie to avoid sex with her husband. She did, and the unhappy couple divorced a year later. Apparently Keaton is still playful, as subsequent owners report a playful ghost who fiddles with the lights, water faucets, doors, wall hangings, and so on.

Subsequent owner Pamela Mason once said, "This is so typical of everything out here—the minute they built it they wrecked their lives and couldn't live in it." She lived in the home for 25 years after her highly publicized late–60s divorce from English actor James Mason. She was one of palimony lawyer Marvin Mitchelson's first high-profile clients. She and her ex-husband starred in the 1950s television show *The James Mason Show*, and she also appeared solo in the 1960s television series *The Panic* and *The Accused*. She hosted early chat shows—*The Pamela Mason Show* in 1965 and an interview program featuring female guests, *The Weaker Sex (?)*, in 1968. On June 29, 1996, the 80-year-old had a fatal heart attack in her sleep inside Buster's beloved mansion.

(Reverse to Hartford. Right to Benedict Canyon. Left to:)

917 Benedict Canyon Drive, Charlotte Pickford death site

Toronto mother Charlotte Smith pushed her daughter Gladys into Canadian stage productions at the age of five after her husband, who operated a fruit stand on a ferry, was hit in the head with a pulley and killed. When Gladys came to Hollywood and was

renamed "Mary Pickford," mother Charlotte changed her name as well and become her manager. Charlotte also managed son Jack and younger daughter Lottie, and a worshipping Mary bought this home for her mother even before she had bought *herself* a home.

When Charlotte died of cancer on February 1, 1928, at this home, Mary was so overcome with grief that she beat her husband Douglas Fairbanks bloody with her fists and had to be sedated until after the funeral. Mary would never lay eyes on the house again, taking circuitous routes around Beverly Hills to avoid seeing the house for the remaining 50 years of her life. Pickford told friends she spoke with her mother in dreams every night of her life.

(Benedict Canyon to:)

910 Benedict Canyon Drive, Marion Davies studio bungalow

William Randolph Hearst built Marion Davies a 14-room "bungalow" to use as a studio dressing room when she worked at his Metro Studio. Invitations to the celebrity luncheons she hosted in her bungalow were as sought after as invitations to Pickfair. She so loved her "little dressing room" that it was disassembled into smaller pieces and moved in a caravan of ten flatbed trucks every time she moved, first from Metro to Warners, then from Warners to Beverly Hills when she retired.

Although she never actually lived in the house she couldn't bear to part with it. She rented it to Louis B. Mayer immediately after the move, and for ten years Mayer lived there during the numerous separations from his wife Margaret, who was tormented by mental problems that kept her in sanitariums most of the time. Subsequent renters included Ann Miller, David Cameron, and David O. Selznick.

(Benedict Canyon to:)

901 Benedict Canyon Drive, Jerry Giesler home

This was the home of Jerry Giesler, the "Lawyer to the Stars" from the 1930s to the 1960s. He only handled high-profile cases for movie clients that included Errol Flynn's rape trials, Bugsy Siegel's mob problems, Charlie Chaplin's divorces and troubles with the FBI, and mobster Mickey Cohen's scores of problems with the Feds. Geisler also represented Cheryl Crane and Lana Turner after Turner's daughter Cheryl stabbed Johnny Stompanato to death in their Beverly Hills home. In fact, when police arrived at the Turner house the night of the murder Giesler answered the front door. The saying "Get me Giesler!" was heard whenever legal trouble brewed for the stars.

(Benedict Canyon to Sunset. Right to Roxbury. Right to:)

911 North Roxbury Drive, Warner Baxter death site

Warner Baxter appeared in hundreds of films during a 25-year career but is best remembered as "the Cisco Kid." He began as a child star at Paramount in the 1920s, but had his first adult leading role in *Brewster's Millions* (1926). He starred in over 50 movies including *St. Elmo* (1922), *Drums of the Desert* (1927), *West of Zanzibar* (1929), *42nd Street* (1933), and *Kidnapped* (1938). He won the 1929 Academy Award for *In Old Arizona* and starred in the early television series *Crime Doctor*. His last role was in 1949's *Prison Warden*, falling ill as filming was completed.

Suffering from arthritis throughout his life, in April 1951 he endured a frontal lobotomy to alleviate the pain and three weeks later on May 8, 1951, he died at the home he had shared with actress Winifred Bryson for over 30 years. He was 59.

(Roxbury to:)

914 North Roxbury Drive, Pandro S. Berman death site

Pandro Berman came to Hollywood as a teenager and worked as a studio laborer and sometime movie extra. By 25 he was a full-time movie director and producer, and through the 1930s and 1940s his movies featured a who's who that included Katharine Hepburn, Bette Davis, Fred Astaire, Ginger Rogers, Elizabeth Taylor, Gene Kelly, Sidney Poitier, Jimmy Stewart and Glenn Ford.

Berman's movies include the 1930s hits *The Gay Divorcee* (1930), *Swing Time* (1937) and *Shall We Dance* (1939), as well as Hepburn's Oscar-winning performance in *Morning Glory* (1933) and the 1934 film *Of Human Bondage* that turned Bette Davis into a full-fledged star. Elizabeth Taylor worked with Berman as a child in *National Velvet* (1944), and went on to superstardom in other Berman films such as *Cat on a Hot Tin Roof* (1958), *Butterfield 8* (1960), and *Father of the Bride* (1950). His final screen triumph was the controversial 1955 movie *The Blackboard Jungle* that starred Sidney Poitier and Glenn Ford. In 1977 Berman was awarded the prestigious Irving G. Thalberg Lifetime Achievement Award by the Academy of Motion Picture Arts and Sciences for his work. On July 13, 1996, the 91-year-old Berman suffered a fatal heart attack at his home here.

(Roxbury to:)

918 North Roxbury Drive, Jimmy Stewart death site

The charming tudor at 918 Roxbury Drive, bought in 1950 for $89,500 by leading man Jimmy Stewart, was the site of one of the endearing love stories of Hollywood history. A wedding present for his wife Gloria, it was the only home the couple ever owned.

James Maitland Stewart was born in Indiana, Pennsylvania, in 1908, the son of a hardware-store owner, and after studying architecture at Princeton he began doing regional theater with a group that included

The setting for one of the most enduring love stories in Hollywood history, the longtime home of Jimmy and Gloria Stewart.

future Broadway star Joshua Logan, future actors Margaret Sullavan, Mildred Natwick, and Henry Fonda. When Fonda and Stewart signed movie contracts in the early 1930s, they shared a house at 318 Rockingham in Brentwood that they nicknamed "Casa Gangrene." The two quickly became stars, and Stewart was working in films such as *The Murder Man* (1935), *After the Thin Man* (1936), *Seventh Heaven* (1937), *You Can't Take It with You* (1938), and the 1939 hits *Destry Rides Again, Made for Each Other,* and *Mr. Smith Goes to Washington*. In 1940 he won an Oscar for his leading role in the Katharine Hepburn classic *The Philadelphia Story*. In 1942 Stewart left for World War II army service, returning five years later at the age of 38.

His 50-year career included over 100 films such as *Call Northside 777* (1948), *Harvey* (1950), *The Greatest Show on Earth* (1952), *The Glenn Miller Story* (1954), *Rear Window* (1954), *The Spirit of St. Louis* (1957), *The FBI Story* (1959), *How the West Was Won*

(1962), *The Flight of the Phoenix* (1966), and *The Shootist* (1976) with pal John Wayne. Despite such an impressive resumé he is most remembered for his heartwarming portrayal of a tormented George Bailey in the 1946 Frank Capra classic *It's a Wonderful Life*. Although disappointing at the box office, Stewart's first postwar movie went on to epic status, along with its stammering star.

Stewart and Gloria Hatrick McLean wed in 1949, and 45 years later she died in his arms in their beloved home on February 16, 1994, at the age of 75 after a long fight with cancer. It was widely reported that the distraught widower had little interest in life without his wife, and for the remaining few years of his life rarely left the house, even missing the opening of the Jimmy Stewart Museum in his hometown. On July 2, 1997, at the age of 89, the star of some of Hollywood's most famous movies and remembered for some of his most famous roles, died of cardiac arrest in his home here.

After the 1971 earthquake leveled the house on the corner next door Stewart bought the lot to use as a garden that he lovingly maintained for over 25 years. He stubbornly refused literally hundreds of offers to sell "the most expensive garden in the world," but after his death the home was sold for $6 million, an astronomical sum even for Beverly Hills.

(Across the street is the site of:)

921 North Roxbury Drive, Wallace and Noah Beery death site

On April 2, 1946, 62-year-old Noah Beery, Sr., died in his brother Wallace's arms in the foyer of Wallie's home which once stood on this spot. He suffered a fatal heart attack during a birthday party for his brother. The Missouri-born Noah Beery had a modest career in regional theater and turned to the movies only after his young son's 1912 heart illness left the family $8,000 in debt. A bankrupt Beery took a train to L.A. and sold one of his two suits to pay for food, but on his second day looking for work was hired as an extra in Cecil B. DeMille's *Joan of Arc* (1914). Within a few years the leather-faced Beery was in constant demand for "bad guy" roles, and between 1918 (*The Red Lantern*) and 1945 (*This Man's Navy*) starred in over 100 films

Hard-drinking brother Wallace died in the same home of his own heart attack on April 17, 1949, at 64. As a 250-pound teenager, Beery worked as an elephant trainer in the Ringling Brothers Circus, and at 20 he and Noah were cast in the chorus of a flop Broadway show. Within a year, however, he starred in *The Yankee Tourist* and was signed with the original Essanay Studios in New York in 1913. In 1916 he married shy teenager Gloria Swanson—also an Essanay stock player—and according to her memoirs, on their wedding night a drunken Beery raped her on the floor of their hotel suite. It was the only time the two made love, and she divorced him soon afterward.

Beery came to California to work for Mack Sennett's Keystone Studios in 1916 and eventually starred in over 150 films, best remembered for his Oscar-winning performance in 1931's *The Champ* alongside child actor Jackie Cooper. He also starred in a string of such hits as *The Big House* (1930), *Min and Bill* (1930), *Grand Hotel* (1932), *Dinner at Eight* (1932), *Tugboat Annie* (1933), *Treasure Island* (1934), and *Sergeant Madden* (1939). The belligerent Beery had an annoying habit whenever he took part in movie fisticuffs. Rather than throwing the celebrated imaginary "screen punch," Beery enjoyed throwing a real one at whatever unsuspecting actor was in the way. Filming *The Bowery* (1935), he threw a roundhouse punch at unsuspecting co-star George Raft, knocking him out cold, but when Raft came to, a brawl ensued that left both men in the hospital for a week. The Beery home was demolished in the late 1980s so Ricky Schroeder could build this house for his parents.

(Roxbury to the first house on the right in the next block at:)

1000 North Roxbury Drive, Lucille Ball house

This was the last home of Lucille Ball, a television pioneer who made history when she and husband Desi Arnaz created *I Love Lucy* in 1951. The show's success was unbelievable—by 1953 over 11 million families were watching *every* week at a time when there were only 15 million television sets in America. The couple purchased the home in 1955 and shared it until their 1959 divorce, which was allegedly brought on when Lucy found him in bed here with two hookers, ending a 19-year marriage. Lucy then married producer Gary Morton, and the couple shared this home until her death. After years of health problems Lucy became ill here on April 24, 1989, summoning an ambulance for a heart irregularity. It couldn't have helped that she made the ambulance crew wait for almost an hour so she could apply makeup,

Before a 1997 facelift, the former home of *I Love Lucy* stars Desi Arnaz and Lucille Ball was a gorgeous colonial-style mansion.

and the world-famous redhead died during surgery on April 26, 1989, at 77.

The house was put on the market soon after and remained unsold for several years, as the price steadily dropped from $7.8 million to below $3.5 million, reportedly because the house was severely haunted. It was plagued by a litany of unexplained broken windows, furniture moving by itself, loud voices from an empty attic, and household objects moving around inside the empty home. In 1996 the home underwent a complete exterior renovation that may have exorcised Lucy's demons.

(Roxbury past the homes of Terry Murphy and Stanley Kramer [1001], Jack Benny [1002], Kay Gable and Peter Falk [1004], and Eddie Cantor [1012] to:)

1013 North Roxbury Drive, Thomas Mitchell death site

Thomas Mitchell made his debut in the 1934 film *Cloudy with Showers*, but his starring role in *Lost Horizons* (1936) earned his reputation as the premier character actor of the era. He won an Academy Award for his role as a drunken doctor in *Stagecoach* (1939), and later that same year starred as Vivien Leigh's father Gerald in *Gone with the Wind* (1939). Mitchell's other movies included *Mr. Smith Goes to Washington* (1939), *The Hunchback of Notre Dame* (1940), *Three Cheers for the Irish* (1940), *Our Town* (1940), *Flesh and Fantasy* (1943), *Dark Waters* (1944), *High Noon* (1952), and *Pocketful of Miracles* (1961), his final film. Mitchell also won an Emmy for television work and a Tony on Broadway, and he died in his home here from cancer on December 18, 1962.

(Roxbury past the former homes of Betty Grable [1015], and Jeanne Crain [1017] to:)

1019 North Roxbury Drive, George and Ira Gershwin home

Brothers George and Ira Gershwin shared this home for almost 20 years. The lovely estate was the site of the most popular Sunday brunch in Beverly Hills, where dozens of the most famous stars in Hollywood sat by the pool or played tennis. George was a renowned lady's man who had affairs with Greta Garbo, Paulette Goddard, Margaret Manners and Simone Simon. The gorgeous Simon gave him a solid gold key to her home so he could "stop in any time he wished."

On the afternoon of July 9, 1937, Ira found George sitting in agony by the curb, complaining of a vicious headache. Diagnosed an inoperable brain tumor, it led to his death days later on July 11 at a nearby home. A heartbroken Ira moved next door to 1021, where he lived until his death in 1969.

(Roxbury past Ira's home, later owned by Agnes Moorehead [1021], Polly Bergen and Kenny Loggins [1025] to Benedict Canyon. Left to Summit. Right up the hill past the homes of Ronald Colman [1033], and David O. Selznick, Barbara Hutton, Sammy Davis, Jr., and Ed McMahon [1050], and the entrance to the Charlie Chaplin estate [1085]).

Chaplin was a sex addict and voyeur who bedded hundreds of Hollywood stars. He allegedly installed a telescope in his bedroom here that had a view of John Barrymore's bedroom across the hills at his Tower Grove estate, and Barrymore obliged his close friend's odd requests to watch, phoning when he was ready for bed.

(Left at 1085 up the hill past Fred Astaire's home [1129] and note the white stucco fence on your left encircling the hill. At the top of the hill see:)

1143 Summit Drive, "Pickfair" site, Mary Pickford death site

The huge mansion here was built on the site of the most famous home in movie history, the world-renowned "Pickfair." The hilltop estate was purchased by Douglas Fairbanks and Mary Pickford in 1920, at the time just a remote wilderness hunting lodge accessible by dirt roads. Architect Wallace Neff transformed it into a 50-room Tudor chateau atop a 15-acre estate. The couple hosted sumptuous parties and weekly visits by royalty; at one party Marion Davies handed the King of Siam her fur coat, mistaking him for a butler. Meals were served from a different menu every day, and served on a 120-piece china set originally gifted to Josephine by Napoleon in 1807. Pickford and Fairbanks told friends the home was haunted with nightly visits by a spectral young girl carrying a handful of sheet music.

Pickford began as a $5 a day extra in films such as *Her First Biscuits* (1909) at 13, after supporting her widowed mother and two siblings with earnings from stage work that began when she was only 4. Within several years she was a major "child" star although already well into her teens, and she remained a dutiful prisoner to her role as "America's Sweetheart." She played a convincing 9-year-old Little Lord Fauntleroy at the age of 28, and was not permitted to cut her trademark curls until she was 34. In 1919 Pickford founded United Artists with Charlie Chaplin and soon-to-be husband Douglas Fairbanks, and after their marriage, the couple purchased Pickfair.

Pickford left movies after *Secrets* (1932) and lived here through her 1936 divorce from Fairbanks and a subsequent marriage to Charles "Buddy" Rogers. She retired to her bedroom in 1965, taking interviews and visits via the home's intercom system, with guests seated in the downstairs parlor speaking into a phone. She only left the bed for late night strolls around the house, having food, reading materials, and a daily bottle of whiskey delivered to her bed by a butler. She told friends that she was visited by the ghostly woman with the sheet music almost every night until her death here on May 29, 1979, at 86. She said her mother also stopped by nightly.

Singer Pia Zadora and Meshulam Riklis bought the site in 1988 for $7 million, but after termites were found Zadora had it torn down. A six-year construction project left a monstrosity that cost $20 million, but just after completion the couple divorced. Little of the original estate remains standing. Pickford's former husband Rogers moved into a small guest house on the corner of the estate (just below the north gate on Pickfair Way), and the only other reminder of the past glory are the cherub statues atop the gates—all that remain of the once-incredible palace.

(Summit just across the street to the right to:)

1151 Summit Drive, Sammy Davis, Jr., death site

Veteran entertainer Sammy Davis, Jr., died here on May 16, 1990, after a prolonged battle with throat cancer. He was a Broadway star of *Mr. Wonderful, Golden Boy,* and *Stop the World, I Want to Get Off,* and was later renowned for his trademark song "Candyman." He was a founding member of the 1950s Hollywood "Rat Pack" with pals Peter Lawford, Frank Sinatra, and Humphrey Bogart, and was threatened with death by the mob for an alleged affair with white sex symbol Kim Novak during the same period. "Mr. Bojangles" was 75 when he died, but widow Altovise was forced to auction the house and most of their belongings to settle IRS tax claims.

(Left down Pickfair Way to San Ysidro. Left past the last home of Peter Finch at 1348—from which he took a morning stroll to the Beverly Hills Hotel and his fatal heart attack in the lobby—to:)

1107 San Ysidro Drive, Laurence Olivier–Vivien Leigh–Danny Kaye triangle

Laurence Olivier's spectacular 50-year career earned him nine Academy Award nominations and a 1978 Lifetime Achieve-ment Award. In his native England he was knighted Sir Olivier in 1960 and Lord Olivier in 1970, but through all of this bi-ographers suggest that Olivier concealed a lifetime bisexuality. Before his first short marriage to admitted lesbian Jill Esmond ended in divorce, he began an affair with Vivien Leigh during filming of *Fire Over England* in 1936. When Leigh came to the United States to film *Gone with the Wind* in 1938 they were not-so-secretly living to-gether, first at 520 Crescent and later at 9560 Cedarbrook, but at the same time Olivier allegedly rekindled a 15-year affair with young comedian Danny Kaye. Olivier and Leigh rented this home—conveniently close to Kaye's own mansion at 1103 San Ysidro—and the threesome lived here for several years.

The Olivier marriage unraveled as Leigh's mental illness produced week-long fits of hysteria and prolonged depressions highlighted by animal-like rages. The ac-tress fell apart while filming *Streetcar Named Desire,* for which she won the 1948 Academy Award. Her health possibly worsened by knowledge of Olivier's affair with Kaye, Leigh took on the persona of character Blanche Dubois, even off camera. Her ill-ness prevented her from accepting the Oscar, and she "lived" as Blanche for several months before leaving Olivier and returning to England, where she died soon afterward.

(San Ysidro to Benedict Canyon. Right/across onto Ambassador to:)

1719 Ambassador Drive, John Beradino death site

John Beradino was a Los Angeles na-tive who appeared in the *Our Gang* comedies as a child, and after starring in football and baseball in high school earned scholarships to USC in 1936. He played professional baseball with the St. Louis Browns and after four years in the Navy in World War II played for the Cleveland Indians and the Pittsburgh Pirates until a 1953 leg injury ended his career. Beradino was the starting shortstop for an Indians team that won the 1948 World Series.

After leaving baseball, he found work on television shows such as *Superman, The New Breed,* and *I Led Three Lives* before joining the cast of the soap opera *General Hospital* on its first episode which aired on April 1, 1963. For the next 35 years Beradino portrayed chief of staff Dr. Steve Harvey until pancreatic cancer forced him to retire. He earned three Emmy nominations for best actor, and was the first daytime television actor to earn a star on the Hollywood Walk of Fame. He worked on the series until a month before his death, which occurred on May 18, 1996, in his home here. He was 79 years old. The house across the street at 1708 was the longtime home of gossip columnist Hedda Hopper.

(Reverse on Ambassador to Benedict Canyon and notice the gated entrance to the estate at 1230 Benedict Canyon, which can't be seen from the raod. The home can be seen as one drives up the semiprivate driveway just beyond for 1236-1244 Benedict Canyon. On the right just up the driveway notice the lovely English cottage through the trees, site of:)

1230 Benedict Canyon Drive, Elizabeth Montgomery death site

Actress Elizabeth Montgomery came from show-business roots: her mother Elizabeth Allen Montgomery was an actress and father Robert Montgomery the premier leading man of the 1930s who went on to great success as a director. Young Elizabeth made her debut on her father's *Robert Montgomery Presents* and went on to appear in over 200 live television programs during the 1950s. Although she appeared in several films including *The Court Martial of Billy Mitchell* (1957), she was primarily a television star.

Her first series role was as the earth-

bound sorceress Samantha on television's *Bewitched* from 1964 to 1972, which became an instant hit, second only to *Bonanza* in its first season. Playing a witch who tries to become a suburban housewife, Montgomery cast spells with a twitch of her nose. After the series ran its course, she appeared in television movies including *The Legend of Lizzie Borden* (1975), *Black Widow Murders: The Blanche Taylor Moore Story* (1993), and *The Corpse Had a Familiar Face* (1994). She was married to actor-director Robert Foxworth, and tragically died of cancer in the couple's lovely English manor home on May 18, 1995, at 62.

(Continue on Benedict Canyon a very short distance to Leona. Right to the top of the cul-de-sac at:)

1273 Leona Drive, Jean Renoir death site

French director Jean Renoir, son of painter Auguste, died in the modest bungalow at the top of this cul-de-sac on February 12, 1979. Renoir came to the United States in the early 1920s, directing Oscar winners *Swamp Water* (1926), *This Land Is Mine* (1943) and *Diary of a Chambermaid* (1946). He died at 74 after a long battle with Parkinson's disease.

(Reverse to Benedict Canyon. The entire hillside across on the west side was the estate of Thomas Ince and site of:)

Benedict Canyon Drive, Thomas Ince "Peephole House"

The entire hillside opposite on the west side of Benedict Canyon covering from this spot over two miles north was site of "Dias Doradas"—"Golden Days"—a lavish estate built by silent film director and screen pioneer Thomas Ince. He was a true Hollywood titan from 1910 through 1925, producing epics such as *The Battle of Gettysburg* (1914) and *Civilization* (1916). He was also responsible for innovations in filmmaking and advances in script development, direction and editing that are industry standards to this day. The "Inceville" studio sat on 20,000 acres at Sunset Boulevard and the Pacific Ocean in Malibu.

Beginning in 1924 Ince built an extraordinary mansion on the 30-acre site, with the original entrance at 1051 Benedict Canyon. The Spanish-style adobe main house boasted 45 rooms and ten bathrooms with all the luxuries of a palace. The basement held a shooting gallery, a 75-seat movie theater, soundstages and a bowling alley, and Ince added trout streams and a duck-breeding barn. The estate was fully self-sufficient, with its own electric power plant, repair facilities for cars and trucks, and producing fields and orchards. Barely six months after completion the 42-year-old Ince was dead.

His death aboard William Hearst's 280-foot yacht *Oneida* off San Diego on November 18, 1927, allegedly was caused by a love triangle involving Charlie Chaplin, Marion Davies, and Ince. Ince was reportedly shot after Hearst interrupted an on-deck tryst between Davies and Ince, shooting the man he mistook for Chaplin, who he knew was Davies' most recent lover. Though the first "bulldog" edition of the *L.A. Times* trumpeted "Producer Shot on Hearst Yacht," every copy somehow disappeared from *every* archive in the Hearst empire, and subsequent stories reported that Ince had died at his estate on November 19 from ulcer problems.

Silence secured a lifetime contract for columnist Louella Parsons, who was also on the cruise, and Ince's widow Elinor was given Hollywood's Hotel Elysee—a Hearst property—shortly after the death. Elinor sold "Dias Doradas" to producer Carl Laemmle two years later, and his servants soon discovered a secret "storage room"—to which only Ince had a key—that concealed a passageway snaking above the guest bedrooms. Over each bed was a quarter-sized peep hole hidden in the ornate ceiling carvings. Ince was apparently a Peeping Tom. The estate

was demolished in 1951 to make way for a housing development.

(Benedict Canyon to Beverly Estate. Right to curve at 1315, site of:)

Below 1375 Beverly Estates Drive, Montgomery Clift crash site

Late on Saturday night, May 13, 1956, as he tried to negotiate this sharp curve, Montgomery Clift was in a car crash that nearly ended his career and his life. He had just left a dinner party hosted by Elizabeth Taylor and Michael Wilding at their home at 1375 for friends Rock and Phyllis Hudson and actor Kevin McCarthy. For over a year the notoriously bad driver Clift had been under studio orders not to drive at all, but for some reason he didn't use his chauffeur that evening and drove himself to Taylor's home.

Leaving the party, Clift followed close friend McCarthy down the steep hill, almost rear-ending him just before McCarthy lost sight of Clift's headlights. He had smashed into a telephone pole at this corner, suffering near-fatal head and face injuries. Waiting for the ambulance, Taylor comforted her friend Clift, saving his life by removing two dislodged teeth from his throat. When she saw photographers arrive she screamed at those assembled that if anyone took pictures of the injured man she would see they never worked again. No pictures were taken.

(Beverly Estates up the hill, and notice across the canyon to your left the tile roof of the Valentino estate "Falcon Lair" in the trees to the left of the fence running up the hillside. On the hillside directly to the left of that point, across the small canyon, is a modern new home built on the site of the Sharon Tate murders. Beverly Estates to Tower Grove. Left to:)

1611 Tower Grove Road, Vickie Morgan–Alfred Bloomingdale "love-nest"

Alfred Bloomingdale, Diners Club founder and advisor to Ronald Reagan, met actress Vickie Morgan when she was 17 and he was 54. The teenager soon became his mistress, joining him and his many hookers for wild sex parties. Morgan was his favorite partner since she let him engage in his favored sadomasochism games. He particularly enjoyed whipping her bloody. Many of the couple's sex parties allegedly took place at this house, rented from 1980 and used until Bloomingdale's 1982 death. Although he had promised during his life to take care of Morgan after his death and had contracts drawn up outlining those wishes, his incredibly bitter widow cut Morgan off immediately after his death. Morgan moved to a rented condo in Studio City where she was murdered in 1983.

(Reverse down Tower Grove past Beverly Estate Drive to the intersection with Seabright at 1400, site of:)

1400 Tower Road, John Gilbert death site

This chateau was built on the site of a 1920s mansion owned by John Gilbert, the greatest of the silent stars. MGM's biggest star earned $20,000 weekly starring in 150 films including *The Merry Widow* (1924), *The Long March* (1925), and *La Bohème* (1926). To help placate on-again off-again girlfriend Greta Garbo, he built a lovely log cabin in the trees above the house where the enigmatic star lived for four years. The site included a man-made mountain stream running past the cabin. She refused repeated pleas of marriage and left him at the altar four times, leading Gilbert into a long battle with alcohol.

As his career fizzled and his alcoholism grew worse Gilbert resumed an old affair with a then-married Marlene Dietrich, who was in bed with the drunk 40-year-old on January 9, 1936, when he suffered a heart attack and choked on his own tongue. She left before police and reporters arrived. The original Spanish-style hacienda was demolished in 1983, and subsequent residents of the property have included Miriam Hopkins, David O. Selznick and Jennifer Jones, and Sammy Davis, Jr. This mansion—once owned by Elton John—was built on the site, and was used as a set for the 1997 Martin Lawrence–Charlie Sheen comedy *Money Talks*.

(Tower Grove to 9900 Beverly Grove, and notice the house above you at:)

1270 Tower Grove Road, Heidi Fleiss home

In 1990, a Beverly Hills dentist bought this house from actor Michael Douglas as a gift to his daughter Heidi. Unknown to her father, Heidi was a hooker working for Hollywood's Madam Alex, and by 1992 Heidi Fleiss was using her house as the headquarters for her *own* growing escort service, sharing the house with Victoria Sellers, the daughter of *Pink Panther* star Peter.

Heidi managed a group of 250–300 beautiful women providing the Hollywood "A-list" with companions for up to $1,500 a night. Her booming business evaporated on April 6, 1993, when undercover police recorded Fleiss closing some "business" at the Rangoon Racquet Club (9474 Little Santa Monica). Her taped admissions led to her August arrest while she took out the garbage here. Although the names in her three "black books" were not revealed, some famous names, including actors Charlie Sheen and Jack Nicholson, were identified as past Fleiss clients. Fleiss was convicted of tax evasion and money laundering and sentenced to 37 months in jail, along with an 18-month sentence on pandering charges.

(Beverly Grove to Beverly Estates. Left down to Benedict Canyon. Right to

Clear View. DO NOT STOP UNLESS THE LIGHT IS RED, or pull up Clear View to see the blue house at:)

1543 Benedict Canyon Drive, Macdonald Carey death site

For over 30 years Macdonald Carey was Dr. Horton on the soap opera *Days of Our Lives*, winning two Emmys, but he also starred in 50 films including *Shadow of Doubt* (1943), *Wake Island* (1942), and *The Great Gatsby* (1949). Carey died at his home here of cancer on March 21, 1994, at the age of 81.

There was a bizarre appearance during the May taping of the emotional scene when Carey's television wife was told that Carey's "Dr. Horton" character was dead. As a stunned cast and crew watched, a blue light appeared on every studio monitor, visible for everyone to see. The light came to rest next to Carey's favorite on-set chair as the scene was taped, fading from view as the touching scene ended, evidently one final appearance by Carey on his beloved set.

(Benedict Canyon to:)

1579 Benedict Canyon Drive, George Reeves murder site

Iowa native George Keefer Brewer Bessolo debuted as one of the Tarleton twins in *Gone with the Wind* (1939), and starred in *So Proudly We Hail* (1943) and *From Here to Eternity* (1953), but he is best-remembered as "Superman." George Reeves' June 16, 1959, death here is one of Hollywood's greatest mysteries. It was well-known at the time that Reeves had been having a long-standing relationship with Toni Mannix, the wife of MGM public relations director and studio "fixer" Eddie Mannix, who not only let the affair persist but actually bought this home for the actor. After a 1958 breakup with Mannix, Reeves soon became engaged to Lenore Lemmon, a New York party girl and socialite.

According to Lemmon, during a party Reeves abruptly got up and went to his bedroom, where he shot himself in the head with a pistol. Although everyone at the house was drunk—Reeves' own blood alcohol level was *three times* the legal limit—police accepted the curious story. Suspicions were raised when no fingerprints were found on the gun and two other bullet holes were found in the walls, but the death was still classified as an "indicated suicide." His disbelieving mother kept his body on ice for five years waiting for some evidence to turn up, but when none surfaced she buried him in an unmarked urn in an Altadena cemetery.

Just before his death Reeves filed complaints with police and prosecutors naming Toni Mannix as the source of threats and attempts on his life which began just after he broke off with her. He survived three near misses with oncoming trucks that all disappeared into the night; he was run off nearby canyon roads twice; and on still another occasion found all of the brake fluid drained from his car.

The house is still visited by his spirit, which has been seen wandering the upstairs bedroom by residents and passersby alike. Toni Mannix spent her final years sitting in front of a flickering television screen watching *Superman* reruns over and over.

(Continue on Benedict Canyon past 1905, the last home of actor Brandon Lee, son of martial artist and movie star Bruce Lee. The younger Lee was killed in a freak accidental shooting on the set of the 1993 movie The Crow. *Benedict Canyon to:)*

2017 Benedict Canyon Drive, Shannen Doherty–Dean Factor home

Cosmetics heir Dean Factor and actress Shannen Doherty lived here during their tempestuous 1992-1993 romance. During that time, the pair provided countless tabloid stories detailing car accidents, public drunkenness, arguments and fistfights with fans and friends alike. In his request for court protection from Doherty, Factor alleged that the stormy relationship reached a peak when she physically assaulted him and threatened him with a gun in the driveway of this house.

(Benedict Canyon to Easton. Right on the narrow street winding up the hill, and notice in the trees above 9820 Easton the turreted estate site of:)

Above 9820 Easton Drive, Paul Bern murder site

During the 1920s and 1930s the house at 9820 was the garage and servants' quarters for the turreted mansion still visible in the treetops above, now reached only by a private entrance up Easton at Rimmele Road. In the early 1930s this then-remote estate was owned by Paul Bern, a respected MGM director and close friend of Irving Thalberg. Although short, bald and potbellied, the 42-year-old Bern had a string of beautiful lovers including Clara Bow, Lila Leeds, and Joan Crawford. When Bern and 20-year-old beauty Jean Harlow announced wedding plans in the summer of 1932, the world was stunned, but their astonishment turned to horror when Bern was found shot to death inside the couple's home on September 5, 1932, just two months after their marriage.

When a butler found the nude body, the first people called to the house were MGM studio head Louis B. Mayer, his assistant Irving Thalberg, and their fixers Howard Strickling and Whitey Hendry. The group spent over three hours at the scene before calling police, making sure it looked like a suicide instead of a murder. They planted a phony suicide note implying

Director Paul Bern was found dead in the second-floor bedroom on the left; the night before, servants heard loud arguments by the pool on the lower right. In the 1920s, the secluded estate was at the end of a winding dirt road.

that Bern had killed himself because he couldn't perform sexually and had beaten her on their wedding night, a fact they knew to be untrue. They did know, however, that the public would immediately feel sympathy for Harlow and that what they knew of Bern's past would have seriously hurt Harlow's career.

The secret kept by the studio was that Bern had a common-law wife—Dorothy Millette—who had been in a New York insane asylum for ten years in a state of dementia, supported financially the entire time by Bern. Unfortunately, Millette had awakened from her fantasy world in May of 1932 looking for her "husband" Paul, and when she found him in Hollywood, she began pressuring Bern to re-marry her.

The household staff identified Millette as the woman who surprised Bern with a visit here on the night of his death, and also reported the sounds of loud arguing at the pool. The next day, police found a broken champagne glass next to the pool, and a wet bathing suit—much too large for Harlow but fitting Millette. Bern's wet bathing suit was found near the body, indicating that after an argument by the pool, Millette snuck up behind Bern as he changed into dry clothes and shot him in the back of the head. But Strickling and Hendry arranged with D.A. office pals that none of Bern's staff testified at the inquest, and Millette committed suicide the next day by jumping off a steamer into the Sacramento River. The public never learned about Millette's existence, about the physical evidence, or of the deceit of the MGM executives. To this day Bern is remembered as a perverted wife-beater who killed himself.

Subsequent owners have reported hearing the sounds of beatings, of a crying female voice and loud sobs coming from the corner of the bedroom where Bern's body was found. In 1966 hairstylist Jay Sebring lived in the house, and was told by terrified houseguest Sharon Tate that the strange noises had kept her up all night and that she had seen the ghost of "a creepy little man"

she "knew" was Bern. Running down the stairs she was frozen in her tracks by the specter of herself as a bloody corpse tied to the post at the bottom of the stairs! In 1969, as he was in the process of buying the home from director Milo Frank and his actress-wife Sally Forrest, Sebring was visiting Sharon's nearby canyon home when the Manson "Family" came calling.

(Reverse to Benedict Canyon. Right to:)

2570 Benedict Canyon, Roseanne Barr–Tom Arnold trashed rental house

Roseanne Barr once described herself and husband Tom Arnold as the upper class' worst nightmare: "white trash with money." She wouldn't get an argument from record company executive Sydney Proffer, who rented this Benedict Canyon home to the couple in 1990. According to a subsequent lawsuit filed by Proffer, the couple left damage including broken windows, flame-scorched and badly stained floors, torn wallpaper and ripped and ruined upholstery, broken furniture, punched-out walls, a scuffed tennis court, and a dented security gate. In addition, household items such as towels and silverware were missing, costing a reported $225,000. Suits and countersuits were settled a year or so later.

(Benedict Canyon to Hutton. Right to:)

2620 Hutton Place, Rachel Roberts Harrison suicide site

British actress Rachel Roberts won three British Academy Awards, for *Saturday Night and Sunday Morning* (1960), *This Sporting Life* (1963), and *Yanks* (1980), but had less success with her ten-year marriage to actor Rex Harrison. Roberts was his fourth ex-wife, and after their divorce she somehow believed that she and Rex would remarry. According to biographers, the amoral Harrison let her believe the fantasy so he could continue the affair during his subsequent marriage. By late 1980, however, she realized that remarriage was a fantasy.

On November 26, 1980, she set up a blanket on top of the hillside visible above this canyon home and took a huge dose of barbiturates that would have killed her in a few minutes. For some unknown reason, though, shortly after taking the drugs she walked down to the house to have a donut and some wine. But she unfortunately forgot that liquid lye was being saved in the wine bottle and in a gruesome accident took a mouthful that killed her almost immediately. It was the second time that Harrison was a cause of a lover's suicide—25 years earlier Carole Landis did the same thing, for the same reason.

(Reverse to Benedict Canyon. Left to Cielo. Right to Bella. Right to top of hill and note the white gates adorned by the name "Falcon's Lair," site of:)

1436 Bella Drive, Rudolph Valentino haunted "Falcon's Lair"

The hilltop hacienda behind the flower-covered walls was the last home of Rodolpho Alfonzo Rafaelo Pierre Filibert Guglielmi di Valentina d'Antonguollo, better known as Rudolph Valentino. The star of such films as *The Sheik* (1921) and *Blood and Sand* (1922), his sultry tango in *The Four Horsemen of the Apocalypse* (1923) made female moviegoers faint.

His offscreen success with the ladies was slightly less impressive; lesbian first wife Jean Acker locked him out of their hotel room on their wedding night and never consummated the marriage that lasted only two weeks. Valentino later married Natacha Rambova, a pretentious faker from Utah whose real name was Winifred Kimball Shaughnessy deWolf Hudnut. He built this estate for her, naming it after a movie the couple was writing on the life of El Cid that they had entitled *The Hooded Falcon*. In

Built by Rudolph Valentino for his wife Natacha Rambova and named for a movie they were writing together, "Falcon's Lair" was never a happy home—she divorced him as construction was completed, and he died soon after. Subsequent owners haven't fared much better.

1925, just a month after completing the mansion, she left him and a distraught Valentino tried to kill himself here. He wore her slave bracelet until his death at 31 caused by peritonitis contracted during a trip to New York. After his death over 200 women claimed to have had children fathered by the star, and two distraught Japanese fans leapt to their deaths into a live volcano. He was buried wearing Rambova's slave bracelet.

Questions regarding Valentino's sexual preference dogged him his entire life; the fact that he favored corsets and never dated a heterosexual woman fueled those rumors. After he died his bosses tried to groom his younger brother Alberto to take his place. After seven painful nose jobs failed to produce a good copy, they gave up trying to replace "The Great Lover," and a scarred Alberto returned to Italy.

Several subsequent residents have reported a strong presence of Valentino pervading the estate, of hearing 1920s music echoing through the remote hilltop and loud footsteps echoing empty hallways. His beloved guard dog "Kabar" died a month after Valentino and allegedly still prowls the estate as well. Standard Oil heiress Millicent Rogers bought the home in the 1930s but left during her first night after Valentino's ghost stalked her through the halls.

The last owner was heiress Doris Duke, who bought the house in 1953. Duke, whose father James Buchanan Duke founded the American Tobacco Company and actually built Duke University, was dubbed "The Richest Girl in the World" after she inherited $100 million at the age of 13. She once boasted, "I can buy anything I see," but the 80-year-old died all alone in Valentino's old bedroom, allegedly suffering a fatal heart attack on October 29, 1993.

Eyebrows were raised when her ponytailed high-school dropout butler-turned-best-pal Bernard Lafferty was named the executor of her estate. Lafferty stood to inherit millions of dollars and would control the biggest charities in the United States, but

family friends cried foul and charged that the elderly matron had been swindled by Lafferty. A family nurse also claimed that Lafferty and the family doctor had conspired to kill Duke through the use of "massive sedation." All the conflict didn't stop Lafferty from going on an incredible spending spree, buying $35,000 watches, luxury cars, and bizarre renovations to various Duke estates. In early 1996 he struck a deal with the estate for a lump-sum payment of $4.5 million and an "allowance" of $500,000 a year for life. Just a few months later Lafferty himself was found dead in the brand-new, 30-room Bel Air mansion he had just bought with his newfound wealth.

The original Valentino stable is located below at 10051 Cielo, a secluded spot where Ingrid Bergman and Roberto Rossellini spent quiet afternoons literally "in the hay." Their scandalous 1950 relationship—both were married at the time and allegedly loving-family types—led to ugly divorces that ended her U.S. movie career and forced the couple to retreat to Europe where they were later wed.

(Reverse at the cul-de-sac below the estate. Return to look over the small canyon over Cielo Drive and see the huge white mansion on the bluff across the way which was built on the site of:)

10050 Cielo Drive, Sharon Tate–Manson Family murders site

Beautiful actress Sharon Tate and several friends were murdered on August 9, 1969, by members of the Manson "Family" in a hilltop mansion that once stood on the hill across the small canyon from the Valentino estate. Killed along with the nine-months pregnant Tate—wife of director Roman Polanski—were Jay Sebring, coffee heiress Abigail Folger, her boyfriend Woytek Frykowski, and local teenager Ronald Parent, who was visiting a friend who was the caretaker on the estate.

Tate had bit parts in television shows including *The Beverly Hillbillies, The Man*

The Manson Family killers gained access to the Tate estate by scaling the hillside to the right of the gate in this photo.

from U.N.C.L.E. and *Petticoat Junction*, and movie roles in *The Wheeler Dealers* (1963), *The Sandpiper* (1965), and *The Americanization of Emily* (1965). She also starred in Polanski's camp classic *Fearless Vampire Killers* (1967) and *Valley of the Dolls* (1968).

At the time of the murders the estate's entrance gate was at the top of the street that runs up the side of the hill to the site. The killers crept up the hillside around the gate to enter the secluded estate, after which they shot and stabbed the hapless residents while the nearby neighbors slept. The entire estate was razed in early 1994 to make way for the huge mansion that now sits on the spot. The only thing remaining is the telephone pole by the gate, which was climbed by murderer Tex Watson on the night of the murders so he could cut the phone wires.

(Reverse from Bella to Cielo. Left down the hill past the stable site to Shadybrook. Right to Hillgrove. Right to Maybrook. Left to Angelo. Right a block to Sunbrook. Right to top of cul-de-sac on right at:)

10106 Sunbrook Drive, Dr. Timothy Leary death site

During his 75 years Timothy Leary went from West Point cadet to Harvard professor to leader of the 1960s drug culture to convict to fugitive, but still fascinated almost everyone with whom he came in contact. Born in Springfield, Massachusetts, Leary attended West Point before spending four years in the army and receiving an undergraduate degree from the University of Alabama and graduate degrees from Washington State University and the University of California at Berkeley. It was while a Harvard professor of psychology that Leary began experimenting with hallucinogenic drugs. The use of students in LSD drug experiments forced Harvard to fire the controversial teacher, and his mantra "tune in, turn on, drop out" became the motto of an entire generation of 1960s hippies.

In 1970 his wife and friends in the radical Weather Underground helped Leary escape from a California prison where he was serving a ten-year term for marijuana possession, and he spent the next four years on the run. For several years he hid out in Algeria with fellow fugitive Eldridge Cleaver before he was arrested in Afghanistan and returned to prison. Upon his release he settled in L.A. to become a fixture on the concert circuit and an obsessive computer nerd. After being diagnosed with inoperable prostate cancer in 1995, Leary chronicled his illness on his internet web page, highlighted by a picture of Leary lighting a joint. His death was announced on his internet page with the simple statement "Timothy has passed" appearing on May 31, 1996. Surrounded by family and friends, his last words were reportedly "why not" and "yeah." It was reported in 1997 that the drug guru's ashes were launched into outer space in a private satellite, where they were released into the cosmos that seemed to be his home. *Star Trek* creator Gene Roddenberry's ashes were reportedly also on the flight.

(Reverse to Angelo. Right as Angelo winds up the hill to the corner at 1300 and note the English Tudor on your left across the canyon that belonged to writer P.G. Wodehouse [1315], and at 1330 the entrance to an estate that director Fred Niblo rented to Jules Styne, Katharine Hepburn, Gloria Swanson and Rupert Murdoch. Carefully pull to the curb and note the mansion and gatehouse on the left up the hill:)

1363 Angelo Drive, Frances Marion– Thomas Thomson haunted house

The imposing castle-like gatehouse (originally 1441 Angelo) fronts a beautiful estate that was designed for screenwriter Frances Marion and her cowboy-star husband Fred Thomson by world-renowned architect Wallace Neff in the 1920s. When "Enchanted Hill" was built, their closet neighbor was their friend "Rudy" Valentino's "Falcon's Lair" a mile away. No expense was spared building the lavish house—the barn, floors and stalls for Fred's horse were made

The upper reaches of Angelo Drive are reached by a narrow dirt road that has remained virtually unchanged for over 50 years.

The extraordinary mansion built by screenwriter Frances Marion and her movie star husband Fred Thomson is still allegedly visited by Thomson's ghost. When the estate was built their nearest neighbor was Valentino's "Falcon's Lair," over a mile away.

of imported mahogany! As the home neared completion, Thomson accidently stepped on a rusty nail in the barn and contracted tetanus, dying an agonizing death at his home on Christmas Eve, 1928.

Marion told friends that for several evenings after the funeral he appeared at the end of her bed, standing and watching her. She immediately sold the house and never returned. Subsequent owners have been regularly visited by the lamentable Thomson. Houseguests clearly hear bootsteps trailing the path between Thomson's upstairs quarters through the main house and into his favorite lower-level den. The footsteps stop at the entrance to the den. Studio head Sherry Lansing and her director-husband William Friedkin owned the estate during the 1990s.

(Proceed on Angelo further up the hill and carefully reverse in the area where the semiprivate driveways leave the street, and return back down Angelo. The numbering on Angelo can be confusing, so pay attention; numbers increase from

1000 to 1820 at Brooklawn. Just past that point is the entrance to 1801 Angelo, built by Jack Warner and now owned by David Geffen. Across at 1802 is the former home of Hedy LaMarr and later Humphrey Bogart and Lauren Bacall. Continue on Angelo to Chevy Chase, right and notice the house on the corner of 1027 Chevy Chase which was owned at various times by Greta Garbo, Orson Welles, George and Ira Gershwin, and Gary Cooper. Chevy Chase to Ridgedale. Left through Bridle Path to:)

1025 Ridgedale Drive, "The Wizard of Oz" death site

On September 18, 1949, after a morning playing golf with best friend Clark Gable at the Bel Air Country Club, 59-year-old actor Frank Morgan returned to his home here and suffered a fatal cerebral hemorrhage as he stood at the front door. Born Francis

"The Wizard of Oz" died here—the last home of Frank Morgan.

Phillip Wupperman, Morgan starred in over 100 movies as a member of MGM's stock company during his 30-year career, including *The Mighty Barnum* (1935), *Tortilla Flats* (1942) and *The Miracle of Morgan's Creek* (1944). Although he was twice nominated for Academy Awards, Morgan is best-known for his role as the Wizard of Oz in the 1939 MGM classic movie. He was just getting underway in a role as Buffalo Bill in the western classic *Annie Get Your Gun* (1940) when he earned his role as the Wizard. Actor Louis Calhern took over the Buffalo Bill role from Morgan.

Besides his role as the Great and Powerful Wizard of Oz, Morgan played four other roles in the same movie: the fortune-teller Dr. Marvel, the cranky Emerald City doorman, the Emerald City cockney cabdriver, and the Wizard's spear-carrying guardian. In an uncanny coincidence, during filming a tailor's tag was discovered sewn into the sleeve of the black overcoat worn by Morgan as Dr. Marvel after it was turned inside-out to dry. The coat, which was purchased at an L.A. thrift store for $1 because it was the only one they found that fit Morgan, was originally made by a Chicago tailor for a local writer. When stunned filmmakers approached the writer's widow, she confirmed that the coat had in fact belonged to her late husband L. Frank Baum. The then unknown writer wrote a series of short stories for neighborhood children that he called *The Wizard of Oz.*

Morgan was the younger brother of another longtime MGM stock player, character actor Ralph Morgan. The house across the street at 1026 belonged to actor Fredric March and his actress-wife Florence Eldridge.

(Reverse to Hanover. Right and immediately notice the gorgeous mansion on the left above the hillside covered with flowers, site of:)

1029 Hanover Drive, Anita Stewart suicide site

"Anna" Stewart was a 14-year-old extra at Vitagraph Studios in Brooklyn, working for her director brother-in-law. She became an overnight sensation from her first role in 1917's *The Girl Philippa,* becoming the first movie actress to become a star with no acting experience (Joan Crawford was the second). *The Goddess* serials (1918) made her an international star, and she was hired by Louis B. Mayer, who shamelessly badgered her into leaving while she was recovering from a nervous breakdown caused by overwork. The Anita Stewart Picture Company was the first-ever production deal ever made with an actress. Mayer produced *Virtuous Wives* (1918), *Rose o' the Sea* (1922) and dozens of others with Stewart's company. At the time she owned the grandest mansion in Hollywood at 2000 DeMille, which was later owned by Charlie Chaplin and Cecil B. DeMille. On May 4, 1961, the long-forgotten 66-year-old Stewart took a massive overdose of barbiturates in the bedroom of this lovely mansion and was found dead by her sister.

(Hanover to Carolwood. Left to:)

355 Carolwood Drive, Walt Disney home

Famed animator Walt Disney lived with his family on Carolwood for over 30 years. The creative genius behind every major cartoon character developed during the early 1900s and the driving force behind the concept of family theme parks, the private Disney was however a strange and quirky man. The terribly moody, Disney didn't consummate his marriage until well after his honeymoon, and he was subject to black moods that lasted for months at a time. He could be extremely vengeful, responding to one animator's strike by firing his entire company and hiring replacements for every employee. Disney circled his entire estate here with a fully operational miniature steam train with scale-model tunnels and buildings that he rode alone for hours at a time, sitting quietly in the miniature engine with a train hat and whistle simply cruising in circles. After his death the family removed the weird train set.

Disney's longtime housekeeper, Thelma Howard, a crusty chain-smoking local woman, worked for Disney for 30 years before she died on June 10, 1994, at 79. A no-nonsense woman described by Disney as "the real Mary Poppins," the family caller her "Fou-Fou." Beginning in the early 1950s Disney gave Howard annual gifts of company stock, warning her never to sell it. She took his instructions to heart, never knowing what her shares were worth or how many she had. When she died, stunned executors found a stock portfolio worth over $10 million. She left half to a Thelma Pearl Howard Foundation and the other half to her institutionalized son from an early marriage. The cranky housekeeper had indeed become a fairy godmother.

Lillian Disney, widow of Walt, died in the house after suffering a stroke exactly 31 years to the day after her husband's death, dying on December 15, 1997. It was Lillian who gave us "Mickey Mouse," convincing her husband that his choice—"Mortimer Mouse"—seemed "too formal." In 1923 she was hired by Disney as his first secretary, marrying the artist in 1925.

(Carolwood past the homes of Clark Gable [325], Constance Bennett and Barbra Streisand [301], Gilbert Roland and Loretta Young [280], and George Harrison, Burt Reynolds and Loni Anderson [245] to Monovale. Left to Whittier. Right to:)

906 Whittier Drive, Ella Fitzgerald death site

Ella Fitzgerald was born in Newport News, Virginia, but grew up near New York City mimicking the voices of the popular torch singers of the day. After she won a 1934 amateur concert at Harlem's Apollo Theater, she began singing with Chick Webb's big band in such venues as the Savoy Ballroom and the Plaza and in concert halls around the world. By the age of 20, Ella was a huge star and by the age of 60 was recognized the world over as "The First Lady of Song," elevating jazz to a level never before heard. According to music producer Quincy Jones, Fitzgerald "invented the music." Among her hits were a popular rendition of "Lady Be Good" and "Songbook" anthologies of the likes of Gershwin, Porter, and Rogers and Hart. She released over 250 albums during her incredible career.

Fitzgerald retired from performing in 1994 and spent the last years of her life suffering with complications from diabetes—she lost both legs below the knees and most of her sight. The ultimate "Jazz Singer" suffered a stroke and died in her sleep in this mansion on June 15, 1996, at the age of 79.

(Whittier to Sunset. Right to:)

10000 Sunset Boulevard, Judy Garland home

The estate behind the tall stucco walls at 10000 Sunset surrounded by the humorous statues out front was rented by Judy Garland and husband Vincente Minnelli after her June 20, 1950, suicide attempt (her sixth) in a nearby rented Hollywood Hills home. For over a year the couple lived here while she recuperated. Howard Hughes and Terry Moore lived here for several years after the Minnellis left, and according to Moore, the pair were secretly married while they were in residence. That claim has never been proven, however.

(Continue to South Carolwood. Left and notice the mansion on the corner at:)

10100 Sunset Boulevard, Jayne Mansfield's "Pink Palace"

Everytime singer Engelbert Humperdinck tries to paint his mansion another color, Jayne Mansfield's favorite pink has returned to her beloved "Pink Palace." The 35-room mansion with a heart-shaped pool and matching jacuzzi remains a haunted, garish pink to this day. Gifted with a genius I.Q. of 163 and a striking 40-21-35 figure, Mansfield debuted in *Female Jungle* (1954) and had

bit parts in *Pete Kelly's Blues* (1955) and *Hell on Frisco Bay* (1956). She got only dumb-blonde roles, however, and was never able to distance herself from her looks. Purchasing the estate from Rudy Vallee in 1960, Mansfield was living in the home with Mickey "Mr. Universe" Hargitay when she was decapitated in a freak Louisiana car accident on June 29, 1967, at 34.

Humperdinck felt Mansfield's presence immediately after moving in, and reportedly came face-to-face with her ghost as he descended the main stairwell. As the stunned singer watched, the sad-looking vision vanished and has reportedly not returned. Mansfield's original intricate "J" and "M" scrollwork is still visible in the middle of the massive iron gates facing Sunset.

At the end of the South Carolwood cul-de-sac you can see the lovely "Owlwood" estate which sits on the hill behind the gates. It was originally built for studio mogul Joseph Schenck, who shared the home with his young mistress Norma Jean Baker for several years. After moving out, the renamed Marilyn Monroe so despised Schenck that she never again uttered his name out loud. The home was later owned by Sonny and Cher, and Tony Curtis.

(Sunset to Baroda. Right to:)

200 North Baroda Drive, Gary Cooper death site

Gary Cooper grew up in Helena, Montana, and came to L.A. in 1925 to work as a cartoonist. Some old Montana chums working as cowboy extras got him jobs as a stunt man and trick rider until he was given the lead in *The Winning of Barbara Worth* (1927). Immediately noticed by millions of female fans, he became an overnight star.

His films include *Children of Divorce* (1927) with then-lover Clara Bow, *The Virginian* (1929), *The Texan* (1930), *The Spoilers* (1930), *Desire* (1936), *Beau Geste* (1939), *Pride of the Yankees* (1942), *Sergeant York* (1941), *Distant Drums* (1952), and his last film, *The Adventures of Marco Polo* (1965). Though he was dogged by rumors of homosexuality during his early years in Hollywood—he allegedly carried on an open affair with fellow actor Andy Lawler while dating Lupe Velez—he had well-publicized affairs with stars like Bow, Tallulah Bankhead, Evelyn Brent, Countess Dorothy Taylor de Frasso, and Patricia Neal. He died at his longtime home here on May 14, 1961, from cancer at the age of 61.

(Baroda to:)

261 Baroda Drive, Henry Mancini death site

Henry Mancini started as a pianist for Glenn Miller in 1930 at the age of 17. During his long career he wrote some of the most famous songs in history, many featured in both the finest—and silliest—of movies, from *Breakfast at Tiffany's* to Abbott and Costello comedies. Mancini's movie songs included the scores for *Victor/Victoria, Pink Panther, Hatari, Home Before Dark,* and *Charade,* and television theme songs including "Peter Gunn" and "Mr. Lucky." He earned 14 Oscar nominations, 4 Oscars, and 26 Grammys. Married for 50 years to singer Ginger O'Connor, he died at his beautiful home on June 14, 1994, at 70 after a battle with cancer.

(Baroda to Delfern. Left to:)

250 Delfern Drive, Bugsy Siegel home

This home was built as a fortress by Bugsy Siegel and was his L.A. headquarters until the time of his 1947 murder. Bugsy designed hidden liquor and gun cabinets and concealed rooms secreted behind movable bookcases. It also featured an escape tunnel that led from his bedroom closet down to the basement so that he could exit the house if he were ever attacked. Siegel was arrested here for the 1939 murder of his old friend Harry Greenberg and was discovered by police cowering in the attic. He sold his stronghold to help finance the Las Vegas Flamingo Hotel fiasco, moving to a smaller—and much less safe—house on nearby Linden Drive.

(Delfern to the bottom of the hill just before Sunset Boulevard, and notice the gorgeous white mansion on your left at:)

100 Delfern Drive, Anita Louise death site, Eva Gabor last home

This lovely mansion was built in 1938 for studio president William Goetz and his

This Bel Air mansion was the last home of Anita Louise and Eva Gabor.

wife Edie, the daughter of Louis B. Mayer. Subsequent owners have included David Niven, Audrey Hepburn, Frank Sinatra and Mia Farrow, Anita Louise, and Eva Gabor.

Anita Louise—born Anita Louise Fremault in New York City—was a one-time child star whose blonde beauty made her a star in the 1930s and 1940s, described as "the most beautiful woman in Hollywood." As an infant, she was the model for the "Post Toasties Girl" cereal boxes, appeared in her first movie at six, and by eight was a Broadway veteran. At 13, she played her first adult role in *Just Like Heaven* (1930), and she starred in such movie classics as *Anthony Adverse* (1936) with Claude Rains and Fredric March, *Louis Pasteur* (1934) with Paul Muni, *A Midsummer Night's Dream* (1935) with James Cagney, *Marie Antoinette* (1938), *Going Places* (1939), *These Glamour Girls* (1939), and *Wagons Westward* (1940). She also starred in several television series such as *My Friend Flicka* in the 1950s and made

guest appearances in 1970s shows including *The Mod Squad* and *Mannix*.

Once married to producer Buddy Adler, Louise suffered a stroke and died here on April 25, 1970, at the age of only 53. Her pallbearers were Henry Fonda, Anthony Quinn, Ricardo Montalban, Jim Backus, and Robert Stack.

Eva Gabor lived here for almost 20 years. The youngest of the three Gabors, Eva came to the United States with her sisters Magda and Zsa Zsa in the 1930s. Eva is best-remembered for her role as farm wife Lisa Douglas on television's *Green Acres*. Though trashed by critics at the time, the campy 1960s comedy has become wildly popular in syndication, and helped make Eva a household name. Married five times and for years linked romantically to good friend Merv Griffin, Gabor died on July 4, 1995, of complications from a broken hip suffered in a fall at her home here.

Tour 9: Beverly Hills Flats, South of Sunset

Begin Tour 9 at 512 Palm Drive, in the first block north of Santa Monica Boulevard, facing south. Please note that the intersections in the Flats below Sunset all have stop signs. Be careful crossing and obey speed limits.

512 Palm Drive, Jean Harlow death

Gorgeous "Platinum Blonde" Jean Harlow was known by adoring fans and friends alike as the "Baby." When the youthful but beautiful 15-year-old was placed in a Chicago boarding school, she escaped by eloping with wealthy young Charles McGrew. Financed by McGrew's inheritance, the couple moved to Beverly Hills and bought a home near here at 618 Linden Drive. While dropping off a friend at an audition, she was noticed by a studio agent. Given small parts in Laurel and Hardy comedies, she next starred in Howard Hughes' *Hell's Angels* (1931) and soon divorced McGrew. An almost unbelievable leap to superstardom followed as she starred in her signature film *Platinum Blonde* (1931) and a string of classics including *Public Enemy* (1931), *Scarface* (1932), *Red-Headed Woman* (1932), *Red Dust* (1932), *Dinner at Eight* (1932), *China Seas* (1935), and *Libeled Lady* (1935).

Harlow's home life was dismal though; she lived under the watchful eye of her obsessive mother "Mama Jean" and her gold-digging stepfather, Marino Bello. The couple spent Harlow's money faster than she made it, and kept young Jean working like a horse. Her 1932 marriage to director Paul Bern shocked everyone except the friends who knew of her troubled home life, but the marriage that got her out of the gloomy house left her in the middle of Bern's scandalous murder just two months later. After Bern's death, Harlow moved into the all-white 214 South Beverly Glen mansion with her extended family and into a six-month marriage to cameraman Harold Rosson. She than rekindled an old relationship with longtime lover William Powell, who suggested she take this smaller house in 1936 to escape from her mother and stepfather.

On May 28, 1937, Harlow collapsed in Clark Gable's arms as the duo filmed *Saratoga*. Her Christian Scientist mother allowed no visitors, a doctor missed the early signs of uremic poisoning, and by the time Gable and Frank ("The Wizard of Oz") Morgan broke into the home on Louis B. Mayer's direct orders on June 6 it was too late. A wasted Harlow died the next morning at 26 years old. Her appalling mother told the press that "Bill Powell bought the room where she will lie forever," and though he knew nothing of the $30,000 Forest Lawn crypt she had selected ($400,000 today) he paid for it.

(Palm to:)

Gorgeous Jean Harlow died inside this home because her Christian Scientist mother delayed calling doctors, who compounded the error by misdiagnosing symptoms of the uremic poisoning that killed her.

508 and 718 North Palm Drive, Marilyn Monroe homes

This small cottage at 508 was Marilyn Monroe and Joe DiMaggio's home during their nine-month marriage which ended on October 6, 1954, with a huge press conference on the front lawn. DiMaggio drove away through a throng of 250 reporters while a distraught and tearful Marilyn met the press and cameras from around the world.

Up the street at 718 Palm Drive, Marilyn had earlier shared a home with her married mentor Johnny Hyde, the 5'3" head of the William Morris Agency. Although she remained his mistress for two years, she steadfastly refused to marry him, and the relationship ended when he suffered a fatal heart attack at the home on December 17, 1950. At his funeral she threw herself sobbing onto the casket, although she had been ordered not to attend. When she returned to the house, she discovered that Hyde's furi-

ous family had thrown all of her belongings into the street.

Marilyn's agent Charlie Feldman lived across the street from the Monroe–DiMaggio house at 509 Palm. Feldman was often the host when Massachusetts congressman John F. Kennedy visited Hollywood, and hosted a fateful dinner party in 1951 for the Kennedys, the Peter Lawfords, and the DiMaggios. During the evening, Kennedy's flirtation with Monroe was so obvious to everyone present that an enraged DiMaggio grabbed his wife by the arm and abruptly left the party. It was the beginning of an affair that would end in Monroe's tragic death. The home was later owned by comedian Paul Lynde, the longtime "center square" in television's *Hollywood Squares*. He suffered a fatal heart attack here on January 11, 1982, at the age of 55.

(Palm to Santa Monica. Right to Maple. Right to:)

511 North Maple Drive, Dean Martin death site

Son of an immigrant barber, teenager Dino Paul Crocetti began singing at his father's Steubenville, Ohio, spaghetti parlor. When he joined a Cleveland band he became Dino Martini, and further shortened his name to Martin after he met Jerry Lewis in 1946 when the duo shared a New Jersey nightclub stage. According to Martin, "we started horsing around, and doing anything that came to our minds," and the pair was soon headlining and earning $5,000 a week. From 1946 to 1956 Martin and Lewis paired in 16 comedies that featured Martin's suave straight man playing to Lewis' clowning, although offscreen they were not friends. In 1956, soon after completing *Hollywood or Bust,* the pair announced their breakup.

During the same period Martin had such song hits as "That's Amore," "Memories Are Made of This," and "Everybody Loves Somebody," and as an actor starred in 60 movies, from *My Friend Irma* in 1949 to *Cannonball Run II* in 1984. In between he starred in the hits *The Young Lions* (1958), *Sergeants Three* (1962), *Four for Texas* (1963), and *Robin and the Seven Hoods* (1964). He also had an eight-year television run on his *Dean Martin Show.* The cast of *Robin and the Seven Hoods* included Martin and pals Frank Sinatra, Sammy Davis, Jr., Shirley MacLaine and Peter Lawford, a Hollywood clique that was soon widely recognized as "The Rat Pack." The group's image helped to perpetuate the myth that Martin was an alcoholic living in a liquor-induced haze—a carefully crafted persona he borrowed from friend Phil Harris—though he actually lived quietly, eating dinner nightly at the nearby Villa Capri Restaurant. At 3:30 A.M. on Christmas Day, 1995, Martin died of acute respiratory failure alone in bed at home at 78. His only companion was his longtime housekeeper.

Martin was married three times. His second union produced a son, Dean Paul "Dino" Martin, a handsome singer-actor romantically linked with Olympic skater Dorothy Hamill. Dino was killed piloting a National Guard jet in 1987, a tragedy that haunted the elder Martin until his death.

(Maple to:)

720 North Maple Drive, George Burns and Gracie Allen deaths

Grace Ethel Cecile Rosalie Allen married fellow vaudevillian Nathan Birnbaum in 1926, and the couple's burlesque partnership evolved into one of the lasting love stories in Hollywood history. Gracie Allen and George Burns were 1930s radio stars turned movie and television legends. Their *George Burns and Gracie Allen Show* became the longest running show in television history at 298 episodes until heart trouble forced Gracie into an early 1958 retirement.

Gracie reportedly suffered through several youthful infidelities during their 30-year marriage, and whenever Gracie caught George he gave her an expensive present. She once told friends, "I wish George would find a new girlfriend; I could use a silver fox jacket." She was felled here by an August 28, 1964, heart attack, dying shortly thereafter with George at her side.

On July 10, 1994, Burns fell in the tub and suffered a head injury that led to several 1995 strokes and eventually to his death here on March 9, 1996, at 100. At 98 Burns told a friend, "There's not a thing I do now that I didn't do when I was 18, which goes to show how pathetic I was at 18." When asked what his doctor thought about his six daily cigars and numerous martinis, he replied, "My doctor's dead." Until his death, Burns visited Gracie's Forest Lawn crypt once a week, and was buried in a crypt beneath her's "so she could keep top billing." He was buried with $1,000 cash and three cigars in one pocket, and a deck of cards in the other "in case a bridge game comes up." The house was originally owned by actress Pauline Frederick, who rented it to Chico Marx and later to his brother Harpo.

The set used for the 1950s *The George Burns and Gracie Allen Show* was an exact replica of his home where the couple lived for almost 50 years.

(Maple to Lomitas. Hard left to Elm. Left to:)

722 North Elm Drive, Jose and Kitty Menendez murders site

This was the site of the gruesome shotgun murders of Jose and Kitty Menendez on August 20, 1989. Jose, head of Carolco Pictures, was shot nine times and his wife Kitty five times while the two watched television in the den. Their sons, 22-year-old Lyle and 19-year-old Eric, were charged with the killings after private confessions they made to a psychiatrist were furnished to police.

In the family computer investigators also discovered a screenplay written by Eric based on a teenager who murders his parents for insurance money. Their defense was that the killings were justified self-defense that followed years of physical, mental and sexual abuse at the hands of both parents. It may have been difficult to convince a jury, though, since when they were gunned down Mom was filling out Eric's UCLA parking permit and Dad was eating strawberries and cream. In 1994 their first trials ended in hung juries, but a 1996 retrial resulted in guilty verdicts, and life sentences for both.

(Elm to Elevado. Right to intersection with Alpine, and notice the lovely cottage on the corner on your left at:)

632 North Alpine Drive, Theda Bara home

The house at the corner at 632 Alpine was the longtime home of Theodosia Goodman, the Ohio-born daughter of a tailor, who became world famous as Theda Bara. In 1915 she was a Fox Studios bit player of dubious talent when director Frank Powell picked the unknown actress to play the role of Theda Bara—an anagram for "Arab Death." His publicists told reporters that Bara was the daughter of an Egyptian potentate, that she could see the future, and that she was poison to men. The "frightfully evil woman" appeared in public, her face painted deathly

Top: The site of the grisly 1989 Menendez murders, where Eric and Lyle Menendez shotgunned their parents to death as they watched television in a den at the rear of the house. *Bottom:* Silent movie temptress Theda Bara lived in quiet retirement here until her 1955 death.

white and with black rings around her eyes, and she was never photographed without her trademark snakes and skulls. Her contract also stipulated that Bara could not go out in public except at night. The gullible public ate it up as Bara was cast as an evil temptress in 45 movies between 1915 and 1919.

Bara's first vehicle, *A Fool There Was* (1916), featured the birth of word "vamp," which was short for "female vampire," and the immortal line "kiss me, you fool." When the public finally tired of the charade, the studio fired her in 1919 and Bara married *Ben-Hur* director Charles Brabin. The Brabins were well-known in Beverly Hills social circles until her cancer death here on April 7, 1955, at 62. The house on the right behind the hedges was the home of Donna Reed, who died from cancer at 65 on January 14, 1986.

(Right on Alpine to:)

801 North Alpine Drive, Marie Dressler death

Marie Dressler had hundreds of Broadway roles and was a Mack Sennett comedy

star, but her career ended during a 1920 Broadway labor strike when she was blacklisted by the studios. Rescued from obscurity when director Alan Dwan gave her a small role in *The Joy Girl* in 1927, she was than tapped for a small part in *Anna Christie,* a so-so 1930 film better known for Greta Garbo's first spoken words: "Gimme a viskey, ginger ale on the side … and don't be stingy baby!" Posters and newspapers the world over screamed "Garbo Speaks" but Dressler stole the show and earned an Academy Award nomination for her supporting role.

During the next five years she won Oscars for 1930's *Min and Bill* and 1932's *Emma*, as well as starring in *Tugboat Annie* (1933), *Dinner at Eight* (1933), and *Christopher Bean* (1933). During 1931 and 1932 former has-been Dressler was the country's number one box office draw. It was rumored at the time that the openly lesbian Dressler and the actively bisexual Garbo were lovers, but neither star ever confirmed the stories. Dressler suffered a heart attack here on July 28, 1934, and died at 65.

(Alpine to Lomitas. Left to Crescent. Right to:)

After a comeback from obscurity to 1930 Oscar winner, Marie Dressler purchased this mansion, where she allegedly entertained lovers that included Greta Garbo.

812 Crescent Drive, Vincente Minnelli death site

Vincente Minnelli was MGM's premier musical director from the late 1930s through the 1950s, a master of crafting musical numbers in nonmusical movies. It was while directing *The Ziegfeld Follies* (1944) that Minnelli married his co-star Judy Garland, and fathered daughter Liza. Subsequent Minnelli hits included *Meet Me in St. Louis* (1944), *The Pirate* (1948), *An American in Paris* (1951), *The Band Wagon* (1953), and *Gigi* (1958), for which he won an Academy Award for direction. Other Minnelli treasures include *Brigadoon* (1954), *Father of the Bride* (1950), and *The Bad and the Beautiful* (1952). On July 25, 1986, the celebrated director suffered a fatal heart attack at 83 and died here. Although immensely talented and a celebrated director with hundreds of film successes, Minnelli is known to many simply as the former husband of Garland and father of Liza.

(Crescent to intersection with Sunset and Canon. Directly in front is Will Rogers Memorial Park, the site of:)

Will Rogers Memorial Park, George Michael arrest site

On April 8, 1998, an undercover police officer arrested 34-year-old singer George Michael in the public restroom in the middle of Will Rogers Park here. Michael and his partner Andrew Ridgeley rocketed to stardom in the 1980s as the duo Wham!, and his 1986 solo album *Faith* sold more than 10 million copies with songs like "I Want Your Sex."

The public restroom in the park is literally a world-famous gay cruising spot. According to police, at 4:48 P.M. on a Tuesday afternoon, Michael was seen standing next to a stall, exposed and "committing a lewd act." The arresting officer reported that Michael stood against the wall and masturbated in front of him! He was arrested when he walked out of the bathroom, handcuffed and taken to the police station where he was booked for investigation of misdemeanor lewd conduct. In an interesting twist, the plaque at the park honoring humorist Rogers offers his famous quote, "I never met a man I didn't like."

(Take a hard left on Canon to:)

609 North Canon Drive, Chester Morris home

Chester Morris appeared in over 80 films during a 30-year movie career, best-remembered as Captain Queeg in *The Caine Mutiny* and for creating the lead character in the 1940s and 1950s movie serial *Boston Blackie*. During his entire Hollywood career he lived in this lovely Canon Drive home, but on September 11, 1970, Morris checked into a New Hope, Pennsylvania Holiday Inn and shot himself to death, apparently despondent over career problems. He was 69 at the time of his suicide, and still owned his home here.

(Canon to:)

603 North Canon Drive, Ben Turpin death site

New Orleans comic Ben Turpin was a child vaudeville star when he was discovered by Essanay Studios in 1907. He is remembered for his bushy mustache highlighted by permanently crossed eyes, the result of years of vaudeville eye-crossing gags. Turpin's studio took out an insurance policy from Lloyd's of London in case they ever uncrossed.

Turpin made immensely popular parodies of such silent stars as Chaplin, Valentino, Harold Lloyd and cowboy star Tom Mix in *The Shriek of Araby* (1923), *The Reel Virginian* (1924), and *Three and a Half Weeks* (1924). When talkies arrived, Turpin appeared in Lubitsch's *The Love Parade* (1929), provided the legs for the W.C. Fields vehicle *The Million Dollar Legs* (1932), and made

At the height of his 1950s fame, *Boston Blackie* star Chester Morris lived here before a 1970 suicide.

his final appearance in the 1940 Laurel and Hardy comedy *Saps at Sea*. Two weeks after filming ended, Turpin died here on July 1, 1940, at 70.

(Canon to Carmelita. Right to Beverly. Right to:)

619 North Beverly Drive, Lita Grey Chaplin house

Lillita MacMurray debuted at 11 in Chaplin's *The Kid* (1920) with four-year-old Jackie Coogan (whose final role was "Uncle Fester" on TV's *The Addams Family*). In 1924 Chaplin renamed her Lita Grey, gave the now 15-year-old the lead in *The Gold Rush*, and on November 26, 1924, married the pregnant teenager in Mexico. The marriage was a publicity nightmare, since Grey was his second child bride—his first wife Mildred Harris was also 15 when they wed. Chaplin and Grey's son Charles was born on May 5, 1925, but to avoid a statutory rape

charge, the baby was hidden until given an "official" birth date of June 28. By 1927 the 17-year-old mother of two divorced Chaplin in a bitterly contested battle that not only cost Chaplin a fortune, it turned his jet black hair a glaring white almost overnight. For the rest of his life Chaplin had to dye his hair black. The divorce settlement required that Chaplin purchase this mansion for Grey and the children.

Subsequent owners included Jose Iturbi, Jack Benny, and heiress Evelyn Walsh McLean, eccentric wife of *Washington Post* editor Edward McLean and somewhat of a Hollywood gadfly. She owned the Hope Diamond, a 45-carat midnight blue stone that allegedly carries its own curse. It has brought sorrow to every owner from the time it was worn by Marie Antoinette. Soon after McLean got the rock her eight-year-old son Vinson ran from his nannies into the street and was struck and killed by a passing truck. The heartbroken McLean never took the stone out of her jewelry box again, keeping it hidden in a bureau drawer for ten years.

(Beverly to:)

706 Beverly Drive, Rosalind Russell death site

Built by silent-screen star Mary Boland, this mansion was the home of actress Rosalind Russell and her husband of over 30 years, movie agent Frederick Brisson. Russell debuted in 1934's *Evelyn Prentiss* and later appeared in *The President Vanishes* (1934), *Reckless* (1935), *China Seas* (1935), *The Women* (1939), *His Girl Friday* (1940), *The Velvet Touch* (1948), and *Gypsy* (1962). Nominated for four Academy Awards, she succumbed here after a long battle with cancer complicated by arthritis on November 28, 1976, at 69.

(Beverly to Lomitas. Left to Rodeo. Left to:)

732 North Rodeo Drive, Lupe Velez suicide site

Tempestuous *Mexican Spitfire* star Lupe Velez called this Rodeo Drive hacienda "Casa Felicitas," her "Happy House." It was far from that. Real name Guadalupe Velez de la Villalobas, Velez is best-remembered for the 1940s *Mexican Spitfire* series which included *Mexican Spitfire* (1939), *Mexican Spitfire in Mexico* (1941), *Mexican Spitfire at Sea* (1942), and *Mexican Spitfire Sees a Ghost* (1943).

She was equally famous for her off-screen antics, including firing a pistol at Gary Cooper when he broke off their year-long relationship and stabbing Johnny *(Tarzan)* Weissmuller with a fork when she found him dining with another woman at El Mocambo. Pregnant by actor-playboy Harald Ramond, the devout if confused Catholic decided that suicide was the solution, leaving a pathetic note imploring "How could you, Harald, fake such a great love for me and our baby when all the time you didn't want us?" She was found on December 14, 1944, and according to studio writers was lying peacefully on her eight-foot by eight-foot white bed in a room filled with candles and flowers. The reality was not as pretty: After a big Mexican dinner Velez took 80

The longtime home of actress Rosalind Russell and director Frederic Brisson was also the site of Russell's 1976 death.

Mexican Spitfire star Lupe Velez committed suicide in the mansion she called her "Casa Felicitas" or "Happy House."

Seconal tablets, and either the dinner or the drugs made her violently ill. As she ran to her bathroom she slipped on the tiles, fell onto the toilet, and broke her neck. The tragic 32-year-old was found with her head submerged in the commode.

(Rodeo to:)

725 North Rodeo Drive, Gene Kelly death site

To make ends meet at the University of Pittsburgh, Gene Kelly gave dance lessons for 50 cents an hour and becoming so popular that he opened the Gene Kelly Studios of Dance before going to Broadway in 1938, and Hollywood in 1940. He debuted opposite Judy Garland in *For Me and My Gal* (1942) and was soon choreographing his own pictures including *Take Me Out to the Ballgame* (1949), *On the Town* (1950), and *An American in Paris* (1952), which featured an amazing 17-minute ballet that won him a special Oscar. His follow-up *Singin' in the*

Rain (1954) was his last great musical. Through the 1960s and 1970s Kelly directed such features as *Gigot* (1962) and *Hello, Dolly!* (1969), and made cameo appearances in films such as *That's Entertainment* (1974) and *Xanadu* (1980).

Kelly narrowly escaped death during a Christmas Eve 1984 fire that destroyed much of the home. His son dragged him to safety. Plagued by health problems and weakened by a series of strokes, the dancing legend died here on February 2, 1996, at 83.

Joseph Kennedy, Sr., rented a house several doors away in January 1926 after buying the FBO Studio. His movie investment allowed him to carry on an affair with Gloria Swanson, with whom Kennedy had a four-year relationship. In 1929 Kennedy called her so often from around the country that he had the largest private telephone bill in the entire United States. In 1930, Swanson saw that Kennedy gifted a writer a Cadillac and charged *her* personal account, though at the time he was worth $200 million. When she asked him about it, his

Singin' in the Rain legend Gene Kelly almost burned to death in a 1984 fire here before dying of natural causes in 1996.

response was to hang up on her and never speak to her again.

(Rodeo to:)

602 North Rodeo Drive, Jean Hersholt death site

Danish-born Jean Hersholt was one of the most successful actors in history, with a 50-year career studded with starring roles in classic movies, but he is also remembered for his philanthropic endeavors on behalf of the acting community that earned him the love and respect of the entire industry. The Academy of Motion Pictures Arts and Sciences pays tribute to Hersholt during the Oscar presentations each year with the prestigious Jean Hersholt Humanitarian Award.

In 1914 Hersholt arrived from Denmark and was immediately hired by producer Thomas Ince. His silent film roles included *Tess of the Storm Country* (1922) with Mary Pickford, Erich von Stroheim's classic film

Greed (1924), *Stella Dallas* (1925), *The Four Horsemen of the Apocalypse* (1926), *The Student Prince* (1927), and *13 Washington Square* (1928). In the heyday of the silents, Hersholt was one of the most recognizable in the world. Later starring roles were in *Grand Hotel* (1932), *The Mask of Fu Manchu* (1932), *Dinner at Eight* (1933), *Christopher Bean* (1932), *The Country Doctor* (1936), *Heidi* (1937), *Alexander's Ragtime Band* (1938), and *Stage Door Canteen* (1943).

Hersholt's charity work included several terms as president of the Academy of Motion Picture Arts and Sciences, almost 20 years as the president of the Motion Picture Relief Fund, and he was instrumental in the building of the Motion Picture Home, a retirement community in the Encino hills for retired movie people. During his lifetime, he also accumulated the largest collection of Danish writer Hans Christian Andersen's papers in the world, which he donated to the Library of Congress "in gratitude for what this country has meant to me and my family."

After a long battle with cancer, Hersholt died in his home here on June 3, 1956, at the age of 69. His grave just outside Forest Lawn–Glendale's main mausoleum is one of the most impressive on the property, decorated by a bronze statue of a horseman standing just outside the building.

(Rodeo to Santa Monica. Right to Camden. Right to:)

606 North Camden Drive, Leslie Howard last home

Leslie Howard was born Leslie Stainer, the son of a wealthy London stockbroker, and after army service during World War I spent ten years starring in English and Broadway stage productions. After making his film debut in *Outward Bound* (1930), he became one of the top romantic leading men in the world. His starring roles included *Devotion* (1931), *Of Human Bondage* (1934), *The Scarlet Pimpernel* (1935), *Romeo and Juliet* (1936), *Pygmalion* (1938), *Gone with the Wind* (1939) playing Vivien Leigh's husband, *Intermezzo* (1939) with Ingrid Bergman, and his final film, *Spitfire* (1943).

Howard spent his Hollywood years living in this home with his wife and children. On June 2, 1943, he was flying between Portugal and England aboard an English Overseas Airways plane when it was attacked by Nazi fighter planes and shot down over the English Channel. Howard and 13 fellow passengers were killed amid rumors that the patriotic Howard had been on a spy mission for England when his plane was attacked. He was 49 when he died.

(Camden to Lomitas. Left to Bedford. Left and immediately on your left at the corner see:)

730 North Bedford Drive, Johnny Stompanato murder site

Contrary to the popular legend, Lana Turner was *not* discovered at Schwab's Drug Store—then 15-year-old Julia Jean Mildred Francis was sipping a coke at the Top Hat Café when *Hollywood Reporter* publisher William Wilkerson saw her and introduced her to his agent Zeppo Marx. Marx renamed her Lana Turner for *They Won't Forget* (1937) and when audiences howled their approval at

Lana Turner's teenaged daughter stabbed mobster Johnny Stompanato to death in the second floor bedroom above the front door.

her wardrobe, she immediately became "The Sweater Girl" and an overnight pinup sensation. She starred in films like *Dr. Jekyll and Mr. Hyde* (1941), *The Three Musketeers* (1948), *The Postman Always Rings Twice* (1946), and an Oscar-nominated role in *Peyton Place* (1957). However, Turner's personal life was tumultuous to say the least.

She was married eight times, and during the late 1950s took up with mobster Johnny Stompanato, a former Mickey Cohen bodyguard who battered her physically, emotionally and verbally during their four-year relationship. When Turner returned from the 1957 Academy Awards, Stompanato savagely beat her for not inviting him. A year to the day later, on Good Friday Eve, April 5, 1958, the volatile union ended in the second-floor bedroom here (behind the grating above the front door) when he was stabbed in the chest by Turner's 15-year-old daughter Cheryl Crane. Her first phone call was to lawyer Jerry Giesler, who answered the door when police arrived to investigate. After the killing, the Turners moved around the corner to 619 Canon.

Although the Bedford house is known as the Turner house, she didn't live here for very long. The family stayed longest at 120 South Mapleton after Turner married Lex "Tarzan" Barker, but when she found that he had sexually abused Cheryl for years she divorced him.

(Bedford to:)

722 North Bedford Drive, Adolphe Menjou death site

Adolphe Menjou was the picture of the suave and debonair European man with his slick hair and trim mustache, but he was actually born in Pittsburgh and educated at Indiana's Culver Military Academy and New York's Cornell University. After dropping out of Cornell, Menjou was waiting on tables at his father's New York restaurant when he got an extra role in a Vitagraph silent movie, *The Man Behind the Door*

(1915). After serving in Europe in World War I he went to Hollywood and had small roles in *The Three Musketeers* (1921) with Douglas Fairbanks, *The Sheik* (1921) with Rudolph Valentino, and *Bella Donna* (1923) with Pola Negri. When his well-trimmed mustache earned him repeated villain and nobleman roles, he decided to *live* the part, wearing expensive spats, an ascot tie, and a walking stick. The carefully crafted image earned him hundreds of movie roles and was with him until he died. His role as a wealthy Paris bon vivant in Charlie Chaplin's *A Woman of Paris* (1923) made him a star.

Other Menjou movies included *The Marriage Circle* (1924), *Broadway After Dark* (1924), *The Swan* (1925), *The Grand Duchess and the Waiter* (1926), *The Front Page* (1930), *A Farewell to Arms* (1932), *Little Miss Marker* (1934), *The Mighty Barnum* (1934), *Sing, Baby, Sing* (1936), and *A Star Is Born* (1937). He may be best remembered for his later roles as a crafty political boss in *State of the Union* (1948), a Communist henchman in *Man on a Tightrope* (1953), and a disheveled eccentric in Disney's *Polyanna* (1960), his final feature film.

Menjou was a fervent anti–Communist who aided Senator Joseph McCarthy's House Un-American Activities Committee in their film industry witch-hunt during the late 1940s. He supplied the Committee with dozens of names of Hollywood actors he thought to be Communist sympathizers, alienating him from other stars for the rest of his career. Menjou died at his home from chronic hepatitis on October 30, 1963, at the age of 73.

(Bedford to:)

622 North Bedford Drive, Harry Crocker death site, Greta Garbo hideaway

Harry Crocker was a Hollywood pioneer whose career began with roles in Charlie Chaplin silent films *The Circus* (1914) and *The Pawnshop* (1915), later working as a production assistant to Chaplin on *City Lights* (1921). Crocker's lifelong friendship with newspaper tycoon William Randolph Hearst earned him a job as Hearst's assistant and aide-de-camp, and he later became the movie columnist for the Hearst's *Los Angeles Times*. His "Behind the Makeup" column was the first Hollywood "gossip" column.

His ties to Hearst made Crocker the toast of Hollywood, allowing him to squire such movie stars like Joan Crawford, Mary Pickford and Greta Garbo to premieres and parties inaccessible to other reporters. Crocker became the reclusive Garbo's closest Hollywood friend, and she usually stayed incognito at this house for months at a time while unknowing fans and reporters camped out at her other addresses. She considered this to be her "other" Hollywood home because reporters did not discover her secret until after his death.

When Hearst died in 1951 Crocker lost his job and the clout it had always brought, and the party invitations quickly vanished.

He suffered a fatal heart attack at his home on May 28, 1958, forgotten by all his Hollywood friends. One of the half-dozen friends who attended his funeral was his old friend Garbo, but no photographers showed up.

(Bedford to:)

616 North Bedford Drive, Carmen Miranda death site

Comedienne and actress Carmen Miranda—born Maria de Carmo Miranda da Cunha Sebastian in Portugal and raised in Brazil—rose from a dirt-poor immigrant to become Brazil's biggest musical star of the 1930s. "The Brazilian Bombshell," adored by her countrymen, came to the United States in 1939 and became an overnight sensation. She debuted in 1940's *Down Argentine Way*, immediately recognized for her overdone South American costumes and fruit basket headgear. She starred in such hits as

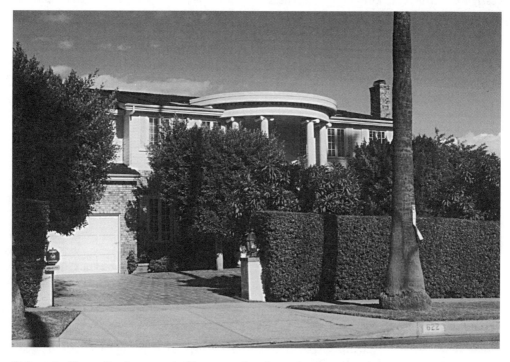

Columnist Harry Crocker never told anyone that Greta Garbo routinely stayed in his house here for months at a time.

Copacabana (1947), *That Night in Rio* (1943), *Weekend in Havana* (1941), and *Scared Stiff* (1953).

Just a few hours after filming a "comeback" role on *The Jimmy Durante Show* on August 5, 1955, Miranda was found dead here, reportedly from a heart attack, although she supposedly kept the hollowed-out four-inch heels of her dancing shoes filled with a stash of cocaine, which may have killed the 40-year-old.

(Bedford to:)

512 North Bedford Drive, Clara Bow party house

This was the 1920s home of "The IT Girl"—Clara Bow, remembered as much for personal escapades as for her on-screen credits, which included *Wings* (1927), *Children of Divorce* (1927) and dozens of other films. A 10-year-old Bow once awoke to find her psychotic mother holding a knife to her throat and threatening to kill her; she never once slept through an entire night during her life, and inherited the mental problems that plagued her mother. At 16 she won a *Motion Picture Magazine* contest and a trip to Hollywood, where she soon became the consummate Jazz Baby, nicknamed "The IT Girl" by writer Anita Loos.

Bow starred in such films as *Kiss Me Again* (1925), *Mantrap* (1926), *Kid Boots* (1927), and the classics *Children of Divorce* (1927) and *Wings* (1927), and her signature *IT* (1927). Along the way she had dozens of offscreen lovers that included Gilbert Roland, Bela Lugosi and Gary Cooper, all of whom were entertained in her bizarre "loving room" that was done in oriental themes with red and black lacquered walls and had no light of any kind.

Bow met the 1927 USC football team during a publicity appearance, and the players began visiting her here. One quiet freshman linebacker named Marion Morrison would later become better known as John Wayne. Rumors of nude football games and

Clara Bow's modest ranch house boasted an all-red "loving room" and allegedly was the site of wild parties for the USC football team.

backyard orgies led USC coach Howard Jones to declare, "Clara Bow is off limits to all members of this football team," but the wild stories were undoubtedly false.

Bow fled Hollywood after a 1930 nervous breakdown, marrying cowboy star Rex Bell and moving to Nevada, where she was known to dye her cows' fur red to match her own hair, and ballooned to over 200 pounds on a five-foot body. As worsening mental problems led to a divorce, she returned to L.A. and died in her Culver City bungalow while she watched a 3:00 A.M. movie in 1965. The poor girl still couldn't sleep.

(Bedford to Santa Monica. Right to Roxbury. Right to:)

518 North Roxbury Drive, Gilbert Roland death site

Gilbert Roland was born Luis Antonio Damaso de Alonso in Juarez, Mexico, and was trained as a bullfighter. When his family moved to the United States, he combined the names of actor John Gilbert and serial star Ruth Roland to become Gilbert Roland and quickly became a star as "Armand" in the 1927 version of *Camille.* During the 1930s he starred in *She Done Him Wrong* and *The Last Train from Madrid,* in the 1940s — *Sea Hawk, Captain Kidd, The Bullfighter and the Lady,* and had hundreds of supporting roles through the 1950s and 1960s.

When paunchy producer Joe Schenck learned of Roland's five-year dalliance with his wife Norma Talmadge, he hired a mob pal to kidnap and castrate the youth at his home here. When Talmadge intervened, the contract was canceled, although the affair lasted several more years. On May 15, 1994, Roland died here after a long battle with cancer at 88.

(Roxbury to:)

800-802 North Roxbury Drive, Lionel Barrymore haunted house

This former home of screen legend Lionel Barrymore is reportedly still visited by a spectral guest who may be Barrymore. The

The last home of actor Gilbert Roland.

oldest son of British stage icon Maurice Barrymore and sibling of John and Ethel, Lionel was never the huge star that John became but worked more steadily than his incorrigible brother. He started movies in 1909, starring in such early silents as *The Musketeers of Pig Alley* (1912) and *Judith of Bethulia* (1914), and by the late 1920s was the top character actor in the business. He won an Oscar for his starring role in *A Free Soul* (1931), and starred in all 15 *Dr. Kildare* movies from the late 1930s through the 1940s. After 1940 Barrymore acted from a wheelchair due to chronic arthritis and hip injuries, and he is perhaps most remembered for his role as the cantankerous, wheelchairbound Mr. Potter in Frank Capra's 1946 masterpiece *It's a Wonderful Life*. Subsequent owners of this home report repeated ghostly appearances, although nobody's sure if it's Lionel or not. Whoever is haunting the house enjoys playing with the doors and lights in empty rooms.

(Roxbury to:)

822 North Roxbury Drive, Marlene Dietrich home

Maria Magdalena van Losch was a German film extra when director Josef von Sternberg spotted her dancing in a revue and gave her the lead in his 1930 film *The Blue Angel*. He brought her to the United States, changed her name to Marlene Dietrich ("Mar-lay-na," she told reporters) and cast her in *Morocco* (1930) with Gary Cooper. She signed an incredible Depression-era contract that paid $125,000 per picture at a time when an experienced studio seamstress was paid $21 per week.

Josef von Sternberg filled an almost "Svengali" role for the bisexual Dietrich, who left a husband and child in Germany and moved to L.A. with Sternberg. She publicly denied that the two were lovers, although they were, and he was forced to endure regular visits here by her lesbian lovers who included Mercedes de Acosta and

Greta Garbo. When her family was finally allowed to join her here, her husband was put in an apartment and daughter Maria moved in with Dietrich and von Sternberg. The steel bars were installed after the 1932 Lindbergh kidnapping threw Hollywood to the grip of panic as stars feared their children would also be targeted. A month later extortionists threatened to kidnap Maria, though they never showed up to collect the ransom that they had demanded.

(Roxbury to Sunset. Left to Linden. Left on Linden just past the "Y" intersection of Linden and Whittier at:)

808 North Linden Drive, Sidney Korshak death site

Described as "one of the great hidden figures of 20th-century organized crime," Sidney Korshak was an enigma. Although his client list included Gulf and Western, Hilton and Hyatt hotels, and the Los Angeles Dodgers, Korshak was also called "the most important contact that the Mob had to legitimate business, labor, Hollywood and Las Vegas."

Sidney Korshak was born in Chicago, and opened a law practice there with his brother Marshall in 1930. Although it was rumored that he was Al Capone's chauffeur during law school, he was apparently introduced to his lucrative mob clientele by Capone associate Jake "Greasy Thumb" Guzik, and by the mid–1930s Korshak was working for the likes of Tony Accardo, Paul Ricca, and Capone's cousins. Although his mob connections were well-publicized— mob union organizer Willie Bioff once testified that Korshak was "our man" during one mob trial—Korshak remained in the background, avoiding publicity, scandal, and most importantly, jail. He worked in Vegas during the 1950s, but in 1960 he moved to Beverly Hills, buying a Bel Air mansion at 10624 Chalon Road and filling it with priceless antiques and Picasso and Monet paintings. Amid the quiet trappings of huge wealth, however, men with machine guns guarded the front door.

Korshak's power was well known around the world. According to Bob Evans' 1994 book *The Kid Stays in the Picture,* "a nod from Korshak and Teamsters change their management … a nod from Korshak and the Dodgers can play night baseball." When friends at Paramount Studios wanted Al Pacino to star in their gangster epic *The Godfather,* but were unable to convince MGM Studio management to release him from a prior commitment, Korshak made one phone call, Pacino was free, and the movie was made. Coincidentally, soon afterward construction problems that had plagued the build of the MGM Hotel in Las Vegas mysteriously ceased. When comic Alan King tried to check in to a five-star Paris hotel, the staff insisted they were full. As King was complaining to Korshak in Los Angeles from a phone in the hotel lobby, a clerk knocked on his window to tell him that his room was ready.

Although virtually all of his mob associates were eventually murdered—including Willie Bioff, Gus Greenbaum, Sam Giancana, Bugsy Siegel, Jimmy Hoffa, Johnny Roselli and dozens of others—the powerful Korshak survived to "retire" to this house in the 1980s. On January 17, 1996, he suffered a fatal heart attack and died there at the age of 88. Coincidentally, brother Marshall had died just a day earlier at his Chicago home. The Korshak brothers took whatever secrets they kept with them to their graves.

It was near this curve on Whittier Drive near Linden that singer Jan Berry had a near-fatal automobile accident on April 12, 1966, running his '65 Corvette Stingray into the back of a parked gardener's truck. Berry—half of the Jan and Dean singing team—spent two months in a near-death coma, suffering severe brain damage and paralysis and ending his singing career.

(At the "Y" intersection of Whittier and Linden—comic Buddy Hackett lives in the northern corner of the intersec-

tion—bear left on Linden. Directly on your left, with the turret-like front, see:)

810 North Linden Drive, Benjamin "Bugsy" Siegel "hit" site

"Bugsy" Siegel's girlfriend Virginia Hill rented this mansion after he had pawned his 250 Delfern Drive estate to finance his Las Vegas Flamingo Hotel venture. The Flamingo was actually named after Hill, whom Bugsy had nicknamed "Flamingo" for her flaming red hair. At 10:45 P.M. on June 20, 1947, a mob assassin crept up the driveway to the house next door, stood in the bushes and fired a .30-30 hunting rifle through the side living room window at Siegel. Bugsy was sitting on a couch reading the paper a scant ten feet away, and was killed immediately when four of the nine point blank shots hit him in the head as he chatted with mob pal Al Smiley and Hill's younger brother. The 41-year-old mobster's body sat on a blood-soaked coach with the newspaper at his feet, four holes in his head, and his eyeball lying on the floor across the room.

Just before the shooting, as the group had returned from dinner and entered the house, Siegel mentioned that he was certain that he smelled flowers, an odd comment since the house never contained any flowers and nobody else smelled anything. According to Virginia Hill, though, family superstition claimed that if flowers were smelled and there were none around it was a sure sign of impending death.

(Linden to:)

803 and 805 North Linden Drive, Howard Hughes plane crash site

Better known for his later-in-life eccentricities, Howard Hughes was a skilled airman, the holder of flight records including a record around-the-globe trip in 1938. He also received the prestigious Harmon Award in 1937, awarded annually to the top-rated flyer in the world. On July 7, 1946,

Bugsy Siegel was shot as he sat in the family room on the left. His killer stood in the bushes next to the driveway and fired through the window.

Hughes was flying an experimental F-11 aircraft built by his Hughes Aircraft, and as he returned to the airfield he lost power and crashed in a ball of flames into the two houses at 803 and 805. Hughes nearly died from severe injuries that included a crushed chest, splintered breastbone, 12 broken ribs, fractured collarbone, a severely bruised heart, a broken neck, back and nose, and dozens of severe cuts. A Marine sergeant pulled him from the burning wreckage, but painkillers used during the grueling recovery started Hughes on a lifetime of drug abuse.

Just behind these houses at 806 Whittier is the villa designed by horror star Lon Chaney, known as "The Man of a Thousand Faces." Sadly, cancer killed Chaney on August 26, 1930—the week that the house was finished. For years Chaney's ghost was repeatedly seen sitting on his favorite bench at the bus stop at the corner of Hollywood and Vine. As a young actor Chaney waited daily on that very bench for jobs, and when he became a star often hired young actors he found waiting at the same spot on the same

bench. His ghost was seen regularly until a new bench was installed 15 years after his death.

(Linden to:)

718 North Linden Drive, Lilyan Tashman–Edmund Lowe home

Ziegfeld Follies headliner Lilyan Tashman starred in such early films as *Manhandled* (1924), *So This Is Paris* (1926), and the original *No, No, Nanette* (1930). Her $1 million (worth over $20 million today) wardrobe was copied in stores throughout the United States and Europe and sold millions of "Tashman hats, gowns and jewelry." Openly lesbian, Tashman was one of the most sexually aggressive women in Hollywood—once making a blatant sexual request of Irene Mayer Selznick, daughter of mogul Louis B. Mayer, in the bathroom during a party. Her studio arranged a marriage between Tashman and homosexual leading-man Edmund Lowe in 1930, after which the couple led their separate lives inside this mansion, with Lowe's homosexual lovers and Tashman's lesbian girlfriends often visiting together. The pair were also well-known for the all-night orgies they hosted here, inviting an "A-list" of men and women.

The jealous Tashman was fiercely protective of her lovers, once getting into a screaming hair-pulling fight with Constance Bennett when she thought Bennett was making passes at a girlfriend in a Beverly Hills restaurant. Her most famous lover was Greta Garbo, who broke off a four-year affair in 1930 after growing tired of Tashman's fierce jealousy. The heartbroken Tashman died just a month later on March 21, 1934, of a cerebral hemorrhage at the age of 33.

(Linden to:)

705 North Linden Drive, David Begelman home

This was the last home of producer David Begelman, whose Hollywood story was a sad tale of greed, shame, and personal disgrace. He began as an agent representing Paul Newman, Judy Garland and Barbra Streisand, and as the head of Columbia Pictures during the '70s supervised the blockbusters *Close Encounters of the Third Kind*, *Kramer vs. Kramer*, and *Shampoo*. In 1977 he was charged with forging a check to actor Cliff Robertson, a tawdry tale recounted in the 1982 book *Indecent Exposure*. A humiliated Begelman still operated on the fringes of the movie business into the 1990s, though, but his August 7, 1995, suicide in an L.A. area hotel came amid a swirl of financial misdealings and lawsuits.

At the time, investigators were accusing Begelman of embezzling millions of investor dollars for personal reasons, and on August 4, 1995, the court attached everything he owned, including his home and all of his personal belongings. On August 7, the 73-year-old checked into the Century Plaza Tower Hotel, borrowing the name Bruce Vann from a friend. When his wife Annette found her husband's pistol missing from

Producer David Begelman's beautiful, but heavily mortgaged, Beverly Hills mansion. On the day of his suicide it was attached by the bank.

here, she and some friends—including actress Suzanne Pleshette—sped to the hotel, but when the group and security guards entered room 1081 at 10:30 P.M. they found Begelman shot through the head. A note lying nearby said simply, "My real name is David Begelman."

(Linden to:)

601 North Linden Drive, Errol Flynn–David Niven house

Errol Flynn rented this house from 1938 to 1940 while he filmed movies that included *The Adventures of Robin Hood* and *They Died with Their Boots On*, sharing the house with his close pal David Niven. According to *The Hollywood Reporter*, when they were here the pair lived "a life which is a trespass against all good taste." Niven dubbed the house "Cirrhosis-by-the-Sea," and it was the site of their infamous Sunday parties featuring a houseful of very young women. Soon after Flynn moved out of the home he was charged in several statutory

rape cases involving underage girls.

(Linden across Santa Monica Boulevard to:)

135½ South Linden Drive, Ethel Mae Barrymore death site

After an acclaimed Broadway career that lasted from 1909 to 1940, Ethel Mae Barrymore—sister of John and Lionel Barrymore—followed her brothers into the movies in the early 1940s. Already a grandmother when she retired from the stage and moved to L.A. in 1940, Ethel Mae eventually starred in over 30 movies including *Rasputin and the Empress* (1933), *Spiral Staircase* (1946), *Young at Heart* (1947) and *None But the Lonely Heart,* for which she won the Academy Award in 1944. Her final films were *The Story of Three Loves* (1953) and *Johnny Trouble* (1957), after which she retired to her little apartment here. Confined to bed due to chronic heart problems and arthritis, after listening to her beloved Dodgers play the Braves in a June 17, 1959,

The weekend parties hosted here by young actors David Niven and Errol Flynn were legendary—as were the young ages of Flynn's dates.

doubleheader, Ethel asked friends gathered in her bedroom, "Is everybody happy? I want everybody to be happy, because I'm happy." She then quietly closed her eyes and died at the age of 79.

(Linden to Charleville. Left to McCarty. Right to Olympic at:)

355 South McCarty Drive, Pier Angeli suicide site

Gorgeous Pier Angeli was one of James Dean's few female lovers, but their respective studios ended their heated relationship when she was picked as the first "MGM Star of the Future" in 1952. The bisexual Dean sat outside the Beverly Hills church during her 1954 wedding to Vic Damone, loudly revving his motorcycle's engine, before roaring away as the couple emerged after the ceremony.

Angeli starred in several good films such as *The Devil Makes Three* (1952) and *Somebody Up There Likes Me* (1956) but her career fizzled during a very public seven-year

custody battle with then-ex Damone. She eventually turned to alcohol and attempted numerous suicides, and was successful on her fifth try, taking an overdose of barbiturates in her apartment here on September 10, 1971, at 39.

(Olympic left to Roxbury. Right to:)

465 South Roxbury Drive, Eleanor Powell death site

Eleanor Powell was discovered dancing on an Atlantic City beach at 13 and was cast in the Broadway hit *George White's 1935 Scandals*. MGM quickly gave her a seven-year movie contract and her first film— *Broadway Melody of 1936*—made her an immediate star. Billed as "The World's Greatest Female Tap Dancer," Powell also starred in *Born to Dance* (1936), *Broadway Melody of 1938* (1938), *Honolulu* (1939), *Lady Be Good* (1941), and *Ship Ahoy* (1942). Her 1937 starring role in *Rosalie* earned her a spot in the world-famous forecourt at Grauman's Chinese Theatre, where Powell embedded a pair

The site of former sex symbol Pier Angeli's 1971 suicide.

of her tap shoes in cement along with her hand and footprints. "The Queen of Tap Dancers" died in quiet retirement in her home here on February 11, 1962, of ovarian cancer at 69.

(Roxbury bearing left at the fork to Bedford. Left to:)

141 South Bedford Drive, Joan Bennett–Jennings Lang love-nest

When young starlet Joan Bennett married producer Walter Wanger, the insecure and insanely jealous director (*I Want to Live*) was over twice her age. He hired private detectives that trailed Bennett 24 hours a day, and on December 13, 1951, Wanger learned from them that Bennett had been having an affair with manager Jennings Lang. Their favored trysting spot was a downstairs apartment in this small apartment building here at 141.

Later that day, Wanger saw his wife's Cadillac parked in the Rexford Drive lot at Lang's MCA Corporation offices at 9370 Santa Monica, walked up to Lang as Bennett got into her car, shot Lang twice in the groin. Wanger was sentenced to six months in an honor farm and upon his release he and Bennett reconciled and remained married for years afterward. The incident was the inspiration for the classic Billy Wilder comedy *The Apartment* (1960).

(Bedford to Wilshire. Right to Peck. Right to:)

144 South Peck Drive, Billionaire Boys Club murder site

On the night of June 6, 1984, local hustler Ron Levin was shot to death in his apartment in this duplex. The gruesome murder was the basis for several books and television movies relating to what became known as the "Billionaire Boys Club Murders." The BBC was founded by Joe Hunt—actually Chicago-born hustler Joe Gam-

sky—and some prep school buddies from Beverly Hill's prestigious Harvard School. The company eventually bilked investors out of millions of dollars from their ultra-plush Wilshire Boulevard offices, but when Levin shorted Hunt in a similar deal of his own, Hunt had him killed.

Levin was murdered by Jim Pittman, the former bodybuilder doorman at Hunt's apartment who had become the BBC security chief. After forcing Levin to write Hunt a $1 million check, Pittman shot him in the head, but soon after the body was dumped in Soledad Canyon the check unfortunately bounced. Levin's disappearance was reported to police by cosmetics heir Dean Factor, a friend who first had discovered him missing. Police had no clues to the killer's identity until Levin's own father incredibly found Hunt's handwritten seven-page murder checklist in his son's trash along with other BBC papers. The paper trail led grateful police to the murderers, but not before Hunt hatched an even dumber scheme than the Levin murder.

A month after the Levin killing Hunt directed some BBC pals to drive to San Francisco, kidnap member Reza Eslaminia's father, and bring him in a steamer trunk back to L.A. in a rented truck. Brain surgeon Hunt figured the family would pay a handsome ransom for the return of the elderly man, but stuffed in the trunk for the ride to L.A., he suffocated when the airholes were taped shut. The group hid the body in a rented house at 155 North Beverly Glen before dropping it near Levin somewhere in Soledad Canyon in the nearby Angeles National Forest. Reza Eslaminia and Arben (Ben) Dosti—son of an influential *L.A. Times* food writer and critic—were both convicted and will be incarcerated at Folsom Prison for the next half-century or so. Hunt sits on death row for planning some of the dumbest murders in L.A. history.

(Peck to Charleville. Left to Elm. Left to:)

123 South Elm Drive, Chico Marx death site

Leonard "Chico" Marx was the oldest of the Marx Brothers, and during years of vaudeville work affected the overdone Italian accent he featured during his movie career. As a young man, his continuous womanizing earned him the name "Chicko" (1910 slang for chasing "chickens," or women) but a spelling error on a vaudeville playbill forever changed his name to "Chico." For over 20 years he shared star billing with his brothers Groucho (Julius), Harpo (Adolph Arthur), Zeppo (Herbert), and Gummo (Milton). Chico died in his small apartment here on October 11, 1961, from heart disease at 74, after wasting several fortunes fighting a compulsive gambling problem that dated back to his youth. In his later years big brother Groucho paid the usually broke Chico's bills.

Just to the left on Wilshire Boulevard at Beverly Drive is the world-renowned Regent Beverly Wilshire Hotel, the luxurious setting of the 1992 hit movie *Pretty Woman*. Stars Richard Gere and Julia Roberts shared the penthouse suite during the movie. Michael Douglas has allegedly had problems with several pretty women at the hotel. According to reports, in 1992 his wife Diandra first caught him in a Regent Beverly Wilshire room with a young friend of theirs, and after a noisy and public scene in the lobby, she stormed off and filed for divorce. When Michael checked into a sexual addiction rehab clinic, the couple reconciled, but in 1995 Diandra again caught the philandering Douglas at the same hotel with yet another family friend. She again filed for divorce.

Tour 10: Bel Air

Begin Tour 10 on St. Pierre Road, just west of Beverly Glen, and as it begins to wind up the hill, notice on your left the intricate stone-work covering the entire hillside, surrounding a series of pools and waterfalls. Continue to the top of the hill to the estate home at:)

414 St. Pierre Road, Johnny Weissmuller home and ruins

On the corner as you proceed up the hill on St. Pierre Road notice the eerie remains of the once-gorgeous terraced gardens and pools from the estate of former *Tarzan* star Johnny Weissmuller. The entire lower acreage here is covered with hand-carved concrete and marble walkways with intricate stonework, and a huge water complex featuring several pools of varying sizes once fed by a man-made stream.

The main building of the old Weissmuller estate is at the top of the hill on your left at 414 St. Pierre. Badly burned in a late 1980s fire, it has remained a fire-scarred hulk surrounded by a chain-link fence for over 15 years. As of early 1998, the once-impressive pink Italianate manse and surrounding grounds remain just another haunting reminder of the fleeting nature of Hollywood fame and fortune. At different times, Mick Jagger, and John and Michelle Phillips have also lived in the house.

(St. Pierre to the crest of the hill, and notice the mansion across the intersection on the corner facing you at:)

345 St. Pierre Road, Errol Flynn statutory rape site

The mansion at 345 was built by silent star Colleen Moore and rented in the early 1940s to wealthy playboy Freddie McAvoy— a one-time Olympic bobsled champion— and his actor-friends Bruce Cabot and Stephen Raphael. The group used the estate as a party house. They and Cabot's pal Errol Flynn hosted one of the trio's infamous parties on September 27, 1942, the fallout of which was one of two statutory rape charges filed against Flynn during that very busy month. In both cases, charges were brought involving sex with teenaged girls.

According to 15-year-old Nebraska runaway Betty Hanson, she went to the party with some Warner Bros. employees she knew, and after watching Flynn play tennis retreated to an upstairs bedroom and had sex with the star. Even though the statutory rape charge was thrown out by the county grand jury, the district attorney's office proceeded with a trial against Flynn. The second accusation was made by 16-year-old Peggy Lee Satterly, who alleged that Flynn had attacked her aboard his yacht *Sirocco* during an evening cruise off Catalina. Satterly, who had worked as an extra on Flynn's movie *They Died with Their Boots On* (1941), actually did date Flynn, but her case was lost when the jury was shown that had she been beneath Flynn as she claimed, she would not have been able to see the "beautiful full moon" through the porthole that she had testified to seeing. After a month-long trial and a worldwide media frenzy,

Flynn was acquitted at both trials, and a beat reporter for the *L.A. Times* introduced the phrase "in like Flynn" to describe Flynn's success with the ladies. One teenage fan from New York actually collected money for what he called The American Boy's Club for the Defense of Errol Flynn. His name was William S. Buckley, later a right-wing senator and ultraconservative writer.

Incredibly, during Flynn's second trial he took an interest in pretty young teenager Nora Eddington, who was tending the cigar counter at the Los Angeles courthouse where his rape trial was being held. His pal and stunt double Buster Wiles later said that during the trial, Flynn had to be convinced by pals *not* to bed the teenager. He was forced to wait at least until the trials were over. Within months Flynn had arranged a meeting, and the pair were subsequently married in Mexico in August 1943. Interestingly, the loving couple had a baby daughter just four months later.

Flynn's craving for teenaged girls was well known, and when he died on October 14, 1959, the 50-year-old was living openly in Canada with 16-year-old Beverly Aadland. His life is best summed up in his autopsy which stated, "The blood alcohol level of 0.35% [three times the legal limit] would appear not to have been unusual for the deceased to have been able to handle without difficulty."

The 345 house was later rented at various times by Marlene Dietrich, Greta Garbo and Robert Stack, who so loved the place he bought the backyard pool tract and built a mansion on the spot (now at 321). The mansion at 356 was rented by the Beatles during their 1964 U.S. tour.

(Bear to the right as St. Pierre, right continues onto St. Cloud, and the first mansion on the left side at the top of the hill is:)

364 St. Cloud Road, Althea Flynt death site

When Althea Leasure was 9 years old, her father murdered her mother, both of her grandparents and a family friend, and then committed suicide. She was immediately sent to a Catholic orphan's home, where she was repeatedly sexually molested by her guardians. By the late 1960s, the then 15-year-old was living on the streets of Columbus, Ohio, dabbling in marijuana, LSD and heroin, and working as a stripper at the Columbus Hustler Club. The Hustler Club was the brainchild of local bartender Larry Flynt, who planned a countrywide string of clubs and dreamed of publishing his own bawdy women's magazine. Within a few years of meeting Leasure, Flynt had taken her as his girlfriend and installed her as the editor-in-chief of his own *Hustler* magazine, by then the third-largest-selling men's magazine in America. By 21 she was one of the highest paid female executives in the country.

In 1977 Larry and by-then wife Althea had bought this Bel Air mansion, which was originally built for Errol Flynn and later occupied by Robert Stack, Tony Curtis, and Sonny and Cher. She also joined Flynt's decades-long fight against what he felt were unfair restrictions of the constitutional right to freedom of speech. But after Flynt was shot by a reader angered over a biracial photo spread in his magazine on March 6, 1978, left paralyzed and confined to a wheelchair, Althea began using drugs again and enjoying the Hollywood party lifestyle. By 1983 she was a hopeless addict. It may have been a shared needle, or perhaps a tainted blood transfusion, but by the mid–1980s Althea was diagnosed with AIDS, and retreated yet further into her murky world of drugs. On June 27, 1987, she left Larry in their bed to take a bath, and late that afternoon was discovered submerged in the water, dead at only 34 years old.

In the 1996 film *The People vs. Larry Flynt* starring Woody Harrelson as Flynt, rocker Courtney Love gave a remarkable portrayal of Althea Flynt in an Oscar-nominated performance.

(Reverse back to St. Pierre, and continue to the right down the hill past the

homes of Andrea Leeds [303], Robert Mitchum [268], and Ann Sothern [214] to Bel Air. Right to:)

268 Bel Air Road, Ernst Lubitsch death site

German director Ernst Lubitsch suffered a fatal heart attack at his home here on November 30, 1947, at the age of 55. Lubitsch studied acting under European stage legend Max Reinhardt and became a top German stage star. He later began producing films, including *Carmen* (1918), which became the biggest movie in European history and earned him the reputation as the greatest filmmaker on the continent. He later discovered Pola Negri and starred her in his controversial classic *Madame DuBarry* (1918) before Mary Pickford brought him to the United States to direct her in *Rosita* (1922).

Over the next 25 years, Lubitsch worked for several studios and was responsible for some of the most famous movies in history, including such classics as *The Student Prince* (1927), *The Love Parade* (1929), *Monte Carlo* (1930), Greta Garbo's *Ninotchka* (1939), Maurice Chevalier's *The Merry Widow* (1934), *To Be or Not to Be* (1942) and *Heaven Can Wait* (1943). In 1946 he received a Special Academy Award for his "contributions to filmmaking during twenty-five years of filmmaking." Lubitsch was known for mixing subtle humor with imaginative situations, giving his movies an implausible Cinderella-like quality that came to be called "The Lubitsch Touch."

The great director battled heart ailments for most of his life, suffering a fairly severe heart attack in October 1947 at a party at his neighbor Otto Preminger's house at 333 Bel Air Road. He survived, but a month later suffered his fatal heart attack during an afternoon lovemaking session on the couch in his den here. He died just a week after completing his final film, *That Lady in Ermine* (1948). The home across the street at 325 belonged to actress Mary Martin, and later writer Dashiell Hammett.

(Bel Air to:)

783 Bel Air Road, Jeanette MacDonald–Nelson Eddy home

The gorgeous estate named "Twin Gables" was purchased by musical star Jeanette MacDonald after her 1937 marriage to actor Gene Raymond. She was discovered by Ernst Lubitsch, paired with Maurice Chevalier in *The Love Parade* (1929) and later in *The Merry Widow* (1934). Her musicals *Monte Carlo* (1930) and *Love Me Tonight* (1932) made her a star, and she was teamed with rising young singer Nelson Eddy in *Naughty Marietta* (1935). The twosome became an immediate hit, following in eight films including *Rose Marie* (1936), *The Girl of the Golden West* (1938), *Sweethearts* (1938), and *I Married an Angel* (1942).

MacDonald's legion of fans were stunned by her surprise 1937 wedding to the hard-drinking Raymond, since everyone was expecting her to wed her co-star and lover Nelson Eddy. Although Eddy was shattered by her marriage to Raymond, he remained MacDonald's lover as her marriage eventually collapsed. During the summer of 1938, Eddy learned that MacDonald was being beaten by Raymond and confronted him in the driveway of this mansion. He beat Raymond almost to death—only a surprise visit by director Woody Van Dyke stopping the beating. After separating from Raymond, MacDonald and Eddy rekindled their affair while rumors circulated that Raymond had taken a Hollywood house with a 19-year-old male extra. For some reason the Raymonds never divorced, even as Raymond's beatings reportedly continued, as did his relationships with younger men. When Eddy drove by the home in 1942 and again saw Raymond assaulting MacDonald in the driveway, he again left Raymond bloody on the ground. The strange marriage lasted until MacDonald's death in 1965. Raymond died in 1998. The home was later owned by Mamas and Papas founders John and Michelle Phillips, and also by singer Sly (of the band Sly and the Family) Stone.

(Reverse on Bel Air to Copa de Oro. Right to Stone Canyon. As you approach the intersection of Stone Canyon and Chalon Drive a short distance ahead, on the left [west] side of the street notice the large walled estate and stucco mansion at:)

685 Stone Canyon, Don Simpson death site

Producer-director Don Simpson and Jerry Bruckheimer paired on 1980s megahits including *Flashdance, Beverly Hills Cop I* and *II*, and *Top Gun*, grossing over $1.4 billion dollars worldwide. Simpson earned $10 million for *Top Gun* alone. During the 1990s, the pair followed with *Days of Thunder* (1990), *Crimson Tide* (1994), *Dangerous Minds* (1995), and *The Rock* (1996).

A friend said Simpson had two speeds, "full throttle and crash and burn," and he lived a high-octane lifestyle abusing drugs and hiring Madame Alex's high-priced hookers to satisfy his hard-core bondage and pain fetishes. In a 1996 interview, Heidi Fleiss stated that Simpson was Alex's "bread and butter client," and in the 1996 book written by several L.A. hookers, *You'll Never Make Love in This Town Again*, his chapter is entitled "Don Simpson: An Education in Pain." It describes his personal preference for erotic beatings, sexual torture, whippings, bathroom games, and more, all of which took place in this Stone Canyon home. In and out of detox dozens of times, a 1995 doctor's report "confirmed initial diagnosis of Risk of Sudden Death."

In August 1995, Simpson's 44-year-old doctor-friend Stephen Ammerman, who was staying at the house while he tried to help Simpson off drugs, was found dead in the poolhouse here. Interestingly, an autopsy showed a pharmacy of drugs in *his* system, including cocaine, Valium, morphine, and antidepressants. On January 18, 1997, just four months after Ammerman's death, Simpson himself finally "crashed and burned." His nude body was found on the bathroom floor, dead from an overdose of the same combination of drugs that had killed his former doctor. During the three years before his death, Simpson had been issued prescriptions for over 15,000 pills of all types, and police found almost 2,500 in his bedroom. He was 52.

(Continue through the stop sign at Chalon Road and continue past the Bel Air Hotel to Tortuoso. Right past the home of comic Red Buttons [778] to:)

780 Tortuoso Way, Kim Novak– Sammy Davis, Jr., love-nest

A lovely hilltop mansion here has been the longtime home of 1950s sex symbol Kim Novak, star of such movie hits as *Vertigo* and *Picnic*. The house is famous for her all-purple bedroom and infamous as the setting for the romance between Novak and entertainer Sammy Davis, Jr., the most controversial love affair of the 1950s. Novak, the first studio-created sex goddess, was the personal obsession of tyrant studio czar Harry Cohn. When Cohn was informed of the rumored affair between Novak and Davis, he reputedly suffered the first of three rapid-fire heart attacks that eventually killed him. During the conservative 1950s, interracial relationships were taboo and meant certain career suicide in Hollywood. The two nonetheless carried on a well-publicized affair that lasted until Davis allegedly received death threats from some "friends" of fellow Rat Packer Frank Sinatra. Just months after ending the affair, Davis wed Mae Britt, another beautiful, blue-eyed blonde actress.

The Novak mansion was caught in the middle of the worst brush fire in Beverly Hills history on November 6, 1961. What became the fifth-costliest blaze in U.S. history began on the west side of Beverly Glen at 8:15 A.M. on November 6 and was soon blown west across the 405 freeway and south past Sunset Boulevard. Completely out of control within minutes of starting, it eventually destroyed over 650 estates—if it occurred today it would consume *3,000* homes. Most of the damage was centered in the Stone Canyon/Bellagio area of Bel Air, destroying every home on Bellagio Place and severely damaging every home on Bellagio and Sarbonne roads. A miraculous exception to the Sarbonne Road carnage was Red Skelton's house at number 801 which was spared when the firewall inexplicably changed direction after burning within a foot from the home. Skelton was also protected by two fire engines dispatched to the home from close friend Walt Disney's studios. Burt Lancaster's home at 980 Linda Flora was destroyed, Zsa Zsa Gabor lost millions of dollars in priceless Renoir and Picasso oil paintings when her 11001 Bellagio house burned to the ground, and neighbor Joan Davis at 10971 Bellagio lost everything.

On the west (other) side of the 405 freeway comic Joe E. Brown lost a priceless sports-memorabilia collection at 1044 Bundy Drive and Joan Fontaine's 404 Fordyce Road mansion was a total loss. Wire services widely distributed a picture of actress Novak hosing her house while standing on the roof amid a firestorm of flames. Singer Barry Manilow owns the huge estate at 800 Tortuoso Way.

(Reverse to Stone Canyon. Right to:)

1120 Stone Canyon Road, Ava Gardner–Howard Hughes home

In addition to a list of young stars kept hidden away in one of 43 rented Hollywood apartments, Howard Hughes particularly enjoyed seducing stars who were either married or recently separated. His affairs with Billie Dove, Elizabeth Taylor, Susan Hayward, and Jane Russell occurred while each was married or had just ended a long-term relationship.

The buxom Ava Gardner was more of a challenge. After watching her first screen test Louis B. Mayer howled, "She can't act. She can't talk. She's terrific!" She married

and divorced Artie Shaw at 18, had an affair with Frank Sinatra featuring public fistfights, and survived a short marriage to Mickey Rooney that ended in a 1947 separation that had Hughes calling the next day.

While the pair was dating, Hughes became furious when his spies reported to him of Gardner's affair with a bullfighter in Spain, whom she met while filming there. Hughes confronted her in her home here and slapped her to the floor. Turning to leave, he was oblivious as an enraged Gardner marched up behind him and clobbered him on the head with a 20-pound bronze statue, knocking him unconscious. He was saved when a maid heard the commotion and pulled Gardner off Hughes.

(Reverse on Stone Canyon past the former homes of Bette Davis [1100], Peggy Lipton [910], Dean Martin [850], and Leonard Nimoy [801]; past the Chalon intersection to Bellagio. Right past homes of Georgia Frontieri [10410], Robert Montgomery [10430], the movie set of 9 to 5 [10431], Edgar Rice Burroughs and Brian Wilson [10452], Joseph Pasternak [10451] and Rex Fountain [10475] to Siena Way. Right to:)

642 Siena Way, Linda Darnell last home

This lovely home, which was originally numbered 646, was the home of Texas-born Linda Darnell, who was brought to Hollywood by her mother at the age of 15. After six months of auditions Darnell was hired as a 20th Century–Fox Studios contract player with small roles in such movies as *Hotel for Women* (1939) and *Daytime Wife* (1939) opposite Tyrone Power. After moving on to bigger roles in *Star Dust* (1940), *Brigham Young* (1940), and *Blood and Sand* (1941), Darnell became known as one of Hollywood's young beauties. Although she showed a special flair for portraying sultry vixens on camera, she was still living with her mother and family in a Brentwood home at 534 Avondale Road bought with her earnings. In 1944, Darnell escaped by marrying cameraman Pev Marley and moving into this lovely Bel Air mansion as her film roles became bigger.

Through the 1940s and 1950s, Darnell starred in a series of successful films but never became a huge box office draw. Her movies included *Summer Storm* (1944), *Hangover Square* (1945), *Fallen Angel* (1946), *Forever Amber* (1947), and the two Joseph Mankiewicz classics, *Unfaithfully Yours* (1948) and *A Letter from Three Wives* (1949). By the mid–1950s her movies were not box-office winners, and though just in her early thirties her once-promising movie career was a distant memory and she earned a living doing regional and dinner theater appearances.

Darnell died during a visit to her former personal secretary's Chicago-area home. After she and her hosts watched a television screening of her breakthrough film *Star Dust* on April 9, 1965, Darnell was somehow trapped in her room during a house fire and burned over 80 percent of her body. She died in a Chicago hospital the following Sunday, April 11, 1965, at the age of 43. The Sienna Way estate was Darnell's last Hollywood home.

(Continue on Siena Way to Chalon. Left just past Dolo Road, and as Chalon curves to the right, notice the lovely stucco and tile home below the road on the left at:)

10744 Chalon Road, Henry Fonda death site

Henry Fonda's career lasted over 40 years, highlighted by an Oscar-winning performance in 1981's *On Golden Pond* alongside real-life daughter Jane. Patriarch of an acting family that also includes son Peter (1969's *Easy Rider*) and granddaughter Bridget (1996's *It Could Happen to You*), Fonda

died here on August 12, 1982, of heart failure at 77. Robert Redford's former home is at 10745, now owned by writer-producer Neil Simon.

10778 Chalon Road, George Getty suicide site

The lovely mansion at 10778 was once owned by actor Brian Keith, and in the early 1970s the 23-room house was owned by J. Paul Getty's oldest son George. The elder Getty became the world's richest man after he discovered oil in the Middle East in 1953, but his personal life was a dismal failure. He was married five times, and though each marriage produced a son, Getty was so removed from his family—usually with one of his dozens of mistresses—that he did not attend any of his sons' weddings. Although worth billions he once refused to pay a $3.2 million ransom for a grandson, after which the kidnappers cut off the grandson's ear and mailed it to a Rome newspaper.

Getty's family was fully dysfunctional. Son Jean Ronald was married five times and son Jean Paul II survived alcohol and heroin addictions (wife Talitha died in 1971 of a heroin overdose). Grandson J.P. III survived his kidnapping ordeal only to wind up a blind quadriplegic after a 1981 methadone overdose.

Third son George Franklin Getty referred to his unfeeling father as "Mr. Getty," and called himself "the vice president in charge of failure." As he grew older he exhibited increasingly manic behavior, abusing alcohol and drugs. In June 1973, George consumed a massive quantity of drugs and was found dead next to the pool here. The press was told that he had fallen during a poolside barbecue, struck his head on the grill and died. The coroner ruled the death a probable suicide, but investigators hired by the Getty family concluded that it was an "unfortunate accident."

For beautiful views of the Bel Air Country Club and surrounding neighborhoods, reverse to Bellagio and drive around the club to the next tour stop, or proceed with the directions noted.

(Chalon to Sarbonne. Left past homes of Tony Curtis [737] and Howard Hughes [619] to Bellagio. Right as Bellagio joins Roscomare for a short distance and bear left to stay on Bellagio a block past the Bellagio/Roscomare split on the left [west] side to:)

10914 Bellagio Road, Jim Backus home

Jim Backus' career lasted over 60 years on stage, in movies and on television, but he is best-remembered as the voice of the myopic 1960s cartoon character Mr. Magoo and for his role as the dense millionaire "Thurston Howell III" on TV's *Gilligan's Island* from 1964 to 1967. He also starred in dozens of movies, the most famous of which was *Rebel Without a Cause* (1955). Backus died in his Bel Air mansion on July 3, 1989, at the age of 73 from the effects of pneumonia and Parkinson's disease.

(Bellagio a short distance on the right [east] side to:)

10957 Bellagio Road, Alfred Hitchcock death site

In 1941 Alfred Hitchcock rented a house at 609 St. Cloud from actress Carole Lombard but was so upset after her 1942 death in a wartime plane crash that he moved out and purchased the only home that he ever owned. Sentiment seems curious from a man who was one of the most peculiar in Hollywood history. Hitchcock's 40-year career began in 1918 as a title-card writer for Lasky Studios in London. Coming to Hollywood in 1936, his résumé eventually included dozens of classics including *Rebecca* (1940), *Suspicion* (1941), *Rear Window* (1954), *Dial M for Murder* (1954), *Strangers on a Train* (1955), *Vertigo* (1958), *North by Northwest* (1959), *The Birds* (1961), and *Psycho* (1960).

Hitchcock was known for his unusual treatment of his female stars, all of whom— Joan Fontaine in *Rebecca* (1941), Ingrid Bergman in *Spellbound* (1946), *Notorious* (1947) and *Under Capricorn* (1950), Grace Kelly in *Rear Window* (1955), Tippi Hedren in *The Birds* (1964) and Janet Leigh in *Psycho* (1963)—were strikingly Aryan, young, athletic, very beautiful, and blonde. He repeatedly bragged to friends about a torrid affair with Bergman, which was patently false, and boasted that Kelly joined him in his avocation for voyeurism, a story that Kelly biographers claim is true.

He allegedly rented Kelly a nearby canyon home visible across the golf course from this Bellagio house, and she allowed him to watch her private "activities" through a telescope in his den. Grace's Philadelphia "Main Line" breeding and cleverly cultivated screen image was of an elegant innocence, but the reality was that she had scores of affairs with countless Hollywood power brokers—both married and unmarried—all of whom could help her to the stardom she so privately craved but publicly abhorred.

She reputedly had affairs with most of her leading men, including Gary Cooper in *High Noon* (1952), Clark Gable in *Mogambo* (1953), and William Holden in *The Bridges at Toko-Ri* (1955). She carried on a fling with Bing Crosby that took place while his wife was dying of cancer. When Kelly teamed with Crosby and Holden for *Country Girl* (1954), she carried on with *both* married men at the same time. Her career was almost destroyed when she became involved with a very married Ray Milland during the filming of *Dial M for Murder* (1954). Milland's 25-year marriage was a well-known Hollywood love story, and when rumors of his affair with Kelly surfaced, both fans and the studios alike responded with disgust. Kelly later said of Hollywood, "I know of no other place in the world where so many people suffer from nervous breakdowns, where there are so many alcoholics, neurotics and so much unhappiness."

Demanding on all of his starlets, the

enigmatic Hitchcock took particular interest in tormenting Tippi Hedren, the only one who ever publicly stood up to him. During filming of *The Birds*, Hitchcock ordered live birds tied to her hair, hands and arms under the guise of ensuring realism, a directive that nearly cost Hedren an eye when the birds began pecking uncontrollably. At the same time he allegedly gifted her 9-year-old daughter Melanie Griffith a lifelike doll of her mother lying in a coffin! For over 40 years Hitchcock lived in this Bellagio house with wife Alma and their daughter before dying in the house of heart failure on April 29, 1980, at 81.

(Bellagio to:)

11001 Bellagio Road, George Sanders home

Handsome Russian-born George Sanders played the hero in the original *The Saint* and *The Falcon* movie serials of the 1930s and 1940s, but is best remembered for badguy roles in over 100 films. His films included *Rebecca* (1940), *The Picture of Dorian Gray* (1945), *Village of the Damned* (1960), and *All About Eve*, for which Sanders won the 1950 Best Actor Oscar. He was married four times; among his wives were actresses Benita Hulm and two of the Gabor sisters, Zsa Zsa and Magda. Despite his screen success, Sanders spent most of his life under psychiatric care for depression, and on April 25, 1972, he committed suicide in a hotel room during a Spanish vacation. He left a note saying, "Dear World, I am leaving because I am bored. Love, George." He made his Hollywood home here for many years, and was still the owner when he died.

(Bellagio to Chalon. Right to Roscomare. Left to:)

1153 Roscomare Road, Martha Raye last home

Martha Raye's 50-year career began as a singer and dancer with Jimmy Durante and Joe E. Louis at the Trocadero in 1936. When Bing Crosby saw her one evening, he hired her and cast Durante in his movie *Rhythm on the Range*. She was an overnight sensation, later starring in *Hellzapoppin*, *Waikiki Wedding* and scores of World War II films. She also worked tirelessly for the USO visiting WWII troops and doing USO shows around the world. Her wild exploits during her travels alongside actress Carol Landis became the movie *Three Jills and a Jeep*. After several years of strokes, circulatory problems and related illnesses, Raye died on October 19, 1994, at 78. Because of her work with the army, Raye was given a full military funeral at Fort Bragg, North Carolina.

Up Roscomare are homes of Alan Alda (1231), Jake (the workout guy) Seinfeld (2112), Bruce Lee (2551), and Colleen Gray (2841). High up at 2928 is the death site of comic Wally Cox, former *Mr. Peepers* star and star of television's *Hollywood Squares*. He suffered a heart attack at home on February 15, 1973, at 48.

(Reverse on Roscomare to Chalon. Right past the Dye School onto Linda Flora to:)

830 Linda Flora Drive, Burt Lancaster death site

Burt Lancaster built this home after his estate at 890 was destroyed in the devastating 1961 Beverly Hills fire. From rolling in the surf with Deborah Kerr in *From Here to Eternity* (1953) to his Oscar-winning role as *Elmer Gantry* (1960), Lancaster was the consummate movie star. Other Lancaster movies included *The Killers* (1946), *Come Back, Little Sheba* (1952), *Judgment at Nuremberg* (1961), *Birdman of Alcatraz* (1962) and his final role as a country doctor in *Field of Dreams* (1989). After battling back from a 1990 stroke, he suffered a fatal heart attack at home on October 21, 1994, and was dead at 80. Every home between Roscomare and the freeway was destroyed in the 1961 fire.

(Linda Flora to Bellagio. Left to Sunset. Right to:)

11001 Sunset Boulevard, Truman Capote death site

New Yorker writer Truman Capote wrote the murder classic *In Cold Blood*, but is remembered for his eccentricities more than for his prodigious talent. On August 23, 1984, Capote died while visiting his close friend Joanna Carson—Johnny's first ex—at her estate here. Death was caused by liver disease worsened by a three-day bender on a potpourri of drugs and alcohol. Capote once said of himself, "I'm an alcoholic, a drug addict, a homosexual, and a genius. I can be all four and still be a saint."

(Many automobile accidents have occurred in this area:)

West on Sunset, the Bentley Drive intersection was the site of the March 5, 1981, death of composer Yip Harburg. His lyrics graced hundreds of Broadway plays and movies but he was most-celebrated for creating the music for *The Wizard of Oz* (1939). He suffered a massive and instantly fatal heart attack while driving west on Sunset just before entering the intersection with Bentley. With a dead Harburg sitting behind the wheel, the car slowly cruised through the intersection and collided head-on with a car waiting at the light.

East on Sunset, the UCLA curve is synonymous with Jan and Dean's 1964 song "Dead Man's Curve." Everyone has an opinion of the *real* location described in the song about a deadly Corvette crash. Some describe a spot on Sunset and Carolwood; some say it was here at the UCLA curve; and some a curvy stretch of Whittier Drive (the actual site). In 1968, Dean *was* in a serious accident when he lost control of his Corvette and hit a garbage truck. But while the songwriters have said that the song does indeed describe the UCLA curve, *that* crash didn't happen there. It happened on Whit-

tier Drive in nearby Holmby Hills. Because of serious head injuries, "it was years before [Jan] could remember an entire song lyric." Also, they couldn't have been describing the Whittier accident because they released the record almost four years before the accident that spawned years of debate.

So many serious accidents occur at UCLA that it's been regraded regularly over the years. For much of the 1940s and 1950s this was the most dangerous spot on Sunset Boulevard, at the time a much sharper curve on a windy two-lane road out to the beach, until it was finally regraded for safety reasons. This spot has been the site of numerous terrible wrecks, several almost killing well-known movie names including Mel Blanc and Joe E. Brown. The first prominent "victim" of the curve was Einer Hanson, a dashingly handsome Swedish emigrant who was brought to the United States from Sweden by Louis B. Mayer in 1925 along with his constant companion Greta Garbo and his longtime lover, director Mauritz Stiller. He became an instant star after his first role, and followed up with nine movies in his first 18 months in America. He did seven films in 1927 alone, including *The Woman on Trial* (1927) with Pola Negri. Although he was a huge star, he was also a violent alcoholic and was uncontrollable when he became drunk. On the evening of June 3, 1927, Hanson convinced Garbo and Stiller to come along to a party in Santa Monica, where Hanson got wildly drunk. When he decided to go to a party at Clara Bow's Beverly Hills home—Bow and Hanson had starred in her classic film *Children of Divorce* in 1926—an argument ensued when they declined the invitation to come along due to his condition. He jumped into his car and sped off, and early the next morning his crumpled body was found behind the wheel of his demolished sports car in a ditch alongside the Sunset Boulevard curve.

Milton Sills had starred in the silent films *Burning Sands* (1922), *Savage* (1921), and *Adam's Rib* (1923), but by 1930 a once-flourishing career ended with a last bit part in *Man Trouble* and the forgotten star was about to lose his Beverly Hills mansion to foreclosure. On September 15, 1930, he got into his special-designed Rolls-Royce, sped to this spot, and committed suicide by intentionally accelerating off the road and over the steep hillside. He was dead at the age of 48, officially of a heart attack, but more likely a suicide.

On December 6, 1939, wide-mouthed comedian Joe E. Brown (star of *Hollywood Canteen* and *Around the World in 80 Days*) sideswiped another car on the curve in front of the home of child actress Jane Withers at 10731 Sunset and careened down the embankment across the street before coming to rest 275 feet away. Nearly dead, Brown suffered serious face and chest injuries and a broken back and spent the next year encased in a cast from his hips to his neck. Youngster Withers was in her yard with her mother, and the two comforted Brown until police arrived. Brown is most-remembered for his role as a crazed millionaire in love with Jack Lemmon in 1959's *Some Like It Hot* with Marilyn Monroe and Tony Curtis.

On January 24, 1961, cartoon voice legend Mel Blanc lost control on the curve, struck a car and left the road. Barely surviving the accident, the voice of hundreds of cartoon characters spent over a month in what was thought to be a terminal coma. However, one morning when a doctor asked the lifeless Blanc, "Hey Bugs, how you doin' today?" Blanc woke up and answered the startled doctor in Bugs Bunny character, "Ehhhhh, fine doc." Blanc spent almost a year in the hospital recovering from injuries sustained in the near-fatal crash.

Tour 11: Westwood and Century City

Begin Tour 11 on South Mapleton, in the block south of Sunset Boulevard. Pass at the corner of South Mapleton and Sunset the former home of Lana Turner and Lex Barker (120) and next door the one-time home of Judy Garland and Vincente Minnelli (130) to:

232 South Mapleton Drive, Humphrey Bogart death site

The greatest star in movie history died here of throat cancer on January 14, 1957, at 58. "Bogie's" trademark lisp was not an affectation—while escorting an AWOL prisoner to a navy prison during World War I, Bogart was punched in the mouth with handcuffs, slashing his lip and face. Surgery left Bogart with his trademark droopy-lipped delivery. After the war he began working off-Broadway, and was starring in *The Petrified Forest* when Warner Bros. called him to work in the movie version. He became an overnight star but his reputation as a feisty drinker kept him off most Hollywood party lists.

Bogart was living here with Lauren Bacall at the time of his death. Nearing the end of a year-long battle with cancer—during which time Bogart continued smoking and drinking, wanting to live his life to the fullest even if it did indeed kill him—he was visited by a steady stream of Hollywood notables. The night he died, as his closest friends Spencer Tracy and Katharine Hepburn left the room, Bogart replaced his trademark "so long kids" with a solemn "Goodbye Spence. Goodbye Kate." An hour later he was dead. Bacall sold the home to director-writer Ray Stark. The bogus police car in front was a gift from a studio friend and has been there forever.

(South Mapleton to Charing Cross. Left to:)

10231 Charing Cross Road, Jack Benny death site

For over 30 years legendary comic Jack Benny lived on the estate behind these gates, and he died here on December 26, 1974, at 80 after a long battle with cancer. Benny once said that his success came from his ability to mirror the failings we all see in ourselves and acquaintances. His decades-long insistence that he was only 39 years old was one of show business' most famous ongoing bits. Benny's father—Meyer Kubelsky—was a Russian immigrant who so loved music that he gifted his son Benjamin with a $50 violin for his eighth birthday. Within a month the boy was giving concerts at a local music hall, and by the age of 18 the renamed Jack Benny was playing on the vaudeville circuit. During one musical performance, Benny told a joke, and was hooked after hearing the audience laugh. He never really gave up his violin, but from that moment on he was a comedian first, musician second. His violin soon became just another prop.

By 1926 he was starring on Broadway in *The Great Temptations* and was the emcee at the most prestigious vaudeville theater in the world, the Palace Theater. In 1932 he moved to Hollywood and began working in radio, by 1936 becoming the most popular radio performer in the country. His radio show—which paid him over $1 million a year—stayed on the air until 1955, when he began doing television. Along the way, the versatile comic starred in dozens of movies including *Broadway Melody of 1935* (1936), *College Holiday* (1936), *Man About Town* (1939), *Love Thy Neighbor* (1940), *To Be or Not to Be* (1942), *Hollywood Canteen* (1944), and his final film, *A Guide for the Married Man* (1967). His last appearance came just a month before his death, in a television special entitled *Jack Benny's Second Farewell*, a "retirement" celebration that took place just two months after his first *Farewell* special.

(Reverse on Charing Cross to Mapleton. Left to:)

323 South Mapleton Drive, Alan Ladd home

Diminutive Alan Ladd's screen image was much larger than his actual height of 5'4". He was more confident on film than in life, constantly haunted by insecurities that led to serious depression. He was living here when he died on January 29, 1964, at 50, the official cause an "accidental" overdose of alcohol and drugs which may or may not have been a suicide. Less than a year earlier, though, a despondent Ladd had shot himself in the chest with a rifle. According to the studio, he was shooting at a burglar and missed.

In the 1950s, Ladd's next-door neighbor was best friend Bing Crosby. Crosby's reputation as a happy-go-lucky nice guy was a huge facade—in reality he was a cold, controlling man who routinely battered his children for the most minor sins. Several of his

children were suicides later in life. Chronically unfaithful to wife Dixie Lee, Crosby used Ladd's pool and cabana for his many extramarital trysts. Even as Dixie lay dying of cancer at home, Crosby entertained then-girlfriend Grace Kelly at Ladd's pool. After Dixie's 1951 death Crosby began dating again within weeks, enjoying his now-public pool parties with Kelly, Mona Freeman, or Rhonda Fleming.

The Crosby mansion was one of three estates razed for the huge Aaron Spelling mansion at 594. The massive chateau is over 60,000 square feet in size, so large that local ordinances forced Spelling to place "Exit" signs at the ends of the hallways.

(Mapleton at the Spelling estate at the intersection with Club View. Right to Beverly Glen. Right to:)

343 South Beverly Glen, Juliet Prowse death site

Juliet Prowse was born in India and raised in South Africa, and studied ballet until she grew to 5'8" and was told she was too tall. Famed for her sultry good looks and long dancer's legs, Prowse made her movie debut in the 1960 musical *Can-Can* with Frank Sinatra. She also starred in *G.I. Blues* (1960) with Elvis Presley, carrying on a torrid affair while she was also dating an enraged Sinatra. Briefly engaged to Sinatra in 1962, Prowse broke it off at the last moment.

Prowse toured in dozens of stage musicals and appeared in several Broadway productions. On September 14, 1996, she lost a two-year battle with pancreatic cancer and died at her home at the age of 59.

(Continue on Beverly Glen a short distance to Bainbridge. Left on Bainbridge to Loring. Left to:)

225 South Loring Drive, Lloyd Bridges death site

Lloyd Bridges moved from stage to Hollywood in the late 1930s, and his handsome good looks led to a debut in *The Lone*

Lloyd Bridges' longtime home, the site of his 1998 death.

Wolf Takes a Holiday (1941) and roles in such memorable films as *Here Comes Mr. Jordan* (1941), *Talk of the Town* (1942), *Sahara* (1943) with Humphrey Bogart, and *A Walk in the Sun* (1945). Among over 50 film credits was a role in a 1942 Three Stooges short entitled *They Stooge to Conga*, but his most notable movie role was in the 1950 classic *High Noon* with Gary Cooper. In 1957 he earned the role for which he is most remembered: scuba diver Mike Nelson from the long-running television series *Sea Hunt*. Bridges starred in six other television series as well: *The Lloyd Bridges Show*, *The Loner*, *San Francisco International Airport*, *Joe Forester*, *Paper Dolls*, and *Capital News*, as well as dozens of miniseries and television movies, including *Roots*.

In recent years Bridges earned a reputation as a fine comic actor as well, starring in a series of wacky comedies including *Airplane* (1980), *Airplane II* (1982), *Cousins* (1989) and a recurring role in the 1990s movies *Hot Shots* and *Hot Shots Part Deux*. Bridges' sons Beau and Jeff have also carved out highly successful movie and television careers. On March 10, 1998, the 85-year-old

star died at his longtime home here of natural causes.

(Continue on Loring to Comstock. Left to:)

424 Comstock Avenue, Fanny Brice death site

Comedienne Fanny Brice was born Fannie Borach in New York's Lower East Side in 1892 and was a teenage Ziegfeld Follies star doing comic impressions of classic ballet dances. During her Broadway and burlesque career she starred alongside such stars as Will Rogers, W.C. Fields, Eddie Cantor, and Willie Howard. The "Baby Snooks" character that she created for Ziegfeld made her a huge radio star in the 1920s.

Brice left burlesque for Hollywood in 1916 to appear in the silent film *My Man* (1916), and during her 30-year career starred in movies that included a later sound remake of *My Man* (1928), *The Great Ziegfeld* (1936), *Everybody Sing* (1938), and *Ziegfeld Follies* (1946). She was married three times, her first

Former Ziegfeld Follies and movie star Fanny Brice's last home, where she suffered a fatal 1951 cerebral hemorrhage.

to a Springfield, Massachusetts, barber she met during a vaudeville tour, to stockbroker Nicky Arnstein, who embezzled $5 million during their marriage, and finally to Broadway producer Billie Rose. Brice suffered a massive cerebral hemorrhage at this home and died shortly afterward on May 30, 1951, at the age of 51.

(Continue on Comstock to the intersection at Wilshire Boulevard. On your right note the high-rise condominium building at 865 Comstock Avenue, site of:)

865-75 Comstock Avenue, Wilshire Comstock Apartments, Freddie Prinze death site

Freddie Prinze was a hugely popular stand-up comic and television star of 1974's *Chico and the Man*, but he couldn't make *himself* laugh. His depression first surfaced in a suicide attempt at 17 when a girlfriend left him, but several others followed. A chance 1973 spot on *The Tonight Show* led to his television "Chico" role and rocketed Prinze to a stardom he was ill-equipped to handle. The extremely insecure actor wasted millions of dollars on alcohol and drugs and liked playing Russian roulette in front of horrified friends.

On January 28, 1977, the 22-year-old actor sat on a couch in his condo here, scribbled "I must end it. There's no hope left. I'll be at peace. My decision totally. Freddie Prinze" on a scrap of paper, and shot himself in the head with a .357 magnum. Although he was depressed over a pending divorce (from comic Ernie Kovac's daughter Mia), in the week prior to the shooting he had signed contracts that would earn him over $7 million and had seemed in good spirits. The conflicting evidence forced the coroner to classify Prinze's cause of death as "undetermined."

(Comstock across Wilshire to Club View. Left to:)

1353 Club View Drive, Jean Harlow haunted home

Early in her career Jean Harlow purchased this home for mother "Mama Jean" and her gold-digging stepfather Marino Bello, reportedly so that she could put an end to Bello's nightly visits to her bedroom requesting sex. The unsavory Bello also pressured Harlow to date his mobster pals, one of whom passed out samples of Harlow's pubic hair to his friends after the dates that Bello arranged for him. Bugsy Siegel bragged to friends that he had bedded the beautiful starlet.

Harlow was visiting her mother here

Jean Harlow purchased this house for her mother and stepfather, and was visiting here when she was told by Louis B. Mayer that her husband Paul Bern had been found dead in their Benedict Canyon estate. It is allegedly still visited by a crying female spirit.

on the night of the mysterious 1932 murder of her husband Paul Bern at the couple's nearby Benedict Canyon home. Louis B. Mayer's self-serving autobiography described Jean trying to kill herself by leaping from the balcony in front of the house, saved only by Mayer grabbing her off the railing. It was clearly a fabrication—Mayer and his studio flunkies were much too busy "cleaning up" Bern's death scene. Irving Thalberg gave Jean the horrible news here. As his wife Norma Shearer waited in her limousine at the curb, she watched Harlow faint when she heard the terrible news.

One of many secrets the studios kept from the public about the day of Bern's murder was that Marino Bello was hunting with Clark Gable that weekend. Meyer and his fixers kept that tidbit from the public to protect Gable—no star would be publicly tied to a character as shady as Bello, although Gable like him personally. Subsequent owners of this house have described the distinct sounds of a moaning woman, and loud groaning emanating from what was Harlow's bedroom. Noisy footsteps are also heard from within rooms once occupied by the tragic star.

The home across the street at 1352 was shared by one of the movies' most famous canine stars and his trainer's family. "Rin-Tin-Tin" died in the house in 1932, allegedly in the arms of his neighbor and pal Jean Harlow.

(Club View to Santa Monica. Left past Avenue of the Stars; south at 2025 is the Century Plaza Hotel, site of the August 7, 1995, suicide of producer David Begelman. A block past Avenue of the Stars to Century Park East. Right on Century Park East to:)

2170 Century Park East, #2006, Lana Turner death site

One of the last remaining glamour girls, "Sweater Girl" Lana Turner survived seven turbulent marriages and dozens of

high-profile romances that produced newsprint by the truckload. She was dubbed the "Sweater Girl" after her debut in *They Won't Forget* (1937) and starred in the *Andy Hardy* and *Dr. Kildare* serials of the 1930s and 1940s. Movie roles also included *The Postman Always Rings Twice* (1946), *The Bad and the Beautiful* (1952), and *Peyton Place* (1957). Turner lived in quiet retirement in her condo where she died on June 29, 1995, after a long battle with throat cancer. She was 75 years old.

(Century Park East across Olympic to Galaxy Way, right to:)

10100 Galaxy Way, Bill Bixby death site

Wilfred Bailey Bixby was born in San Francisco and bitten with the acting bug at an early age. Leaving Berkeley to become an actor, his first roles were in the 1960s television series *The Many Loves of Dobie Gillis* and *The Joey Bishop Show*. He is best-remembered for his co-starring role in the 1963 series *My Favorite Martian*, as the unwilling host to space visitor Ray Walston. He followed up in the 1969 to 1972 series, *The Courtship of Eddie's Father*.

Tragedy hit the Bixby family during filming of *Eddie's Father* when Bixby's 6-year-old son died of a throat infection in a hospital waiting room while an attending doctor, according to Bixby, "removed a splinter from the finger of another doctor." Bixby's wife—soap actress Brenda Benet—committed suicide less than a year later. Benet was married to actor Paul (*Donna Reed*) Petersen, but according to Jill Robinson's 1997 *Vanity Fair* article, Benet became involved in a witch's coven in Malibu and left Petersen to marry Bixby. She killed herself at her Malibu house, and according to Petersen, the local coroner called her "the most beautiful corpse he had ever seen."

During the 1970s Bixby made numerous television guest appearances and directed several groundbreaking miniseries such as

Rich Man, Poor Man, and starred in the late 1970s science fiction series *The Incredible Hulk*, playing scientist David Banner alongside hulking alter-ego Lou Ferrigno. After a two-year fight with prostate cancer, Bixby died at his Century City home on November 21, 1993, at the age of 59.

(Galaxy Way to Avenue of the Stars. Right to Santa Monica Boulevard. Left on Santa Monica Boulevard to the intersection with Santa Monica and Beverly Glen, site of:)

Santa Monica and Beverly Glen Boulevards, Ernie Kovacs death

Ernie Kovacs turned a 15-minute New Jersey radio program into international stardom and a huge television career, creating such characters as Percy Dovetonsils, Hecuba Baldspot, and Heathcliff Coldsore. His bizarre humor was usually years ahead of his audiences, but his comic genius was evident.

On January 13, 1962, the brilliant comic was killed here when he lost control of his car while driving down Beverly Glen and turning onto Santa Monica. He was going to PJ's Bar for a drink after leaving a christening party for Milton and Ruth Berle's baby at the nearby home of Billy Wilder. Kovacs' wife, actress Edie Adams, declined the invitation to keep partying and took an earlier ride from another partygoer, which saved her life. Trying to light a cigar while he drove, Kovacs lost control of his wife's station wagon, which skidded out from Beverly Glen across Santa Monica, hit the center divider, flipped, and slammed into a light pole. Killed almost instantly of massive head injuries, the 42-year-old was found with his last cigar clenched in one hand and a lighter in the other.

His grave marker reads "Nothing in moderation." In 1980, his daughter Mia— Freddie Prinze's ex—would herself be killed in a similar accident in the Hollywood hills, thrown through the sunroof of her sports car

and killed instantly when she lost control and ran off the road. She was dead at 23.

(Santa Monica to Westwood Blvd. Left to Coventry, the last right before the overpass. Right to immediate right on Clarkson to:)

10881 Clarkson Avenue, Dorothy Stratten murder-suicide site

The second-floor bedroom in the house on your right was the site of the gruesome August 14, 1980, murder of 20-year old *Playboy* centerfold Dorothy Stratten (born Dorothy Hoogstratten). Paul Snyder, a photographer and erstwhile talent scout, found the 16-year-old beauty working in a Vancouver Dairy Queen and brought her to Hollywood a year later. She was a *Playboy* centerfold within a year of their arrival, but Dorothy and her friends soon tired of Snyder's ill manners and the marriage unraveled as she took up with director Peter Bogdanovich.

Snyder lured Stratten to the house here they once shared allegedly to divide their belongings. In a final act of the ugly breakup of their marriage, when she arrived he strapped her to a bizarre homemade torture rack, assaulted her physically and sexually, and then blew her face off with a shotgun. He then killed himself. Her only movie role had been in *They All Laughed*, which was released a year later. When she was killed, Stratten was living with director Bogdanovich at his 212 Copa de Oro estate, though her apartment was at 262 #1 South Spalding. Ex-boyfriend Bogdanovich later wed Stratten's younger sister Louise. The story was reprised in the 1985 movie *Star 80* starring Mariel Hemingway.

(Reverse to Westwood. Left to Pico. Left to Sepulveda. Right past Santa Monica to Ohio. Right to first intersection at Bentley. The apartment on the left corner at 1436 South Bentley is:)

Playboy centerfold Dorothy Stratten was tortured and murdered by her ex-husband in the second-floor bedroom of this Westwood house.

1436 South Bentley Avenue, Gail Russell death site

Gail Russell was a lifelong friend and reputed lover of John Wayne and was once named as the co-respondent in one of Wayne's divorces. The raven-haired beauty starred in dozens of films including *Lady in the Dark* (1944), *The Uninvited* (1944), *The Angel and the Badman* (1947), and *Night Has a Thousand Eyes* (1948). Extremely insecure and temperamental and suffering from intense stage fright, she was also a heavy drinker, once driving her car through the front window of a Santa Monica coffee shop in a booze-induced stupor. The moody star retreated to alcohol as her career and her marriage to actor Guy Madison both ended, and died of alcoholism in her apartment on August 26, 1961, at the young age of 36. Several days after her death, she was found on the living room floor surrounded by empty vodka bottles.

(Ohio to Westwood. Left to Wilshire. Right one block to Glendon. Right to the office building and parking lot entrance directly on your left. Left and proceed to the top of the driveway and turn right into Westwood Memorial Park:)

1218 Glendon Avenue, Westwood Memorial Park

This small cemetery houses Marilyn Monroe's crypt, a gravesite that probably attracts more visitors than any gravesite in the world. But there are dozens of other well-known movie people resting here as well, and one famous former resident. Actor Peter Lawford was interred here after his 1984 death, but was threatened with eviction when his burial bill went unpaid. A tabloid newspaper bought the rights to photograph the ensuing burial at sea from his widow, offering to pay the bill for the May 19, 1988, event.

At the entrance you will recognize the chapel where Monroe's funeral services were held. Arranged by ex-husband Joe DiMaggio, he so hated the movie friends he blamed for her death that he allowed none to attend, approving the small guest list himself. Only 20 mourners attended the most famous funeral since Valentino's. A distraught DiMaggio sent flowers to the grave weekly for over 20 years. Proceed past the chapel to the left and park to visit the various graves. The following sites can be found:

GRASSY AREA

Singer Minnie ("Lovin' You Is Easy") Ripperton Rudolph
Beach Boy Dennis Wilson (among small markers by tree)
Philosophers and writers Will & Ariel Durant (under tree)
Actress Norma Crane (*Fiddler on the Roof*)
Actress Dorothy Stratten
Actor Lloyd Nolan
Actress Eve Arden (West)
Bandleader Harold Hecht (just below Arden)
Actor Richard Conte (Don Barzini in *The Godfather* [1972])
Actress Dominique Dunne
Actress Donna Reed (Asmus)
Singer Roy Orbison (just below and left of Reed)
Songman Sammy Cahn (five to left of Reed)
Actress Natalie Wood
Studio head Darryl Zanuck
Actor Cornel Wilde (in large group)
Actor Jim Backus (among large group under tree)
Sebastian Cabot (Urn Garden East, near front)

Beginning with the wall at the corner just ahead (southeast corner) proceed counterclockwise to find the following sites:

CORRIDOR OF REMEMBRANCE

Actress Helen Hayes
Singer Dean Martin
Opera star Helen Traubel

CORRIDOR OF LOVE

Writer Oscar Levant

CORRIDOR OF MEMORIES

Actress Marilyn Monroe (in corner of inside section; the empty crypt next door was bought by Hugh Hefner for $35,000 in 1995)
Actor Jay C. Flippen (star of over 50 films, when his leg became infected while filming *Cat Ballou* [1964], he tried to treat it himself, and the leg got gangrenous and had to be amputated)

CORRIDOR OF TRANQUILITY

Jo Rich Corday (notice the marker "Singer who dances"—there are critics everywhere!)
Carlotta Laemmle
Writer Nunnally Johnson (producer of *The Three Faces of Eve* [1957] and *The World of Henry Orient* [1964])
Drummer Buddy Rich

CORRIDOR OF DEVOTION

Actress Anita Louise (Marks)
Agent and movie playboy Gregory Bautzer

SANCTUARY OF TENDERNESS

Songwriter Harry S. Warren (Oscar-winning composer of "I Only Have Eyes for You," "You'll Never Know," and "You'll Never Know How Much I Love You," the opening notes of which grace his crypt)

OUTSIDE WALL OVERLOOKING GRASSY AREA

Actress Heather O'Rourke (child star of *Poltergeist I, II* and *III*, as noted on her crypt, also co-starred in television's *Happy Days* in 1982, she died at the age of 12 on the operating table after being stricken with congenital intestinal problems during a family camping trip)
Actor Peter Lawford resided in the crypt directly above O'Rourke until his reburial.
Writer Truman Capote

SMALL GRASSY AREA

Agent Swifty Lazar (left of outside wall against wall)
Actor John Cassavetes (under tree)
Eva Gabor (just to the left of Cassavetes)
Industrialist Armand Hammer (family mausoleum)

SANCTUARY OF SERENITY

Actor John Boles

Top: Marilyn Monroe's is probably the most-visited grave in the world. *Bottom:* The grave of murdered *Playboy* centerfold Dorothy Stratten.

Actor–murder victim Victor Killian's ashes were scattered in the area in the corner rose garden. Among the other famous names buried here are Richard (*Voyage to the Bottom of the Sea*) Basehart, Philip Dorn, Christopher (*Rat Patrol*) George, Stan Kenton, Edith Massey, Marvin Miller, Frank Tuttle, Frank Zappa and Estelle Winwood.

(Exit to Glendon. Right across Wilshire to intersection with Glendon, Lindbrook, and Tiverton. Soft right on Tiverton to one block to Weyburn. Right to:)

10749 Weyburn Avenue, Ted Healy death site

Born Charles Earnest Lee Nash in Kansas in 1896, Ted Healy began in vaudeville wearing blackface to imitate the famous stars of the day. He was a natural talent, but never used a script because he could not remember lines. Between the early 1900s and 1920 Healy was the highest-paid vaudeville star in the world, earning over $8,500 a week doing slapstick for packed theaters around the world.

Healy thought a group of "stooges" working alongside him would make his act even funnier, so he hired Brooklyn comedians Louis Fineberg and brothers Moses and Sam Horowitz to become "Ted Healy's Stooges." Healy also changed their names to Larry Fine, Moe Howard and Shemp Howard so audiences would not know that they were Jewish. "Ted Healy and His Stooges" became immediate stars, filling theaters across North America from 1922 to 1933. In 1933 "The Three Stooges" quit when a temperamental Healy refused to increase their $500 weekly salaries. Healy was soon forgotten. His alcoholism quickly depleted his once vast fortune, and he lived on small roles in low-budget movies for several years.

Alcohol led to his death when on the night of December 21, 1937, a feisty and drunk Healy picked a fight with three young men at the Trocadero nightclub on Sunset Boulevard, and after the group "went outside" the drunken Healy was beaten senseless. He died later that night at his nearby apartment of the injuries incurred in the fight, as well as, according to the coroner, "acute and chronic alcoholism." Although he had made several fortunes during his life, when he died he was broke, so comic Eddie Foy paid for his funeral. He was only 41 years old.

(Weyburn to Selby. Right to Wilshire. Left and notice:)

10787 Wilshire Boulevard, Richard Powell death site

In 1962 Richard Powell moved from his beloved ranch at 3100 Mandeville Canyon to the Marie Antoinette Apartments here as lymph and lung cancer began to take their toll. He and his actress wife June Allyson lived here for the last year of his life. The handsome Powell had starred in dozens of films including *The Cowboy from Brooklyn* (1938), *The Singing Marine* (1939), *The Reformer and the Redhead* (1940), *Right Cross* (1943) with Allyson, and *Johnny O'Clock* (1944). He also starred in the early television series *The Dick Powell Show* in the 1950s.

Powell was one of the victims of *The Conqueror*, the 1954 Genghis Khan saga filmed in a Utah desert chosen because the red sands were similar to the Mongolian setting. Unfortunately it was also just 130 miles from the Yucca Flats atomic testing site where two radioactively "dirty" test bombs were detonated: the 50-kiloton "Dirty Simon" in April 1953, and the 32-kiloton "Dirty Harry" in May 1953. A strong wind blew a huge amount of Dirty Harry's fallout over the St. George movie site; so much so that as late as 1958 Geiger counters were still going wild. Incredibly, during the 1953 filming the crew spent three months living in the contaminated sand that was so irritating that they had to be hosed off every hour. Director Powell even trucked hundreds of tons of the killer sand to his Hollywood soundstages for filming inside shots. As she lay dying of uterine cancer in 1974, Agnes Moorehead was the first to blame the connection between the film site and the illnesses plaguing the cast and crew. Over 130 of the 220-member crew have succumbed to some form of cancer.

(At this intersection:)

Wilshire Boulevard, east of Selby, Jerry Rubin accidental death

Jerry Rubin was the most vocal of the 1960s peace activists, known the world over for his antigovernment, antiwar positions. He and six friends that included Tom Hayden and Bobby Seale were charged with antigovernment activities during the 1968 Chicago Democratic National Convention that ended in full-scale riots when the National Guard was called in by no-nonsense Chicago Mayor Richard Daley, Sr. After a sensational 1969 trial the group—dubbed "The Chicago 7" —was cleared, defended by attorneys Mort Kunstler and F. Lee Bailey. In 1960 Rubin formed the Youth International Party with Abbie Hoffman and Paul Krassner, and their loose-knit group became known the world over as the "yippie" movement.

In his forties and fifties, the former hippie concentrated on more mundane activities. He sold stock, held business opportunity seminars for "yippies" and sold a drink called "WOW" made of kelp, ginseng and bee pollen. On November 14, 1995, he was jaywalking through Wilshire Boulevard traffic 100 yards east of Selby when he was struck by a westbound Volkswagen GTI and seriously injured. Rubin died two weeks later on November 28 at UCLA Medical Center of cardiac arrest resulting from the multiple injuries suffered in the accident. He was 56 years old.

(At Selby, Wilshire to Manning to:)

10701 Wilshire Boulevard, Mary Jennifer Selznick suicide site

The 21-story-tall Crown Towers on Wilshire was the site of the suicide of Mary Jennifer Selznick, daughter of mega-producer David O. Selznick and actress Jennifer Jones. Named after her mother, whom Selznick had stolen from Robert Taylor years earlier, the younger Selznick suffered from severe emotional problems most of her life. On May 11, 1976, the 21-year-old rode the elevator to the top of the building, opened a rooftop hallway window and leapt to her death.

(Wilshire to:)

10660 Wilshire Boulevard, Joe Hunt. Billionaire Boys Club apartment

When 21-year-old Joe Hunt enlisted prep school pals to join his "investment" company they nicknamed it the "Billionaire Boys Club." The BBC paid for two apartments at the Wilshire Manning with money they were supposed to be investing. However, they were just spending it on themselves.

Hunt shared 1505 with Brooke Roberts (daughter of director Bobby Roberts). As his Ponzi scheme crumbled, Hunt committed two murders to try to save the BBC. Hunt's triggerman on the first murder was a gullible bodybuilder who was the doorman of this building. Hunt and several BBC pals are in prison for the murders.

Another past Wilshire Manning resident was Paula Barbieri, a former Victoria's Secret lingerie model and O.J. Simpson's girlfriend at the time he was charged with the Brentwood murders of his ex-wife and a friend. Phone records confirmed that O.J. made several calls to Barbieri here just before and after the murders. The tabloid press reported that she was with singer Michael Bolton in a Las Vegas hotel at the time, but she was among several stars in Vegas for Bolton's charity softball game. When O.J. pressured her to let photographers record their reunion visit after his acquittal, a disgusted Barbieri ended the relationship.

Unable to find model work after Simpson's yearlong trial, she sold her condo and retreated to her family in Florida.

(Wilshire to Westholme, to:)

10590 Wilshire Boulevard, Joseph Cotten death site

The Westholme Apartments was the last home of actor Joseph Cotten, who died in apartment 1202 on February 6, 1994, after a long illness. His 40-year career was ended by a 1981 stroke. He had begun working in Orson Welles' Mercury Theater and starred in Welles' movies *Citizen Kane* (1941), *The Magnificent Ambersons* (1942) and *Journey Into Fear* (1942). Cotten had roles in 200 films including *Shadow of a Doubt* (1943), *The Farmer's Daughter* (1947), *The Third Man* (1949), *Niagara* (1953), *Hush Sweet Charlotte* (1965), *Airport '77* (1977), and *Heaven's Gate* (1982).

(Wilshire to Beverly Glen. Left and note the building on the left on the corner at:)

10401 Wilshire Boulevard, James Caan accident site, Ed Wynn death site

James Caan, star of *The Godfather*, *Misery* and *Honeymoon in Vegas*, borrowed apartment 807 here to relax and read scripts. The corner apartment is three floors below the roof, with a corner balcony covered by glass partitions. At 4:00 A.M. on September 18, 1993, 25-year-old friend Mark Schwartz locked himself out and couldn't rouse the sleeping Caan to get in. Schwartz felt he could jump from the fire escape the 15 feet to Caan's balcony, and leapt from the fire escape window, the small opening left of the balcony. A blood-alcohol level that was five times the legal limit must have seriously impaired the young Schwartz' reasoning, because he missed the railing and plunged 100 feet to his death. His crumpled body was discovered the next morning next to the tree in the corner.

Caan was involved in another bizarre incident on March 10, 1994, at his brother's home at the Royal Sherman Apartments on Ventura Boulevard in North Hollywood. When police arrived, they found Caan being held on the ground by a tenant. During an argument about damage to his brother's car, Caan allegedly brandished a gun, but an apparently much tougher neighbor wrestled the gun away from the movie tough guy, made a citizen's arrest, and held him until police arrived.

The 10401 Wilshire building was also the last home of character actor Ed Wynn, whose son Keenan also had a movie and television career. The elder Wynn, born Isaiah Edwin Leopold in New York City, began entertaining customers at his father's hat shop by putting on the wares and making funny faces. Soon the crowds for his impromptu skits outnumbered the customers buying hats, and at 12 he ran away to join a vaudeville show, taking the stage with a collection of 300 hats and doing improvisation routines at the customers' requests. Wynn was the world's first "improv" comic.

He soon attracted the attention of Florenz Ziegfeld, who hired him in his *Follies of 1914*, and made him a star. For over 25 years Wynn starred in such Broadway shows as *Ed Wynn's Carnival* and *The Perfect Fool*, which became his signature routine, using 400 suits and 800 hats from which he improvised skits. His 1930s radio program was one of the most popular in the United States, and his movies included *The Chief* (1933) and *Stage Door Canteen* (1943), and *The Diary of Anne Frank* (1959) for which he received an Oscar nomination for his supporting role. Through the 1960s Wynn appeared in Disney comedies *Babes in Toyland* (1961), *The Absent-Minded Professor* (1961), *Mary Poppins* (1964), and *That Darn Cat* (1965). His last effort was in *The Gnome-Mobile* (1967) which was being filmed when he died. Wynn succumbed to cancer in his apartment on June 19, 1966, at the age of 79.

Tour 12: Brentwood

Begin Tour 12 at Woodburn Avenue and Sunset Boulevard, just west of the San Diego (405) Freeway. Drive south of Sunset on Woodburn. The garage door visible straight ahead at the fork in the road is the site. Proceed to the left to view the home at:

201 South Woodburn Avenue, Billie Burke death

Mary William Ethelbart Appleton Burke was born in 1884 in Washington State, the daughter of a Ringling Brothers Circus clown. When she was performing in English dance halls in 1896, she came under the wing of theater promoter Charles Frohman, who trained her and brought her back to the New York stage. She was soon the toast of Broadway. When she starred on Broadway she was romanced by both Enrico Caruso—who had 100 red roses thrown on stage every time she appeared—and Florenz Ziegfeld, who won her over with extravagant gifts and married her in 1914. In 1915 director Thomas Ince took one look at the gorgeous redhead and gave her a $300,000 contract (worth $4 million today). She appeared in a dozen Ince movies, including *Peggy* (1916), *Let's Get a Divorce* (1917), and *The Make Believe Wife* (1918) before returning to Broadway. A true diva, when she toured her manager rented a home and had the bedroom decorated to duplicate exactly her bedroom at the Ziegfeld estate in New York.

After the 1929 stock market crash nearly bankrupted Ziegfeld, Burke left for Hollywood and a return to movies. The 50 movies she made after her return made her an immortal star, beginning in *A Bill of Divorcement* (1930) with Katharine Hepburn and including *Dinner at Eight* (1933), *Becky Sharp* (1935), *Splendor* (1935), *Topper* (1937), *The Young at Heart* (1938), *The Bride Wore Red* (1937), *Irene* (1940), *Girl Trouble* (1940), and *Father of the Bride* (1950). Even with such an impressive résumé, Burke will always be remembered for her charming portrayal of Glinda, the Good Witch of the East, in 1939's *The Wizard of Oz*. Her Good Witch character, described as "addlepated, jittery ... a happy combination of naiveté and wit," was not far from the true Billie Burke. She suffered a heart attack at the Brentwood home she shared with her daughter's family on May 16, 1970, dead at the age of 84.

(Reverse on Woodburn to Sunset. Left to Barrington. Right on Barrington. The next stop is left [west] on Crescenda, but if you continue on Barrington past Crescenda Street, at the intersection with Halvern is a lovely large white colonial at the corner at 485 Halvern that was built by singer Nelson Eddy and later sold to Leland Hayward and Margaret Sullavan, still later owned by Fred MacMurray and his wife June Haver. Left [west] off Barrington on Crescenda to:)

The last home of Glinda the Good Witch.

11737 Crescenda Street, Bert Convy death site

Baseball star Bernard Whalen Convy signed with the Philadelphia Phillies out of North Hollywood High School, but quit two years later to study acting at UCLA. He joined Broadway's *Billie Barnes Review* in 1959 and starred in the hits *Fiddler on the Roof, Cabaret,* and *The Front Page* before moving to movies such as *Semi-Tough* and *Hero at Large* in the 1970s. He is best-remembered however as the star of numerous 1970s and 1980s television game shows including *Tattletales* (1977), *Super Password* (1984) and *Win, Lose or Draw* (1986). In 1989 Convy slipped, fell and was knocked unconscious while visiting his mother at Cedars-Sinai Hospital, and was himself diagnosed with brain cancer. He died inside his home here on July 15, 1991, from the effects of the cancer at the young age of 57.

(Crescenda to the intersection with Saltair Drive. Just to the left at the

corner behind the trees and the wrought-iron gating is:)

216 North Saltair Drive, Keenan Wynn death site

Keenan Wynn was the grandson of noted Shakespearean actor Frank Wynn and son of vaudeville, Broadway and movie star Ed Wynn. Comedian Ed named his son Francis Xavier Aloysius James Jeremiah Keenan Wynn, and although typecast as "Ed Wynn's son," Keenan followed his father into the movies with roles in such films as *Dr. Strangelove* (1963) and *Requiem for a Heavyweight* (1958). During his life a *very* lucky younger Wynn survived two plane crashes, a speedboat wreck, a motorcycle accident, and four car crashes before dying in bed at his home here on October 14, 1986, at the age of 70.

After Keenan's death his son Keenan Jr. wrote a book accusing his father of being an alcoholic who tortured his children, inflicted severe beatings and emotional abuse, and looted millions of dollars from

The last house of comic actor Keenan Wynn.

the children's trust funds from their grand-father. Ed Wynn reportedly didn't know the money was missing until almost all of it—$5 million—was gone.

(Saltair a short block to just before Sunset on your right at:)

139 North Saltair Drive, Primula Rollo Niven accidental death

Behind the hedgerow on the west side of Saltair opposite the church is a lovely mansion that was built for Grace Moore, and later rented by Robert Walker and Jennifer Jones, and at other times by Tyrone Power and his wife Annabella. On May 19, 1945, the Powers hosted a party for David Niven and his wife Primula ("Primmie") Rollo, who had just returned from postwar London with their two sons to resume Niven's movie career. Guests included Cesar Romero, Oleg Cassini, Gene Tierney, and Rex Harrison and Lilli Palmer. Niven called the beautiful Rollo his "lovely English rose."

After dinner the party guests played a then-popular version of hide-and-seek called "sardines," a complicated game played in a darkened house. During the game Primmie attempted to hide in what she thought was a closet, but what was in fact an unfinished cellar stairwell. As she stepped inside to hide she fell to the concrete floor below, suffering severe skull fractures and brain injuries. She quickly lapsed into a coma as she lay on the cellar floor, and the 28-year-old died a few days later at a Santa Monica hospital.

The St. Martin of Tours Catholic Church on the left at Sunset and Saltair (or Saltaire, depending on your map), was most recently the site of the Nicole Brown Simpson funeral.

(Saltair to Sunset. Right a short distance to Bundy. Right and you will pass a home on the left at 417 North Bundy:)

The former residence of John Dekker, which was purchased in the 1930s for the

David Niven's new bride fell to her death playing hide-and-seek in this darkened mansion when she stepped into an unfinished cellar stairwell and fell to the floor below.

eccentric writer by his best friend and drinking buddy Errol Flynn. Dekker hosted infamous weekly drinking parties for a select group of friends that were called "The Bundy Street Irregulars." Every Friday night for over 20 years Dekker's benders were attended by an exclusive clique that included W.C. Fields, John Barrymore, Vincent Price, Anthony Quinn, and Humphrey Bogart.

(Continue on Bundy to:)

570 North Bundy Drive, Lee Remick death site

Veteran movie and television star Lee Remick died in her home here on July 2, 1991, from cancer at the age of 55.

Just up the street at 641 North Bundy is a lovely home rented by Bette Davis in 1957 during a tumultuous divorce from actor Gary Merrill. On June 23, 1957, Davis suffered a near-tragic fall in the house, breaking her back when she plunged down some stairs. It was very close to a paralyzing accident, and the lucky Davis recuperated in the Bundy house. Less than a month later, she decided to take a ride on one of her horses at a nearby stable, was thrown off and broke her arm.

(Bundy to Bowling Green. Right to:)

418 North Bowling Green Way, Burt Freed death site

Burt Freed's crew cut and bulky physique earned him hundreds of movie roles, usually as a sinister tough guy or a menacing prison guard type. He starred in such films as *The Desperate Hours* (1955), *Paths of Glory*

(1957), *Billy Jack* (1971), and *Norma Rae* (1979). Freed also made guest appearances in over 200 television shows. He suffered a fatal heart attack in his home here on July 10, 1994, at 74.

(Bowling Green across Sunset onto South Bundy to:)

334 South Bundy Drive, Woody Van Dyke death site

After Woodbridge "Woody" Strong III served in World War I he became a mercenary in Africa, and later spent time as a lumberjack in Canada and a prospector in Alaska. He got a job with director Charles Brabin in *The Raven* (1915) and starred in D.W. Griffith's *Intolerance* (1916), adding "Van Dyke" for European effect. A successful director, Van Dyke was called "One-Take Van Dyke," because he believed the first take was usually the best take, and he was a studio favorite for bringing his films in on time and under budget. He was one of the most respected directors from the 1920s to the 1940s, directing *Tarzan, the Ape Man* (1932) after personally picking Johnny Weissmuller as the lead, and completing William Powell's *The Thin Man* (1934) in just 16 days. Other Van Dyke efforts included Lupe Velez' *Cuban Love Song* (1932), *I Married an Angel* (1942), *Manhattan Melodrama* (1935), *After the Thin Man* (1937), and the enormously popular Jeanette MacDonald–Nelson Eddy musicals of the 1930s and 1940s.

Van Dyke became only the second director enshrined at Hollywood's Grauman's Chinese Theatre, when he and his star Clark Gable were both asked to leave their prints side by side in the fabled concrete "Forecourt of the Stars" for 1936's *Love on the Run*. After a battle with cancer the feisty 52-year-old decided to take his own life, and over several weeks hosted "farewell" dinner meetings with his old friends at his home here. On February 3, 1943, Van Dyke put on his favorite Army uniform and had dinner with his two closest friends, Louis B. Mayer and

Howard Strikling, and was found dead in the same chair the next morning. He was so beloved that Mayer and Strikling ensured that suicide was not mentioned in a single obituary. Even his autopsy report only vaguely described the cause of death to be "primarily cancer of the lung."

(Reverse on Bundy to Kearsage. Right to Westgate. Right to:)

300 South Westgate Avenue, Tod Browning death site

A teenaged Tod Browning was a carnival stagehand fascinated by the sideshow "geeks," the "bearded lady," "dog-faced boy," or bogus "two-headed calf" that were the most popular attractions. He even allowed himself to perform as "The Living Dead," buried for hours at a time in a specially-designed casket before being dug up for throngs of terrified circusgoers. He moved from the circus to vaudeville and then to Hollywood to star in over 50 silent films, after which he directed hundreds of widely recognized films.

During his career Browning worked with every movie legend, beginning with D.W. Griffith on his 1915 epic *Intolerance*. He later directed over a dozen Lon Chaney, Sr., horror movies including *Outside the Law* (1920), *The Unholy Three* (1925), *The Blackbird* (1926), *Road to Mandalay* (1927), *The Unknown* (1927), and *London After Midnight* (1927). His most well-known efforts were the horror classics *Mark of the Vampire* (1932) with Lionel Barrymore, *Dracula* (1931) with Bela Lugosi, and *Freaks* (1932), a cult classic based upon his own childhood sideshow memories.

The elderly Browning steadfastly refused to discuss his incredible career stories with any writers, reporters, or even his closest friends. If anyone mentioned anything or asked him about his life, he would simply get up and leave. Browning moved in with his veterinarian's family in this Brentwood house in 1958, and died on October 6, 1962, at 82, succumbing to cancer of the larynx. He took all of his wonderful stories about the glory days of Hollywood to the grave with him.

(Westgate to Chenault. Left to Lorna. Left to:)

601 Lorna Lane, Billy Haines death– Jimmy Shields suicide

William "Billy" Haines was a major MGM star of dozens of 1920s and 1930s films including *Brown of Harvard* (1926), *Slide, Kelly, Slide* (1927), and *Tell It to the Marines* (1926). At the time Haines and John Gilbert were the two biggest male stars in movies, and Haines the first star who was admittedly gay. Although Haines was one of MGM's leading moneymakers with thousands of female fans, Louis B. Mayer fired him when he refused a demand to dump his lover Jimmy Shields and marry *a woman*. Shields was an MGM bit player who had lived with Haines since the pair met in 1926.

Joan Crawford called Haines and Shields "the happiest married couple in Hollywood." Carole Lombard described Haines as "her closest girlfriend," and once stripped naked in front of him, saying, "I wouldn't do this if I thought you'd get aroused Billy." Haines turned a knack for decorating into a thriving design business, the most popular on the West Coast. Crawford and Lombard were his first two clients, and soon his 8720 Sunset Boulevard office—now the site of Le Dome Restaurant—and an ultra-modern 426 South Canon Drive showroom were packed with movie stars who waited years for him to decorate their homes. He eventually decorated over 400 movie star residences through the years.

Haines and Shields stayed together for almost 50 years, sharing this home for over 20 years before Haines' death on December 26, 1973. After a fight with cancer he died in bed here at 73 with Shields at his side. Utterly inconsolable, the heartbroken Shields committed suicide three months

later, taking a massive overdose of barbiturates in the same bed on March 6, 1974. He left a note tacked to the door instructing the maid not to enter, but to call a close friend who discovered his body. He was 68.

(Reverse to Chenault. Left to Barrington. Right to Gorham. Left to:)

11663 Gorham Boulevard, Ron Goldman home

A block to the left at 11663 Gorham Boulevard is the apartment building where handsome young model and aspiring actor Ronald Lyle Goldman was living when he was murdered alongside Nicole Brown Simpson in June 1994. Goldman was 25 at the time of his murder. Although it was denied during the trial of O.J. Simpson, medical records seemed to indicate that Goldman did in fact know Nicole, and their relationship allegedly infuriated the ex–football star.

(Gorham to Brigham. Right to San Vicente. Right to:)

11700 San Vicente Boulevard, Mezzaluna Restaurant site

As you travel west on San Vicente, on the left several blocks from Brigham is the site of the Mezzaluna Restaurant at the corner of 11700 San Vicente and Dorothy. Young Ron Goldman was a waiter there, the site of the fateful Nicole Brown Simpson family dinner on June 12, 1994. Nicole, her family, and her children by O.J. Simpson shared a family dinner at the popular restaurant before leaving about 8:30 P.M. Shortly afterwards she called the restaurant looking for a pair of eyeglasses left by her mother. Goldman offered to return the glasses and left the restaurant about 9:45 P.M. Some time after that point the two were murdered at Brown's nearby condo. The notorious restaurant and all of its contents were sold at auction in late 1997.

(San Vicente to Montana/Westgate. Left to Dorothy. Right to Bundy. The Nicole Brown Simpson condo is catty-corner across the street to the right. Her unit is the end unit nearest Dorothy, and the murder site the first walkway into the building at 875:)

875 South Bundy Drive, Nicole Simpson–Ron Goldman murders

Nicole Brown was an 18-year-old high school senior working at Daisy's in Beverly Hills when she waited on O.J. Simpson in 1977. Though he was still a year away from divorcing first-wife Marguerite, Nicole quickly became his girlfriend, and after his divorce the couple lived together at his Rockingham Drive estate for five years before marrying on February 2, 1985, at the mansion. Two gorgeous children filled an apparently idyllic life.

However, after repeated abuse at Simpson's hands during the marriage, including a New Year's Eve "911" call in 1989 that ended in her husband's arrest for spousal abuse, Nicole divorced him in 1992. For several years she and her two children lived on nearby Gretna Green, moving into this $700,000 condo in February 1994. But she was still allegedly bothered by her ex-husband's apparent dark side—according to police, in the five months Nicole and their two children lived here she called for 911 emergency assistance on numerous occasions.

The grisly double-murder of 35-year-old Nicole and Ron Goldman occurred inside the gate in front on the north (right) side of the condo, just a short distance from the sidewalk. Their bodies were found at midnight on June 12, 1994, in a gruesome tableau awash in blood. Nicole was lying at the foot of the small stairwell just inside the gate, and Goldman was found among the bushes sitting up against the fence inside and to the right. Both were repeatedly stabbed and mutilated with a large military-style knife while the two Simpson children

Nicole Brown Simpson and Ron Goldman were slashed and stabbed to death inside the front gate at Simpson's Bundy Drive Condo. It has since been redecorated and is now hidden from view.

The murderer of Simpson and Goldman escaped the scene through this gate at the rear of the condo.

slept inside. The killer or killers escaped out the walkway to a gate leading to the alley behind the house running between Dorothy Avenue and Montana Avenue. O.J. was immediately the prime suspect, although he claimed to be at home waiting for a limo at the time of the murders.

(Bundy to San Vicente. Jog left on San Vincente around the park and a quick right to continue on Bundy to Dunoon Lane. Left to Gretna Green. Right to:)

325 South Gretna Green Way, Nicole Brown Simpson home, "911 call" site

After divorcing O.J. in 1992, Nicole Brown moved to this lovely home, the site of another famous 911 call made by Nicole on October 25, 1993. In a recording released after Simpson's arrest for his wife's murder, a distraught Nicole is heard begging for protection from an infuriated Simpson who is heard raging in the background. As in other instances, Nicole refused to press charges, and the incident went unnoticed until after her death. Nicole moved into the Bundy condo in early 1994, a quiet address that would become world famous a few short months later.

(Continue to Sunset. Right a short distance to Kenter Drive. Left on Kenter to Bonhill Drive. Right on Bonhill to Walther Way. Left to:)

675 Walther Way, Lew Ayres death site

Lew Ayres' film career spanned over 60 years but he is remembered for almost sacrificing his career when he declared himself a conscientious objector during World War II. Although the deeply religious Ayres served almost four years as a medic in Europe and earned three medals for bravery in the line of fire, after the war he was shunned by several studios before returning in an Oscar-nominated starring role in the 1948 classic *Johnny Belinda.* He later won the 1976 Golden Globe for Best Documentary for his *Altars of the World*, a study of the various faiths around the world.

Ayres left medical school in 1910 to join a traveling band and was discovered when they played Hollywood in 1928. His first big role came opposite Greta Garbo in *The Kiss* (1929), and he then starred in the film classic *All Quiet on the Western Front* (1930). In 1938 Ayres got the title role in *Young Dr. Kildare* with Lionel Barrymore. During the next four years they made eight *Dr. Kildare* films, but it was at that time that Ayres' wartime troubles interrupted his career. After his triumphant return in *Johnny Belinda*, Ayres went on to star in such films as *Advise and Consent* (1962) and *The Carpetbaggers (1964).*

Ayres was married in the 1930s to actresses Lola Lane and Ginger Rogers, and at the time of his death had been married to third wife Diana for over 30 years. On January 30, 1996, Ayres fell into a coma and died in his home at the age of 88. The nearby house at 654 Walther Way once belonged to "The Girl on the Red Velvet Swing," young Evelyn Nesbit Thaw (see story page 200).

(Reverse on Walther Way to Bonhill. Right to Kenter. Left to Sunset. Right to Carmelina. Left to Twenty-second Helena. Left to:)

12323 22nd Helena Drive, Gene Fowler death site

Gene Fowler was a Denver newspaper reporter when he was made publisher of William Randolph Hearst's *Daily Mirror* in New York. A Damon Runyonesque character known for joining bar fights at the slightest provocation, Fowler was a prolific writer when brought to Hollywood to develop RKO Studio screenplays in the 1930s. During the next decade he wrote several forgettable titles like *Call of the Wild, White Fang* and *Jesse James,* but eventually became the top script editor in the movies.

It was while working on his first movie *States' Attorney* (1932) that Fowler befriended actor John Barrymore. The two became inseparable and Fowler soon joined Barrymore's famed drinking club "The Bundy Street Irregulars," named after their weekly binges at the 417 North Bundy home of John Dekker. Other members were Anthony Quinn, Vincent Price, John Carradine and legendary Hollywood drunks Errol Flynn, W.C. Fields, and Lionel Barrymore. Fowler suffered a fatal heart attack sitting in his garden at his home here on July 2, 1960. During the attack the 70-year-old curmudgeon told his wife, "Agnes, don't let the undertaker rook you."

(Reverse to Carmelina. Left to fifth Helena. Left to end of cul-de-sac at:)

12305 5th Helena Drive, Marilyn Monroe death site

The most debated Hollywood mystery is the death of Norma Jean Baker, found dead in the sleepy little bungalow on the left at the end of this cul-de-sac. The story needs no retelling; it has been told, retold, debated, and "solved" in dozens of books.

This bungalow was the first and only home that Marilyn Monroe ever actually owned, bought in 1961. On August 5, 1962, the 36-year-old star was killed by an overdose of barbiturates, but who gave them to her or why has never been determined. It was common knowledge that Marilyn was in the middle of a heated affair with Jack Kennedy, and allegedly his brother Bobby, and that she was making repeated threats to expose the affairs. Although numerous witnesses placed Bobby Kennedy at this house the day of the mysterious death, and it was apparent that she did not take the drugs of her own volition, the death was classified as an "apparent suicide." A 1997 Donald Spoto book suggested that the death was an accident caused by an improperly administered barbiturate enema. They were routinely prescribed by her psychiatrist Ralph Greenson, and although unethical, Greenson allowed Marilyn's housekeeper Eunice Murray to administer them. Marilyn hated Murray, who was hired by Greenson to spy on Marilyn, and Greenson's clearly improper treatment later earned him a censure from the state board. Although Spoto's theory makes some sense and conforms to some of the physical evidence, there is a growing consensus that there was something much more sinister at work. The Kennedy connection cannot be disputed, and as more and more evidence is uncovered, the role of Bobby, Jack or both has become more and more prominent. Their direct involvement is the basis for the fascinating 1998 book *The Last Days of Marilyn Monroe*, by Donald H. Wolfe.

Robert Slatzer, briefly wed to Norma Jean in 1952, believes that Marilyn has appeared at her former home several times since her death. As he and a friend sat in the driveway on the night of the tenth anniversary of the death, they were astonished to see Marilyn appear in the driveway and walk past the car down the street. When they left the car to follow, she vanished.

The house was rented in 1993 by Guess jeans model Anna Nicole Smith, who also had an overdose problem on February 11, 1994. Staying in a Beverly Hills hotel while earthquake damage to this home was repaired, she and her boyfriend each allegedly consumed near-fatal quantities of prescription drugs and had to be rushed to the hospital. Soon thereafter Smith married a sickly 95-year-old millionaire.

(Reverse to Carmelina. Left to San Vicente. Right to Moreno. Left to:)

513 Moreno Drive, Mickey Cohen bombing site

During the 1940s and 1950s this small home at 513 Moreno was the L.A. home of mob kingpin Mickey Cohen. He was so conscious that his home phones were bugged that the gregarious killer answered incoming calls with a cheerful "Hello everybody!" For most of his West Coast tenure Cohen waged a bitter and bloody turf war with local hoodlum Jack Dragna, each taking turns trying to kill the other. One Dragna attempt occurred in the Moreno house here, when a huge bomb exploded in the early morning hours of February 6, 1950. The enormous sunrise explosion severely damaged the home and several nearby residences but failed to kill Cohen, who was blown out of bed by the force of the blast. After a lifetime of battles with police, various district attorneys and the Feds, Cohen was sent to prison a final time in 1962. After a fellow prisoner beat him almost to death with a bat, Cohen was left disabled for life. He died in prison.

(Return to San Vicente. Left to Twenty-sixth/Rockingham. Right to Evanston. Right to:)

13030 Evanston Street, Rooney-Milocevic murder-suicide site

Mickey Rooney was at the top of his career in 1958 when he married fifth wife Barbara Ann Thomason, a much younger Miss Santa Monica Muscle Beach. They had four children while living here, but during that time she was having an affair with Yugoslavian actor Milos Milocevic, a chauffeur for French actor Alain Delon, whose only screen role was a Russian crewman in *The Russians Are Coming, the Russians Are Coming* (1964). Recognizing Milocevic's severe emotional problems, Barbara confided in friends that the affair had become frightening and she was determined to put an end to it.

On January 31, 1966, while Rooney was hospitalized for a minor operation, the deranged Milocevic became enraged when Barbara decided not to divorce her husband and marry him. After a heated argument in the master bedroom, he shot her in the head several times and then committed suicide. Young Barbara Thomason-Rooney was only 27 when she was murdered. The distraught Rooney never returned to the house, moving to Beverly Hills after the killing.

Nearby at 12921 Evanston is the home of director Harold Ramis, who co-starred with pal Bill Murray in *Ghostbusters* (1988) and directed him in the hit *Groundhog Day* (1994). But none of his movie experiences prepared him for the fear he felt late one evening in 1995 when Ramis had a terrifying encounter with two gun-toting thieves who had broken into his home and held him at gunpoint.

While his children slept upstairs, Ramis was accosted by the armed thieves. During the attack his wife happened to call home from an evening out, and the quick-thinking actor was somehow able to let his wife know that he was in trouble. She immediately called neighbor and friend Martin Mull, who called police. When they arrived at the Ramis home, they found him bound and, though shaken, unhurt. Police later arrested the thieves when they were found in possession of Ramis' credit cards and watch.

(Evanston to Bristol. Left to intersection with Sunset at:)

Bristol Drive traffic circle, Clark Gable accident site

At the height of Clark Gable's fame he was in a car accident here that revealed the kind of power held by the studio "fixers" during the "Golden Age" of the movies. Driving home one late 1935 afternoon in a drunken stupor, Gable was heading to his home at 200 Bristol when he tried to drive *through* the traffic circle instead of around it, demolishing his car among the trees and bringing rush-hour traffic to a standstill. Police contacted Gable's studio, and MGM publicity director and chief "fixer" Howard Strickling went to work. Contacts in the police and D.A.'s office arranged for police to rope off the entire area and quietly hustle Gable away. He was hurried off to a private sanitarium to dry out while Strickling and his squad of fixers kept his name and pictures out of the papers.

It wasn't the first time Strickling's minions had to solve their stars' traffic problems.

In 1928 a drunk Joan Crawford was careening down Hollywood Boulevard when she ran a red light and struck a young woman in a crosswalk. Crawford tried to bribe a policeman and then left the scene before she was later arrested on her way home. Her one phone call was to Strickling, who reportedly went to the young girl's hospital room with $1,000 in crisp new $100 bills (worth about $75,000 today). Any charges and potential lawsuits disappeared.

The house on the north side of the circle—12800—was once the 12812 Sunset home of Betty Martin, ex-wife of comedian Dean. After their divorce, she and their four children lived in the house as she became a somewhat notorious party girl and eventually lost the children to Dean. The 1950s tabloid *Hollywood Confidential* ran a story asserting that she "was one of the hardest drinkers in all Los Angeles," and detailed drunken binges in this house, regular police raids and arrests, neglect for the couple's children, and so on. Though unconfirmed the stories nonetheless were well-circulated.

(Bristol past former homes of Clark Gable [200] and Barbara Stanwyck [409] to:)

426 North Bristol Drive, Joan Crawford "Mommie Dearest" house

When Lucille LeSueur Cassin signed with Metro Studios in 1924, the studio allowed *Movie Weekly* to have a contest to let a fan rename the young star. The winner, an elderly woman in Albany, New York, christened her Joan Crawford, and by 1927 she was on her way to the longest career in movie history. She lived here for 30 years, through three marriages and several children whose lives were detailed in daughter Christina's infamous book *Mommie Dearest*. Crawford was clearly a terrible mother who repeatedly beat her kids black and blue for the most minor transgressions. Friends noticed her often brutal tactics, and in a telling interview, when Crawford was asked if she

The much-redecorated former home of movie star Joan "Mommy Dearest" Crawford.

spanked her children she replied, "Yes, with a capital S. I spank them almost daily. Spare the rod and you have brats."

After buying a Spanish-stucco mansion here in 1929 for $40,000, the home was expanded to 27 rooms that included a movie theater and several guest houses. But she had a peculiar requirement to completely renovate and redecorate the house whenever she remarried. After each of her three divorces—from Douglas Fairbanks, Franchot Tone, and Phillip Terry—the home was completely redone by close friend Billy Haines, transforming the home from Spanish to Mediterranean to Moroccan to contemporary. On the day of each separation Haines' first order of business was to replace all of the toilet seats in the house. Each divorce was then handled the same way: her agent informed her soon-to-be ex-husband that his marriage was over and handed him the keys to a room at the Beverly Wilshire Hotel. His belongings were then gathered and shipped from the home and the locks and phone numbers changed that day.

Alex Madsen's book *The Sewing Circle: Female Stars Who Loved Other Women* de-

scribes Crawford as an earthy bisexual who had a healthy appetite for sex of any kind. In 1935 MGM paid $100,000 ($2 million today) for the negative of a lesbian porn film allegedly made by Crawford when she was 19. According to her children she often slept with their nannies, and among her confirmed female lovers were Barbara Stanwyck, Martha Raye and Greta Garbo. Marilyn Monroe told friends Crawford made a blatant pass at her when she visited the house here, pawing at her breasts as she tried on some of Crawford's dresses.

Subsequently, owners have included Donald O'Connor and Anthony Newley. The wall above the spot where Crawford's bed once stood has a tendency to erupt into spontaneous flames, the fires occurring many times over the years.

During the 1930s Crawford's lover Stanwyck lived nearby at 441 Rockingham during her marriage to alcoholic homosexual Frank Fay, an abusive ex-star twice her age whose legend was fading as fast as her's was rising at the time. Within an hour of their wedding Stanwyck went on the road with a touring play for five months, amid common rumors that the marriage was arranged by her studio to quell very loud and apparently true rumors about her lesbianism. Before she finally divorced Fay, Stanwyck would escape Fay's repeated drunken tirades by fleeing to her lover Crawford's home. She finally dumped Fay. The tumultuous Stanwyck-Fay relationship was the basis for the movie *A Star Is Born* (1937).

(Bristol into Oakmont bearing right. Oakmont is a "private" street with gates which are often not closed. If you continued past the raised gates to the end of the bridle path/tree belt, tucked behind a modern house at 18 is the former:)

18 Oakmont Drive, Joe E. Brown death site

Tucked behind 18 Oakmont at 14 is a gorgeous English stone mansion where wide-mouthed comic Joe E. Brown died at the age of 80 on July 7, 1973, after several strokes. He began as a vaudeville acrobat at the age of 6, moving to Broadway and then to Hollywood in 1925. He made over 150 films including *The Gladiator* (1938), *Wide Open Faces* (1938), *The Circus Clown* (1934), and *Fit for a King* (1937), but is best remembered as a millionaire smitten with a drag ~~Tony Curtis~~ *J. Lemmon* in *Some Like It Hot* (1959) with Marilyn Monroe and Jack Lemmon. The beloved Brown was the first actor to volunteer for USO duty during World War II, then tirelessly logging over 500,000 miles around the world visiting troops in every theater.

(Reverse to Rockingham. Right past the home of superagent Michael Ovitz [457] and the former home of Ed Wynn [441] to:)

426 North Rockingham Avenue, Hal Roach, Jr., death house

During the early 1900s a young Hal Roach was an Alaskan prospector, a mule-skinner in Oklahoma and a Hollywood cowboy extra. He founded Hal Roach Comedy Studios to satisfy the country's huge demand for comedies and for over 75 years wrote, directed, or produced over 1,000 movies. Roach discovered Laurel and Hardy, Ben Turpin, and Harold Lloyd, produced movies for Will Rogers and created the *Our Gang* comedies. His first *Our Gang* gag writer was a young Frank Capra, who later make a name for himself behind the cameras.

After World War II Roach turned his attentions to the new television medium, developing the early hits *Life with Riley* and *The Amos 'n' Andy Show.* He won dozens of television awards, several Oscars, and a Lifetime Achievement Award in 1984. Roach succumbed to heart ailments in his home here on November 2, 1993, at 100. Douglas Fairbanks and Mary Pickford spent their honeymoon at the estate, and writer-director Orson Welles lived here for a short time in the 1940s. Cole Porter lived next door at 420 Rockingham.

(Rockingham to the intersection of Ashford. On the left corner ahead was the site of:)

360 North Rockingham Avenue, former O.J. Simpson home site

O.J. Simpson and his first wife Marguerite Wilson bought the Tudor mansion that once stood at this corner in 1970, and for the next ten years he played football for the Buffalo Bills while Marguerite and their children lived here and O.J. lived in Buffalo. After their 1980 divorce, O.J. continued to live here. The house was the site of a greater tragedy than their divorce when the couple's third child, 2-year-old Aaren, got out of a playpen and drowned in the backyard pool on August 18, 1979. Earlier in April 1979, the *New York Post* had reported that the separated O.J. was still "keeping company with his girlfriend Nicole Brown," who moved in after Simpson's divorce was completed. It was also the site of their 1985 marriage.

According to police responding to a

Probably the most famous mansion in Brentwood, the former estate of O.J. Simpson, which was demolished in 1998.

frantic 911 call from Nicole at 2:45 A.M. on New Year's Eve 1989, they found a battered Nicole, clad only in a bra and sweatpants, cowering in the bushes near the front gate. After she told police that O.J. had beaten her, he was charged with spousal abuse. He pled no contest and was sentenced to community service, a $700 fine, therapy and two years probation. The volatile couple stayed together until their 1992 divorce, after which Nicole rented a house on Gretna Green.

Though he claimed to be waiting at the house for an airport limo at the time of his wife's June 12, 1994, murder, he was charged in her death and the death of her friend Ron Goldman. Important circumstantial evidence incriminating Simpson was found by police at the home, including a trail of blood droplets on the south driveway and the now legendary "bloody glove" uncovered down the walkway that ran the length of the same side of the house. His white Bronco, parked on the north side of Ashford, also contained suspicious bloodstains.

After a warrant for his arrest was issued a week later Simpson returned to the site following the bizarre "slow-speed" chase during which he had threatened suicide. While a nation watched transfixed, boyhood pal Al Cowlings drove the car into the driveway while helicopters hovered overhead. After a nine-month trial Simpson was acquitted of both murders on October 3, 1995, returning here again followed by a throng of onlookers, helicopters and tabloid photographers.

A visit to the site raised some interesting questions in Simpson's defense, however, leaving an equal number of questions that prosecutors failed to answer. How could Simpson have gotten through the neighbor's yard (to the south on Rockingham) to scale the fence where he allegedly dropped the bloody glove next to the garage, when the neighbor's security system would have seen him and the fence is (even still today) blocked by an eight-foot high densely packed line of shrubs? And how could the limo driver park facing the gate and use the intercom and not see the Bronco? And why wouldn't Simpson have simply entered the estate through the service entrance at the rear of the house if he wanted to remain undetected? He used that same gate to exit the house unobserved while over 500 press corpsmen were camped out in front in the days after the killing. He simply walked out back and drove away. The site of the murder-night dance recital, the Paul Revere Junior High School, is located south of Sunset on Allenford, just east off of Rockingham.

In July of 1998 the house was sold at auction for $3.95 million, and the new owner almost immediately had the entire site bulldozed to make way for a new home. He was reportedly trying to deter the thousands of still-interested fans who continued to flock to the notorious site.

(Rockingham past former homes of Zasu Pitts [241], Greta Garbo, Claudette Colbert and Bette Davis [301], Shirley Temple [227 and 209], and Michelle Pfeiffer and husband David (Picket Fences) Kelley [201]. Pfeiffer and Kelley were so incensed by the Simpson media and tourist circus that they moved out, renting the house to Melanie Griffith and Antonio Banderas. Continue to Sunset.)

12824 Sunset Boulevard, John Colton–Mercedes de Acosta house

During the 1930s homosexual writer John Colton shared his house at the corner at 12824 Sunset with lesbian writer Mercedes de Acosta so she could be closer to her lover Greta Garbo. Mercedes was raised on New York's ritzy Upper East Side in a Broadway theater family, and by 20 the free spirit was celebrated not only as a talented writer but also known for an interest in Buddhism and for slicking her hair and dressing as a man. Her earliest romantic affairs were with Broadway actresses Katharine Cornell, Elizabeth ("Bessie") Marbury, and Isadora Duncan.

When RKO studios brought her to Hollywood in 1929 to write screenplays for Pola Negri, the sultry de Acosta began an intense ten-year affair with bisexual Garbo, who turned exclusively to women after ending her long relationship with John Gilbert. Whenever Garbo moved—she had 14 homes in ten years in Hollywood—an obsessed Mercedes moved nearby. The inseparable couple were known as "The Garbos" by the movie set, and when Garbo moved to nearby 301 North Rockingham, de Acosta moved in here with Colton.

At that point de Acosta even began taking control of Garbo's career, acting as her agent and recommending to stunned studio moguls Louis B. Mayer and Irving Thalberg that Garbo should play *male* characters like Hamlet and Dorian Gray. Thalberg's reply: "You must be out of your mind." Feminist author Alice B Toklas once said of de Acosta, "Say what you want about Mercedes, but she had the three most important women of the twentieth century." After Garbo and Dietrich, the speculation was that the third was either Gertrude Stein or Eleanor Roosevelt.

Tour 13: Pacific Palisades, Santa Monica and Malibu

Begin Tour 13 at Sunset Boulevard and Mandeville Canyon Road.
Right on Mandeville Canyon to Boca de Canyon. Left to:

13176 Boca de Canyon Lane, Lionel Stander death site

Gravel-voiced actor Lionel Stander had a 70-year stage, movie and television career, from Broadway to Frank Capra's *Mr. Deeds Goes to Town* (1937) to television's *Hart to Hart*. By 25 he had appeared in 30 major productions including the original *A Star Is Born* (1937) and *The Last Gangster* (1937). Stander was the loudest critic of Sen. Joe McCarthy and his 1950 House Un-American Activities Committee, which led to him being blacklisted for much of the 1950s.

To escape the sentiment in Hollywood he settled in Italy and starred in 50 spaghetti westerns before returning in the late 1970s for a role as "Max" the chauffeur on the Robert Wagner television series *Hart to Hart* from 1979 to 1984. Through the 1990s he reprised the role in half a dozen *Hart* television movies, the last of which—"The Locket"—filmed the month he died. On November 30, 1994, Stander lost a long fight with lung cancer, dying at his longtime home here at 86. Coroner's records stated the death was caused by "lung cancer due to cigarette smoking."

Nearby at 1630 Mandeville Canyon is the last home of movie comic John Candy, the 350-pound star of such movies as *Stripes* (1981), *Summer Vacation* (1984), and *Planes, Trains and Automobiles* (1990). Candy, 43,

suffered a fatal heart attack on March 4, 1994, while filming a movie in Mexico. Further beyond at 3099 Mandeville Canyon is the reportedly haunted former home of Barbara Stanwyck and Robert Taylor.

(Reverse to Sunset. Right to:)

13043 Sunset Boulevard, Everett Sloane suicide site

On August 6, 1965, 55-year-old actor Everett Sloane committed suicide in his home by taking a massive overdose of barbiturates. Sloane was a protégé of Orson Welles in his Mercury Theater and starred in the radio thriller *War of the Worlds*. He entered the movies in Welles' cinema classic *Citizen Kane* (1941) and also appeared in other Welles' films, *The Lady from Shanghai* (1948), *Journey Into Fear* (1942) and *The Magnificent Ambersons* (1942). By the 1960s his career was at a standstill, and in a final indignity just days before his death the once-great star was relegated to providing the voice of "Mr. Magoo" in *Mr. Magoo's Holiday Festival*.

(Continue just past Allenford to San Remo. Hard right up the hill to D'Este. The hacienda catty-corner on the left at 1501 San Remo was formerly numbered:)

13515 D'Este Drive, Lionel Atwill estate, party site

The original mad scientist, Lionel Atwill starred in 25 horror films from 1918 to 1946 including *Mystery of the Wax Museum* (1933), *The Devil Is a Woman* (1935), and *Dr. X* (1932). But Atwill was closer to "Dr. Jekyll and Mr. Hyde." Cultivating an image as an erudite country gentleman by buying Old English Master paintings and expensive antiques, he was obsessed with murder trials that he attended when he wasn't working, and he also hosted and choreographed huge sex parties at this house.

During the 1930s a large European contingent came to Hollywood, bringing along their freewheeling sexual attitudes. Many, like Greta Garbo, Mercedes de Acosta, and Marlene Dietrich, settled in this area of Brentwood, which became a virtual European stronghold. Atwill was soon favored by the group for his well-organized sex parties. All guests had to bring a letter from a doctor certifying a clean bill of health to gain entrance, and after dinner all guests ceremoniously removed everything but jewelry. The group was then paired or grouped according to their individual sexual desires for parties that lasted the entire weekend.

Atwill's 1940 Christmas party included several underage girls, and a 16-year-old Minnesota farmgirl named Sylvia claimed that she had become pregnant at the orgy, though she couldn't specify the father. The Sylvia problem earned Atwill a perjury conviction and probation, and never escaped his label as a sex fiend. His final films were *House of Dracula* (1946) and *House of Frankenstein* (1946). During all of this time Atwill somehow managed to stay married to actresses Mary Louise Cromwell, Phyllis Relph, and Elsie MacKay, and writer Paula Pruter. He died in the mansion on April 22, 1946, from pneumonia.

(D'Este left to Capri. Left and notice the home directly in front between the fork of Monaco [left side] and Capri [right side].)

The entrance to the former hacienda of Lionel Atwill, the site of his well-attended weekend orgies.

1940 Monaco Drive, Rod Serling house

Immortal sci-fi writer Rod Serling lived in this house during his time in L.A. The ingenious producer of *The Twilight Zone* and *Rod Serling's Night Gallery* purchased the home from theater diva Virginia Bruce. The home earned a place in the tour due to Serling's preoccupation with death and the occult. If any house is haunted, it should be this one.

(Capri right to first house on the right:)

1465 Capri Drive, Carole Landis suicide site

Like thousands of young beauties trying to become stars, lovely Carole Landis, born Francis Lillian Mary Ridste, worked the casting couch circuit bedding men who promised to help make her a star. She had dozens of failed relationships, and two of her four disastrous marriages before she turned 25 didn't last two weeks. She typically wore all four of her wedding rings to remind her not to get married again. She had small roles in *Blondes at Work* (1938), *Broadway Melody of 1938* (1938), *Topper Returns* (1941) and *One Million B.C.* (1940), but she never became a star. Her numerous and very public affairs with married studio bosses kept her in disfavor with the "Hollywood wives club" and ensured that her career would never get off the ground.

Although he was married to Lilli Palmer at the time, actor Rex Harrison repeatedly promised to marry her during their two-year affair, and a gullible Landis believed him. Openly distraught over the doomed relationship, her own mounting debts, and a stagnant career, Landis had dinner with Harrison here on July 4, 1948. After he left the house, she packaged Rex's love letters and left them by a friend's garage and penned the note "Dearest Mommie, I'm sorry, really sorry to put you through this. But there is no way to avoid it. I love you

darling. You have been the most wonderful Mom ever. Everything goes to you. Look in the files, and there is a will that decrees everything. Good bye my angel. Pray for me. Your Baby." She then took a huge overdose of Seconal and died in the house.

Harrison found her body the next morning curled up on the bathroom floor, dead after a fourth suicide attempt. In each of the previous three tries, Landis followed a pattern well-known to her friends, of leaving messages that she was about to kill herself, after which she was saved by the expected response. But she forgot that on a July Fourth holiday weekend nobody would be home. Her messages, which as usual were sent, got no response. The picture of the dead 28-year-old lying by the toilet was a well-publicized portrayal of a Hollywood movie tragedy.

Harrison's petulant attitude and his indifference to Landis' tragic death doomed his U.S. career. The *Hollywood Reporter* spoke for Landis' friends, saying, "we don't remember an actor, foreign or domestic, who has breached so many rules of good taste … the wonder of the whole thing is that he hasn't had his face smashed by now." Persona non grata, he was forced to return to England to find work. A minor U.S. career that reemerged in the 1970s would be tarnished yet again by the similar suicide of fourth wife Rachel Roberts in 1980.

(Capri to Romany. Right to Amalfi.)

Nearby at 1461 Amalfi is the pink mansion built by *Sunset Boulevard* writer Vickie Baum, later shared by Greta Garbo and Mercedes de Acosta before they sold it to David Niven in 1930. His well-attended Sunday pool parties included very popular card games in the men's dressing room. Their popularity came from a full-length one-way mirror giving players an unobstructed view into the women's dressing room.

(Amalfi left past former home of Ronald

Reagan and Nancy Davis [1258] and Pavia to Napoli. Left across Sunset on Napoli to:)

868 Napoli Drive, David Wayne death site

David Wayne was a classically trained theater actor who received the first Tony Award for his 1947 Broadway portrayal of the feisty leprechaun in *Finian's Rainbow.* Wayne's stage and film career lasted over 50 years, including roles as Ensign Pulver in *Mr. Roberts* (1954) and as the preening Kip Lurie in the 1949 Tracy-Hepburn classic *Adam's Rib.* He also had a recurring role as the Mad Hatter in the campy 1960s television series *Batman*, and portrayed the muddled Dr. Amos Weatherby in the 1978–1982 sitcom *House Calls.* The 81-year-old star died at his home on February 9, 1995, after a long battle with lung cancer.

(Napoli past the homes of Dabney Coleman [715], Michael Keaton [828], and Shelly Long [905] to the "Y" intersection with Toulon. Right on Toulon a short block to Amalfi. Left to:)

788 Amalfi Drive, James Whale suicide site

Acclaimed director James Whale was best known for creating such stylish 1930s horror classics as *Frankenstein* and *The Invisible Man.* He was imported from England in 1925 to direct a movie version of his stage hit *Journey's End*, based upon his experiences in a World War I German POW camp. Other Whale hits included *Waterloo Bridge* (1931), *Frankenstein* (1931), *The Old Dark House* (1932), *The Invisible Man* (1933), and *The Bride of Frankenstein* (1935). It was a shock to the industry when Whale walked away from the movies in 1941, allegedly to "pursue other interests like painting."

The reality was that his career ended when he refused to publicly disavow his homosexuality and leave live-in lover David

Lewis, who was Irving Thalberg's former assistant. Whale shared his home with Lewis, and after several health setbacks drowned himself in the pool on April 29, 1967. His death at 60 was the subject of speculation for years since Lewis kept the suicide note a secret—a note that ended with the comment "No one is to blame." The home was later purchased by actress Goldie Hawn.

(Reverse to Amalfi to Sunset. Left down the hill into Pacific Palisades. On the left side, tucked into a cluster of homes at 14238 Sunset [Do Not Stop Here], is:)

14238 Sunset Boulevard, Robert Walker death site

Handsome leading man Robert Walker starred in 25 films including *Winter Carnival* (1939) and the war-era movies *Bataan* (1943), *See Here Private Hargrove* (1944), *Thirty Seconds over Tokyo* (1944), and *The Clock* (1945). Walker, childhood sweetheart Jennifer Jones and their two children lived an idyllic Beverly Hills life, first in a 139 Saltair Drive mansion and later at a lovely 635 Perugia Way estate. Pictures of the loving household were frequently in the pages of movie magazines, but the Walkers idyllic life was thrown into a nightmare of alcohol abuse and subsequent mental illness after Jones was literally stolen away by director David O. Selznick. Friends of the couple and movie fans the world over were shocked when movieland's allegedly most loving couple divorced in 1943 and Jones married Selznick.

Walker never truly recovered from the heartbreak, and after several bouts with alcohol and numerous stays in sanitariums, moved to this rented Pacific Palisades house to get his life together. However, he suffered a nervous breakdown on August 27, 1951, and a doctor tried to calm the struggling 32-year-old by giving him a shot of the sedative sodium amytal, a drug Walker had used countless times before. For some reason, however, after being given the shot Walker simply stopped breathing and died on his bed. It seemed to be a merciful ending to the poor man's tragic love story.

(Sunset Boulevard to the entrance to Will Rogers State Historic Park at 14400 Sunset:)

14400 Sunset Boulevard, Dennis Wilson house

The house across on the south side of Sunset Boulevard hidden in the trees was once Will Rogers' private hunting lodge, and former Beach Boy Dennis Wilson's home during the late 1960s. While he was living there Wilson somehow befriended Charles Manson and his weird extended "Family." For several months before the gruesome August 1969 Tate and LaBianca murders that put five Family members on death row, a large group of the Family moved in and lived here with Wilson.

Using the secluded house as a base of operations, during the four-month visit they cleaned Wilson out of more than $100,000 cash, food, clothes, and a number of Beach Boys Gold Records that they stole and pawned. The Manson women used Wilson's Rolls-Royces to go on food-stealing missions and destroyed a brand new, uninsured Ferrari when a drug-addled Family member got in a Chatsworth car wreck.

(Sunset right past Chautauqua to Hartzell. Right to:)

740 Hartzell Street, Francis X. Bushman death site

When 83-year-old Francis Bushman slipped in his bungalow kitchen here on August 24, 1966, striking his head on a countertop in a fatal accident, his neighbors thought that he was simply an unfortunate old man. Few remembered that Bushman's fame once rivaled that of even Valentino, a close friend who coincidentally died forty

years to the day earlier. Bushman was the biggest of the silent stars, living in a 50-room mansion at the peak of posh Whitley Heights that boasted the U.S.'s first in-ground pool. He starred in over 450 movies between 1911 and 1920, becoming a premier leading man worshipped by millions of women the world over. The Hollywood press "paired" Bushman with every unattached starlet in town, and he was called "The Most Beautiful Man in the World."

His career ended almost overnight when he was served with divorce papers by a wife whose existence was known only by scheming studio heads who also kept the couple's five children a secret from his millions of adoring female fans. She and the kids had lived quietly on a Manassas, Virginia, estate until the expected publicity explosion that resulted from the revelation. The stunning and scandalous divorce papers named popular star Beverly Bayne as the corespondent in the divorce, and disgusted fans the world over avoided his movies by the millions.

A quietly resigned Bushman retired with his huge fortune and married Bayne, spending his remaining years making over 2,500 anonymous appearances on radio and television soap operas. He and Bayne moved to this small Pacific Palisades bungalow in the 1950s, the present house the result of an extensive 1970s renovation. His Forest Lawn crypt says simply, "Francis X. Bushman, The King of the Movies."

(Reverse to Sunset. Right to Swarthmore. Left to Hamden. Left to:)

713 Hamden Place, Louise Peete murder site

On December 10, 1944, the body of elderly Margaret Logan was found buried in the backyard by neighborhood dogs digging for squirrels. She had been shot in the head and her skull had been crushed. It was quickly learned that Mrs. Logan had been allowing parolee Louise Peete to live in her home after Peete's release from a prison term for an earlier murder conviction. When police confronted the young woman, she blamed Logan's elderly husband, who had recently died in a home for the insane. It was an excellent alibi except for the 40 similarities police noted between Logan's murder and the earlier killing committed by Peete, and on April 11, 1947, she became the first woman executed in California's brand new gas chamber at San Quentin.

(Reverse to Sunset. Left around sharp curve at Las Casas to Arno. Left around the corner to the intersection with Aderno. Left a short distance and turn right on Aderno, and proceed to the second house on the left at:)

219 Aderno Way, Hugh O'Connor suicide site

Hugh O'Connor, adopted son of *All in the Family* star Carroll O'Connor, had a re-curring role on the elder O'Connor's 1990s television series *Heat of the Night*. Young O'Connor fought drug problems for 15 years and by 1995 was addicted again to crack cocaine. His wife left with their infant son for her father-in-law's beach house. Soon afterward, on the morning of his third wedding anniversary on March 28, 1995, Hugh called his long-suffering father, who begged his son to get help. Hugh replied, "No, I think I'm going to cap myself today ... I gotta go. So long."

A panicked O'Connor called local police, but when police SWAT teams arrived here they heard a gunshot from inside this home. They found the forlorn 32-year-old sitting on the living room couch with a bullet wound in the head. He had killed himself with a single shot from a .45 caliber revolver.

His infuriated father publicly identified his son's drug supplier, and Harry Persaigian was arrested on drug charges. He was convicted after a 1996 trial at which a shaken elder O'Connor testified, and sentenced to a

Despondent over ongoing drug problems, actor Hugh O'Connor committed suicide in this Pacific Palisades home.

year in jail. O'Connor has urged other families to take similar action against people who provide drugs to addicts, in the hope that his success against Persaigian would keep other sons from the same fate.

(Continue around the block on Aderno back to the Arno intersection. Go left on Arno down to the stop sign, and continue left a short distance to Trino Way. Right to:)

250 Trino Way, Gene Raymond death site

Raymond Guion made his Broadway debut in 1920 and later starred in a number of stage hits, including a two-year run in *Cradle Snatchers* alongside a young Clark Gable. After a dozen years on stage and in radio, he came to Hollywood and became an RKO stock player in 1935. Over the next 30 years the renamed Gene Raymond played second leads in dozens of major films and starring roles in a like number of B movies.

His 1930s movies included *Red Dust* (1932) with Jean Harlow and Clark Gable, *Ex-Lady* (1933) with Bette Davis, and *Brief Moment* (1936) with Carole Lombard. Other later Raymond films include *Hooray for Love* (1935) with Ann Sothern, *The Bride Walks Out* (1936), *That Girl from Paris* (1936), and his last major film, 1954's *The Best Man*.

His film career was overshadowed by his surprising and reportedly tumultuous 1937 marriage to actress Jeanette MacDonald. MacDonald married the hard-drinking Raymond even while she maintained a torrid affair with her co-star Nelson Eddy. On several occasions Eddy beat Raymond almost to death after he was told that Raymond had been beating MacDonald. The Raymond-MacDonald marriage somehow lasted until her death in 1963. On May 3, 1998, Raymond died in his Pacific Palisades home of pneumonia at the age of 89.

(Reverse to Sunset. Left to Castellamare, the last right just before Sunset reaches

Pacific Coast Highway. Castellamare winds up the hill and around the corner to the Posetano intersection, in front of which, built into the hillside is a two-door garage at:)

17531 Posetano Road, Thelma Todd murder site

The streets in this section of Pacific Palisades received their names from locales on the Italian island of Sicily, the birthplace of the mob. The Castellammare neighborhood here is named after the Sicilian fishing village of Castellammare del Golfo, the infamous birthplace of the "Vendetta." It was a vendetta that apparently claimed the life of comic actress Thelma Todd, who was found dead in the right-side garage here on December 18, 1935. Feisty "Ice Cream Blonde" Todd's death has been debated since the gorgeous star was found dead in her car inside this garage. She was found curled up in a bloody mess on the front seat of her car. The garage is unchanged to this day.

Todd was a sixth-grade teacher in Massachusetts when she won several local beauty contests and ended up in Hollywood. She starred in several Laurel and Hardy comedy hits including *Unaccustomed As We Are* (1929) and *Chickens Come Home* (1930), but a comedy serial with close pal ZaSu Pitts made her a star. Pitts raised several of her friend Barbara LaMarr's kids after LaMarr's drug-related death. The fresh-faced and bubbly Todd was a favorite of Groucho Marx, who featured her in his movies *Horse Feathers* (1932) and *A Day at the Races* (1937).

Todd used the garage owned by manager and ex-lover Roland West, whose ex-wife Jewel Carmen owned the large house above the garage. He was in love with Todd and shared an apartment above her nearby café. Though Todd was severely beaten and was discovered in her blood-spattered car with a broken nose and ribs, police and the coroner classified the death a suicide. Curiously, Todd spent her last days with mobster Lucky Luciano, also a lover at the time. Todd repeatedly

Actress Thelma Todd was found murdered in her car behind the garage on the right on a cool December night in 1935.

Porto Marino, right and carefully reverse at the top of the hill. Note the building below at the intersection:)

17575 Pacific Coast Highway, Thelma Todd Café, haunted

The building at the base of the hill was the site of Thelma Todd's fashionable "Sidewalk Café" in the early 1930s. Though Todd owned the building, her partner in the popular restaurant was her ex-lover Roland West. The building remains unchanged to this day, featuring the original leaded glass doors and the imported tilework that Todd installed. Her apartment on the upper right side of the second floor overlooked the ocean, while West lived in the apartment on the other side of the building. The third-floor upper level was the area Lucky Luciano wanted to transform into a casino. Todd's refusal may have led to her death. Subsequent residents and visitors have reported regularly meeting Thelma's ghostly presence inside her apartment. She has been repeatedly seen standing in front of her old windows staring out over the ocean.

declined Luciano's entreaties that she let him open an illegal casino in the upper floor of her café, and when she said, "over my dead body" he responded, "That can be arranged." She was dead within a week.

Some biographers place the blame on West, maintaining that he locked the garage with a drunken Todd still inside to punish her for her infidelities, not realizing she would be killed by the fumes from the car. Hal Roach, a lifelong friend of West's, reported that on his deathbed West made such a confession to him.

(Reverse to Sunset. Right to Pacific Coast Highway. Right under the walkway to

Just north up the Pacific Coast Highway is the location of a September 8, 1935, auto accident that ended the career of noted choreographer and director Busby Berkeley. Returning home from a party, a drunken Berkeley crossed the median and slammed into another car, killing three members of a local family. Charged with three counts of second degree murder, Berkeley retained attorney Jerry Giesler, who navigated through three trials, orchestrating two hung juries and a mistrial for his unemployed client. His first trial began on the day that Todd's body was discovered.

The site of Thelma Todd's "Sidewalk Cafe," where Todd was living in the second-floor oceanview apartment when she died in 1935. Both the cafe and the garage where she died remain unchanged to this day.

(Pacific Coast Highway north to Coastline. Right to:)

18424 Coastline Drive, Gary Busey overdose site

On May 4, 1995, Malibu police responded to a 911 call that actor Gary Busey's girlfriend had placed from this rented home. The 50-year-old Busey has been nominated for an Oscar for his role in *The Buddy Holly Story* and played villain roles in *Die Hard* and *Lethal Weapon II*. Police discovered that Busey had ingested a near-fatal accidental overdose of cocaine and quickly rushed the unconscious actor to the hospital where he was admitted in serious condition. When an additional 11 grams of cocaine was found in his shirt pocket, police obtained a search warrant for the house. A subsequent search found a half gram of cocaine, four grams of marijuana and reportedly some drug-laced mushrooms. After a week-long hospital stay, Busey was released to face several drug charges.

(Reverse to Pacific Coast Highway. Right on PCH to Bonsal. Right to:)

5820 Bonsal Drive, Michael Landon death site

A lavish Mexican hacienda behind the flower-bedecked gates belonged to Michael Landon, who began his career in *I Was a Teenage Werewolf* but is best-remembered as "Little Joe" on the television series *Bonanza*. Landon lost a long battle with stomach cancer and died in his home here on July 1, 1991. He was 56 years old.

Returning south on Pacific Coast Highway, pass Topanga Canyon Rd. (Rte. 27) on the left. Take a sidetrip into Topanga Canyon Park, set of the television show *M*A*S*H**, or continue on Topanga Canyon Road. to Old Topanga Canyon Road. in the heart of still-funky Topanga Canyon. The old house at 964 Old Topanga Canyon was the site of an obscure murder on July 25, 1969, that led to some of the most famous killings in L.A. history. Gary Hinman, a 23-year-old musician, was murdered in the house on the orders of Charlie Manson, after being tortured for two days and later killed when he refused to sign over his VW minibus to Manson. The crazed Manson's attempts to free the follower charged with Hinman's murder led to his bizarre "Helter Skelter" plan that led to the Tate-LaBianca killings a month later.

(Reverse to PCH. Left past Sunset to Chautauqua. Left to LaCumbre. Left to end of block at Alma Real. Left to Altata. Left to:)

14948 Altata Drive, Cameron Mitchell death site

Character actor Cameron Mitchell is best-remembered for his role as "Happy" in the stage and screen versions of *Death of a Salesman*. He debuted in 1945's *They Were Expendable*, and starred in *Okinawa, Powder River, Garden of Evil, All Mine to Give,* and such films as *Les Misérables* (1952), *Carousel* (1956) and *What Next, Corporal Hargrove?* (1957). During the 1950s Mitchell starring in 200 foreign films before returning to the United States for a final television role as drunken cowhand "Buck Cannon" in the 1970s western series *High Chaparral*. On July 15, 1994, he succumbed to lung cancer in his home at 75.

On nearby Toyopa Drive see the last home of cartoon voice wizard Mel Blanc at 266, character actor Ed Prentiss at 267 and Walter Matthau at 278.

(Altata to Toyopa/Corona del Mar intersection. Straight on Corona del Mar around to Chautauqua. Right to PCH. Left past Sunset/Chautauqua to Entrada. Left to East Channel. Left to:)

639 East Channel Drive, Leo Carrillo death

Leo Carrillo's remarkable 60-year career began in 1900 but is highlighted by his role as "Pancho" in the 1950s television serial *The Cisco Kid*. Often paired with fellow cowboy star Andy Devine, Carrillo also starred in the classics *City Streets* (1933), *The Barretts of Wimpole Street* (1934), *Viva Villa!* (1934), *One Night in the Tropics* (1940), *Crime, Inc.* and *Manhattan Melodrama* (1934). The latter was watched by John Dillinger and his "Woman in Red" girlfriend before he was gunned down by FBI men outside the Chicago movie theater. Carrillo suffered a fatal heart attack at his home here on September 11, 1961, at 81.

(Reverse to Entrada. Left to Kingman/ Seventh. Right to Adelaide. Right to:)

144 Adelaide Drive, Mary Miles Minter death site

Silent star Mary Miles Minter lived in seclusion here for over 50 years until her death on August 8, 1984, at the age of 82. Her role as the "next Mary Pickford" ended with the scandalous fallout from the William Desmond Taylor murder. The world-famous director was murdered in his Los Angeles bungalow in 1922, shot to death at the height of Minter's popularity.

An enthralling murder mystery, the still-unsolved crime has generated dozens of theories over 70 years and numerous suspects but was never solved. The long list of suspects included his first wife, who was abandoned by Taylor; his chauffeur, who was likely Taylor's ex-convict younger brother; disgruntled studio drug dealers who hated Taylor for his vehement anti-drug posturing; Mabel Normand, the last person to see him alive; or most likely, Minter's stage mother Charlotte Shelby, who knew about the scandalous affair between Taylor and her 16-year-old meal ticket. After studio fixers cleaned up the crime scene, it

Child-actress Mary Miles Minter was a central figure in Hollywood's first real scandal, the 1922 murder of director William Desmond Taylor. After her career was ended by the fallout she lived here with her mother, who remains the prime suspect in Taylor's unsolved killing. Both Minter and her mother died in the house.

became impossible for police to solve the crime.

Minter was ruined when police found underwear with her "M.M.M." monogram and juicy love letters on her handmade butterfly stationery. Her performance at Taylor's funeral was almost absurd—she threw herself sobbing on the casket and kissed the corpse on the lips, and swore to the other mourners that she had heard Taylor say, "I shall always love you, Mary." Her career over, Minter married her Beverly Hills milkman, and as her weight ballooned to over 200 pounds would only respond to questions if she was addressed as Mrs. O'Hildebrandt. Minter's mother lived here as well, and died here in 1957, taking her secrets about the Taylor affair to the grave.

The house across the way at 145 Adelaide was shared by author Christopher Isherwood and his longtime companion Don Bachardy. Isherwood was a novelist, writer and essayist who arrived with the large Eu-

ropean contingent in the late 1930s, who met on Sundays at the nearby 165 Mabery Drive home of Salka and Peter Viertel. Isherwood and Bachardy moved here in 1953, living together until Isherwood's bizarre 1983 death. While hosting a party, he choked to death on a toothpick hidden in a canapé, and died at the age of 50.

(Adelaide to Seventh. Right to San Vicente. Right to Ocean. Left to the intersection of Ocean Avenue and Alta at:)

535 Ocean Avenue, William Holden death site

The Shorecliff Towers condos were actor William Holden's last home, living in the fifth floor front unit 5B. Born William Franklin Beedle in O'Fallon, Illinois, Holden earned the nickname "Golden Boy" after his 1939 debut in the film of the same name. Holden never chose a bad role during his 40-year career, and is remembered for his work in *Meet the Stewarts* (1942), *Sunset Boulevard* (1950), *Born Yesterday* (1950), *Stalag 17* (1953)—for which he earned an Academy Award—*The Country Girl* (1954), *Sabrina* (1954), *The Proud and the Profane* (1956), *Love Is a Many-Splendored Thing* (1955), and dozens of others.

Prior to his death Holden had fallen in love with Stephanie Powers, star of television's *Hart to Hart*. The pair shared a love of the outdoors and his Mount Kenya nature preserve, but the hard-drinking Holden fought a losing battle with alcoholism. The 63-year-old actor died here on November 16, 1981, found dead on the floor in his bed-

A drunken William Holden bled to death after falling from his bed and hitting his head on the bedside table in his fifth floor front Shoreham Towers apartment.

room. He had apparently fallen out of bed in a drunken stupor and gashed his head on the bedside table. Though he tried to stop the bleeding, Holden was unaware of the seriousness of the injury and soon bled to death.

(Ocean Avenue a few blocks to the intersection with Palisades, and for a better view of several beachfront sites, stop along the park on your right [beach] side of Ocean. Proceed to the walkway along the cliff over the ocean for a beautiful view of the beach, the nearby Santa Monica Pier, and the beachfront houses located below at 707, 705 and 625 Palisades Beach Road. The first house, located at 707, is the huge Tudor below and almost directly across from Palisades Drive. It was the site of:)

707 Palisades Beach Road, Irving Thalberg death site

Sickly and beset with respiratory and heart problems, 20-year-old Irving Thalberg somehow still helped his friend Louis B. Mayer build the biggest studio in Hollywood history—Metro-Goldwyn-Mayer. He was Mayer's number two man at the tender age of 23, responsible for MGM's list of stars and all of the decisions on every aspect of production. He personally oversaw production of *Ben-Hur* (1926), *Grand Hotel* (1932), *Mutiny on the Bounty* (1935), discovered the Marx Brothers, and once boasted, "I, more than any person in Hollywood, have my finger on the pulse of America." Even so, he is also famous for telling Mayer not to produce *Gone with the Wind*, saying, "Forget it Louis, no Civil War picture ever made a dime."

Although just five feet tall, Thalberg was nonetheless a tenacious negotiator. Edward G. Robinson ran out of one contract meeting with Thalberg and threw up in the hallway. As tough as he was, however, he also enjoyed cross-dressing, fond of wearing wife Norma Shearer's dresses and shoes around the house. She told friends they wore each other's clothes to eat dinner. Their beachside mansion was the first home in California with air conditioning, installed to alleviate Thalberg's breathing problems. The house was also soundproofed so waves wouldn't disturb his sleep.

The Thalbergs spent Labor Day of 1936 playing bridge on a hotel verandah in Monterey, and by the time they returned to L.A. a week later Irving had a serious cold. Against his doctors' advice he attended an MGM premiere on a cool fall night, and his cold quickly led to pneumonia. A week later on September 14, 1936, he died here at the age of 33. Shortly after his death Shearer moved to a Beverly Hills Hotel bungalow, leaving this mansion empty—but still fully staffed by three full-time maids, a butler, a crew of four gardeners, and a poolman—until she sold the house 19 years later.

Unchanged since it was built in the 1920s, Irving Thalberg's Santa Monica mansion was the first in L.A. with central air conditioning. After his death, his widow Norma Shearer left the fully staffed house empty for almost 20 years.

(The next house north [to the right] was the site of:)

705 Palisades Beach Road, Douglas Fairbanks death site

In 1919 Douglas Fairbanks and Mary Pickford built this beachside home as the companion to their incredible "Pickfair" mansion. The couple called this cottage "Fairford," and they spent virtually every weekend here enjoying the ocean. Fairbanks often interrupted his neighbors' parties by appearing at his second-floor balcony, jumping to the awnings below, and bouncing off of them into his pool.

After divorcing Pickford, he lived with Lady Sylvia Ashley until his death here from heart failure on December 12, 1939, at 56. While his body lay in state on his ornately carved bed in front of the window overlooking the ocean, his 150-pound mastiff "Marco Polo" whined and cried, refusing to move. Lady Ashley lived in the home until her later death here.

(Notice the blue beachhouse tucked between several other large houses to the north [right], the site of:)

625 Palisades Beach Road, Peter Lawford home, John F. Kennedy–Marilyn Monroe love-nest

The blue beachfront mansion at 625 Palisades Beach Road was built by Louis B. Mayer and over the years has had numerous celebrity tenants including Leslie Caron, Warren Beatty and Abbe Mann. The most famous former owner was Peter Lawford, who allegedly lent his digs to pals Bobby and John Kennedy for trysts with Lawford's Hollywood friends. The most famous coupling was between John Kennedy and Marilyn Monroe, who allegedly met here several times during an affair that lasted from 1954 into his presidency, ending just before her mysterious death. The lovebirds were regular clients of several Malibu motels including the Holiday House Motel, and a secluded motel where Sunset Boulevard meets the Pacific Coast Highway. Prior to his election J.F.K. was an unknown congressman from Boston, so a preelection appearance with a Hollywood star warranted less attention than after the national campaign.

Tucked in among a row of beachfront mansions, Peter Lawford's was reputedly the site of several Marilyn Monroe–John F. Kennedy trysts.

(Return to Ocean Avenue, and proceed left [east] on Palisades Avenue to:)

226 Palisades Avenue, Jackson Browne–Darryl Hannah home

Darryl Hannah (*Splash, Roxanne, Attack of the 50-Foot Woman*) and singer Jackson Browne ("Doctor My Eyes," "Rock Me on the Water") shared this home for several years. On September 23, 1992, it was site of the boisterous swan song of their long-running affair. According to reports Browne and Hannah allegedly physically assaulted each other during a violent quarrel here. Though Browne subsequently denied any assault and no charges were filed—though police were called to quell the disturbance—*People* magazine reported that Hannah had suffered bruises, a black eye, a broken finger and other injuries. She took refuge with her close friend John F. Kennedy, Jr., after the breakup with Browne.

(Palisades to Seventh. Right to Montana. Right to Ocean. Left to the Oceana Apartments on your left, site of:)

849 Ocean Avenue, Stan Laurel death site

Arthur Stanley Jefferson Laurel was born in the tiny English village of Ulverson in 1890 into a longtime theater family. Young Stan followed the family tradition working in the circus, on vaudeville, and in London burlesque shows. After spending several years as Charlie Chaplin's understudy in London music halls, in 1910 the renamed Stan Laurel toured the United States with the Fred Karno Vaudeville Troupe alongside his pal Chaplin. It was during that time that Laurel perfected his distinctive walk by wearing huge oversized shoes with the heels removed.

Although Hal Roach has gotten credit for discovering Laurel and Hardy, it was Stan who actually discovered Ollie. Prior to meeting Laurel, Hardy's movie roles were primarily as movie "heavies," but when Stan envisioned a comedy twosome in 1922, he hired Oliver as his partner and gave him a three-year contract. By the time the original deal ended, the duo was hugely popular, and both comics signed huge contracts directly with Roach. Immortalized in 105 Roach comedies, Laurel and Hardy actually made more movies apart than together: Hardy made 215 films without Stan and Laurel made 76 without Oliver. But their Hal Roach comedies—at one time filmed in almost a dozen different languages—are movie legend.

After a 1955 diabetic stroke, Laurel retired here to the Oceana Apartments with his last wife Ida, a rather quiet end to a tumultuous personal life. He had countless extramarital affairs, as he was almost incapable of resisting a woman with an accent. He married eight times and was sued by a ninth who wanted to become a legal rather than common-law wife. Virginia Rogers was number two, three and seven, and last wife Ida was number four and eight. After Hardy's 1957 death, Laurel refused interviews for the rest of his life, and after several

The legendary Stan Laurel died quietly at his home here in the Oceana Apartments.

strokes, on February 23, 1965, he began failing rapidly. Laurel said to his nurse, "I'd rather be skiing than doing this." His nurse asked, "Oh, Mr. Laurel, do you ski?" and he replied, "No, but better be doing that than having these needles stuck into me." With his typically perfect timing, as if on cue he died that very instant. He was 65, the same age as Oliver Hardy when Hardy had died in 1957. At his funeral, the mortuary played the Laurel and Hardy theme song in the background for the mourners.

(Continue on Ocean past the entrance to the Pacific Coast Highway and Santa Monica [10] Freeway as it winds along the beach and entrances to several beachfront hotels and parking lots and becomes Barnard. The next stop is on Fraser Avenue, which is just one block before the intersection with Ocean Park Drive. However, you will have to turn around at Ocean Park and return back

[northbound] on Barnard to enter Fraser, as southbound entrance is prohibited by a median. Enter Fraser from Barnard, and proceed to the third house on the left at:)

139 Fraser Avenue, Margaux Hemingway death site

Actress and model Margaux Hemingway was the granddaughter of Ernest Hemingway, who had committed suicide at his Idaho home when he was in his early sixties. The older sister of actress Mariel Hemingway, Margaux first gained public notice as a teenaged model and cover girl who earned a $1,000,000 contract to promote the Faberge perfume "Babe" in 1975. She made her movie debut in the 1976 hit *Lipstick* as a rape victim stalking her attacker, but she never became as celebrated an actress as her sister. Her only other credits were low-budget 1980s films like *Over the Brooklyn Bridge, Killer Fish, Mass in C Minor, They Call Me Bruce?,*

Margaux Hemingway overdosed in her second-floor apartment at the rear of this lovely Santa Monica cottage, just a block from the beach.

and *Inner Sanctum*. In 1990, she attempted to revive her stalled movie career by posing nude in *Playboy*, but was not successful.

Hemingway's career was regularly disrupted by ongoing problems with eating disorders and alcoholism, culminating with a prolonged stay at the Betty Ford Center in 1988. After living in Idaho for several years she had returned to L.A. just three weeks before her death, renting the second-floor studio apartment on a tree-lined street a half block from the beach, in a cute pink and burgundy house with the white picket fence. The entrance is visible at the back of the house on the driveway.

On July 1, 1996, friends who had been unable to reach her by phone used a ladder to look into a window, and saw Hemingway dead on the floor. She was 41 years old, and had been dead for several days from what the coroner described as acute Phenobarbital intoxication.

The actress' death continued a bizarre legacy of suicide in the Hemingway family. Her paternal great-grandfather committed suicide in the 1920s, followed by her famous grandfather's death in the 1960s. Ernest Hemingway's sister killed herself in the late 1960s, and another brother followed suit in the late 1980s. Margaux's suicide came just a day before the thirty-fifth anniversary of the suicide of her father.

(Frazer to Nielsen Way. Right and you can return to a beachfront drive by proceeding right on Ocean Park back to Barnard, and returning northbound on Barnard. Continue on Barnard and or Ocean to any of the several entrances to the Pacific Coast Highway for a ride along the beach. The garage entrances to the beachfront homes located along Palisades Beach [Thalberg at 707, Fairbanks at 705, Lawford/JFK at 625] can each be seen, but as previously mentioned, they are better viewed from above on Ocean Avenue. Return to the

Pacific Coast Highway, passing these three locations proceeding to 415 Palisades Beach Road:)

You can view all that remains of the incredible beachfront "cottage" built in 1928 by William Randolph Hearst for his lover Marion Davies. The site of hundreds of famous Hearst-Davies' parties, her "Ocean House" originally boasted 125 rooms, 55 bathrooms, 40 fireplaces, and featured an Olympic-sized swimming pool hand cut from Italian marble that sat right on the beach. The interior was stuffed with priceless 15th and 16th century European antiquities. The main building was razed in 1960, leaving only the servants' quarters and a guest house, which are now used as a private swim club. The still-large building remaining nonetheless represents less than one-tenth of the original house. The handwrought marble columns and portico that once encircled the front door at Marion's fabulous dream house can still be seen today gracing a lovely fountain at Little Santa Monica Boulevard in Beverly Hills, where they were moved when the house was torn down.

(PCH to:)

321 Palisades Beach Road, Marlene Dietrich–Mercedes de Acosta love-nest

After moving to Hollywood in 1929 to work for RKO studios, New York screenwriter Mercedes de Acosta shared a Brentwood house with homosexual writer John Colton just down the block from her lover Greta Garbo's home. In 1932, during one of Garbo and de Acosta's numerous breakups during a ten-year union, de Acosta engaged in a short but intense affair with Marlene Dietrich. It was Dietrich who rented this secluded (at the time) Santa Monica beach house from Marion Davies for trysts with de Acosta.

Of their first evening at the beach, de Acosta wrote Dietrich, "Wonderful One,

It is one week today since your naughty hand opened a white rose: Last night was more wonderful and each time I see you it grows more wonderful and exciting." Dietrich and de Acosta remained on-again, off-again lovers throughout the early 1940s.

If you wish to view the beachfront houses from the beach and don't mind a hike, park at one of the beach lots between the Santa Monica Pier and here, and you can walk the beach. It's a good idea to have a feeling for where they are located from the text, however.

(Continue on the Pacific Coast Highway to San Vicente. Right to Twentieth. Right to:)

517 Twentieth Street, Royal Dano death site

Royal Dano's gaunt good looks earned him hundreds of character roles during a 40-year career, most often cast in western roles and usually the villain. He starred in CBS' pioneering 1950s television show *Omnibus* portraying Abraham Lincoln, and co-starred in over 125 films. Some of his better-known movies include *Carrie* (1952), *The Adventures of Huckleberry Finn* (1960), and *The Outlaw Josey Wales* (1976) with Clint Eastwood. His final screen appearance was in the 1990 sci-fi laugher *Spaced Invaders,* cast as a bumbling farmer battling Martian invaders. Dano succumbed to pulmonary fibrosis at his Santa Monica home here on May 15, 1994, at 71.

(Twentieth to:)

1338 20th Street, Evelyn Nesbit Thaw death site

On January 17, 1967, a frail elderly woman died at the Casa Contenta retirement home of heart disease. The anonymous 81-year-old died in obscurity, though 50 years earlier Evelyn Nesbit was a central character in the biggest sex scandal of the 20th century. Evelyn was then a 16-year-old

Broadway chorus girl when she met 48-year-old playboy Stanford White in 1901. He was a renowned architect with a portfolio including churches, New York University's Romanesque campus, Pennsylvania Station, and his crown jewel Madison Square Garden. When the couple met she was a teenage virgin so beautiful that local photographers often posed her as an angel in magazine and newspaper ads. The two embarked on a clandestine three-year affair, meeting at his offices, his beachfront mansion or in one of his hotels, and were often seen in public together.

The relationship would have remained a secret had Nesbit not married railroad heir Harry Thaw after the affair ended, and for some reason told the psychotic millionaire about White. Thaw soon became obsessed with the thought that his wife had been seduced by White and had become "damaged goods." Adding to Thaw's venom, White had blackballed him from several exclusive private clubs in the years earlier. When Thaw and his new bride happened upon White at the rooftop restaurant at Madison Square Garden in 1904, he took his revenge. Thaw walked up to the unsuspecting White, calmly shot him three times in the forehead, walked back to his table and calmly ate lunch while he waited for the police to arrive. During Thaw's trials, the White-Nesbit sexcapades became front-page news the world over.

For 20 years Thaw shuffled through numerous insane asylums while his mother engineered several appeals, and during which time Nesbit divorced him. She had a minor movie career but her once-extraordinary looks vanished almost overnight during the early 1920s. The now-homely star was forced into guest appearances with touring vaudeville dancers, drawing crowds wanting a quick 25-cent look at the lead player in the world-renowned scandal.

One such visitor was writer Orson Welles, who came upon Nesbit "performing" in a seedy Jersey nightclub in 1938. Their alcohol-laced encounter was the basis for one of the opening scenes in his classic *Citizen Kane* (1939), when a newspaper reporter interviews a now-elderly Susan Kane in a sleazy bar in Atlantic City. By the mid 1940s Nesbit had faded into total anonymity. Her story was the basis for the 1955 movie *The Girl on the Red Velvet Swing*, so-named for a well-told story of a naked Nesbit riding a red-velvet swing that hung over the grand piano in White's New York penthouse.

For the last 20 years of her life Nesbit shared a Brentwood home with her son Russell at 654 Walther Way (near the Haines-Shields site), and shortly before she died told her last interviewer, "Stanny was lucky, he died. I lived." Her Holy Cross Cemetery marker simply reads "Mother, Evelyn Florence Nesbit."

(Twentieth to Wilshire. Left to:)

2222 Wilshire Boulevard, Clyde Bruckman suicide site

Clyde Bruckman was an award-winning sports editor for the *Los Angeles Examiner* who was hired in 1917 by his close friend Buster Keaton to write movies. He directed such Keaton classics as *The General* (1927) and *The Cameraman* (1928), and directed Laurel and Hardy's *Leave 'Em Laughing* (1928), Harold Lloyd's *The Freshman* (1925) and W.C. Fields' *The Fatal Glass of Beer* (1933) and *The Man on a Flying Trapeze* (1934).

A violent alcohol problem ended his once-bright career and reduced Bruckman to poverty, and on January 4, 1955, the 60-year-old Bruckman was turned down for a job writing for The Three Stooges by old friend director Jules White. He drove over to pal Keaton's home and borrowed a .45 caliber pistol, telling Keaton he was going hunting. Later that day Bruckman left a typed note for his wife at their modest home at 934 6th in Santa Monica and went to Bess Eiler's Wilshire Café. Without paying his 50-cent dinner tab—he had no money in his pockets—Bruckman quietly walked to the men's room and shot himself in the head. Some stories place the suicide in a phone booth outside the restaurant, but they are unsubstantiated.

Tour 14: San Fernando Valley

Begin Tour 14 at 11917 Vose Street in North Hollywood, just east of the Hollywood (170) Freeway, between Laurel Canyon Boulevard and Lankershim, and just north of Vanowen Boulevard, at:

11917 Vose Street, Frank Zappa death site

Baltimore-born Frank Zappa started as a drummer in high school garage bands and was thrown off his high school band for smoking while he marched. His later garage band The Mothers of Invention achieved huge cult status during the 1970s with such albums as *Lumpy Gravy, Burnt Weeny Sandwich,* and *Weasels Ripped My Flesh.* He once called his music "sonic mutilations," and his early 1980s send-up "Valley Girl," recorded along with daughter Moon Unit, introduced the entire country to catch phrases like "fer shur" and "gag me with a spoon." He later won a 1987 Grammy for his more mainstream album *Jazz from Hell.*

On December 4, 1993, he lost a long battle with prostate cancer and died in his maze-like home here that he once described as "early Rumpelstiltskin." His children Moon Unit, Dweezil, Ahmet and Diva were at his side. He was 52 years of age.

(Vose east to Lankershim, right [south] bearing right on Colfax Avenue at Victory-Lankersham Boulevard intersection/fork. Continue south on Colfax past Oxnard Street to Burbank Boulevard left several blocks to Beck, right to the intersection with Killion. The modest duplex on your right at the corner is:)

11537 Killion Drive, Herve Villechaize suicide

Herve Villechaize will always be remembered as "Tattoo" on the 1980s hit television series *Fantasy Island,* standing next to Ricardo Montalban in a tiny white tuxedo hollering "Boss, de plane, de plane!" from the roof. But after he was fired during a contract holdout after the show's third season, he was unable to find work except in regional television commercials. He was also plagued by health problems, and on September 4, 1993, the diminutive star committed suicide at his home here.

At 3:00 A.M. Villechaize sat on the back porch of his home and tried to shoot himself in the chest with a pistol, recording the event on a portable tape deck. Incredibly, the first shot missed and blew out the picture window at the rear of the house. Villechaize can be heard on the recording muttering, "Oh, shit…" before firing a second shot into his heart. He died minutes later in his wife's arms.

During the 1980s and early 1990s his personal problems were regular tabloid fodder, and Villechaize's problems on the *Island* set were well-known. As his life spiraled out of control, he began carrying guns onto the

"Tattoo" shot himself to death on the back porch of this modest San Fernando Valley duplex.

set, and hung a sign on his dressing trailer proclaiming himself "The Sex Doctor." When he was inside the sign was turned to read, "The Doctor is IN." After his dismissal from the series, one fascinating tabloid story described Tattoo's fondness for walking into his wife's shower covered head to tiny toe with chocolate pudding.

(Return to Burbank Boulevard. Right one block past Cahuenga to Auckland. Right to end of the block just before Chandler Boulevard. to:)

5421 Auckland Avenue, Oliver Hardy death site

The son of a wealthy Georgia land-owner, Oliver Hardy began his career singing and dancing on Mississippi River show-boats, and appearing in local vaudeville companies during vacations from his law studies at the University of Georgia. When the Lubin Company filmed in Atlanta in 1913, the 300-pound singer was hired, and he appeared in several comic shorts before join-ing the Pathé Film Company in 1915, then headquartered in Ithaca, New York. Between 1918 and 1925 he worked for Vitagraph Films in New York City.

Hardy first worked with Stan Laurel in 1919, but it wasn't until Hardy had a role in a 1926 comedy directed by Laurel that Laurel hired Hardy to be his partner. The Laurel and Hardy career spanned some 150 films, and at one time their later Hal Roach comedies were released in English, Spanish, German, French, Danish, Italian, and Chinese to satisfy their worldwide audience.

Known as "Babe" to family and friends, Hardy had continual health troubles that eventually led to a heart attack and stroke suffered on September 12, 1956. The once-graceful comic was left paralyzed and un-able to speak for the remaining year of his life. Because he needed constant nursing care, Hardy and his wife Lucille—who had been a script girl on his movies prior to their 1940 marriage—moved in here, a home that Oliver had earlier bought for his mother-in-law. He died on the morning of August 7, 1957, and though the pair were not close

Probably the most famous face in comedy history, Oliver Hardy died at this modest bungalow that he purchased for his mother-in-law years earlier.

offscreen, a tearful Stan Laurel was the last visitor at Hardy's bedside.

(Auckland to end of block at Chandler Boulevard. Right one block to Cahuenga. Left to intersection of Magnolia. Left three blocks to Biloxi Avenue. Right to end of block at Otsego Street to house on the corner to your right at:)

5103 Biloxi Avenue, Joe Besser death site

Columbia contract player Joe Besser starred in dozens of comedies including *Hey, Rookie!* (1944), *Talk About a Lady* (1945), and *Abbott and Costello Meet the Keystone Cops* (1955) before being tapped as a third of The Three Stooges after Shemp Howard's 1955 death. He appeared in 20 Three Stooges features from 1956 to 1958, leaving after Columbia surprisingly fired them after 25 successful years. He starred on *The Joey Bishop Show* from 1962 to 1969 and made hundreds of sitcom appearances through the 1970s.

Besser died here on March 1, 1988, of heart failure at the age of 80.

You will pass nearby Solomon "Shemp" Horowitz' home at 10522 Riverside (just east of Cahuenga Boulevard) traveling to the next stop. It was Shemp and not younger brother Jerry ("Curly") who was the original third Stooge. In 1922 comic Ted Healy hired Shemp and his older brother Moe to work with Larry Fine and become "Ted Healy's Stooges." When the trio was hired to do movies in 1933 Shemp left to go solo and was replaced by his younger brother Jerry, known to all as "Curly." Before rejoining the trio in 1946 after a stroke felled Curly, Shemp starred in 100 films of his own and headlined the *Shemp Howard Show*.

He was a family man who loved the local boxing matches, and returning from a Hollywood fight with friend Al Winston on November 22, 1955, Shemp was sitting in a cab enjoying a cigar. Winston noticed Howard leaning over spilling ashes on his leg and told him, "Hey Shemp, sit up straight, you're burning my suit." Shemp didn't respond.

Joe Besser, replacing Shemp Howard as the last "Third Stooge," died at his beloved Valley home here in 1988.

With one of his beloved cigars clenched in his mouth, he had suffered a heart attack at the age of 60.

(Right on Biloxi in front of Besser house to Cahuenga. Left/south a short distance to:)

5114½ Cahuenga Boulevard, Helen Walker death site

Massachusetts-born Helen Walker began in regional theater and as a teenager starred on Broadway in the late 1930s. Discovered in the Broadway production of *Jason*, she was hired by Paramount and starred with Alan Ladd in 1942's *Cute Eyes*. The lovely actress skyrocketed to fame with starring roles in such wartime efforts as *The Good Fellows* (1943) and *Abroad with Two Yanks* (1944), but at the height of her popularity was involved in a car accident that ended her career.

Returning from a Palm Springs New Year's Eve party in 1946, a soldier that she had picked up hitchhiking was killed and Walker seriously injured when she was involved in a car accident on a lonely stretch of desert highway. Although she was absolved of blame, her near-fatal injuries and highly publicized lawsuits left her with little money and no more starring roles. Although she appeared in small roles in late 1940s to early 1950s films like *Duffy's Tavern* (1944), *Call Northside 777* (1948) and *My Dear Secretary* (1952), by the time of her final role in 1955's *The Big Combo* her meteoric career was over at the young age of 34. A 1960 house fire destroyed all of her belongings, and only a benefit arranged by Hugh O'Brian, Dinah Shore and Ruth Roman kept Walker afloat.

Just after the fire, the ill-fated actress contracted throat cancer, and after a seven-year battle she died at her rented home here on March 10, 1968, at the age of 47. After so much bad luck it almost seemed a merciful end to a sad life.

(Continue south on Cahuenga just past the Ventura [101] Freeway to Riverside. Right to Cartwright. Left to:)

4445 Cartwright Avenue, Perc Westmore death site

Born Percival Harry Westmore in London, "Perc" came to the United States just after World War I and began working in the family's popular Hollywood hair salon, concentrating on makeup. By the 1940s an appointment at his "House of Westmore" was the most sought-after ticket in Hollywood, and Perc became the chief makeup man for Warner Bros. Most of the top stars refused to work unless he was present. Success didn't bring happiness though, as several unsuccessful suicide attempts were each hidden by studio fixers. On September 30, 1970, the 65-year-old retiree suffered a fatal heart attack on the front lawn of his small Valley home.

(Continue on Cartwright to end of block at Moorpark. Right a block to Lankersham. Right on Lankersham to Camarillo. Left and proceed under freeway as Camarillo becomes Riverside Drive again. Continue a block past the freeway to Farmdale. Left to:)

4729 Farmdale Street, Don "Red" Barry shooting death house

Rugged character actor Don "Red" Barry was discovered by John Wayne and Mickey Rooney playing in L.A. for a Texas all-star football team. He soon became a top cowboy star, with a career lasting from 1936 into the 1970s. Born Donald Michael Barry de Acosta, he was best remembered as the star of the 1940s serial *The Adventures of Red Ryder,* but also appeared in dozens of movies including *Rio Lobo* (1970), *The Crowd Roars* (1937), and 13 *Jesse James* movies from 1935 to 1950. The handsome star was also a renowned ladies' man, with well-publicized affairs with actresses Joan Crawford, Linda Darnell, Susan Hayward, Lana Turner, and Jil Jarmyn. His love life was a busy one—at one point Jarmyn sued Hayward over a fistfight that began when Jarmyn discovered

Barry and Hayward in bed on November 4, 1955.

Barry shared his home with actress-wife Peggy Stewart, and on the afternoon of July 17, 1980, the disturbed 68-year-old was shot to death by police during an altercation inside. They were called when he became enraged during a dispute with his wife, and since he forced and cajoled police into shooting him, the death was ruled a suicide.

(Reverse on Farmdale or go around the block and back to Riverside. Left to Colfax. Left to Moorpark. Left two blocks to Irvine. Right to:)

4318 Irvine Avenue, Peg Shannon death site

Peg Shannon was a Ziegfeld Follies and Broadway star who was brought to Hollywood in 1931 by MGM to replace Clara Bow as the "IT Girl." She starred in over 30 films including *This Reckless Age* (1932), *Ellis Island* (1935), *The Woman* (1938), and *The Adventures of Jane Arden* (1938), but when real superstardom didn't materialize and her career stalled due to her own erratic behavior, she retreated to alcohol and eventual obscurity.

On May 11, 1941, she was found dead in the kitchen of her San Fernando Valley home here, sitting at the table with a burnt cigarette in her mouth, literally having drunk herself to death at 32. Her despondent husband of only ten months sat in the same chair three weeks later and shot himself in the head, leaving a note that said, "I am very much in love with my wife, Peggy Shannon. In this spot she passed away, so in reverence to her, you will find me in the same spot."

(Continue on Irvine to Valley Spring. Right to Colfax. Left to:)

4171-D Colfax Avenue, Vickie Morgan murder site

Gorgeous model Vickie Morgan was bludgeoned to death with a baseball bat in her condo here on July 7, 1983, by her some-time roommate Marvin Pancoast. She had been the longtime mistress of millionaire Alfred Bloomingdale, satisfying his kinky sex needs during a 12-year relationship that lasted until his death in 1982. His widow immediately shut her off, and Morgan sued for $11 million in a 250-page deposition describing all of the erotic stories of Bloomingdale's sex life. Although she had written promises from Bloomingdale to care for her for life the penniless Morgan lost her lawsuit, the judge ruling that their relationship amounted to prostitution and his monetary promises payment for services rendered.

(Continue on Colfax as it dead-ends at Acama Street, go left a block to Troost Street, and go left back to Valley Spring. Right six blocks on Valley Spring to Tujunga. Right on Tujunga to the large intersection at Ventura Boulevard. Right to Radford. Right over the L.A. River to Valleyheart Drive. Left to Agnes. Right to:)

4312 Agnes Avenue, Aneta Corsaut death site

Lovely Aneta Corsaut starred with Steve McQueen in the 1958 sci-fi thriller *The Blob* and had hundreds of movie and television roles. But Corsaut is best known for her long-running role as schoolteacher Helen Crump, Andy's girlfriend on the 1950s and 1960s television series *The Andy Griffith Show*. Corsaut died at her home here on November 6, 1995, from heart ailments at the age of 62.

(Agnes to Woodbridge. Left to Laurel Canyon. Right past the Ventura [101] Freeway to Hesby. Left to second house on your left at:)

12116 Hesby Street, Ida Lupino death site

Ida Lupino was born into an English family with a 200-year acting tradition, debuted on the London stage at the age of 15 and starred in 60 movies during a 40-year career. Calling herself "the poor man's Bette

Ida Lupino, one of the first female Hollywood power brokers, died at her home here in 1995.

Davis," the headstrong Lupino was Holly-wood's first female director. Her roles mirrored her personality, portraying strong women in such films as *They Drive by Night* (1940) with Bogart and Raft, *High Sierra* (1941) with Bogart, and *Out of the Fog* (1941) with John Garfield.

The independent Lupino started her own production company, tackling subjects not wanted by Hollywood, like unplanned pregnancy in *Not Wanted* (1949), polio in *Never Fear* (1950), and bigamy in *The Bigamist* (1953). Her work opened doors for generations of female writers and directors that followed. Lupino suffered a fatal stroke during a long battle with colon cancer and died here on August 3, 1995, at the age of 77. Lupino's first Hollywood friend was Thelma Todd, who was murdered in December 1935 after attending a party at the Trocadero Restaurant hosted by Ida's famous father Stanley Lupino.

(Continue on Hesby several blocks to end, and proceed right a short block to Ot-sego Street. Left on Otsego to Whitsett. Left on Whitsett under the Ventura [101] Freeway three blocks to Sarah

Street. Left one block on Sarah Street to the intersection of Rhodes Avenue at:)

12354 Sarah Street, Nicholas Colasanto death site

Rhode Island–born Nicholas Colasanto enjoyed a 30-year stage and movie career, but achieved international fame playing the cheerful but dimwitted "Coach" on the 1980s television hit *Cheers*. His hilarious portrayal of the bumbling but lovable bartender helped make the show the most popular on television and earned Colasanto yearly Emmy nominations. The 61-year-old suffered a fatal heart attack at his home here on February 12, 1985, at the height of the show's— and his—popularity.

(Sarah around block back to Whitsett. Right a few blocks to Kling. Left to Teesdale. Right to:)

4709 Teesdale Avenue, Sharon Gless home siege site

This home was used as a home and office by *Cagney and Lacey* star Sharon Gless.

"Coach" of *Cheers* **fame died here.**

On March 30, 1990, an obsessed lesbian fan arrived here and announced to Gless' publicist that she had a rifle and was looking for Gless. Joni Leigh Penn held the assistant hostage for a full day while she described to SWAT team negotiators her plans for a murder-suicide with Gless. The obsessed stalker eventually surrendered and was arrested.

The nearby Studio City Golf Center on Whitsett is a favorite of the stars and is the only golf practice range within miles. You can usually find Sylvester Stallone or any one of dozens of other celebrities hitting balls there. Also nearby at 12750 Hortense is the former home of Lon Chaney, Jr.

(Continue on Kling to Coldwater Canyon. Right past the freeway to Chandler. Right several blocks to Goodland. Right to:)

5309 Goodland Avenue, Dorothy Lamour home

Mary Leta Dorothy Slaton was born in the charity ward of a New Orleans hospital and began her showbiz career singing with bandleader Herbie Kay during the 1930s. Renamed Dorothy Lamour, she made over 60 motion pictures during a 50-year career, but is most known as Bob Hope and Bing Crosby's sultry, sarong-wearing sidekick in half a dozen *Road* pictures the trio made during the 1940s. She first wore her trademark wraparound dress in her debut movie role in 1936's *Jungle Princess,* and she played similar roles in her next two films, John Ford's *The Hurricane* (1937) and *Beyond the Blue Horizon* (1938).

Lamour became a comedy star trooping around the world with Hope and Crosby, playing the exotic straight-woman to Hope's playboy character and Crosby's character as the crooning pal begging for her attention. Their first effort was *Road to Singapore* (1940), and the trio followed with *Road to Zanzibar* (1941), *Road to Utopia* (1945), *Road to Rio* (1948), and *Road to Hong Kong,* a 1962 remake widely regarded as Lamour's only movie flop.

Although best known for her comedy persona, Lamour also starred in dozens of plays and movie dramas, including *Johnny Apollo* (1940), *A Medal for Benny* (1945), *The Greatest Show on Earth* (1952), and her final movie role as an elderly murder victim in *Creepshow 2* (1987). Quietly retired at her home here, Lamour suffered a fatal heart attack on September 21, 1996, dying soon afterward at a nearby hospital. She was 81 years old.

(Reverse to Chandler. Right and reverse direction by making a U-turn through the bridle path running down the middle of Chandler. Proceed west on Chandler past Fulton and again reverse at the turnaround in the bridle path. Just before the intersection with Fulton note the yellow vine-covered cottage across from Nagle at:)

13330 Chandler Boulevard, Richard Webb suicide site

Richard Webb, former star of the 1950s television serial *Captain Midnight,* committed suicide in his home here on June 10, 1993. Despondent over failing health, the 77-year-old actor shot himself to death. Although he starred in 75 films and 200 television shows, he was forever known for his "Captain Midnight" serial role that ran from 1954 to 1958. The show spawned hundreds of commercial tie-ins, from Captain Midnight decoder rings to dinner plates, and his fan club was the biggest in the world.

(Proceed right on Fulton to:)

4524 Fulton Street, Jerome "Curly" Howard home

Jerome Lester Howard's last home was at 4524 Fulton, demolished by a 1990s earthquake. Called "Babe" as a child, when he joined brother Moe's comedy trio, he shaved his head and mustache and became "Curly." His alcohol problems and married life weren't as funny as his movies: a 1935 marriage was annulled, a second ended in 1940 after two years, and a third in 1946 lasted three months. Each divorce cost him a large chunk of his once-huge fortune.

By 1946 his personal life caught up with him, and on May 6, while filming their ninety-seventh comedy—*Half Wits Holiday*—he had a stroke that left him unable to walk or talk. He was replaced by older brother Shemp. During his recovery Curly met Valerie New-man, a caring and loving partner who nursed him for the rest of his life. His first post-stroke role was in *Hold That Lion* (1947), the only time all three Howard brothers—Moe, Shemp, and Curly—appeared together on film. After a second stroke in 1949, his health slowly declined until a cerebral hemorrhage killed him at home on January 18, 1952. Curly was only 48 years old.

(Fulton to Ventura. Left a block to Long-ridge. Right to:)

4124 Longridge Avenue, Lou Costello, Jr., accidental death

Like "Curly" Howard, Louis Francis Cristillo's life wasn't as funny offscreen as it was on. Better known as Lou Costello, the larger half of Abbott and Costello lived in this home for over 20 years. During the 1940s and 1950s Costello would walk outside and sign autographs for the tourist buses that stopped in front of the house every hour on the hour. But the house was the site of a personal tragedy that many felt actually "killed" the rotund Costello. On Novem-ber 4, 1943, Costello's adored 2-year-old son Lou Jr. died when he somehow got out of his playpen next to the backyard pool, fell into the pool and drowned.

When he left the house that afternoon to tape his weekly radio show, Lou promised "Butch" that he would say "hello" during the show. Even after being told of the accident before going on the air, the anguished Costello somehow went ahead with the live taping, saying a tearful "good-night" to

Butch as it ended. The audience was unaware of the tragedy, and gave Costello a huge stand-ing ovation for what they thought was just part of the performance. The heartbroken comic was never the same after his son's death, and the last years of his life were spent in bitter feuds with the IRS and with his former best friend Bud Abbott. Both feuds continuing until his March 3, 1959, death.

(Longridge to Valley Vista; catty-corner across to the right is:)

4031 Longridge Avenue, William Conrad death site

Rotund William Conrad was the orig-inal voice of Marshall Dillon on the 1940s *Gunsmoke* radio series, and starred in *East Side, West Side* (1948) and *The Naked Jungle* (1954). His greatest acclaim, however, came from his two television series, *Cannon*, which ran from 1971 to 1976, and *Jake and the Fatman*, which ran from 1987 to 1993. His booming voice was perfectly suited for voiceover work, and Conrad provided voices for dozens of Disney movie characters and for the television series *The Fugitive*. He suffered a fatal heart attack at his home here on February 11, 1994, and died soon after at the age of 73.

John Wayne rented the lovely home after his 1951 divorce from his eccentric sec-ond wife Esperanza Baur Diaz Ceballos, whose nickname was "Chata." Chata was a bit actress in the Mexican movie industry, and it was rumored that she was a high-priced Mexico City call girl when she met Wayne in 1941. The couple was introduced by actor Ray Milland, who "dated" Chata whenever he was in Mexico. After divorcing his first wife, Wayne married the unstable Chata in 1943, but after eight years of her al-cohol-related antics and her frightful tem-per, Wayne endured a difficult and very pub-lic divorce from the hot-tempered Mexican beauty. He moved back to his nearby En-cino mansion after the proceedings. He had to wait for some repairs, since Chata had

This longtime Valley estate of legendary John Wayne was almost burned to the ground by one of his angry ex-wives during a particularly ugly divorce.

tried to burn the house to the ground in his absence.

(Longridge to:)

3737 Longridge Avenue, Susan Hayward–Jess Barker assault

Oscar-winner Susan Hayward and her actor-husband Jess Barker moved here on Christmas Eve 1946. The fairy-tale marriage reached an ugly climax on the night of July 16, 1953, when a drunken Barker assaulted Hayward in a vicious beating that began inside the house and spilled into the driveway as she tried to flee. Than he dragged her into the backyard and tried to drown her in the pool.

Their divorce turned into a bitter two-year custody battle over the couple's twins, which led a distraught Hayward to attempt suicide here on April 26, 1955. She took a massive overdose of sleeping pills, but police who had been alerted by her mother arrived at the last minute and saved her life. Hayward than moved two doors down the street to 3801.

(Reverse to Valley Vista. Left past Woodman to Hollyline. Left up the hill to immediate left on Witzel on up the hill onto Sherwood to:)

3862 Sherwood Place, Greenberger home, Roy Radin murder

In 1983 Laney Jacobs lived here, and appeared to her neighbors as just another Valley divorcée. But, unbelievably, she was in fact L.A.'s biggest drug dealer, working for Colombian cocaine lord Carlos Lederer. She was later implicated in the 1983 murder of producer Roy Radin, who was producing the movie *Cotton Club* at the time his bullet-riddled body was found in a remote central coast canyon on May 13, 1983. Jacobs ordered the murder, convinced that Radin was behind the theft of $100,000 and a kilo of cocaine from a safe hidden in her garage. To her chagrin, she later discovered that a lowly drug courier was the culprit and that Radin had nothing to do with it. Escaping incognito to Florida just before she was to be arrested for the Radin murder, she was later implicated in the mysterious murder of the wealthy surgeon she had married there. The ex–Mrs. Greenberger is presently in prison in California.

(Reverse on Sherwood and Witzel to Valley Vista. Left to Beverly Glen. Left to first left on Millbrook to:)

14341 Millbrook Drive, Sorrell Booke death site

Sorrell Booke received classical theater training at the Yale School of Drama and starred on Broadway for over 20 years. Booke had dozens of movie roles before leaping to stardom as Sheriff Jefferson Davis "Boss" Hogg on the 1980s television sitcom *The Dukes of Hazzard*. After *Dukes* left the air, Booke traveled the country to hundreds of auto shows yearly alongside the "General Lee" car from the series.

Booke spent years restoring his beloved home here, making auto show appearances whenever additional renovations to the house were needed. After the 64-year-old lost a battle with cancer and died here on February 11, 1994, he was buried wearing his cherished toolbelt. His carpentry crew served as his pallbearers.

(Reverse to Beverly Glen. Right to Valley Vista. Left just past the intersection of Van Nuys Boulevard to the second house on the right at 14527, originally numbered 14511:)

14511 Valley Vista Boulevard, reputed Marilyn Monroe home

According to longtime residents, when this Valley Vista home was purchased in the mid–1960s it was discovered that it was owned by Paramount Studios, and borrowed at one time by Marilyn Monroe. Neighbors reportedly told the buyer that while Marilyn lived at the house, she was visited several times by young Massachusetts congressman John Kennedy, who once arrived via a helicopter that landed on a knoll above the home. Letters between the two were allegedly found inside the house, but, unbelievably, they were thrown away. Much of the story is unverifiable but fascinating local lore.

(Actor Barry Sullivan died at his home on nearby Round Valley Road, a secluded site that is surrounded by hedges and not visible from the road. To see the Sullivan site, proceed on Valley Vista a short distance to Madelia Avenue, and go left up the hill to Round Valley Road. Go left on Round Valley— it is a very narrow street so proceed carefully—as it winds around to 14687. To continue, proceed carefully on Round Valley back down the hill to Valley Vista, and go left to the Sullivan site. If you choose not to view the site, continue on Valley Vista to the Doug McClure site as directed after the Sullivan text.)

14687 Round Valley Road, Barry Sullivan death site

Veteran actor Barry Sullivan died at his 14687 Round Valley Road home on June 6, 1994 of heart problems and respiratory failure. The 70-year-old had starred in 40 movies, including the original version of *The Great Gatsby* (1949), *The Bad and the Beautiful* (1952), *Jeopardy* (1953), *Tell Them Willie Boy Is Here* (1969), and *Oh, God!* (1977). He also had hundreds of television roles.

(Proceed west on Valley Vista to Stone Canyon. Left to Stonesboro. Left to:)

14936 Stonesboro Place, Doug Mc-Clure death site

A teenaged Doug McClure worked at a Nevada cattle ranch and competed in weekend rodeos for extra cash. His first role was in the late 1950s television series *Men of Annapolis*, and after starring in *The Overland Trail* he quickly became one of the most popular of the screen cowboys. In 1962 he became Trampas on *The Virginian* and then reprised the role in its spin-off program *The Men from Shiloh*. His movie roles included *The Enemy Below, Shenandoah*, and *Beau Geste*. McClure died of lung cancer in his home here on February 5, 1995, at the age of 59.

(Reverse to Stone Canyon and back to Valley Vista. The site of James Dean's final home is nearby, but the original building is no longer standing. To see the Dean site go right on Valley Vista a short block to Kester, and go left a block to Sutton. Go right on Sutton to the end of the block on the left at 14611 Sutton Drive. If you choose not to view the Dean site, continue on Valley Vista to the Richard Arlen site as directed after the Dean text.)

14611 Sutton Drive, James Dean's final home

James Dean starred in a few 1950s television commercials and only three movies, but his almost unbelievable legacy is rivaled only by that of Marilyn Monroe. Dean rented a small log cabin that once stood behind this home from Nicco Ramanos, the maître d' at Dean's favorite Hollywood hangout, the Villa Capri Restaurant. On the sunny Saturday morning of September 30, 1955, Dean and a pal left here in his new Porsche Spyder to travel to a Santa Barbara car race. Just hours after getting a speeding ticket on the Hollywood Freeway less than five miles from here he was killed when a local teenager ran into the Porsche at a

secluded rural Paso Robles intersection. The 23-year-old actor had done just three movies—*East of Eden* (1954), *Giant* (1955) and *Rebel Without a Cause* (1955)—and, incredibly, at the time of his death just one—*East of Eden*—had been released, but his popularity has been extraordinary.

Dean's crushed and blood-spattered Porsche went through a succession of owners, all of whom had terrible luck while they owned the haunted wreck. Used by police for a short time in safe-driving presentations, it fell off stage supports on three separate occasions, seriously injuring spectators each time. The police sold the car. Traveling on a flatbed to a car show a few months later, it somehow worked free of its moorings and fell to the roadway, causing an accident that left three people dead. Still another man was killed in an accident after adding pieces of the car's engine to his own car. Traveling to California in 1959, the haunted Porsche vanished from a sealed and locked trailer. When the trailer was opened upon its arrival in L.A. it was found to be empty. The mystery car has not been seen since.

(Reverse on Kester to Valley Vista. Go right past Sutton Place just before the intersection with Noble Avenue at:)

15063 Valley Vista Boulevard, Richard Arlen death

Born Van Mattimore in rural Virginia, Richard Arlen ran away from home at 17 to join the Royal Canadian Air Force as a pilot. After World War I, Arlen immigrated to Hollywood, and was working for a film lab when he was hit by a studio delivery truck. After leaving the hospital, Paramount rewarded him with small parts in silent movies. His first major role, in the 1927 silent masterpiece *Wings*, made him a star, and the film won the first Academy Award. It also made stars of the other lead actors: Clara Bow, Buddy Rogers, and newcomer Gary Cooper. In the ensuing 40 years Arlen starred in over 250 movies including *Manhattan Cocktail*

Richard Arlen became a star when he was hit by a studio delivery truck as he crossed a Hollywood street in 1920.

(1928), *Thunderbolt* (1929), *Mutiny in the Arctic* (1941), *Kansas Raiders* (1951), *Warlock* (1959), and *Fort Utah* (1961). On March 29, 1976, he succumbed at his home here after a long battle with emphysema.

(To get to the other side of the San Diego [405] Freeway on Valley Vista, continue to Sepulveda. Right to Ventura. Left under the freeway to Densmore. Left to Woodvale. Right to High Valley Place/High Valley Road intersection. Right on High Valley Place to:)

16133 High Valley Place, Jack Carson death site

John Elmer "Jack" Carson starred in 225 films, usually cast in comedies but also in serious films such as *A Star Is Born* (1937), *Cat on a Hot Tin Roof* (1958), *Bringing up Baby* (1938) with Katharine Hepburn, *Mr. Smith Goes to Washington* (1941) with James Stewart, *Mildred Pierce* (1945) with Barbara

Stanwyck, *Rally 'Round the Flag, Boys!* (1945) and *Strawberry Blonde* (1941). He died in his Valley home here on January 2, 1963, at the age of 62. Coincidentally, Carson died within minutes of his lifelong best friend Dick Powell, who also died of cancer.

(Reverse to High Valley Road. Right on High Valley past Royal Mount Drive as High Valley changes to Clear Valley Drive, and proceed around to the right to Meadowridge Way. Left on Meadowridge to Contera Road. Left on Contera a short way to Sapphire Drive. Left on Sapphire across Hayvenhurst Drive and continue up the hill to the stop sign at Ballina. Go left to continue on Sapphire past the first sign saying "Mandalay 16200" a block to the second sign saying "Mandalay 16300." Right on Mandalay, and notice the large stucco house, the second on the left at:)

16254 Mandalay Drive, Robert Kardashian home

Robert Kardashian was O.J. Simpson's golf buddy, business partner and personal attorney at the time of Nicole Simpson's June 14, 1994, murder. After O.J.'s highly publicized return to L.A. to face a day-long police interrogation the next morning, he somehow escaped the media frenzy at his surrounded Brentwood estate to hide out at this Encino hills home that Kardashian had purchased for his then-fiancée. For several days, Simpson, then-girlfriend Paula Barbieri and an entourage of friends, lawyers, doctors, nurses, psychiatrists and hanger-ons sequestered themselves in the secluded mansion. According to Dominic Dunne's later *Vanity Fair* article, on the evening before Nicole Brown Simpson's funeral the sounds of Simpson-Barbieri lovemaking "woke up the household."

When an arrest warrant for the Brentwood murders was issued on June 17, police

and D.A. staffers were told that Simpson would return from a secret location (unknown to police at the time, the secret location was this house) and surrender to them at noon that day. When he failed to do so he became the most high-profile fugitive in U.S. history.

Incredibly, O.J. and old pal Al Cowlings allegedly eluded the houseful of people, loaded O.J.'s white Bronco with personal possessions, and fled the house for an ill-fated trip to Nicole's grave that became the world-famous "slow-speed chase" over miles of L.A. freeways. The chase, broadcast live over national television, ended when the pair returned to O.J.'s Brentwood mansion, where Simpson surrendered and was arrested. Kardashian reportedly sold this house soon afterward.

Simpson's first Los Angeles–area home is nearby in the Encino hills. It is somewhat difficult to find, and is most easily reached by taking Sepulveda Boulevard south from Ventura Boulevard to Mulholland Drive at

This is reputedly the Encino home where O.J. Simpson hid after sneaking out of a Brentwood mansion surrounded by hundreds of media people; he and pal Al Cowlings left here for the famous "slow-speed chase" down the freeway.

the top of the Encino hills. Right on Mulholland to Elvido, left to Elvill Drive and left to 3005 Elvill, which O.J. Simpson purchased while still a USC football star. Simpson and his high school sweetheart Marguerite purchased the home in 1972 and lived there until 1978 when they moved to the now world-famous Rockingham mansion in Brentwood. They were divorced soon after the move amid vague but repeated stories that O.J. had abused his wife.

According to police, they were called to the Sherman Oaks home numerous times by Marguerite, though no written record of the complaints or calls survives. Subsequent purchaser Gloria Pall reported that when she took possession of the home it was in shambles. According to real-estate agent Pall, every door in the home was kicked in or broken, all of the locks had been broken and all of the appliances cracked and broken. There were also numerous holes in the walls, as if someone had punched a hand through the board.

(Continue around the block on Mandalay to Sapphire. Left the short block to the Ballina Drive intersection. Left on Ballina to Hayvenhurst Drive. Left a short distance on Hayvenhurst Drive to Lanai Road. Right on Lanai up the hill and back down to the stop sign at Hayvenhurst Avenue. Right on Hayvenhurst to Libbet Avenue. Left on Libbet to Petit Avenue. Right on Petit a short distance to Ashley Oaks Road. Left on Ashley Oaks a block to Tara Drive, and right on Tara to:)

4543 Tara Drive, Clark Gable–Carole Lombard home

During the 1930s this lovely house was the centerpiece of the secluded 50-acre ranch owned by director Raoul Walsh, who sold it to Clark Gable after Gable's 1939 marriage to Carole Lombard. Lombard had to pay for the place because he was virtually

broke after a recent divorce. The gated entrance was originally on Petit Drive, and the then-isolated house was surrounded by acres of orchards, fields, barns and trees.

Gable and Lombard shared their beloved ranch until January 16, 1942, when the 34-year-old Lombard was killed in a plane crash while returning from a World War II–bond rally in her home state of Indiana. Wanting to return as quickly as she could, Lombard took the flight against the wishes of her superstitious mother, who became terrified after noticing that the flight number was her "bad luck" number. Gable never got over Lombard's death and for ten years wouldn't allow anyone to enter her bedroom here. On November 4, 1960, he was changing a tire on his favorite tractor here when he was stricken with a massive heart attack, dying soon afterward. Although he remarried twice after Lombard's death, his last wife Kay Spreckles buried him next to Lombard in a private section of Forest Lawn Glendale. Spreckles bore him his only son just four months later.

In the 1980s the Gable ranch was subdivided into the neighborhood now surrounding the home, which remains unchanged to this day. Its most recent owner was deposed bond billionaire Michael Milken.

(Reverse to Petit. Left to Ventura Boulevard. In the 1930s this entire area was covered for miles around by farms and orchards, one of which stood at 17221 Ventura. Now covered with commercial properties—for this reason not worth driving by—it was the site of:)

17221 Ventura Boulevard, Ross Alexander suicide site

In the spring of 1935, actor Ross Alexander married beautiful Broadway star turned movie actress Aleta Alexander and moved into a home at 7347 Woodrow Wilson in the Hollywood Hills. At the time, Aleta was having problems getting her movie career to the level of her former Broadway experience, and for some reason within four months of their wedding he began seeing other women. When the fragile Aleta discovered his secret during the summer of 1935 she committed suicide by shooting herself with one of his hunting rifles on the front lawn of their home.

Thirteen months later, the guilt-ridden Alexander himself committed suicide. Now the site of a retail store, at the time the actor owned a small ranch on the site of 17221 Ventura Boulevard. On a cool fall day in 1936, Alexander climbed into the hayloft of his barn and shot himself in the head with the same rifle his wife had used barely a year earlier.

(From Petit and Ventura, left on Ventura to Balboa. Left a short distance to Rancho. Right to the gated entrance to:)

17100 Rancho Street, Ann Sheridan death site

Clara Sue Sheridan was born in Denton, Texas, and was a student at the North Texas State Teacher's College when her sister sent her picture to a Paramount Studios "Search for Beauty" Contest. She won a two-year contract and was featured in the film *Search for Beauty* (1934), a story appropriately about a small-town girl trying to become a movie star. She went on to become one of MGM's top leading ladies, becoming a star after her 1939 role in *Dodge City* opposite Errol Flynn and Olivia de Havilland. Sheridan starred alongside such stars as Humphrey Bogart, Zachary Scott, Ronald Reagan, Jack Carson, Jack Benny, James Cagney, Cary Grant, and Gary Cooper in the classic films *Behold My Wife* (1935), *San Quentin* (1937), *Letter of Introduction* (1938), *They Drive by Night* (1940), *The Man Who Came to Dinner* (1942), *George Washington Slept Here* (1942), *Edge of Darkness* (1943), *The Unfaithful* (1947), *Stella* (1950), and *The Opposite Sex* (1956).

Several times during her movie career the fiercely independent Sheridan either

went on strike or refused to work if she felt she was not getting good roles or was not making enough money. Such acts of disobedience were unheard of during the days of the studio system when the studios owned all of the rights to their actor-employees, using and trading them at will. Sheridan was known as Hollywood's "Oomph Girl" during World War II, and was married to three actors: Edward Norris, George Brent and Scott McKay. After a career spanning almost 35 years she died of cancer at her home here on January 21, 1967, at the age of 51.

(Continue on Rancho to the intersection with Louise Avenue.)

In 1951 John Wayne purchased the large estate on the left side at the intersection of Louise and Rancho. The lovely colonial home set back from the road on the hillside at 4750 Louise is still standing (for the best view, proceed left/south on Louise and the house is immediately on the left and can be seen through the gates). Wayne purchased the mansion with his second wife "Chata," but when he returned after a two-month movie shoot in Hawaii, he discovered that during his absence his wife had shared the mansion with hotel heir Nicky Hilton, a young L.A. playboy and former husband of Elizabeth Taylor. The Wayne's ensuing divorce was a media extravaganza, and at one point Chata tried to burn this house down. Mike Conner owned the estate at the northeast corner of the same intersection at 4810 Louise, while just up the road at 4875 Louise is a huge estate originally built by Al Jolson and Ruby Keeler, later owned by Don Ameche, and most recently by Kirstie Alley and Parker Stevenson.

(Proceed across Louise on Rancho to:)

17349 Rancho Street, Edward Arnold death site

Edward Arnold was born Gunther Edward Schneider in New York in 1890, and by 10 was touring with the renowned Ben Greet

Shakespearean Players. He joined the Essanay Company in 1915, debuting in the 1916 silent film *The White Alley.* He was one of the most celebrated character actors in movie history, starring in films like *Diamond* (1935), *Sutter's Gold* (1936), *Come and Get It* (1936), *Mr. Smith Goes to Washington* (1939), *Mrs. Parkington* (1944), and *Command Decision* (1948). During World War II he became a leader in the Hollywood war effort, doing hundreds of bond tours and public appearances. On April 26, 1956, the beloved star suffered a fatal cerebral hemorrhage and was found dead in his Encino home here at the age of 66.

When Arnold lived here during the 1950s the Valley was still largely unpopulated, covered by thousands of acres of farmland, orchards, and fruit groves. The quiet area drew numerous Hollywood luminaries such as Gable and Lombard, Lucille Ball and Desi Arnaz, Barbara Stanwyck, Harpo Marx and dozens of other stars who purchased the then-secluded ranch properties.

Nearby Rancho Drive residents include rocker David Crosby at 17351, Dana Carvey at 17333, and Smokey Robinson at 17085.

(Continue on Rancho to Encino Avenue. Right on Encino across Ventura Boulevard a short distance to the intersection with Embassy Drive. The rustic cottage-style mansion set behind the trees on your left is:)

5065 Encino Avenue, Phil Hartman murder-suicide site

Phil Hartman was born in Canada but raised in Connecticut and in Southern California, where he was a high school class clown doing imitations of John Wayne, Jack Benny and Lyndon Johnson. He studied graphic design in college, and after several years of doing album cover–art for rock bands, in 1975 he began appearing in local clubs and with the L.A.–based comedy troupe The Groundlings. He collaborated

This rustic cottage-style mansion was comic Phil Hartman's dream home—his drug-addicted wife murdered him in their second-floor bedroom.

with fellow member Pee Wee Herman on Herman's *Pee-wee's Big Adventure,* and in 1986 joined the cast of television's *Saturday Night Live.* Hartman was famous for his dead-on impersonations of almost 75 famous faces including Frank Sinatra, Jimmy Stewart, Ed McMahon, Bill Clinton, and Phil Donahue. In 1995 he joined the cast of the weekly sitcom *NewsRadio,* playing the egotistical anchorman Bill McNeal, and appeared in such movies as *House Guest, Blind Date, The Coneheads, Sgt. Bilko, Three Amigos,* and *Jingle All the Way* with Arnold Schwarzenegger.

Like scores of his fellow comedians Hartman's private life was not so funny. His ten-year marriage to 40-year-old wife Brynn was marked by frequent fights and several separations, and it was rumored that his wife was fighting a losing battle with drugs. She was reportedly to have entered a rehab clinic the first week of June 1998, but on the evening of May 28, 1998, after allegedly informing his wife that he was considering ending the stormy marriage, he went to bed in the couple's lovely mansion here. He never woke up.

At 6:20 police received a 911 call from the Hartman home here, placed by a male acquaintance of Brynn Hartman's, telling them that Hartman had been murdered by his wife. When police arrived and began removing the couple's two young children from the home, Brynn locked herself in the bedroom and put a bullet into her own head. She was found lying atop Hartman, who had been killed with several gunshots to the head while he slept sometime the previous night. He was 49 years old.

(Reverse to Ventura. Right past White Oak Avenue to Avenida Hacienda. Left on Avenida Hacienda to the end of the block at Tarzana Drive, and notice the tree-covered property above, the site of:)

18230 Tarzana Drive, Edgar Rice Burroughs "Tarzana" estate site

During the early 1900s, "Tarzan" creator Edgar Rice Burroughs used the millions of dollars earned from his amazingly successful

Once the centerpiece of an estate covering tens of thousands of acres, writer Edgar Rice Burroughs' huge mansion stood at the top of the hills among the trees. The gatehouse remains.

book character that spawned movies, comics, and hundreds of commercial tie-ins to purchase tens of thousands of acres of valley real estate in this area. He lived in a massive estate that stood at the top of the hillside in front of this intersection, on a property covering 15 tree-covered acres. He named his ornate grounds "Tarzana."

Today, all that remains of the Burroughs estate are the neglected ruins of the pool area amid acres of weed-infested lily ponds and gardens just over the top of the hill, and a home that once served as servants' quarters and a gatehouse around the corner on Mecca Avenue. Still standing in 1998, it can be seen by taking a right on Tarzana a short distance to Mecca, and taking a left on Mecca.

In the 1940s, Burroughs began selling off portions of his huge estate in a planned subdivision that is still called Tarzana. Burroughs died at his estate in 1950. Just east of Avenida Hacienda at 18354 Ventura Boulevard is a small stucco office that Burroughs used in the 1930s and 1940s as a personal office. After his death, his ashes were buried beside those of his mother underneath the walnut tree that still stands outside of what used to be the window of Burrough's private office.

Tour 15: Far San Fernando Valley

Begin Tour 15 at the 19700 block of Ventura Boulevard at Corbin. Left or south to Redwing. Right to:

19853 Redwing Street—Woodland Hills, William "Bud" Abbott death site

William Alexander "Bud" Abbott toured the burlesque and vaudeville circuits for 15 years before teaming up with fellow vaudevillian Louis Cristello, better-known as Lou Costello. The pair became the most successful comedy team in the history of the movies, starring in dozens of comedies and the most successful weekly radio show in the world during the 1930s and 1940s. The pair took their seasoned and perfectly-timed "Who's on First?" vaudeville routine to the movies, and it has become an immortal piece of baseball Americana, permanently exhibited on tape at the Baseball Hall of Fame in Cooperstown, New York.

Sadly, Abbott and Costello were estranged both professionally and personally at the time of Costello's 1959 death, which left Abbott heartbroken. Bud died at his Valley home on April 24, 1974, at the age of 75 from heart disease.

(Redwing to Oakdale. Left to Queen Victoria. Left to Queen Florence. Right to:)

4852 Queen Florence Lane—Woodland Hills, Lee J. Cobb death site

Lee J. Cobb starred in over 80 films during a 40-year Hollywood career but is perhaps best remembered for creating the role of Willy Loman in the Broadway classic *Death of a Salesman* in 1949, a performance he recreated in a landmark 1966 television performance. Cobb starred in dozens of classic films including his debut in *Golden Boy* (1939), *The Song of Bernadette* (1943), *Boomerang* (1947), *Johnny O'Clock* (1947), *On the Waterfront* (1954), *12 Angry Men* (1957), *The Brothers Karamazov* (1958) and *Exodus* (1960).

At the height of Cobb's stardom he testified before Senator Joseph McCarthy's House Un-American Activities Committee and admitted to having briefly joined the Communist Party during his early stage career. The public and industry backlash led to a near-fatal heart attack, and a blacklisting that nearly bankrupted Cobb. He survived the episode, slowly regaining his public image in part from a long-running role as Judge Garth in the 1960s television hit *The Virginian*. During the latter part of his career, Cobb starred in *How the West Was Won* (1963), *The Man Who Loved Cat Dancing* (1973), and his final movie role in *The Exorcist* (1973).

On February 12, 1976, Cobb died in his Woodland Hills home of cancer at the age of 64.

(Reverse to Oakdale. Right to Ventura. Left to Topanga Canyon Boulevard. Left to:)

4201 Topanga Canyon—Woodland Hills, Chester Conklin home

Chester Conklin was born in rural Iowa in 1888, and for most young men at that time the only way out of a small town was to join the circus, which he did. After spending ten years as a Ringling Brothers clown, in 1913 Conklin began making silent movies for the original Vitagraph Studio in New York. Mack Sennett hired him to join his original *Keystone Cops* movie troupe, and sporting his trademark walrus mustache Conklin quickly became a huge star and a particular favorite with the fans. In addition to his *Cops* roles, Conklin often filmed two or three other movies every week. Some of Conklin's other film credits include *Greed* (1924), *Say It Again* (1926), and *Dough and Dynamite*, a 1919 silent that featured young English comedian Charlie Chaplin.

Conklin's star began to fade with the advent of sound, and he spent his remaining years living quietly in a Long Beach apartment, taking small extra roles in a series of big movies including *The Virginian* (1929), *The Great Dictator* (1940)—given a small part by his old friend Chaplin—and *The Perils of Pauline* (1947). His considerable fortune gone, the once-major star earned a meager living with his bit roles and working as a department store Santa during the Christmas holidays. By the early 1960s he was staying at the nearby Motion Picture Country Home and Hospital, a home for retired, indigent or ailing performers located nearby at 23588 Mulholland Drive in Woodland Hills.

In 1965 he tired of his quiet life there, eloped to Las Vegas with a hospital guest at the age of 77 and moved into this quiet Woodland Hills house, where he died on October 12, 1971, of emphysema and prostate cancer. The former silent screen legend was 83 when he died.

(Reverse on Topanga Canyon. Right past the Ventura [101] Freeway to Victory.

Left past Shoup to Sale. Left a block to Sylvan. Right to:)

22612 Sylvan Way—Woodland Hills, Buster Keaton death site

In 1924 Buster Keaton was making $5,000 a week as the screen's foremost movie comedian, but much of his understated comic genius was lost on moviegoers in the 1920s. Two failed marriages cost him millions of dollars and led to a humiliating 1934 bankruptcy and a slow journey into obscurity. In 1937 he was forced to take work at MGM as a $100 a week gag writer, the lowest rung on the studio ladder. He survived his remaining years making European appearances and television commercials at home.

In the 1960s the world finally began to recognize Keaton's genius, and his films were earning the acclaim that had eluded him during his youth. His final marriage to Eleanor Norris was a happy one, lasting from 1940 until his death in 1966, during which time the couple lived in this sleepy bungalow nicknamed "The Keatons." It was a quiet retreat where Buster spent his time playing with his model trains and feeding his chickens. A lifelong chain-smoker, Keaton died from lung cancer on February 1, 1966, at the age of 70. He was buried at Forest Lawn Hollywood Hills with a rosary in one pocket and a deck of cards in the other.

(Sylvan to Fallbrook. Right past Victory and Sherman to Roscoe. Right to Topanga Canyon Boulevard. Left to Chase. Left to Hanna. Right to cul-de-sac at Michale at:)

22100 Michale Avenue—West Hills, Judith Barsi murder site

Judith Barsi was a child actress with roles in dozens of 1980s television shows including *St. Elsewhere*, *Family Ties*, and *Growing Pains*, and several movies such as *Jaws: The Revenge*. On July 27, 1988, the 11-year-old rising star was shot to death in the garage of her northwestern L.A.–county home by her deranged father, who also murdered her mother and younger sister. Obviously despondent over the couple's pending divorce, the berserk elder Barsi laid the bodies of his family in the garage and set them on fire with gasoline. Standing next to the pyre, he committed suicide by shooting himself to death so he would be burned with his family.

(Reverse to Topanga Canyon. Right to Vanowen. Left to:)

17811 Vanowen Drive—Northridge, Louise Carver death site

Louise Carver was one of the first female silent stars, moving from vaudeville to stardom working for Mack Sennett and Hal Roach in the early days of slapstick comedy. During a 20-year career Carver was featured in 350 comedy shorts, appearing with Harold Lloyd, Buster Keaton, Laurel and Hardy, and the Keystone Cops. During some weeks up to five or six short features were filmed. She also co-starred in 25 Laurel and Hardy features in her typical role as the brutish wife browbeating her wimpy husband. On March 8, 1958, Carver died in her San Fernando Valley home from a heart attack brought on by emphysema. Her young age—only 42—led to rumors that the death may have been caused by drug use.

Tour 16: Locations Off Maps

The Tour 16 stops are usually a short distance from other tours, but too far or out of sequence to be included. Directions follow each entry.

Westchester Golf Course—Marina del Rey, William Lennon murder site

William Lennon, the father of Diane, Peggy, Kathy and Janet—the singing "Lennon Sisters"—was murdered on August 12, 1969, but because of the more famous Tate/LaBianca killings the same week his death was relegated to the back pages. At noon on a warm August day the 53-year-old Lennon was seen arguing with a man in the parking lot of the Marina del Rey golf course where he worked as a golf pro. When the man pulled a hunting rifle from his trunk Lennon tried to run away, but was shot in the back by the unidentified man. The shooter then coolly walked up and shot the elder Lennon in the head.

It was later determined that the killer was an obsessed fan who for years had been stalking the sisters with letters and phone calls and following them to their concerts. The deranged man was convinced that he was married to one of the singers, and was found dead several months later in a car in a Northern California state park, a suicide victim. Ballistic tests proved that the rifle he had used to kill himself was the same gun used to murder Lennon.

(On Westchester and Lincoln Boulevard, just north of Los Angeles International Airport [LAX])

12214 Aneta Street—Culver City, Clara Bow death site

"IT Girl" and movie flapper Clara Bow's flamboyant lifestyle made her the subject of wild and often unfounded rumors that helped lead to an early retirement from the movies. Though married to 1930s cowboy star and Nevada Lieutenant Governor Rex Bell, her undiagnosed mental illness likely caused most of her problems. She died in obscurity in this bungalow watching late-night television on September 27, 1965, at the age of 60.

(Near Howard Hughes Airport in Culver City, west of the San Diego [405] Freeway between Centinella Boulevard and Inglewood, just north of LAX airport)

6001 Centinella Avenue—Culver City, Hillside Memorial Park

Near LAX and adjacent to the San Diego (405) Freeway, Hillside Memorial Park if full of celebrity graves. The most stunning is the hillside mausoleum and waterfall visible from the freeway, the grave of Al Jolson. The egotistical Jolson designed his own memorial to feature a marble sepulcher covered by a tiled canopy, a life-sized statue of himself in his role as *The Jazz Singer*, and an eternal waterfall. Jolson was even more arrogant in death than he was in life.

Inside the main mausoleum Jack Benny and wife Mary Livingston are at the end of the Hall of Graciousness. Just to their left is Eddie Cantor and nearby is Jeff Chandler, buried under real name Ira Grossel. Singer Percy Faith is in a small outside garden, as is the *Fugitive* star David Janssen, in a vault garden left of the main hall. George Gessel is three drawers above David Janssen, and Dick Shawn is in the same small wall. Michael "Little Joe" Landon is in a crypt just behind and outside the main hallway. Proceed through the lobby court to the family rooms outside on the left to find his crypt, which looks like a walk-in closet. *Bonanza* co-star Lorne Greene is buried just beyond Landon outside to the right. Greene's flat headstone is opposite a doorway behind the main mausoleum. *Twilight Zone—The Movie* accident victim Vic Morrow is buried in the Mt. Olive section (block 5) of the cemetery.

The ornate grave personally designed by *Jazz Singer* star Al Jolson, featuring a lighted waterfall, a granite sarcophagus beneath a hand-tiled cupola, and a life-sized statue in the courtyard.

(Hillside is at the 405 Freeway and the Centinella Boulevard)

5835 West Slausen Avenue—Culver City, Holy Cross Cemetery

Holy Cross is also close to LAX, just northeast of Hillside and even more full of celebrity graves. It is very large, so concentrate on just a few of the 20 very large and very crowded sections: the Grotto, Holy Cross and Main Mausoleum sections. To follow the directions to the next marker, assume you are facing up the hill toward the main mausoleum at the marker described. "Rows" are described as horizontal rows versus vertical, so use the horizontal orientation.

The Grotto section is up the hill to the left as you enter the cemetery grounds through the main gate, featuring a lovely grotto altar at the top of the hill. Park adjacent the altar area, and notice just to the right of the altar the kneeling angel and bonsai tree placed by Rita Hayworth's family after her 1987 death from the effects of Alzheimer's disease. Her headstone just in front of the statue says, "To yesterday's companionship and tomorrow's reunion." Just to the right of Hayworth are soap star Macdonald Carey and actress Bonita Granville (Wrather), star of *Youth Runs Wild* (1944) and *Love Laughs at Andy Hardy* (1946). Her funeral plans were an exact copy of her best friend Hayworth's.

Walk just above and behind the Hayworth statue to the St. Joseph section to find Jimmy Durante in the second row in from the street (#6, Tier 96). About 25 yards

The grave of Rita Hayworth, who died from complications of Alzheimer's disease in 1987. Her family also planted the bonsai tree just behind the grave.

beyond Durante, nine or ten markers down the row from the tree next to the road are Pat O'Brien (#62, Tier 56), Spencer Tracy's childhood pal and star of *Knute Rockne, All-American* with Ronald Reagan, and Edmund O'Brien (#50, Tier 54). Further down the treeline is John Leslie "Jackie" Coogan, child star of Chaplin's *The Kid* (1920) and *Oliver Twist* (1921) who went on to later fame as "Uncle Fester" in television's *The Addams Family*.

Return to the front of the altar area, and notice to the left of the Grotto altar a raised area that is called St. Anne's Garden. As you enter the section from the altar, in the fourth row close to the right side are Sharon Tate and her unborn child (#6, Tier 152). To the right of the Tate family in the same row are James and Marian Jordan, radio's *Fibber McGee and Molly* from 1935 to 1956 (#1, Tier 153). In the tenth row almost to the back, seven spots from the right are Charles Boyer, French-born star of *The Garden of Allah* (1936) and *Algiers* (1938), his wife Pat Paterson and son Michael Boyer, who killed himself in his Beverly Hills house (#5, Tier 186). Just two days after his wife of 44 years died from cancer, the elder Boyer

committed suicide as his son had. Behind the unfortunate Boyer family is early movie star ZaSu Pitts, Thelma Todd's movie partner and best friend (#1, Lot 195).

The hillside below the altar also has several interesting movieland graves. Begin at the top of the hill below the altar, and walk down the hill to row three (the third from the top), and in from the road about 11 graves find Bela (*Dracula*) Lugosi. In the same row five in from Lugosi is the Crosby family, crooner Bing and first wife Wilma "Dixie Lee" (#1, Tier 119). Bing had himself buried nine feet deep so that second wife Kathryn can be buried with him if she wishes. Below in row six, six graves from the street is *The Wizard of Oz* (1939) "Tin Man" Jack Haley (#2, Lot 100). Below Haley in row seven next to the street is Walter Brennan.

Across the street down the hillside in Sacred Heart Section D walk to the large tree about halfway down the hill and a short distance in from the road between the Grotto and that hillside. You can also see a waste receptacle shaped like a tree trunk near the road roughly even with the large tree. In the second row behind the tree (near marker 313) find early race-car driver Barney

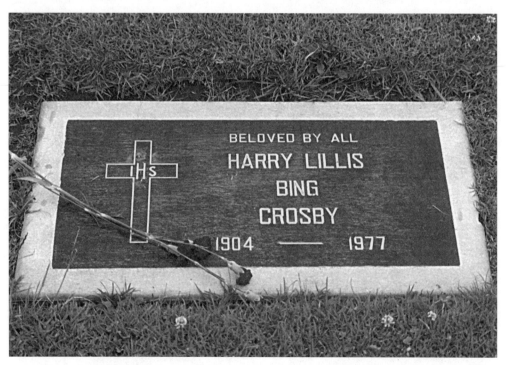

Top: The grave of actress Sharon Tate and her unborn son, murdered by the Manson Family in 1969. *Bottom:* Crooner Bing Crosby was apparently "beloved by all" except the sons that he tormented, two of whom have committed suicide in the years since.

Top: Here Dracula remains dead. *Bottom:* The anonymous grave of "The Tin Man," Jack Haley.

The most powerful woman in Hollywood for almost forty years lies beneath this secluded Holy Cross marker.

Oldfield, who in 1913 drove a car at the even-today amazing speed of 133 miles an hour. From Oldfield, walk down the hill four rows, and walk about ten markers to the right toward the road and the waste receptacle and you will find mega-powerful Hearst gossip columnist Louella Parsons (Martin; near marker 263), who literally ruled Hollywood for 20 years, making and breaking careers with a single well-read column. She also ruined movies, once saying about the movie version of *A Midsummer Night's Dream*, "Shakespeare or no Shakespeare, there should be some kind of entertainment in films of this kind." Married to alcoholic surgeon Howard "Docky" Martin, Parsons once told party guests not to awaken Martin after he had passed out under their piano during a party, "leave him alone, he has surgery at seven in the morning." On the opposite side of this section, under and just to the left of the largest tree to the right near

the road is *Keystone Cops* star Edgar L. Kennedy (near marker 224), and up six rows from the tree and a dozen markers to the left is Gene Lockhart (near marker 279), star of *Miracle on 34th Street* (1947) and *The Man in the Gray Flannel Suit* (1956). His daughter June played Timmy's mom on the *Lassie* television series for over ten years. William Lundigan (#3, Lot 269), Sara Allgood, and Mary Astor are also nearby in this area.

The next area is over the right, just beyond this area, in Section M, below and directly in front of the Main Mausoleum. Drive over to the lower border street and notice the large crucifix and evergreen trees, the grave site of Rosalind Russell (#2, Lot 536). Russell was allegedly given the grave site by a local bishop after her years of charity work on behalf of the Catholic church; her grave is surrounded by the graves of dozens of Carmelite priests and nuns. Down a row in front of Russell and three markers away is actress Gia Scala, buried under he real name of Giovanna Scoglio, a 1972 suicide victim. Three rows below Russell and five to the left is studio head Joe Schenck. Five or six rows further down (eight rows up from the street below Russell), and five markers in from the right curb is the grave of Evelyn Nesbit Thaw, under the simple inscription "Mother." She can be found beneath the third small tree up from the curb. Thaw's life was forever changed by the fallout of a 1906 shooting in New York, when her husband murdered her former lover, world-famous architect Stanford White. In the same section are John Ford (#5, Lot 304, to the left of the crucifix, four rows down and 25 over), writer Gene Fowler (#3, Lot 792, upper left of same section as Ford), and actor Frank Lovejoy, star of *The Best Man* (1960).

Proceed up the street on the right side of this section toward the Main Mausoleum, and park by the side of the road to the right of the building, roughly even with the mid-

dle of the small roundish grassy area to the left and in front of the building. On your right, ten rows down the hill, under a small tree, is the legendary director Mack Sennett (Section N, #1, Lot 490), under a marker that simply says "Beloved King of Comedy." The creator of the slapstick movie genre, more than any other man Mack Sennett is responsible for the early popularity of comedy.

Inside the main entrance of the Main Mausoleum at the end of the foyer behind the altar is singer Mario Lanza, the "American Caruso." The arrogant alcoholic died of a heart attack at 38. To his left is comic actress Joan Davis (Block 46, crypt D-1). Bandleaders Lindley "Spike" Jones (Block 70, crypt A-70, near the top) and Jose Iturbi (Block 16, crypt E-1) are also in the mausoleum. *The Wizard of Oz* scarecrow Ray Bolger is in Block 35 (crypt F-2), Scott Brady is in Block 156 (crypt B-7), and Jack "Lash" LaRue is in Block 69 (crypt E-3).

The central player in the biggest sex scandal of the early 1900s—the murder of architect Stanford White—was buried under her maiden name rather than the name of her killer husband.

Irishman Mack Sennett came to America in the late 1800s and founded the biggest comedy factory in the world, producing the most popular comedies in movie history. He truly was "The King of Comedy."

(Holy Cross is east of the 405 Freeway, north of Slausen and east of Sepulveda/Jefferson Boulevard, reachable off the 405 Freeway. or the Marina [90] Freeway. which ends below the cemetery. From Hillside Memorial Park, exit right on Centinella north to Sepulveda, right to Slausen, right up the hill to the entrance on the left)

6433 Holt Avenue—Culver City, Delores Jackson death site

Delores Martes Jackson was married to Michael Jackson's older brother Tito, an original member of The Jackson Five. Divorced in 1993 after 21 years of marriage, on August 27, 1994, the 39-year-old woman was pulled from the pool behind her businessman boyfriend's home, dead of a variety of injuries. According to 59-year-old Donald Bohana, he was swimming with Jackson and left on a short errand, returning to find her dead in the pool. Initially classified accidental, an autopsy later concluded that Jackson's death was caused by "asphyxia due to drowning, alcohol intake and blunt force traumatic injuries." A coroner's investigation indicated that the bruises, abrasions and lacerations on her body suggested she had been the victim of a "non-accidental ... assisted drowning," and the D.A.'s office reopened the case.

Her surviving children filed a wrongful death suit against Bohana in 1994, detailing almost 60 injuries suffered by Jackson before her death. Ex-husband Tito filed another wrongful death suit against Bohana on May 17, 1996, alleging that Bohana drowned Delores in his pool after assaulting her. According to *People* magazine, Bohana's attorney called the allegations "a whole lot of garbage."

(East/south from Hillside Memorial on Centinella ½ mile to second light at Sherbourne, left up the hill and bearing right onto Sixty-fourth Street to Holt. Right to site)

13999 Marquesas Way, Basin C-110— Marina del Rey, Dennis Wilson accidental death site

Drummer Dennis Wilson was the only surfer in the Beach Boys and also the most free-spirited. He was a drug and alcohol abuser who eventually became unable to even perform in public. His bizarre life ended when he drowned in a boat slip here on December 28, 1983. He was visiting friends on the yacht *Emerald*, which was his until it was repossessed by his bank, and after spending the afternoon drinking, Wilson began diving by the boat to pick junk off the bottom. After several dives, Wilson failed to surface, and his body was discovered some time later. With a blood alcohol level of 0.26 he was literally too drunk to remember to hold his breath underwater and he drowned. He was married to Shawn Love, allegedly the illegitimate daughter of his cousin and fellow band-member Mike Love.

(In the Marina del Rey marina, near Washington and Lincoln [Route 1]. On the west side, off Via Marina between Panay Way and Tahiti Way)

28 Club House Drive—Venice Beach, Christopher "Zero" Murder

Another murder committed by members of the Charles Manson Family occurred on November 4, 1969, about the same time that Manson was being linked to the more famous Tate-LaBianca slayings. Family member Christopher "Zero" was found dead in this house of a fatal head wound in the company of six Manson women who all claimed that he had died playing Russian roulette. The death gun was found without fingerprints—not even Zero's—and amaz-

ingly none of the uncooperative friends admitted to police that they had seen him do it. Because of the lack of evidence, no charges were ever filed.

(On Venice Beach, west of Pacific/Ocean Ave. between Rose Avenue and Venice Boulevard)

Venice Beach Pier—Venice Beach, Mrs. Douglas Shearer suicide

Like it still does today, a sunny Sunday afternoon lured thousands of people to the rides and shops of Venice Beach Pier on June 14, 1930. The pier was packed with beachgoers when the wife of famed MGM sound director Douglas Shearer walked up to a shooting gallery amidst a crowd of people. Paying her nickel she grabbed one of the target pistols and shot herself right between the eyes in front of hundreds of horrified onlookers. It was reported by the *Hollywood Citizen News* that the 25-year-old woman was despondent over her failing marriage to Shearer and by the recent death of her mother.

Several years earlier, his sister Norma Shearer's husband Irving Thalberg got Doug a job as a studio animal trainer. Realizing that the advent of sound was upon them, an enlightened Shearer became an expert on the subject, soon the only man in Hollywood with any information and the first of the studio "soundmen." During a long career he went on to win an incredible 12 Academy Awards for sound during his career.

(Venice Beach Pier is located on the beach in Venice, at the end of Washington Boulevard)

8612 Rindge Street—Venice Beach, Loretta Young–Clark Gable love child birthplace

When Loretta Young and Clark Gable starred in *Call of the Wild* (1935) she was a single 22-year-old and he a 35-year-old twice-divorced star. Rumors soon arose that the pair were engaged in a torrid affair during filming in the Washington mountains, quickly followed by whispers of a pregnancy. Both stars issued denials, and Young reportedly left for Europe for an extended rest. In reality she had secretly moved into a rented bungalow in Venice Beach, where on November 6, 1935, she gave birth to Gable's child, secretly attended by studio doctors. The infant was moved to an orphanage until a studio-arranged adoption allowed Young to reclaim her child 19 months later.

Young's adopted little girl bore an uncanny resemblance to Gable and was never allowed in public without a hat covering the bulging ears that were identical to his. Young consistently denied the rumors, saying, "It was a rumor then, it's a rumor now. I guess it will always be a rumor. And that's the end of it." Daughter Julie Lewis' 1994 book exposed the true story, however.

(South of Manchester (Route 42)/Pershing intersection, adjacent Waterview. Much of the area was demolished to make way for nearby LAX runways; all that remains of the area above 7600 Rindge are crumbling streets and sidewalks and haunting streetlights. It is now called Vista del Mar Park)

Queen Elizabeth cruise ship, haunted

Moored in Long Beach since 1967 and open daily to tourists, the *Queen* was the grandest ship at sea, christened on May 27, 1936, and veteran of over 1,000 Atlantic crossings during a 30-year career that included service as a transport during World War II. During the war she was camouflaged and painted gray, earning the prophetic nickname "The Gray Ghost." According to manifests, almost 100 people died aboard ship during her various cruises, some of whom are apparently still hanging around. Over the years hundreds of employees and visitors have reported strange sightings of

ghostly inhabitants aboard ship. The first class pool area is particularly busy, with clear sounds of splashing guests and laughing children heard frequently by tour guides, workers and sightseers alike. Phantom wet footprints also regularly appear next to the pool in front of awestruck visitors.

The sounds of rushing water and agonizing screams have been repeatedly heard within the empty bow area of the otherwise silent ship. The noises may be the spectral remains of a wartime collision with a small British cruiser that killed over 300 men, most of them housed in the bow section that suffered the most damage. A longtime employee killed in a 1966 fire drill reportedly still "works" in the shaft alley area where he died, dressed in his familiar blue overalls and smiling at visitors and staff alike.

(Moored at the pier in Long Beach)

2686 Bayshore Drive—Newport Beach, John Wayne last home

In a 1970 interview, John Wayne said, "I would like to be remembered—well, the Mexicans have an expression, 'Feo, Fuerte y Formel,' which means: he was ugly, he was strong, and had dignity." Perhaps the most recognized and beloved movie star in the history of Hollywood, Wayne was discovered by director John Ford playing football for Southern Cal, and had a career that spanned over 60 years and hundreds of renowned movie roles. Wayne was a true folk hero, the most consistently popular actor in the history of Hollywood, top ten in 19 of 20 box office polls between 1949 and 1968. His films have grossed an incredible $800 million (over $8 billion today), a record that may never be broken.

Born Marion Michael Morrison in Winterset, Iowa (also the site of the 1995 movie *The Bridges of Madison County*), he grew up in Glendale, and earned a football scholarship to Southern Cal based on his 6-foot 4-inch 260-pound size. The football team's popularity gave Wayne the chance to hobnob with movie stars, and he was part of the infamous team parties held at the Beverly Hills home of Clara Bow. Wayne worked during the summers at Fox Studios prop department and had small roles in a few films until starring in *The Big Trail* (1929) alongside Gary Cooper. Wayne quickly became the country's top western star, with a credit list including *Riders of Destiny* (1933), *Stagecoach* (1939), *Red River* (1948), *She Wore a Yellow Ribbon* (1949), *High and Mighty* (1954), *The Searchers* (1956), *Rio Bravo* (1958), *The Alamo* (1960), *The Man Who Shot Liberty Valance* (1962), *El Dorado* (1967), *True Grit* (1969)—which earned him his only Best Actor Oscar—and *The Shootist* (1976), his final film. His war films were equally popular, including *The Fighting Seabees* (1944), *They Were Expendable* (1945), and *The Sands of Iwo Jima* (1949), which earned him an Academy Award nomination for Best Actor.

Wayne and third wife Pilar moved to this Newport Beach mansion in 1965 after they sold their Encino estate to Walt Disney's daughter. Living nearby Wayne's beloved yacht *The Wild Goose*, the couple were the unofficial king and queen of the Orange County social register. Wayne lost a long battle with stomach cancer on June 11, 1979, dead at the age of 77.

(Near the marina at Newport Beach, just off Route 1)

Newport Beach Marina—Newport Beach, John Wayne's haunted yacht, *The Wild Goose*

John Wayne so loved his treasured *Wild Goose* that he made special arrangements for its eventual sale prior to his death. Knowing he would never see his yacht again, Wayne sold it to Santa Monica lawyer Lynn Hutchins for $750,000 just weeks before his 1979 death. When Wayne was told after the sale closed that the *Goose* needed a $40,000 engine repair, he paid for it even though he was not obligated to do so, because, as he put it, "I gave him my word. I wouldn't sell

anyone a turkey." Hutchins and many of his visitors are certain that Wayne still enjoys his beloved ship, a converted navy trawler. Ghostly footsteps, apparitions of a tall gentleman wandering the cabins, and clearly heard laughter from empty rooms are just some of the manifestations that have continued over the years.

(Moored at the marina in Long Beach, near the Queen Mary)

221 Moonstone Court—El Porto— Manhattan Beach, William Haines assault site

Billy Haines was fired by MGM head Louis B. Mayer when he wouldn't forsake his male lover for his then-thriving career. For years studio fixer Howard Strickling had covered for the openly homosexual Haines by promoting various "girlfriends" and a long "engagement" to actress Pola Negri, but Mayer became fed up when Haines was caught in a vice raid at a local Y.M.C.A. He immediately canceled Haines' contract and blacklisted him from studio employment for life. Haines opened the most popular interior decorating firm in Los Angeles (located in the building now housing Le Dome Restaurant at 8720 Sunset in Hollywood).

Before leaving the movies Haines was involved in a well-publicized incident near his Manhattan Beach summer home on the night of June 1, 1936. A 6-year-old local boy told police that he had been approached at Haines' beach house by Haines, his boyfriend Bill Shields and director George Cukor. According to Haines, the boy was simply visiting while Cukor dyed his white poodle purple on a lark, and that nothing had occurred during the visit. Outraged neighbors didn't believe the story, however, and the next night a group of Ku Klux Klansmen entered the mostly gay beach area, and as Haines and some friends were leaving his house they were severely beaten. Shields was left with head injuries and a concussion. When his name came up in police and press reports, busy fixer Strickling made sure that it was removed.

(In Manhattan Beach, near Artesia Boulevard and the ocean)

2600 Nicholas Canyon Drive—Malibu, Manson home, "Family movie" set

During March of 1969, in the spring before the Tate-LaBianca killings, Charles Manson rented a small house in the hills above Malibu. During the next several months, his "Family" moved in, and while living there the group filmed a poorly made but fairly well-distributed porn film featuring most of the family members. After evicting Manson because of complaints from neighbors and for nonpayment of rent, the owner found that the house had been left in shambles. Frighteningly, lying next to the trashed pool where most of the filming had occurred was a blood-soaked machete.

(Nicholas Canyon is in the hills above Malibu)

3704 Carbon Canyon Drive—Malibu, Richard Jordan death

Richard Jordan was a classically trained Shakespearean actor and veteran of over 100 plays who also had a long and successful television and movie career. He received the 1976 Golden Globe for his role in the groundbreaking television miniseries *Captain and the Kings*, and starred in movies such as *Lawman* (1970), *Interiors* (1978), *Dune* (1984), *The Hunt for Red October* (1990), and *The Friends of Eddie Coyle* (1973). His last movie was Ted Turner's *Gettysburg*, and he was to have starred in *The Fugitive* (1993) before illness sidelined him. Jordan died at his Malibu home on August 30, 1993, from a brain tumor at the age of 56. *Gettysburg* was released a month later.

(Carbon Canyon Drive is off of the Pacific Coast Highway just north of

Las Flores Canyon Road in the Carbon Beach area south of Malibu)

12551 Ocean Breeze Drive—Garden Grove, Cinnamon Sands–David Brown murder case

Early on the morning of March 19, 1985, police found young mother Linda Brown shot to death in her small Anaheim home. She was murdered in a home shared—in true hillbilly style—with her 16-year-old sister Patti, her husband David, their infant daughter, both of her husband's parents, and his 15-year-old stepdaughter Cinnamon Sands. According to another sister, Cinnamon murdered Brown and also took a shot or two at her, and the teenager was subsequently convicted and jailed for 27 years.

Several years later, though, a now-repentant convict Cinnamon told cops that Patti had actually helped her shoot Linda, and that the crime had been planned by their father. David allegedly forced her to confess to the murder to prove that "she loved him," and the gullible teenager agreed to do so. It was also discovered that for years the loving father—again in true hillbilly style—had been sleeping with *both* teenagers, one his sister-in-law and the other his own stepdaughter. His dead wife had allegedly "sold" Patti to him for his sexual needs for $5,000, and following the murder he actually married her. David was found guilty and sentenced to life in prison, and Patti joined Cinnamon in the Women's lockup. As one might expect, the happy family saga ended up as a 1992 television movie entitled *Love, Lies and Murder*.

(Ocean Breeze is in Garden Grove, near Anaheim, off Brookhurst off the Garden Grove [22] Freeway)

9828 Newville Avenue—Downey, Karen Carpenter death site

Richard and his younger sister Karen Carpenter made the most successful love songs of the 1970s, prom anthems such as "Close to You," "We've Only Just Begun," "Yesterday Once More," "Rainy Days and Mondays," and so on. But personal demons haunted both superstars.

Richard managed to beat a near-fatal drug addiction, but Karen spent her life desperately fighting a losing battle with anorexia nervosa, obsessed about food and her weight even though she rarely weighed more than 80 pounds. She was visiting her parents at their Downey home when her body finally gave up the struggle, and she was found dead in her brother's second-floor bedroom closet on February 3, 1983. She was only 32 years old.

(Southeast of L.A., near the 605 and 5 Freeways intersection. Newville is between Florence and Firestone west of the 605)

Forest Lawn Memorial Park— Glendale

Over a million people a year visit Forest Lawn Memorial Park, entered by passing beneath the largest wrought iron gates in the world. The cemetery was designed in 1917 by Dr. Hubert Eaton as a group of "great parks, devoid of signs of earthly death and filled with towering trees, sweeping lawns, splashing fountains and beautiful statuary." Eaton's system includes Forest Lawn parks here in Glendale, in nearby Hollywood Hills, in Cypress, in Covina Hills and in Sunnyside. Eaton filled his parks with replicas of classic works of art—Forest Lawn Glendale boasts the largest collection of marble statuary in America. He envisioned a cemetery where the stars could be embalmed in the mortuary, laid out in one of a dozen viewing rooms, have a service in one of the chapels, and be transported to the grave site without ever having to be driven "through crowded city streets under the stares of curious onlookers." In Glendale are perfect reproductions of Michelangelo's *David* and his soulful *Pieta*, as well as statues

of George Washington and *The Great Republic*. Forest Lawn Glendale is a large park, and it is worth the time to stop in the Memento Shop (yes, they have a gift shop) for a detailed map.

Most of the Hollywood stars of note are buried in and around the Great Mausoleum and the smaller Freedom Hall Mausoleum at the very top of the property. Begin in the area around the Freedom Hall and work your way down. As you proceed up the hill past the gift shop you will pass the Wee Kirk o' the Heather Chapel, and at the top of the hill on your left note the Forest Lawn Museum, which is definitely worth a stop, and the Church of the Recessional chapel. Both chapels have hosted some of the biggest funerals in Hollywood history, from Jean Harlow's to Carole Lombard's to Spencer Tracy's and Humphrey Bogart's.

On your left on Cathedral Drive at the top of the hill notice the Mystery of Life statue. In the private garden area just to the left as you stand in front are stage star Earl Carroll and his companion Beryl Wallace, who were both killed in a 1948 plane crash, and bandleader Abe Lyman, who wrote the hit "I Cried for You." To the right side is actor Warner Baxter, better known as "The Cisco Kid," and the star of *42nd Street* (1933). In the back of the garden is another little known but recognized actor, S.Z. Zakall, who starred in *Casablanca* (1942) as the chubby waiter in Humphrey Bogart's bar. Comedian Charlie Ruggles is next to Zakall, and his director brother Wesley Ruggles is buried next to him. In the last columbarium on the left, on the right wall beneath a statue of a woman under a seashell you'll find Humphrey Bogart beneath a small marker with a vase to the right side. Bogart's ashes were buried with the gold whistle given him by wife Lauren Bacall after filming *To Have and Have Not*, when she said, "If you want me, just whistle. You know how to whistle? Just put your lips together and blow."

To Bogie's right is actor Victor McLaglen, star of *What Price Glory* (1926) and *The Informer* (1935), and near McLaglen is hillbilly comedienne Judy Canova, star of *Hit the Hay* (1945) and *Singin' in the Corn* (1946). Former Twentieth Century–Fox production chief Buddy Adler is in the corner garden on the right, and adjacent to Adler, closest to the entrance, is a marble monument of three women and four small children. This is the grave of the family Pickford: former "America's Sweetheart" Mary Pickford, her brother Jack, her sister Lottie, and her mother Charlotte.

Across the road on the hillside you can find Terry Kath, former lead singer of the band Chicago, who accidentally shot himself in the head during a San Fernando Valley party, lovely actress Merle Oberon, star of *Wuthering Heights* (1939), *Mary Tyler Moore Show* star Ted Knight, remembered as the bumbling Ted Baxter, and actor Robert Alda, father of Alan.

Continue toward the Freedom Hall Mausoleum ahead, and just before on your left see the Court of Freedom. Just to the left of the entrance to Freedom Hall you will notice a little mermaid sitting alone in a garden on top of a rock, the barely marked grave site of Walt Disney. Enter the Garden of Everlasting Peace adjacent Disney's grave, and you can find Errol Flynn on your right under a statue of a woman on a pedestal, and in the garden to the right of the George Washington statue next to a marble bench the grave of Spencer Tracy. At the end of the area is a wall plaque memorializing baseball great Casey Stengel. Just across the road, near the tree trunk–shaped garbage can, you will find actress Lilli Palmer, an Austrian actress who starred in *Thunder Rock* (1942) and *The Rake's Progress* (1945). Palmer was married to philandering actor Rex Harrison when his then-mistress Carole Landis committed suicide when she realized that he was not going to leave Palmer and marry her.

Near the Statue of Immortality actress Joan Blondell (*A Tree Grows in Brooklyn* [1945]) is buried, and near the Greek statue is actor Robert Taylor. In the Columbarium

This enchanting statue of a young mermaid is the only sign of the otherwise unmarked grave of legendary Walt Disney.

of Honor is producer Jerry Wald, and near the entrance is Clarence Brown, who directed such classics as *National Velvet* (1944) and *The Yearling* (1946). Charlotte Shelby, the stage mother of silent screen actress Mary Miles Minter and who likely murdered director William Desmond Taylor to stop his affair with her daughter, was originally interred just outside the Columbarium of Honor, but Minter had her mother's body exhumed so that the bizarre couple could be cremated together. Nearby is director George Cukor (*Little Women* [1933] and *The Philadelphia Story* [1940]) and singer Sam Cooke, shot to death in a seedy Los Angeles motel in 1964.

Inside the Freedom Mausoleum, in the middle in Heritage Hall, you will find actor Alan Ladd and his actress wife Sue Carol Ladd, and just below Ladd's crypt is the "IT Girl" Clara Bow and her cowboy star ex-husband Rex Bell. Crooner Nat King Cole is also next to the Bells. Also in this area are singer Jeanette MacDonald and George and Gracie (Allen) Burns. He had himself buried beneath his loving wife so "she could always have top billing." In the Columbarium of Victory at the end of the hall is *Porgy and Bess* (1959) star Dorothy Dandridge. Blues singer Clara Ward is interred in the Sanctuary of Commandments. Downstairs in the lower level you will find "King of the Movies" Francis X. Bushman in the Sanctuary of Gratitude, Chico Marx in the Sanctuary of Worship, his brother Gummo across the hall in the Sanctuary of Brotherhood, and The Three Stooges' Larry Fine in the Sanctuary of Liberation.

Proceed from the Freedom Mausoleum to the Great Mausoleum below. As you return to the Great Mausoleum passing the Wee Kirk o' the Heather Chapel, you can see the beautiful "The Finding of Moses" fountain. Near the fountain in the Whispering Pines section here are vaudeville star Rosetta Duncan, half of the Topsy and Eva comedy duo, actress Jane Darwell, and Susan Peters, whose promising career was cut short when she was accidentally shot

while hunting with her husband, actor Richard Quine in the late 1940s. Just up the hill is Lurene Tuttle, star of the 1950s television program *Life with Father*. Along the crest of the hill above Tuttle are writer Theodore Dreiser and his companion and then wife Helen Richardson, and just to their right actors Jack Oakie, Andy Clyde— who for years played Hopalong Cassidy's sidekick "California" in dozens of movies— and Fay Holden, who played the mother in *The Hardy Boys* movie series. Actor Edward Everett Horton, whose 50-year career included everything from serious leading roles to playing the Indian Chief on television's *F Troop* during the 1960s to the voice of *Rocky and Bullwinkle's Fractured Fairy Tales*, is buried in this area. The maker of cowboy star Tom Mix (very close to marker 986) has his autograph and a copy of his diamond-encrusted belt buckle. Mix was killed when he ran his Cord sportster off an Arizona desert highway in 1940 and was thrown under the car.

The Great Mausoleum houses some of the most famous names in Hollywood history—some in public areas, and some in private areas. The public entrance is near the Last Supper Window, and the private areas are entered through Holly Terrace. Near the spectacular Last Supper Window you will find songwriter Carrie Jacobs Bond and the founding family of the Forest Lawn group, the Eatons, in the private room on the right. Inside the nearby Sanctuary of Trust on the left side you will find Clark Gable, Carole Lombard, and her mother Elizabeth Peters, who was killed along with Lombard in a 1942 plane crash. Producer David O. Selznick is at the end of the hallway past Gable and Lombard, and also in the same alcove is Lon Chaney, Sr., behind an unmarked crypt featuring a simple urn. Also there are Will Rogers, Jack Pickford, Charles Mack, and Frank Joyce. Across the hall in the main Sanctuary of Vespers is singer Russ Columbo, who was accidentally shot to death just prior to announcing his engagement to Carole Lombard. Around the corner

Together even in death, Clark Gable is buried next to Carole Lombard even though he married twice after her 1942 death in a Nevada plane crash.

in Sanctuary of Benediction is actress Marie
Dressler, and next to her is theater magnate
Alexander Pantages. Across the aisle in the
same alcove is Sid Grauman, founder of
Grauman's Chinese Theatre and creator of
the famous forecourt of the stars featuring
handprints and footprints in concrete. At the
end of the aisle in an ornate marble crypt purchased by William Powell, Jean Harlow rests
with the awful stage mother who drove her
there. Irving Thalberg and Norma Shearer
are next door, and Jack Carson and Theda
Bara are just down the hall in the next alcove.
If you walk through the public areas of either of these wonderful mausoleums, you are
sure to come across names you will recognize.

*(Forest Lawn—Glendale is located at
1712 South Glendale Avenue, south of
the Glendale [134] Freeway, and east
of the Golden State [5] Freeway. From
the Golden State, east on Glendale
Boulevard, right onto Forest, and left
on Glendale Avenue to entrance)*

Forest Lawn Memorial Park— Hollywood Hills

Forest Lawn Hollywood Hills is the
second largest in the Forest Lawn system,
and the easy access off the Hollywood/Glen-
dale Freeway makes it an easy tour stop. It
features replicas of Boston's Old North
Church and the awe-inspiring Liberty Mural.
In 1978, Kenneth Bianchi and Angelo
Buono—the "Hillside Stranglers"—left several bodies in the area of Forest Lawn, either
on the hillside next to the freeway offramp
or up in the hills in nearby Elysian Park.

Most of the interesting Hollywood
graves can be found either in the Court of
Remembrance or Hall of Memory sections.
If you begin in the Court of Remembrance,
note just to the left of the entrance the monument over the grave of actress-legend Bette
Davis near the road. Entering the court, in
a corner of the first section on your right you
will find actor Charles Laughton in the first
alcove to the right at the top of the stairs,

and three spots away, circus legend Clyde
Beatty. Beatty, who began as a lion tamer in
a traveling circus, was gored during performances over 100 times during his 40-year
career, leaving his face a mass of frightening
scars. Across from Beatty is composer Albert
Hay Malotte, who wrote the score for Disney's *Lady and the Tramp*.

As you walk toward the back on your
right facing the court note the ornately decorated family plot of the Liberace family,
where the entertainer, his mother, and his
brother George are all buried. Lifelong homosexual Liberace—born Wladziu Valentino Liberace—publicly denied his sexual
preference for years, often filing lawsuits
when it was publicized. When his longtime
boyfriend Scott Thorson filed a palimony
suit in 1982, Liberace won because, according to the court, their relationship "amounted
to prostitution." He attempted to continue
the deception even after his death, having
ordered that his body be quickly moved to
L.A. for burial. It was never mentioned that
Liberace may have died from the effects of
the AIDS virus. When the rumors arose the
county coroner ordered the body retrieved
from here and autopsied, which did indeed
show that the ailing star was killed by the
disease. On the wall to the right of Liberace
are two unknown songwriters whose songs
are known by all: T. Marvin Hatley, whose
marker reminds us that Hatley was "Composer of the Laurel and Hardy Theme Song,"
and Haven Gillespie, who wrote "Santa
Claus Is Coming to Town."

Across the way in Columbarium of Remembrance you can find Ernest Loring
"Red" Nichols, leader of the jazz quintet Red
Nichols and His Five Pennies, whose life
was reprised in the 1959 movie *The Five Pennies*, with Danny Kaye playing Nichols. On
the adjacent wall is Marie Wilson, who
starred in dozens of dumb blonde roles
through the 1940s, and the former husband
and manager of Doris Day, Marty Melcher.

In the Sanctuary of Light behind Liberace you will find actor George Raft's grave
on the wall on the lower right near a statue

of a woman and a child, and next to Raft, actor Freddie Prinze. Across the way is B-movie actress Wanda Hendrix, the former wife of Audie Murphy. In the opposite alcove—the Sanctuary of Reflection—you can find actor Reginald Gardner, and at the end mausoleum in the back, comic Strother Martin, *F Troop*'s Forrest Tucker, and actress Pamela Britton.

Exit to the outside and on your right is director Michael (*The Wild, Wild West*) Garrison, who died after falling from a ladder in his Beverly Hills home. Opera star Tony Martin is near the marble bench nearby. On the outside wall catty-corner to Garrison is pop singer Andy Gibb and Harry Mills, the leader of the singing Mills Brothers. Walk around to the other outside wall (which would be behind the Sanctuary of Remembrance) to find comedienne Lucille Ball (Morton).

Outside the Court of Remembrance, just across Vista Lane from the driveway and next to the curb facing the drive, is actor Jason Nilson Robards, Broadway star and father of actor Jason. Farther down the lawn, across from the water tower, is Ernie Kovacs, under a marker that reads, "Nothing in Moderation." His daughter Mia, who also died in a Hollywood car accident, is buried next to her father. In the nearby Gentleness section you can find actress sisters Amanda (*The Danny Thomas Show*) and Lillian Rudolph, and "Tex" Avery, creator of Bugs Bunny.

Leaving the Court of Remembrance area, make

your way over to the Hall of Liberty, a terraced garden underneath a great mural. As you enter, along the right wall of the first level is the grave of Buster Keaton. Climb the stairs to the last wall, and next to the walkway you will find Stan Laurel alongside his wife Ida K., whose marker reads "Beloved Wife." Laurel was married eight times—he married Ida twice, and Virginia Rogers three times. Just to the left is Ray Bidwell Collins,

The grave site of legendary comic Stan Laurel. His eighth and last wife Ida is interred beneath Laurel.

"Lieutenant Tragg" of the television series *Perry Mason*, and in the same area is William Talman, who played District Attorney "Hamilton Berger" on the same show. His career lasted over 40 years. Across to the left on the same level is actor Rex Ingram, an Illinois doctor who was discovered crossing a Hollywood street in 1921, was cast as Tarzan in a movie filming the next day, and went on to film stardom. In the front of the second (level) garden is bug-eyed comic Marty Feldman, and in the open ground you will find Benjamin Sherman "Scatman" Crothers and Bruce Wayne, the first traffic reporter to use a helicopter for live remote broadcasts.

Over on Memorial Drive in the Enduring Faith section you can find tyrannical director Fritz Lang next to the road on the hillside, and six rows up from Lang, suicide victim Diane Linkletter. Underneath a large tree nearby is Sabu Dastinger, son of an elephant driver from Delhi, who starred in *The Jungle Book* (1942), *Elephant Boy* (1937), and *Song of India* (1949). Sabu suffered a fatal heart attack in Los Angeles in 1963 at the age of 39. His stuntman brother Sheik Dastinger is buried right behind him. In the Sheltering

Hills section you can find Lester "Smiley" Burnett, who starred with Gene Autry in over 80 films, Helen Travolta, actress mother of John, and *Dragnet* star Jack Webb.

Right next to the road in the Murmuring Trees section is the family plot of bandleader Horace Heidt, and above and behind the Heidts, notice Godfrey Cambridge, the 300-pound comic actor who died on the set of the 1976 television movie *Rescue at Entebbe* of a heart attack. Above Cambridge is legendary stuntman Dar Allen Robinson. Across the street about 20 rows up from the road is the family plot of Ozzie, Harriet and Rick Nelson.

(Forest Lawn—Hollywood Hills is located next to the Ventura (134) Freeway in Glendale, just east of the Hollywood (101) Freeway interchange. Exit the freeway at Forest Lawn Drive, and the cemetery is just to the right of the exit.)

980 Stoneridge Drive—Glendale, Robert Reed death site

Robert Reed starred in dozens of movies and television shows but is best-remembered

Robert Reed—best remembered as television's "Mike Brady"—died in this Glendale house from complications of the AIDS virus.

for his long-running role as Mike Brady, forever the father of the mythical Brady family in the 1960s television hit *The Brady Bunch*. A legend in syndication, the show was brought back to the screen in 1995's *The Brady Bunch Movie* with Gary Cole reprising Reed's role. Reed died in his Glendale home from the effects of colon cancer complicated by the AIDS virus in May 1992.

(West of Orange Grove between the 110 and 134 Freeways, south of the Rose Bowl, north of Columbia off Madeline)

240 West Verdugo Avenue— Glendale, "Sunset Murders" site

A Burbank apartment on West Verdugo was shared by Doug Clark and his lover Carol Bundy in early 1980. During the spring of that year the pair cruised the Sunset Boulevard area in Hollywood picking up prostitutes and killing them in what came to be called "The Sunset Murders." Luring their victims into their car, Clark then shot them as they engaged in various sex acts with him and his girlfriend, and then he and Bundy dumped the bodies in the woods. Several bodies were left near the freeway offramp for Forest Lawn Cemetery in Glendale. Two others were beheaded and the bodies were butchered in the Verdugo garage before they were cleaned in the kitchen, given makeup by the fastidious Bundy and frozen prior to their eventual disposal.

The first of their seven victims was picked up at a grocery store at Sunset and LaBrea, which was built on the site of the Charles Chaplin home. Another victim was shot to death in the parking lot of the gas station at Franklin and Highland Avenues, while another was killed in the alley behind the Sizzler Restaurant on Ventura Boulevard in Studio City. Clark actually shot several victims in the head as they performed oral sex on him. Bundy was also charged with the murder of an old boyfriend, shot to death as the pair had sex in a van parked at Sherman Way and Barbara Ann in Studio City. Clark

is awaiting execution at San Quentin and Bundy is serving a life sentence in prison.

(West Verdugo Avenue is the continuation of Riverside/Camarillo Avenue. The location at 240 West is just past Victory Boulevard before the Golden State [5] Freeway underpass)

703 East Colorado Avenue— Glendale, Angelo Buono home, "Hillside Stranglers" murder site

An upholstery shop that once stood at the rear of this lot on Colorado Avenue in Glendale was the site of most of the ten rape-murders attributed to "Hillside Stranglers" Kenneth Bianchi and his cousin Angelo Buono. Buono operated the auto upholstery business and did work for dozens of Hollywood movie stars, living in a home once located in front of the shop. Impersonating police, Bianchi and Buono accosted young women in Hollywood, kidnapped them and brought them to Buono's Glendale home. The terrified women were held prisoner in the basement of the house, repeatedly raped and eventually strangled before their naked bodies were dropped on hillside locations around L.A.

Before the killing spree Bianchi had lived near Buono at 809 East Garfield (Apt. D). Two Hillside victims lived on the street— one in the Bianchi's apartment building (Apt. C) and another across the street at 800 Garfield. Bianchi returned to the Garfield apartment to lure one of the women to her death, and had a chance meeting with the second on a Hollywood street that led to her killing. Buono was sentenced to life in prison without parole, while former pal Bianchi is also imprisoned, but may be paroled for his testimony against his cousin.

(Colorado is east off the Golden State [5] Freeway in Glendale, just east of Glendale Avenue. Garfield is 6 blocks south parallel to Colorado)

1830 Verdugo Vista Drive—Glendale, Paul Wright "White Flame" murders

One of the most celebrated cases handled by Jerry Giesler was his defense of Paul Wright, charged with a double murder that occurred in his Glendale home. During the night of November 9, 1937, the mild-mannered Wright had emptied his nine-shot revolver into his beautiful young wife Evelyn and their best friend John Kimmel after finding them making love on the family piano. Giesler managed an acquittal for Wright, reconstructing from the position of the bodies and the wounds to each that Evelyn was apparently straddling Kimmel when the fusillade of shots rang out.

Wright testified that he had fallen asleep after a night of drinking and dinner shared by the three friends, only to be awakened by the tinkling of piano keys. When he discovered the music was caused by the rhythmic thumping of his wife's feet, he became enraged. Consumed by what Giesler called the "white flame of passion" he blasted the lovers where they sat on the piano bench. The acquittal was the first successful insanity defense ever attempted. The notorious Wright murders quickly became known as "The White Flame Case."

(Verdugo Vista Drive is east off of Verdugo Road, north of the Ventura [134] Freeway near the Verdugo Stengel Field Park)

1318 Sonora Avenue—Glendale, Ray Combs home

Ray Combs was a talented stand-up comic who operated several successful comedy clubs in his native Cincinnati, Ohio, during the early 1980s. In 1988 he was chosen to replace a retiring Richard Dawson as the host of the popular game show *The Family Feud*, a job he held until 1994, when Dawson returned and Combs was unceremoniously let go from his $1 million a year job.

Just two months later he was temporarily paralyzed in a Los Angeles auto accident, which led to an addiction to painkillers. By 1996 his 17-year marriage was foundering, and he sank into depression. His divorce became a real-life "family feud," a battle that began in 1995 and left him banished to the guest house behind the family home. His ex-wife Debbie obtained court orders prohibiting the former star from entering the main house or coming within five yards of her, and she was later awarded custody of the couple's six children.

In May 1996 Combs was fired from another game show job hosting the cable series *Family Challenge*, and a month later lost still another on a third show, *Satellite Bingo*. In late May a Valium overdose landed the 40-year-old in the hospital, and on June 1, 1996, Combs seriously injured himself by banging his head against the walls of the family's Glendale home and hitting himself with a rock. He was taken to Glendale Adventist Hospital for treatment and admitted to the psychiatric ward for observation. Just 14 hours later on June 2 was found dead, hanging by a bedsheet inside the closet of his room. The special safety rod installed in the closet was supposed to break away if someone tried to hang themselves from it, but it tragically did not.

(Sonora Avenue is located east of the Golden State [5] Freeway, a continuation of Riverside Drive. The location is near the Grandview Memorial Park between Glenoaks Boulevard and Kenneth Road)

3280 Larga Street—Glendale, Carl Chessman home

Carl Chessman was a petty criminal turned jailhouse lawyer/author and later gas chamber victim. During a short crime spree between January 13 and 23, 1948, he committed several kidnappings, rapes, armed robberies, and assaults. Caught, convicted and sentenced to death although he had killed none of his victims, he became a cause célèbre after writing four books from his death row cell and years of eventually unsuccessful appeals that ended with his 1960 execution. At the time of his crime spree, Chessman lived on this quiet Glendale street.

(In the Atwater section of L.A., near the Golden State [5] Freeway, south of Glendale Boulevard)

Colorado Boulevard and Arroyo Boulevard—Pasadena, "Suicide Bridge"

The elegant Arroyo Seco Bridge gracefully spans a beautiful dry gulch below Colorado Boulevard in Pasadena known as Lower Arroyo Park. The canyon vistas are as breathtaking today as when construction was completed in 1912, but the span has been the site of over 250 suicides since that time. The nameless souls all leapt from the bridge walkway from a height of over 100 feet into the rock-strewn ravine below. No one has ever survived a leap off the aptly named "Suicide Bridge." To stem the flow of death, county officials installed a row of unscalable metal spikes in 1993, and since that time no deaths have been reported.

Local legend has it that the bridge is haunted by the spirit of a faceless Oriental laborer who was accidentally killed while the bridge was being built when he fell into a 50-foot concrete piling as it was being poured and became forever entombed inside the bridge. His unhappy ghost is blamed for attracting all of those anonymous people to their tragic deaths in the quiet Pasadena canyon below Suicide Bridge.

(Suicide Bridge is at the intersection of Colorado Boulevard and Arroyo Boulevard in Pasadena, just south of the Glendale [134] Freeway, and can be seen from the Glendale Freeway overpass above the Arroyo Park)

1718 West Parkside Avenue—Burbank, Mabel Monohan murder site

On March 11, 1953, neighbors found crippled 64-year-old widow Mabel Monohan dead in her Burbank home, beaten to death and strangled inside the ransacked house. Police quickly arrested a ragtag group of four petty criminals—John True, Jack Santo, Emmett Perkins and Barbara Graham—who broke into Monohan's house because they believed her former son-in-law had stashed thousands of dollars in gambling winnings in the house. The group was eventually convicted of the senseless killing and sentenced to die in the gas chamber at San Quentin.

True turned state's evidence and testified against the group, implicating Graham, but the 25-year-old barfly steadfastly maintained her innocence, saying that on the night of Monohan's murder she was with her sometime husband. After her arrest, Graham's traveling salesman spouse disappeared, refusing to come forward and support her alibi. She was eventually executed. Graham's pathetic story would have been quickly forgotten if independent Hollywood producer Walter Wanger hadn't made the heartwrenching 1956 thriller *I Want to Live,* starring Susan Hayward as the doomed Graham. Although the movie earned Hayward an Oscar and made Graham a cause célèbre, it was not enough to stop her execution.

Moments after she was found guilty, Graham yelled, "All those who want me dead will die violently!" to a crowded courtroom, giving birth to what became known as "Barbara Graham's Curse." Incredibly, within three years of her execution everyone who had a part in her death was dead! The petty thief who tipped police to the foursome was crushed to death in a car accident. Graham's public defender suffered a fatal heart attack less than a month after her execution. Prosecutor Ernest Roll, who seemed obsessed with showing the world that Graham was a "bad seed," died within a year of previously undiagnosed cancer. The presiding judge in the case succumbed to cancer himself less than two years later. True, the ex-con who had fingered Graham, died in a bizarre riverboat accident a year later. The police chief who had coerced the questionable confession from True dropped dead of a heart attack three years later. Finally, Graham's prison warden fell dead of a heart attack two years later.

(Parkside Avenue is just east of the Disney Studios in Glendale, just north of the Ventura [134] Freeway and one block south of Alameda Avenue. The location is between Parish Place and Sparks Street)

2021 Grismer Avenue—Burbank, *Till Death Us Do Part* murder site

The Castillian Apartment complex at the intersection of Grismer and Bonita avenues and Glenoaks Boulevard was the site of an April 18, 1968, murder that became the basis for the 1981 murder mystery *Till Death Us Do Part*. It was written by former Los Angeles district attorney Vincent Bugliosi, who also wrote the renowned bestseller *Helter Skelter* recounting his successful prosecutions of murderer Charlie Manson and his family for the Tate and LaBianca murders. *Till Death Us Do Part* is an equally gripping tale of infidelity, insurance fraud and brutal murder.

As young newlywed Judy Davis Palliko parked her Jaguar convertible inside carport 17 of this complex, she was shot in the head, brutally clubbed and left to die in the front seat of her car. Police immediately suspected her husband Alan, an ex-policeman who operated a local tavern named "The Grand Duke" at nearby 1623 San Fernando Boulevard and who also had become a suspect in a previously unsolved 1966 murder.

On December 11, 1966, firemen pulled Henry Stockton's body out of his burning house at 2723 Ballard Street in the suburb of El Sereno, just south of Pasadena. It was assumed that his death was caused by the fire, but his body bore five bullet holes to the head and chest. It was also soon discovered that his "grieving" widow Sandra was involved in a heated affair with a co-worker and that the two had spent a good portion of Henry's insurance money on a weekend trip to Las Vegas. The co-worker's name: Alan Palliko.

After Judy Palliko's later murder, detectives connected the confusing mosaic of mostly circumstantial evidence, bank transactions and insurance records to convince a jury that Sandra Stockton and Alan Palliko had planned the murders of both Henry Stockton and Judy Palliko for the insurance money. Palliko was also convicted of attempting to murder his first wife Katharine, who was mysteriously hit by a car outside the apartment—not once, but *twice*—and who was beaten almost to death by Alan after she filed for a 1967 divorce. Stockton received a life sentence and Palliko was sentenced to death.

(The Castillian Apartments are at the three-way intersection of 2021 Grismer Avenue, Bonita Avenue, and Glenoaks Boulevard, just east of the Burbank Airport and the Golden State [5] Freeway, north of San Fernando Boulevard. The site of the Grand Duke Bar is south of the apartments at 1623 San Fernando Boulevard just below the McCambridge Recreation Center and Park. The Stockton murder site is located in El Sereno, north of the San Bernardino [10] Freeway, east of the Golden State [5] Freeway, between Huntington Drive to the north and Valley Boulevard, east of Eastern Avenue. It is not far from the El Sereno Recreation Center and Park.)

1927 Midlothian Drive—Altadena, Claude Akins death site

Claude Akins debuted in *From Here to Eternity* (1953), becoming an overnight star who went on to roles in *The Caine Mutiny* (1954) and *Inherit the Wind* (1960) before finding his niche in dozens of 1950s and 1960s westerns including *Rio Bravo* (1958), *How the West Was Won* (1962), and *The Devil's Brigade* (1968). He starred in the 1970s television shows *B.J. and the Bear* (1972 to 1978), the spin-off *Lobo* (1974 to 1977), and *Movin' On* (1979 to 1981). The lovable Akins lost a long battle with cancer and died in his Altadena home on January 27, 1994. His age was reportedly 75, though the family reported him 67.

(Midlothian Drive is north of the Foothill [210] Freeway, several blocks east of Allen Avenue, north of New York Avenue)

1234 Boston Avenue—Altadena, Barbara LaMarr death site

Reatha Dale Watson was visiting L.A. from Yakima, Washington, when she became an instant legend after the 14-year-old runaway was ordered by a judge to leave Los Angeles because she was "too beautiful to be adrift in the big city." She soon became Barbara LaMarr, later starring as Douglas Fairbanks' lover in *The Three Musketeers* (1921), and dozens of other films including *The Prisoner of Zenda* (1922), *Strangers in the Night* (1923), *The Heart of the Siren* (1925) and *Thy Name Is Woman* (1923). She was one of the greatest female stars of the silent era, but went through six husbands and millions of dollars as she almost immediately fell victim to the excesses that claimed the lives of dozens of her friends.

In October of 1925 LaMarr collapsed on the set of her final film, *The Girl from Montmartre,* and by January 20, 1926, "The Girl Who Was Too Beautiful" was dead. She died at the Altadena home of director and close friend William Watson, allegedly from tuberculosis but reputedly from a drug overdose–suicide. The 29-year-old lost her long battle with alcohol abuse and addictions to heroin, morphine, opium and co-

caine that she began using as a teenager. At the height of her fame and fortune, LaMarr stored her drugs inside a solid gold casket that she kept atop a grand piano in her living room. She was married to her sixth husband Jack Dougherty at the time of her death, and after a funeral attended by over 40,000 people she was buried in a crypt around the corner from Rudolph Valentino at Hollywood Memorial Park behind a brass marker that says simply, "With God in the Joy and Beauty of Youth."

(Located north of the Foothill [210] Freeway, between Lake Avenue and Allen Avenue, just north of New York Avenue near the Altadena Golf Course)

5636 Laurel Canyon Drive, #4— Studio City, Ed Wood death site

Quirky "B" moviemaker Ed Wood made bizarre movies like *Glen or Glenda* (1953), *Jailbait* (1954), *Bride of the Monster* (1955) and *The Violent Years* (1957). He is legendary for the 1957 stinker *Plan 9 from Outer Space,* arguably the worst movie ever made. With a budget of $1,200, the film is famous for terrible special effects. Model spaceships dangle from visible string; a shower curtain hangs behind the pilot at the rear of the cockpit; and a clock can be seen on the wall inside an alien spaceship. The backgrounds inexplicably change from daylight to darkness and back again with no explanation, and the entire cast takes overacting to an appalling level. The movie featured Maila "Vampira" Nurmi, who so hated the script that she refused to speak in any of her scenes, so Wood rewrote her character as voiceless. Also appearing was former professional wrestler Tor Johnson, and hopeless drug addict Bela Lugosi in his final film appearance. When he died during filming, Wood replaced him with his chiropodist, a much taller blonde surfer who didn't resemble Lugosi at all and didn't act. According to Wood, however, he "had Lugosi's ears," so that was close enough.

Wood was openly transvestite and favored angora sweaters and women's underwear. He was well-known around his Hollywood office, sauntering down the Hollywood Boulevard sidewalks in pink angora sweaters and pumps smoking a cigarette. Though he served bravely in the Marines during World War II, he wore a pink bra and panties under his fatigues. His fellow infantrymen had promised to shoot him if he was ever wounded so medics or Japanese soldiers would not know of his secret. Chronic alcoholism killed Wood at a modest apartment on December 10, 1978. He was only 54, and unknown except to "bad movie" buffs until the 1994 hit movie *Ed Wood,* starring Johnny Depp as Wood and Martin Landau in an Oscar-winning portrayal of Bela Lugosi.

(North exit off the 101 Freeway west of the 170 Freeway, the site is north of Burbank Blvd.)

10400 Columbus Avenue—Mission Hills—San Fernando Valley, Carl "Alfalfa" Switzer shooting site

Child star Carl Switzer starred as "Alfalfa" in Hal Roach's *The Little Rascals* during the 1930s, but once he outgrew the character in his teens there were no other roles waiting. He retired in obscurity, and by his thirty-first birthday Switzer could only find bit parts and crowd scenes. On January 21, 1959, he was shot to death in a Valley bungalow in an argument over a dog that he had borrowed from a friend and lost during a hunting trip. After Switzer found the dog he demanded friend Bud Stiltz pay him the $50 reward for the dog he himself had misplaced. When Switzer broke a glass-domed clock over Stiltz's head and attacked him with a knife, Stiltz shot him dead. For months afterward the children in the home allowed visitors to view the bloodstained carpet and bullet-riddled walls for 10 cents admission. The killing was ruled justifiable homicide.

(Located southeast of the intersection of the Reagan [118] and San Diego [405] Freeways, a block north off Devonshire Boulevard just east of Sepulveda Boulevard)

11050 Independence Avenue—Chatsworth, Lionel Barrymore death

Lionel Barrymore's 50-year career was eventually destroyed by alcoholism and bad health, and as his career and fortune dwindled he bought a home in far-out Chatsworth and moved there with his lifelong secretary and her family. Barrymore suffered a fatal heart attack in the home on November 15, 1954, dead at 75. He died sitting on the terrace reading *Macbeth* to his companions. A veteran of over 200 films, he is best remembered as the vitriolic Mr. Potter in the Capra classic *It's a Wonderful Life.*

(Located south of the Reagan [118] Freeway, just west of De Soto Avenue, north of Chatsworth Street)

Indian Dunes Motorcycle Park—Valencia, Vic Morrow death site

Indian Dunes Motorcycle Park is a privately owned nature area and one of the few undeveloped areas remaining in L.A. County. It was also the site of an accident on the set of John Landis' *Twilight Zone—The Movie* in the early morning hours of July 23, 1982, that took the lives of former *Combat* star Vic Morrow and two young child actors. According to the Farber-Green book *Outrageous Conduct: Art, Ego and the Twilight Zone Case,* director Landis pushed the safety "envelope" for realism and could be blamed for the unfortunate deaths.

An extremely dangerous stunt in a narrow canyon featured a hovering helicopter, numerous large explosive devices, and running actors. Morrow and the two child stars were used in the scene, and as Morrow ran through the Santa Clara River carrying the children, the helicopter hovering overhead was rocked by a special-effects explosion and fell upon the group. The hapless trio was killed instantly, one child crushed by the craft and the other child and Morrow decapitated by the whirling rotor blades. Lawsuits were later filed by Morrow's daughters—Carrie Morrow and actress Jennifer Jason Leigh—and by the families of the two dead children. They were later settled. After a nine-month trial Landis and four co-defendants were acquitted on a variety of charges involving the tragic deaths.

The Landis incident wasn't the first such accident on a movie set. In an eerie preview of the Morrow accident, a year earlier on the set of the television miniseries *World War III* director Boris Sagal was decapitated when he accidentally walked into a whirling helicopter blade during filming. Sagal was the father of actress Katey Sagal, who played Peg Bundy in the 1990s television series *Married ... with Children.*

(Privately owned preserve located near California Route 5 in Valencia. The accident site is beside a 100-foot-tall cliff that rises above the Santa Clara River inside the park)

15519 Saddleback Drive—Canyon County, Del Shannon suicide

Singer Del Shannon rose from obscurity to fame and fortune after his 1961 hit "Runaway," but after several follow-up songs failed to reach the level of his first he faded into alcoholism. When the 1980s brought a resurgence of interest in 1950s and 1960s music Shannon again appeared at sold-out concerts, enjoying success that let him buy a new ranch home in the hills north of L.A. It was at that new home on February 8, 1990, that Shannon committed suicide, shooting himself to death at 51.

(Approximately 40 miles north of Los Angeles, outside Santa Clarita)

10343 Fairgrove Street—Tujunga, Renee Adoree death site

Renee Adoree—real name Jeanne de la Fonte—had a storybook life reading like a fairy tale, born in a tent in France while her parents worked for a traveling circus, the daughter of a horsewoman and a clown. She spent 15 years as a circus dancer and bareback rider before a vacationing Hollywood director found her and brought her to Hollywood in 1919. Her exotic beauty and effervescent personality enthralled moviegoers, and she starred in *Made in Heaven* (1921), and the John Gilbert blockbusters *Wings* (1923) and *The Big Parade* (1925). Within one year she married and divorced both a movie star (Tom Moore) and a Hollywood agent (William Gill), divorcing each after only three months. Her French accent made her unusable in talkies, and her career soon fizzled. After years of drug and alcohol abuse, Adoree learned she was dying of tuberculosis, and retired to a mountain home above the Burbank studios. She died at home on October 5, 1933, at the age of 35.

(Located north of the Foothill [210] Freeway, north of Foothill Boulevard, east of Commerce Avenue, a block north of Apperson Street. Please Note: Several of the Los Angeles locations are not in areas that are frequented by tourists or travelers. The stories are interesting, but great care should be taken if traveling in these areas. It is not recommended that you stop at sites or get out of your vehicle for pictures, but these stories are included for the sake of interest.)

Boyle Heights, "Night Stalker" capture

Richard Ramirez, a drug addict and devil worshipper held the entire city of L.A. in the grip of panic during a yearlong spree of murder, rape and torture from June 1984 to August 1985. During that time, the dreaded "Night Stalker" left a trail of bodies stretching from nearby Monterey Park north to Pasadena and Northridge. Choosing random houses close to freeways, the late night attacks left 14 people dead and dozens more brutally maimed. The dead were viciously slashed and stabbed to death, most were horribly mutilated, and often the victims had their eyes gouged out.

When fingerprints led police to identify Ramirez he was visiting his family in Arizona. Returning via bus to L.A. on August 31, 1985, he was unaware that his picture was on the front page of every newspaper in the United States. As he bought a soda at Tito's Liquor Store at 819 Towne Avenue near the downtown bus station he was recognized by customers and forced to flee the store. He fled on foot into the nearby Boyle Heights area just east of downtown and tried to break into a home at Percy Street a block west of Indiana but was chased away. He than tried to commandeer a car at the intersection, but was seen by customers in the donut shop across the street and had to run yet again. He jumped a backyard fence on the east side of Indiana on the north side of Percy, by now becoming the stalked instead of the stalker. Fleeing a growing group of pursuers, he jumped another fence between a Percy bungalow and the house directly north on Hubbard and found Fuastino Pinon working under his car in the driveway. When Ramirez tried to start the car and flee, Pinon and his son and the crowd chased him to the east end of Hubbard and held him until police arrived. When they did, a severely beaten "Night Stalker" was crying and begging police to shoot him.

(Located east of downtown L.A. near Calvary Cemetery)

Woodbine Park, Woodbine and Vinton Street—Culver City, Calvin "Snoop Doggy Dogg" Broadus shooting site

Calvin Broadus was allegedly a member of the vicious Long Beach Insane Crips,

and by his nineteenth birthday had spent a year in jail for selling cocaine. After leaving prison in 1991 he debuted his gangster-rap personality "Snoop Doggy Dogg," and in 1993 recorded an album in a local studio. On August 25, 1993, while his debut album *Doggystyle* was selling 5 million copies, Broadus was involved in a shooting that threatened to land him back in jail. Broadus' friend Sean Abrams got into an argument outside Broadus' apartment at the Vinton Palms at 3710 Vinton with 20-year-old street gang member Phillip Woldemarian. Soon afterward, Lee, Broadus and his bodyguard McKinley Lee piled into Broadus' Jeep Cherokee to look for Woldemarian. They found him at the nearby Woodbine Park, and after a confrontation on the sidewalk next to Woodbine Street, Woldemarian was shot twice in the back by Lee.

Charges were dropped against Abrams, and Broadus and Lee were acquitted of first degree murder charges. When the jury couldn't reach a verdict on manslaughter charges, the two were released.

(The Palms neighborhood is south of Rancho Park in Culver City. Woodbine Park is at Woodbine and Vinton, south of National and the nearby 10. Broadus' Vinton Palms apartment is several blocks south of the park near Venice Boulevard.)

3424 Adams Boulevard—Los Angeles, Roscoe "Fatty" Arbuckle house

During Hollywood's "Golden Age" of the early 1900s, Roscoe "Fatty" Arbuckle built this majestic home that today serves as the rectory and parish offices of the Polish Parish of the Catholic Church in L.A. In 1921, after signing the biggest contract in movie history—$3 million a year—he bought an elegant mansion with exquisite mahogany walls, massive handwrought fireplaces and a ballroom covering the third floor. The chandelier in the dining room cost $200,000, and

Roscoe "Fatty" Arbuckle built this multimillion dollar mansion at the height of his 1920s fame, but fallout from the Virginia Rappe scandal cost him his career, his fortune, and this house.

the front door was brought from Spain for $25,000. He lost the home a year later when scandal ended his career. In the '30s Greta Garbo rented the home.

You can usually gain entrance and see the magnificent foyer and first floor living rooms, which now house offices and a gift shop. Another Arbuckle home, also home to Theda Bara, Joe Schenck and Raoul Walsh, is further east at 649 Adams.

Next door at 3430 is the still-opulent former home of director Busby Berkeley, now a condo building. Berkeley's lavishly choreographed movies were fan favorites, but mental problems ruined his life. With his career on a downslide and distressed by his mother's death, Berkeley attempted suicide in his home on June 30, 1946. He slashed both wrists and his throat but survived when his houseboy found him near death. Several months later in September 1946 a Pacific Palisades automobile accident and resulting manslaughter charges dispatched Berkeley into obscurity. He died there in 1976 at the age of 83.

(Adams east of Crenshaw)

2101 South Gramercy Place—Hancock Park, Marvin Gaye death site

Marvin Gaye was the chief Motown star from the record label's inception in Detroit in the early 1960s, with a string of number one soul hits and a marriage to Motown founder Barry Gordy's sister. A bitter divorce drove Gaye to Europe in the early 1970s, where he allegedly picked up a huge drug habit. He returned to the United States in 1984, releasing his comeback album "Sexual Healing" to fabulous reviews. On April 1, 1984, one day before his forty-fifth birthday, he was shot and killed by his own father in his family's L.A. house. Long suffering from substance abuse and recurring mental problems, Gaye was shot during an argument with his minister father. When he allegedly attacked his father in a drug-induced paranoid rage, Gaye Sr. shot his son in the temple. When asked if he loved his son, Gaye replied, "Let's just say I don't hate him."

Ruled justifiable, no charges were filed against Gaye in the shooting.

Less than a block away at the northwest corner of Gramercy and 20th is a charming white clapboard home purchased by Roscoe Arbuckle for his parents in 1918. They were forced to sell the home when Arbuckle lost his career and his millions.

(A block south of Washington Boulevard on Gramercy, west of Western in Hancock Park)

1631 South Wilton Place—Hancock Park, Marion Parker haunted house

On December 15, 1927, 12-year-old Marion Parker was abducted by a neighborhood acquaintance from an elementary school near Hancock Park. Nineteen-year-old college student Ed Hickman kidnapped Marion and immediately killed her and dismembered the corpse. As a frenzied public searched for the missing child during the week following, Hickman drove to numer-ous ransom drop sites with Parker's body propped up in his car so she appeared alive. After being seen and recognized by her father at one of the unsuccessful drops Hickman was arrested, tried and later hanged at San Quentin.

Subsequent owners of Marion's last home report the presence of a friendly ghost inside the house. Childlike in appearance, the happy vision has appeared numerous times in front of residents and visitors. The ghostly visitor likes to play with the lights and the water faucets in empty rooms, and childlike laughter and playful noises are heard from within Marion's old bedroom.

(A block south of Venice, west of Western, three blocks north of Washington, in Hancock Park)

701 South New Hampshire Avenue—Los Angeles, Mary Miles Minter mansion

The enormous 40-room mansion at the corner of New Hampshire and Seventh

Virtually forgotten now, the 1927 kidnap-murder of schoolgirl Marion Parker was the biggest news story of the day. Her home here is reportedly still haunted by the ghost of a playful young girl.

Street—now a church home—was the mansion home of young starlet Mary Miles Minter through the 1920s. Although the estate was paid for with her own massive earnings, Minter shared "Casa de Margarita" with her mother, a sister, a stepsister and several cousins. The extended Minter family, ruled by Minter's unstable stage mother Charlotte Shelby, was in residence here in February 1922, when prominent director William Desmond Taylor was found murdered in his bungalow just seven blocks away at Alvarado and Maryland.

One of the first to arrive at the Taylor murder scene, a hysterical Minter was discovered trying to remove several love letters from Taylor's desk. Within minutes police found other love letters hidden inside a pair of Taylor's boots and several of Minter's monogrammed panties in his bureau. The barely 17-year-old Minter was quickly the center of a full-scale scandal that quickly put an end to her huge career. Her mother, always the prime suspect in Taylor's unsolved murder, lived with Minter for her entire life.

(A block south and west of Wilshire and Vermont in Hancock Park/Koreatown)

325-B North Vermont Avenue—Los Angeles, Mabel Normand–Courtland Dines shooting

Courtland Dines was a wealthy young oil heir who relished spending his considerable wealth on movie stars he took great pains to arrange to meet. He was living in a bungalow court apartment in Los Angeles on New Years' Day 1924, celebrating the day with actresses Mabel Normand and Edna Purviance. Purviance was Charlie Chaplin's former lover and favorite star, and Normand was at the top of her career although battling the negative publicity surrounding her involvement in William Desmond Taylor's recent murder.

During the New Year's Day afternoon Dines ended up wounded, shot in the chest by Normand's chauffeur with Mabel's gun.

When police arrived, all present were wearing underwear and everyone had amnesia. No charges were filed, but the tragic Normand's ties to the Taylor scandal and now a shooting made her a movie curse, and her career was over, as was Edna's. Fortunately, Chaplin supported Edna with weekly checks for the rest of her life.

(At Third Avenue and Vermont in Los Angeles, east of Hancock Park)

Pantages Theater, Seventh Street and Hill Street—Los Angeles, Alexander Pantages rape

During the late 1920s the Pantages Theater was the flagship of the Pantages chain, then the world's largest. The building was also the location of the office of founder and owner Alexander Pantages. On September 9, 1929, a young and acrobatic 17-year-old bit actress named Eunice Pringle alleged to police that she had been raped there by the frail 70-year-old Pantages. Though Pringle had obviously designed a setup, Pantages was somehow convicted after his first trial and sentenced to 50 years in prison. After an appeal he was released, later acquitted with the help of a brilliant defense orchestrated by Jerry Giesler.

The theater was also the site of an April 19, 1913, suicide attempt by actress Cleva Creighton, at the time suffering through a bitter divorce with actor Lon Chaney, Sr., after a 10-year marriage. As Chaney performed onstage, the unstable alcoholic Creighton attempted suicide next to the stage by swallowing a vial of bichloride of mercury. The painful and unsuccessful attempt left her vocal chords, and singing career, ruined. After Chaney divorced her, she died in a private sanitarium a year later.

(On Hill and Seventh in downtown Los Angeles)

9137 South Figueroa Street—Los Angeles, Sam Cooke death site

The former Hacienda (or Polaris) Motel was the site of the mysterious shooting death of crooner Sam Cooke on the night of December 11, 1964. Chicago gospel singer with the Soul Stirrers (alongside Lou Rawls), Cooke went solo with "You Send Me" in 1957, staying on the charts—never dropping off—for an incredible eight years. His songs included "Chain Gang," "Twisting the Night Away," and "Cupid."

Cooke picked up a 22-year-old "model" at a Hollywood bar and brought her to an out-of-the-way motel. When she grabbed his clothes and raced out of their room, the naked Cooke chased her to the manager's office. When he burst inside he was shot to death, mistaken for a robber by the terrified manager. Although Elisa Boyer and the employee told conflicting stories and the wounds suffered by Cooke were questionable, the death was ruled a justifiable homicide.

Days before, Cooke purchased the only home he ever owned in Los Angeles at 2048 Ames Street, a block away from the LaBianca murder site.

(Near the 110 Freeway. between Manchester and Century)

Bibliography

Adams, Alex. *Madam 90210*. New York: Villard, 1993.

Alleman, Richard. *The Movie Lover's Guide to Hollywood*. New York: Harper Colophon, 1985.

Allyson, June, with Frances Spatz Leighton. *June Allyson*. New York: Putnam, 1982.

Altman, Diana. *Hollywood East: Louis B. Mayer and the Origins of the Studio System*. New York: Birch Lane Carol, 1992.

Andrews, Bart. *The "I Love Lucy" Book*. New York: Doubleday, 1985.

Anger, Kenneth. *Hollywood Babylon*. New York: Dell, 1981.

_____. *Hollywood Babylon II*. New York: Dutton, 1984.

Arce, Hector. *Gary Cooper: An Intimate Biography*. New York: William Morrow, 1979.

_____. *Groucho*. New York: William Morrow, 1979.

_____. *The Secret Life of Tyrone Power*. New York: William Morrow, 1979.

Ardmore, Frederick Lewis. *Only Yesterday*. New York: Harper & Brothers, 1964.

Astor, Mary. *A Life in Film*. New York: Delacorte, 1967.

_____. *My Story*. New York: Doubleday, 1959.

Austin, John. *Hollywood's Unsolved Mysteries*. New York: Shapolsky, 1990.

_____. *More of Hollywood's Unsolved Mysteries*. New York: Shapolsky, 1991.

_____. *Hollywood's Greatest Mysteries*. New York: Shapolsky, 1993.

Bacon, James. *Hollywood Is a Four-Letter Word*. New York: Avon, 1977.

_____. *Made in Hollywood*. Chicago: Contemporary, 1977.

Bainbridge, John. *Garbo*. London: Macmillan, 1954.

Bankhead, Tallulah. *Tallulah*. New York: Harper & Brothers, 1952.

Barr, Charles. *Laurel & Hardy*. London: Studio Vista, 1967.

Bashe, Philip. *Teenage Idol—Travelin' Man: The Complete Biography of Rick Nelson*. New York: Hyperion, 1992.

Baxter, John. *Hollywood in the '30s*. New York: A.S. Barnes, 1968.

Beaton, Cecil. *Memoirs of the '40s*. New York.

Beauchamp, Cari. *Without Lying Down: Francis Marion and the Powerful Women of Early Hollywood*. New York: Scribner, 1997.

Behlmer, Rudy. *Inside Warner Bros. (1935–1951)*. New York: Viking Penguin, 1985.

_____. *Memo from David O. Selznick*. New York: Viking, 1972.

Behn, Noel,D. *Lindbergh: The Crime*. New York: Penguin, 1995.

Berg, A. Scott. *Goldwyn: A Biography*. New York: Knopf, 1989.

Berkman, Edward O. *The Lady and the Law: The Remarkable Story of Fanny Holtzman*. Boston: Little, Brown, 1976.

Bernstein, Matthew. *Walter Wanger: Hollywood Independent*. Berkeley: University of California Press, 1994.

Besser, Joe, et al. *Once a Stooge Always a Stooge*. New York: Knightsbridge, 1990.

Blair, Joan, and Clay Blair, Jr. *The Search for J.F.K.* New York: Berkeley, 1976.

Blake, Michael F. *Lon Chaney: The Man Behind the Thousand Faces*. Vestal, NY: Vestal, 1993.

Blum, Daniel. *A Pictorial History of the Talkies*. New York: Putnam, 1973.

Bogdanovich, Peter. *Allen Dwan: The Last Pioneer*. New York: Praeger, 1971.

Bosworth, Patricia. *Montgomery Clift: A Biography*. New York: Harcourt Brace Jovanovich, 1978.

Bowman, William D. *Charlie Chaplin: His Life and Art*. Haskell, NY: 1974.

Brady, Kathleen. *Lucille: The Life of Lucille Ball.* New York: Hyperion, 1994.

Brian, Denis. *Tallulah, Darling.* New York: Pyramid, 1972.

Brooks, Louise. *Lulu in Hollywood.* New York: Alfred A. Knopf, 1982.

Brownlow, Kevin *Hollywood: The Pioneers.* New York: Knopf, 1980.

_____. *The Parade's Gone By.* New York: Knopf, 1968.

_____. *The War, the West, and the Wilderness.* New York: Knopf, 1979.

Burns, George. *Gracie: A Love Story.* New York: Penguin, 1981.

Cahn, William. *The Laugh Makers: A Pictorial History of American Comedians.* New York: Bramhall, 1957.

Capell, Frank. *The Strange Death of Marilyn Monroe.* The Herald of Freedom, 1964.

Capra, Frank. *The Name Above the Title: An Autobiography.* New York: Macmillan, 1971.

Carey, Gary. *All the Stars in Heaven.* New York: E.P. Dutton, 1981.

_____. *Anita Loos: A Biography.* New York: Alfred A. Knopf, 1988.

Carpozi, George. *The Gary Cooper Story.* New Rochelle, NY: Macmillan, 1971.

Carrier, Jeffrey L. *Tallulah Bankhead.* New York: Greenwood, 1991.

Castle, Irene, with Bob Duncan and Wanda Duncan. *Castles in the Air.* Garden City, NY: Doubleday, 1958.

Cerasini, Marc. *O.J. Simpson: American Hero, American Tragedy.* New York: Windsor, 1994.

Chaplin, Charles. *My Autobiography.* London: Bodley Head, 1964.

_____. *My Life in Pictures* London: Bodley Head, 1974.

Chaplin, Lita Grey, with Morton Cooper. *My Life with Chaplin: An Intimate Memoir.* Grove, 1966.

Cheirichetti, David. *Hollywood Director: The Career of Mitchell Leison.* New York: Curtis Books, 1973.

Christian, Linda. *Linda.* New York: Crown, 1962.

Cini, Zelda, and Bob Crane, with Peter H. Brown. *Hollywood: Land and Legend.* Westport, CT: Arlington, 1980.

Coleman, Ray. *The Carpenters: The Untold Story.* New York: HarperCollins, 1994.

Conner, Floyd. *Lupe Velez and Her Lovers*: New York: Barricade, 1993.

Considine, Shaun. *Bette and Joan: The Divine Feud.* New York: Dutton, 1989.

Cooper, Jackie. *Please Don't Shoot My Dog.* New York: William Morrow, 1988.

Cooper, Miriam, and Bonnie Herndon. *Dark Lady of the Silents: My Life in Early Hollywood.* New York: Bobbs-Merrill, 1973.

Corliss, Richard. *Greta Garbo.* New York: Pyramid, 1974.

Crawford, Christina. *Mommie Dearest.* New York: William Morrow, 1978.

Crawford, Joan. *My Way of Life.* New York: Simon and Schuster, 1971.

_____, with Jane Ardmore. *A Portrait of Joan.* Garden City, NY: Doubleday, 1962.

Cremer, Robert. *Lugosi: The Man Behind the Cape.* Chicago: Henry Regnery, 1976.

Crivello, Kirk. *Fallen Angels: The Lives and Untimely Deaths of 14 Hollywood Beauties.* Secaucus,NJ: Citadel, 1988.

Crowther, Bosley. *The Lion's Share: The Story of an Entertainment Empire.* New York: Dutton, 1957.

_____. *Hollywood Rajah: The Life and Times of Louis B. Mayer.* New York: Henry Holt, 1960.

Croy, Homer. *Starmaker: The Story of D.W. Griffith.* New York: Duell, Sloan & Pearce, 1959.

Curtis, Thomas Quinn. *Von Stroheim.* New York: Farrar, Straus & Giroux, 1971.

Davidson, Bill. *Spencer Tracy: Tragic Idol.* New York: E.P. Dutton, 1987.

Davidson, Muriel, and Frank Westmore. *The Westmores of Hollywood.* New York: J.P. Lippincott, 1976.

Davies, Marion. *The Times We Had: Life with William Randolph Hearst.* New York: Bobbs-Merrill, 1975.

Davis, Bette. *The Lonely Life.* New York: Lancer, 1963.

_____, with Michael Herskowitz. *This 'n' That,* New York: Putnam, 1987.

Davis, Dentner. *Jean Harlow: Hollywood Comet.* London: Constable House, 1975.

Day, Beth. *This Was Hollywood.* New York: Doubleday, 1960.

de Acosta, Mercedes. *Here Lies the Heart.* New York: Reynal, 1960.

DeMille, Cecil B. *The Autobiography of Cecil B. DeMille.* Englewood Cliffs, NJ: Prentice-Hall, 1959.

Dody, Sanford. *Giving Up the Ghost.* New York: Evans, 1980.

Donaldson, Norman, and Betty Donaldson. *How Did They Die?* New York: St. Martin's, 1980.

Dowd, Nancy and David Shepard. *King Vidor.* Metuchen, NJ: Scarecrow, 1988.

Dressler, Marie. *My Own Story.* Boston: Little, Brown, 1934.

Dunaway, David King. *Huxley in Hollywood.* New York: Harper & Row, 1989.

Dunne, Dominic. *Fatal Charms and Other Tales of Today.* New York: Bantam, 1987.

Durgnat, Raymond. *King Vidor: American.* Los Angeles: University of California Press, 1988.

Eames, John Douglas. *The M-G-M Story.* New York: Crown, 1971.

Edmonds, Andy. *Bugsy's Baby: The Secret Life of Mob Queen Virginia Hill.* New York: Carol, 1993.

_____. *Frame-Up! The Untold Story of Roscoe "Fatty" Arbuckle.* New York: William Morrow, 1991.

Edwards, Anne. *The DeMilles: An American Family.* New York: Harry N. Abrams, 1988.

_____. *Vivien Leigh: A Biography.* New York: Simon and Schuster, 1977.

Eells, George. *Final Gig: The Man Behind the Murder.* New York: Harcourt Brace Jovanovich, 1991.

_____. *Ginger, Loretta and Irene Who?* New York: Putnam, 1976.

_____. *Hedda and Louella.* New York: Putnam, 1972.

_____. *Mae West: A Biography.* New York: Harcourt Brace Jovanovich, 1982.

Endres, Stacy, and Robert Cushman. *Hollywood at Your Feet: The Story of the World-Famous Chinese Theater.* Los Angeles: Pomegranate, 1992.

Engel, Joel. *Rod Serling: The Dreams and Nightmares of Life in the Twilight Zone.* Chicago: Contemporary Books, 1989.

Everson, William K. *The Films of Hal Roach.* New York: Museum of Modern Art, 1971.

_____. *The Films of Laurel and Hardy.* New York: Museum of Modern Art, 1967.

Eyman, Scott. *Ernst Lubitsch: Laughter in Paradise.* New York: Simon and Schuster, 1993.

_____. *Mary Pickford: America's Sweetheart,* New York: Donald I. Fine, 1990.

Fairbanks, Douglas, Jr. *The Salad Days,* New York: Doubleday, 1988.

_____, with Richard Schickel. *The Fairbanks Album,* Boston: New York Graphic Society, 1975.

Fairbanks, Letitia, and Ralph Hancock. *Douglas Fairbanks: The Fourth Musketeer.* New York: Henry Holt, 1953.

Farber, Stephen, and Marc Green. *Hollywood Dynasties,* New York: Delilah, 1984.

Farr, Louise. *The Sunset Murders.* New York: Pocket Books, 1992.

Fein, Art. *The L.A. Musical History Tour.* Boston: Faber and Faber, 1990.

Feinman, Jeffrey. *Hollywood Confidential.* New York: Playboy Books, 1976.

Finch, Christopher, and Linda Rozencrantz. *Gone Hollywood: The Movie Colony in the Golden Age.* New York: Doubleday, 1979.

Finler, Joel W. *The Hollywood Story.* New York. Crown, 1988.

Flamini, Roland. *Thalberg: The Last Tycoon and the World of MGM.* New York: Crown, 1994.

Ford, Daniel. *Pappy: The Life of John Ford.* Englewood Cliffs, NJ: Prentice-Hall, 1979.

Fountain, Leatrice Joy Gilbert. *Dark Star: The Untold Story of the Meteoric Rise and Fall of the Legendary John Gilbert.* New York: St. Martin's, 1985.

Fowler, Gene. *Father Goose: The Biography of Mack Sennett.* New York: Crown, 1934.

_____. *Good Night Sweet Prince: The Life and Times of John Barrymore.* New York: Buccaneer, 1943.

Fowler, Will. *Reporters: Memoirs of a Young Newspaperman.* Malibu: Roundtable, 1991.

Francisco, Charles. *Gentleman: The William Powell Story.* New York: St. Martin's, 1985.

Frank, Gerold. *Judy.* New York: Harper & Row, 1975.

Freedland, Michael. *The Warner Brothers.* New York: St. Martin's, 1983.

Gallagher, Rachel. *The Girl Who Loved Garbo.* New York: Donald I. Fine, 1990.

Garceau, Jean. *The Biography of Clark Gable.* New York: Little, Brown 1961.

Gardner, Ava. *Ava: My Story.* New York: Bantam, 1990.

Geist, Kenneth L. *Pictures Will Talk: The Life and Films of Joseph Mankiewicz.* New York: Charles Scribner's Sons, 1978.

Giesler, Jerry. *The Jerry Giesler Story.* New York: Simon and Schuster, 1960.

Gifford, Dennis. *Chaplin* (The Movie-Makers Series). Secaucus, NJ: Citadel, 1972.

Gilbert, John. *"Jack Gilbert Writes His Own Story." Photoplay,* June-September, 1928.

Gill, Brendan. *Tallulah.* New York: Harper & Row, 1972.

Gil-Montero, Martha. *Brazilian Bombshell: The Biography of Carmen Miranda*. New York: Donald I. Fine, 1989.

Glyn, Anthony. *Elinor Glyn: A Biography*. Garden City, NY: Doubleday, 1955.

Golden, Eve. *Platinum Girl— The Life and Legend of Jean Harlow*. New York: Abbeville, 1991.

Goldman, Albert. *Ladies and Gentlemen, Lenny Bruce*. New York: Random House, 1971.

Goodman, Ezra. *The Fifty Year Decline and Fall of Hollywood*. New York: Simon and Schuster, 1961.

Graham, Sheilah. *Confessions of a Hollywood Columnist*. New York: Bantam, 1970.

_____. *The Garden of Allah*. New York: 1970.

_____. *Hollywood Revisited*. New York: St. Martin's, 1984.

Griffith, Richard, and Arthur Mayer. *Movies: The Sixty-Year History of the World of Hollywood*. New York: Bonanza, 1957.

Grobel, Lawrence. *The Hustons*. New York: Scribner's, 1989.

Gronowicz, Antoni. *Garbo: Her Story*. New York: Simon & Schuster, 1990.

Guiles, Fred Lawrence. *Hanging On in Paradise*. New York: McGraw-Hill, 1975.

_____. *Jeanette MacDonald*. New York: McGraw-Hill, 1975.

_____. *Joan Crawford: The Last Word*. New York: Birch Lane Carol, 1995.

_____. *Legend: The Life and Death of Marilyn Monroe*. New York: Stein and Day, 1984.

_____. *Marion Davies*. New York: McGraw-Hill, 1972.

_____. *Norma Jean: The Life of Marilyn Monroe*. New York: McGraw-Hill, 1969.

_____. *Stan: The Life of Stan Laurel*. Briarcliff Manor, NY: Stein and Day, 1980.

_____. *Tyrone Power: The Last Idol*. New York: Berkeley, 1979.

Halliwell, Leslie. *The Filmgoer's Book of Quotes*. New York: Signet, 1975.

Harmetz, Aljean. *The Making of* The Wizard of Oz. New York: Alfred A. Knopf, 1977.

Harris, Warren G. *Gable and Lombard*. New York: Simon and Schuster, 1974.

Haver, Ronald. *David O. Selznick's Hollywood*. New York: Knopf, 1980.

Hecht, Ben. *A Child of the Century*. New York: Simon and Schuster, 1954.

Heimann, Jim. *Out with the Stars: Hollywood Nightlife in the Golden Era*. New York: Abbeville, 1985.

Henderson, Robert M. *D.W. Griffith: His Life and Work*. New York: Farrar, Straus & Giroux, 1972.

Henreid, Paul. *Ladies' Man*. New York: St. Martin's, 1985.

Hepburn, Katharine. *Me*. New York: Alfred A. Knopf, 1991.

Hersh, Seymour M. *The Dark Side of Camelot*. New York: Little Brown, 1997.

Higham, Charles. *Bette*. New York: Macmillan, 1981.

_____. *Cecil B. DeMille*. New York: Charles Scribner's Sons, 1973.

_____. *Charles Laughton: An Intimate Biography*. Garden City, NY: Doubleday, 1976.

_____. *Errol Flynn: The Untold Story*. New York: MacMillan, 1980.

_____. *Hollywood Cameramen: Sources of Light*. Bloomington: Indiana University Press, 1970.

_____. *Marlene: The Life of Marlene Dietrich*. New York: W.W. Norton, 1977.

_____. *Merchant of Dreams: Louis B. Mayer and the Secret Hollywood*. New York: Donald I. Fine, 1993.

_____. *Warner Brothers*. New York: Charles Scribner's Sons, 1975.

_____, and Roy Moseley. *Cary Grant: The Lonely Heart*. New York: Harcourt Brace Jovanovich, 1989.

_____, and Joel Greenberg, eds. *Hollywood in the 40s*. New York: Paperback Library, 1970.

Hopper, Hedda. *From Under the Hat*. Garden City, NY: Doubleday, 1952.

Hyams, Joe. *Bogie: The Humphrey Bogart Story*. New York: The New American Library, 1962.

Israel, Lee. *Miss Tallulah Bankhead*. New York: Putnam, 1972.

Jacobson, Laurie, and Marc Wanamaker. *Hollywood Haunted: A Ghostly Tour of Filmland*. Santa Monica, CA: Angel City Press, 1994.

Jordan, Rene. *Gary Cooper*. New York: Pyramid, 1974.

Kanin, Garson. *Hollywood*. New York: Viking Press, 1967.

Kirkpatrick, Sydney D. *A Cast of Killers*. New York: Dutton, 1986.

Kobal, John. *The Art of the Great Hollywood Portrait Photographers*. New York: Harrison House, 1980.

_____. *People Will Talk*. New York: Alfred A. Knopf, 1985.

Kobler, John. *Damned in Paradise: The Life of John Barrymore.* New York: Atheneum, 1977.

Kotsilibas-Davis, James, and Myrna Loy. *Myrna Loy: Being and Becoming.* New York: Alfred A. Knopf, 1987.

Keats, John. *Howard Hughes.* New York: Random House, 1966.

Keylin, Arlene, and Suri Fleischer, eds. *Hollywood Album: Lives and Deaths of Hollywood Stars from the Pages of the New York Times.* New York: Arno, 1979.

_____, and _____, eds. *Hollywood Album 2: Lives and Deaths of Hollywood Stars from the Pages of the New York Times.* New York: Arno Press, 1979.

Kidd, Charles. *Debrett Goes to Hollywood.* New York: St. Martin's, 1986.

Knowlton, Janice, and Michael Newton. *Daddy Was the Black Dahlia Killer.* New York: Pocket, 1995.

Kobal, John. *Rita Hayworth: The Time, the Place, the Woman.* New York: W.W. Morton, 1977.

Koszarski, Richard. *The Man You Love to Hate: Erich von Stroheim and Hollywood.* New York: Oxford University Press, 1983.

LaGuardia, Robert. *Monty: A Biography of Montgomery Clift.* New York: Arbor House, 1977.

LaGuardia, Robert, and Gene Arceri. *Red.* New York: Macmillan, 1985.

Lahue, Kalton C. *Dreams for Sale: The Rise and Fall of Triangle Film Corporation.* New York:, A.S. Barnes, 1971.

Lambert, Gavin. *Norma Shearer.* New York: Alfred A. Knopf, 1990.

_____. *On Cukor.* New York: Putnam, 1972.

Lamparski, Richard. *Lamparski's Hidden Hollywood: Where the Stars Lived, Loved and Died.* New York: Fireside, 1981.

_____. *Whatever Happened to...* Various volumes. New York: Crown, various publication dates.

Lasky, Betty. *RKO: The Biggest Little Major of Them All.* Englewood Cliffs, NJ: Prentice-Hall, 1984.

Lasky, Jesse L. *I Blow My Own Horn.* Garden City, NY:, Doubleday, 1957.

_____. *Whatever Happened to Hollywood?* New York: Funk & Wagnalls, 1975.

Lasky, Jesse L., Jr. *Love Scene: The Story of Laurence Olivier and Vivien Leigh.* New York: Thomas Y. Crowell, 1978.

Lawrence, Jerome. *Actor: The Life and Times of Paul Muni.* New York: Putnam, 1974.

Leaming, Barbara. *Katharine Hepburn.* New York: Crown, 1995.

Lewis, Arthur H. *It Was Fun While It Lasted: A Lament for the Hollywood That Was.* New York: Trident, 1973.

Lewis, Judy. *Uncommon Knowledge.* New York: Pocket, 1994

Lockwood, Charles. *Dream Palaces: Hollywood at Home.* New York: Viking, 1981.

_____. *The Guide to Hollywood and Beverly Hills: The Best.* New York: Crown, 1984.

Loos, Anita. *Cast of Thousands.* New York: Viking, 1977.

_____. *A Girl Like I.* New York: Viking, 1966.

_____. *Kiss Hollywood Good-bye.* New York: Grosset and Dunlap, 1975.

_____. *The Talmadge Girls.* New York: Viking, 1978.

McCabe, John. *Charlie Chaplin.* Garden City, NJ: Doubleday, 1978.

_____. *The Comedy World of Stan Laurel.* Garden City, NY: Doubleday, 1974.

McGilligan, Patrick. *George Cukor: A Double Life.* New York: St. Martin's, 1991.

MacLean, Barbara Barondess. *One Life Is Not Enough.* Los Angeles: Hippocrene, 1986.

Madsen, Alex. *The Sewing Circle: Female Stars Who Loved Other Women.* New York: Birch Lane Carol, 1995.

_____. *Stanwyck: The Life and Times of Barbara Stanwyck.* New York: HarperCollins, 1994.

Mansfield, Stephanie. *The Richest Girl in the World: The Extravagant Life and Fast Times of Doris Duke.* New York: Pinnacle, 1994.

Marinacci, Mike. *Mysterious California: Strange Places and Eerie Phenomena in the Golden State.* Los Angeles: Panpipes, 1988.

Marion, Francis. *Off with Their Heads: A Serio-Comic Tale of Hollywood.* New York: Macmillan, 1972.

Marx, Arthur. *The Nine Lives of Mickey Rooney.* New York: Stein and Day, 1986.

Marx, Groucho. *The Groucho Phile.* Indianapolis: Bobbs-Merrill, 1976.

_____, and Richard Anobile. *The Marx Brothers Scrapbook.* New York: Darien House, 1973.

Marx, Samuel. *Mayer and Thalberg: The Make-Believe Saints.* New York: Random House, 1975.

Mast, Gerald. *A Short History of the Movies.* New York: Macmillan, 1992.

Meade, Marion. *Cut to the Chase: A Biography of Buster Keaton.* New York: HarperCollins, 1995.

_____. *What Fresh Hell Is This? Dorothy Parker: A Biography*. New York: Villard, 1987.

Milton, Joyce, and Ann Louise Bardach. *Vicki: The True Story of Vicki Morgan and Alfred Bloomingdale*. New York: St. Martin's, 1986.

Minnelli, Vincente. *I Remember It Well*. Garden City, NY: Doubleday, 1974.

Moore, Charles, with Peter Becker, and Ragula Campbell. *The City Observed: Los Angeles, A Guide to Its Architecture and Landscapes*. New York: Random House, 1984.

Moore, Colleen. *Silent Star*. New York: Doubleday, 1968.

Morello, Joe, and Edward Z. Epstein. *Gable and Lombard and Powell and Harlow*. New York: Dell, 1975.

_____. *The "IT" Girl: The Incredible Story of Clara Bow*. New York: Delacorte, 1976.

_____. *Lana: The Public and Private Lives of Miss Turner*. New York: Dell, 1971.

_____. *Loretta Young: An Extraordinary Life*. New York: Delacorte, 1986.

Morris, Michael. *Madam Valentino: The Many Lives of Natacha Rambova*. New York: Abbeville, 1991.

Murray, Ken. *The Golden Days of San Simeon*. New York: Doubleday, 1971.

Negri, Pola. *Memoirs of a Star*. Garden City, NY: Doubleday, 1970.

Newquist, Roy. *Conversations with Joan Crawford*. Secaucus, NJ: Citadel, 1986.

Niven, David. *Bring On the Empty Horses*. New York: Putnam, 1975.

_____. *The Moon's a Balloon*. New York: Putnam, 1982.

Noble, Peter. *Hollywood Scapegoat*. London: Fortune, 1950.

Noguchi, Thomas. *Corone*. New York: Pocket, 1983.

Norman, Barry. *The Film Greats*. London: Hodder and Stoughton, 1985.

O'Dell, Paul. *Griffith and the Rise of Hollywood*. New York: A.S. Barnes, 1970.

Palmer, Lilli. *Change Lobsters and Dance*. New York: Macmillan, 1975.

Paris, Barry. *Garbo*. New York: Alfred A. Knopf, 1995.

_____. *Louise Brooks*. New York: Alfred A. Knopf, 1989.

Parrish, James Robert, with Stephen Whitney. *The George Raft File*. New York: Drake, 1973.

Parrish, Robert. *Growing Up in Hollywood*. New York: Harcourt Brace Jovanovich, 1976.

Parsons, Louella. *Tell It to Louella*. New York: Putnam, 1961.

Pascal, John. *The Jean Harlow Story*. Popular Library, 19.

Quirk, Lawrence J. *Margaret Sullavan: Child of Fate*. New York: St. Martin's, 1986.

_____. *Norma: The Story of Norma Shearer*. New York: St. Martin's, 1988.

Ragan, David. *Who's Who in Hollywood: 1900–1976*. New Rochelle, NY: Arlington House, 1977.

Reavill, Gil. *Los Angeles*. Oakland: Compass American Guides, 1992.

Richman, Harry, with Richard Gehman. *A Hell of a Life*. New York: Duell, Sloan & Pearce, 1966.

Roberts, Randy, and James S. Olson. *John Wayne: American*. New York: Free Press, 1995.

Robinson, David. *Chaplin: His Life and Art*. New York: McGraw-Hill, 1985.

_____. *Hollywood in the Twenties*. London/New York: Zwemmer/Barnes, 1968.

Rooney, Mickey. *Mickey Rooney: Life Is Too Short*. New York: Ballantine, 1991.

Rothmiller, Mike, and Ivan Goldman. *L.A. Secret Police: Inside the LAPD Elite Spy Network*. New York: Pocket, 1992.

Russell, Rosalind. *Life Is a Banquet*. New York: Random House, 1977.

Ruuth, Marianne. *Cruel City: The Dark Side of Hollywood's Rich and Famous*. Malibu: Roundtable, 1984.

St. Johns, Adela Rogers. *The Honeycomb*. Garden City, NJ: Doubleday, 1969.

_____. *Love, Laughter and Tears: My Hollywood Story*. New York: Doubleday, 1978.

Sands, Frederick, and Sven Broman. *The Divine Garbo*. New York: Grosset and Dunlap, 1975.

Schatz, Thomas. *The Genius of the System*. New York: Pantheon, 1988.

Schessler, Ken. *This Is Hollywood: An Unusual Movie Guide*, 10th ed., 11th ed. Redlands, CA: Ken Schessler, 1992, 1993.

Schickel, Richard. *D.W. Griffith: An American Life*. New York: Simon and Schuster, 1984.

Schulberg, Budd. *Moving Pictures: Memoirs of a Hollywood Prince*. Briarcliff Manor, NY: Stein and Day, 1981.

Selznick, David O. *Memo from David O. Selznick*. Rudy Behlmer, ed. New York: The Viking, 1972.

Selznick, Irene Mayer. *A Private View*. New York: Alfred A. Knopf, 1983.

Sennett, Mack, and Cameron Shipp. *King of Comedy*. Garden City, NJ: Doubleday, 1954.

Shevey, Sandra. *The Marilyn Scandal*. New York: Jove, 1980.

Shulman, Irving. *Harlow: An Intimate Biography*. New York: Bernard Geis, 1964.

_____. *Valentino*. New York: Trident, 1967.

Sinclair, Andrew. *John Ford: A Biography*. New York: Dial, 1979.

Skal, David J.,and Elias Savada. *Dark Carnival: The Secret World of Tod Browning, Hollywood's Master of the Macabre*. New York: Anchor Books, 1995.

Slatzer, Robert. *The Life and Curious Death of Marilyn Monroe*. New York: Pinnacle, 1974.

Smith, H. Allen. *The Life and Legend of Gene Fowler*. New York: William Morrow, 1977.

Spada, James. *More Than a Woman: An Intimate Biography of Bette Davis*. New York: Bantam, 1993.

_____. *Peter Lawford: The Man Who Kept the Secrets*. New York: Bantam, 1991.

Speriglio, Milo. *The Marilyn Conspiracy*. New York: Pocket, 1986.

Spoto, Donald. *The Kindness of Strangers*. Boston: Little, Brown, 1985.

_____. *Marilyn Monroe: The Biography*. New York: Harper Collins, 1993.

Steiger, Sherry Hansen, and Brad Steiger. *Hollywood and the Supernatural*. New York: St. Martin's, 1990.

Stenn, David. *Bombshell: The Life and Death of Jean Harlow*. New York: Doubleday, 1993.

_____. *Clara Bow: Runnin' Wild*. Garden City, NJ: Doubleday, 1991.

Sternberg, Josef Von. *Fun in a Chinese Laundry*. New York: Collier, 1965.

Stewart, Donald Ogden. *By a Stroke of Luck*. London: Paddington, 1975.

Summers, Anthony. *Goddess: The Secret Lives of Marilyn Monroe*. New York: Macmillan, 1985.

Swanberg, W.A. *Citizen Hearst*. New York: Charles Scribner's Sons, 1961.

Swenson, Karen. *Greta Garbo: A Life Apart*. New York: Scribner, 1997.

Swindell, Larry. *Gary Cooper: The Last Hero*. Garden City, NJ: Doubleday, 1980.

_____. *Screwball: The Life of Carole Lombard*. New York: William Morrow, 1975.

_____. *Spencer Tracy*. New York: World, 1969.

Temple, Shirley. *Child Star*. New York: McGraw-Hill, 1988.

Thomas, Bob. *Bud & Lou: The Abbott and Costello Story*. Philadelphia: Lippincott, 1967.

_____. *Golden Boy: The Untold Story of William Holden*. New York: Berkley, 1983.

_____. *Joan Crawford: A Biography*. New York: Simon and Schuster, 1978.

_____. *King Cohn: The Life and Times of Harry Cohn*. New York: Putnam, 1967.

_____. *Selznick*. Garden City, NY: Doubleday, 1970.

_____. *Thalberg: Life and Legend*. New York: Bantam, 1970.

Thomas, Tony. *Errol Flynn: The Spy Who Never Was*. New York: Citadel, 1990.

_____. *The Films of Errol Flynn*. New York: Citadel, 1968.

Thomson, David. *Showman: The Life of David O. Selznick*. New York: Knopf, 1992.

Tornabene, Lyn. *Long Live the King: A Biography of Clark Gable*. New York: Putnam, 1976.

Torrence, Bruce T. *Hollywood: The First 100 Years*. New York: Zoetrope, 1982.

Tosches, Nick. *Dino: Living High in the Dirty Business of Dreams*. New York: Doubleday, 1992.

Truitt, Evelyn Mack. *Who Was Who on Screen*. New York: R.R. Bowker, 1984.

Vickers, Hugo. *Cecil Beaton*. Boston: Little, Brown, 1985.

Vidor, King. *A Tree Is a Tree*. New York: Garland, Harcourt, Brace, 1952: Hollywood: Samuel French, 1989.

Walker, Alexander. *Fatal Charm: The Life of Rex Harrison*. New York: St. Martin's, 1993.

_____. *Garbo*. New York: Macmillan, 1980.

_____. *Joan Crawford: The Ultimate Star*. New York: Harper & Row, 1983.

_____. *Rudolph Valentino*. New York: Stein and Day, 1970.

_____. *Sex in the Movies*. Middlesex, UK: Penguin, Harmondsworth, 1968.

_____. *Shattered Silents: How the Talkies Came to Stay*. New York: Morrow, 1979.

_____. *Stardom*. New York: Stein and Day, 1970.

Wallace, Irving, et al. *The Intimate Sex Lives of Famous People*. New York: Dell, 1982.

Wanger, Walter. *You Must Remember This*. New York: Putnam, 1975.

Warner, Jack. *My First Hundred Years in Hollywood*. New York: Random House, 1965.

Wayne, Jane Ellen. *Clark Gable: Portrait of a Misfit*. New York: St. Martin's, 1993.

_____. *Gable's Women*. New York: Prentice-Hall, 1987.

_____. *Robert Taylor: The Man with the Perfect Face*. New York: St. Martin's, 1989.

_____. *The Life of Robert Taylor*. New York: Warner Paperback, 1973.

_____. *Grace Kelly's Men*. New York: St. Martin's, 1991.

_____. *Crawford's Men*. New York: Prentice-Hall, 1988.

Webb, Michael, ed. *Hollywood: Legend and Reality*. Boston: Little, Brown, 1986.

West, Mae. *Goodness Had Nothing to Do With It*. Englewood Cliffs, NJ: Prentice-Hall, 1959.

Windeler, Robert. *Sweetheart: The Story of Mary Pickford*. New York: Praeger, 1974.

Wolfe, Donald H. *The Last Days of Marilyn Monroe*. New York: William Morrow, 1998.

Wray, Fay. *On the Other Hand*. New York: St. Martin's, 1989.

Yablonski. Lewis. *George Raft*. New York: McGraw-Hill, 1974.

Yagoda, Ben. *Will Rogers: A Biography*. New York: Alfred A. Knopf, 1993.

Zierold, Norman. *The Moguls*. New York: Coward-McCann, 1969.

_____. *Garbo*. New York: Stein and Day, 1969.

_____. *The World of Yesterday*. New York: Viking, 1943.

Index

Aadland, Beverly 39, 146
A&M Records 88
Abbie's Irish Rose (1946) 86
Abbott, Bud 204, 210, 221
Abbott and Costello 67, 119, 204, 210, 221
Abbott and Costello Meet the Keystone Cops (1955) 204
Abroad with Two Yanks (1945) 205
The Absent-Minded Professor (1961) 167
Academy of Motion Picture Arts and Sciences 131
Accardo, Tony 137
accident: aircraft 123, 138, 139, 151, 225, 236; automobile 5, 14, 17, 23, 24, 89, 106, 118, 128, 138, 150, 153, 154, 161, 166, 178, 190, 205, 213, 238, 239, 248, 249; fall 92, 120, 123, 167, 170, 171, 187, 193, 194; fire 65, 66, 130, 145, 150; shooting 77
Acker, Jean 111
Ackroyd, Dan 48
The Actress (1953) 47
Adams, Edie 161
Adams, Madame Alex 61, 107, 148
Adams, Nick 85, 86
Adams Boulevard 250, 251
Adam's Rib (1921) 153
Adam's Rib (1949) 60, 186
The Addams Family (television series) 69, 128, 226
Adelaide Drive 192, 193
Aderno Way 188, 189
Adler, Buddy 120, 237
Adoree, Renee 10, 249
Adrian, Gilbert 5, 14, 36
Adrian, Iris 45
The Adventures of Huckleberry Finn (1960) 200
The Adventures of Jane Arden (1938) 206
The Adventures of Jessie James (1949) 176
The Adventures of Marco Polo (1965) 118

The Adventures of Ozzie and Harriet 39, 40
The Adventures of Red Rider (1952) 206
The Adventures of Robin Hood (1938) 141
The Adventures of Tom Sawyer (1938) 17
Advise and Consent (1962) 176
After the Thin Man (1936) 100, 172
Afton Place 12
Aftonian Apartments 12
Agnes Avenue 207
AIDS virus, death by 47, 52, 86, 87, 146, 243
Airplane (1980) 157
Airplane II (1982) 157
Airport (1970) 56, 85
Airport '77 (1977) 167
Akins, Claude 246, 247
The Alamo (1960) 234
Albertson, Jack 58
alcohol abuse 9, 12, 22, 123, 141, 146, 147, 153, 154
alcoholism, death by 12, 22, 59, 107, 162, 165, 206, 248, 249
Alda, Alan 152
Alda, Robert 237
Alderman, Myrl 45
Alex, Madame *see* Adams, Madame Alex
Alexander, Aleta 47, 216, 217
Alexander, Ross 47, 216, 217
Alexander's Ragtime Band (1938) 131
Alfred Street 66
Algiers (1938) 226
Ali Baba Goes to Town (1937) 79
Alias Smith and Jones 32
All About Eve (1950) 152
All in the Family (television series) 17, 188
All Quiet on the Western Front (1930) 86
All That Heaven Knows (1955) 48
All the King's Men (1949) 86
Allen, Fred 77
Allen, Gracie 26, 38, 123

Allen, Steve 84
Alley, Kirstie 217
Allgood, Sara 229
Allman, Greg 46
Allyson, June 165
Alpine Drive 124, 125, 126
Alta Loma Drive 56
Altata Drive 192
Alto Cedro Drive 84
Amalfi Drive 185, 186
Ambassador Drive 104, 105
Ameche, Don 217
American Film Institute 81
An American in Paris (1951) 92, 127, 130
The Americanization of Emily (1965) 113
Ammerman, Stephen 148
Amos 'n' Andy (radio and television serial) 180
Amsterdam, Morey 81, 82
Anastasia, Albert "The Executioner" 81
Anchors Aweigh (1945) 80
Anderson, Dame Judith 14, 68
The Andy Griffith Show (television series) 84, 207
Andy Hardy (movie serial) 160
Andy Hardy's Double Trouble (1944) 71
Aneta Street 224
The Angel and the Badman (1947) 162
Angeles National Forest 25, 143
Angeli, Pier 142
Angelo Drive 114, 115
Angels in the Outfield (1951) 38
Animal Crackers (1930) 82
Animal House (1978) 56, 87
Anita Stewart Picture Company 117
Anna Christie (1930) 126
Annabella 170
Annie Get Your Gun (1940) 116
anorexia nervosa, death by 235, 236
Anthony Adverse (1936) 120
anti-Semitism 2, 165

The Apartment (1960) 38, 143
The Apple Dumpling Gang (1968) 45
Arbuckle, Roscoe "Fatty" 3, 7, 20, 51, 52, 75, 97, 250, 251
Arden, Eve 163
Argyle Avenue 27
Argyle Club 49
Arlen, Harold 92
Arlen, Richard 213, 214
Armat, Thomas 1
Armendariz, Pedro 91
Arnaz, Desi 101, 102, 218
Arnold, Danny 57
Arnold, Edward 217, 218
Arnold, Tom 110
Around the World in Eighty Days (1956) 154
arthritis, death by 99
Arthur, Jean 68
Arthur, Johnny 13
Arthur, Roy 79
Ashley, Elizabeth 87
Ashley, Lady Sylvia 195
assault: physical 42, 44, 45, 49, 51, 52, 58, 70, 71, 76, 83, 89, 93, 95, 129, 136, 147, 149, 165, 167, 178, 180, 181, 189, 190, 191, 196, 211, 215, 216; sexual 3, 7, 9, 42
Astaire, Fred 99, 103
Astor, Mary 32, 229
The A-Team (television series) 87
Atwill, Lionell 184
Auckland Avenue 203, 204
Austin, Laurence 62, 63
Austin, William 62
Auto Week (magazine) 25
Avenida del Sol 220
Avenida Hacienda 220
Avery, Tex 241
Ayers, Agnes 11, 66
Ayres, Lew 175, 176

"B" movies 19, 42, 52, 53, 198
Babes in Toyland (1961) 167
Bacall, Lauren 58, 81, 86, 115, 155, 236
Bachardy, Don 193
Back Street (1941) 84
Background to Danger (1943) 90
Backus, Jim 120, 151, 163
Bacon, James 63
The Bad and the Beautiful (1952) 127, 160, 212
Ball, Lucille 44, 101, 102, 218, 241
Banacek (television series) 87
The Band Wagon (1953) 127
The Bank Dick (1940) 22
Bankhead, Tallulah 40, 41, 119
Banksia Place Sanitarium 3
Bara, Theda 124, 125, 126, 240, 251
The Barber Shop (1933) 22
Barbieri, Paula 166, 215
Bardo, John 62
Barker, Jess 211

Barker, Lex 133
Barney Miller (television series) 57
Barnie's Beanerie Restaurant 37
Baroda Drive 118, 119
Barr, Roseanne 110
The Barretts of Wimpole Street (1940) 40, 192
Barry, Donald Red 206
Barrymore, Ethel 137, 141, 142
Barrymore, John 12, 31, 59, 89, 90, 103, 137, 141, 171, 176
Barrymore, Lionel 31, 71, 136, 137, 141, 172, 176, 248
Barrymore, Maurice 137
Barsi, Judith 222
Barthelmess, Richard 15, 16
Baseheart, Richard 165
Bataan (1943) 186
Batman (television series) 186
The Battle of Gettysburg (1914) 105
Baum, L. Frank 14, 116
Baum, Maud 14
Baum, Vickie 185
Bautzer, Gregory 163
Baxter, Warner 99, 236
Bayne, Beverly 187
Beachwood Drive 31, 32, 33
Beahm, Jan Paul 75
beating, death by 17, 30, 49, 189, 190, 191, 206, 207, 231, 245
The Beatles 146
Beatty, Clyde 240
Beatty, Warren 196
Beau Geste (1926) 118
Beau Geste (1939) 91
Becky Sharp (1935) 168
Bedford Drive 132, 133, 134, 135, 143
Beery, Noah 101
Beery, Wallace 67, 90, 101
Begelman, David 140, 141, 160
Behold My Wife (1935) 217
Bel Air Road 147, 148
Bell, Rex 136, 224, 238
Bella Donna (1923) 133
Bella Drive 111
Bellagio Place 151
Bellagio Road 151, 152
Bello, Marino 121, 122, 159, 160
Belmont, Ralf 14
Belushi, John 56, 59
Benedict Canyon Drive 98, 99, 105, 108, 109, 110
Benet, Brenda 160
Ben-Hur (1926) 49, 126, 194
Bennett, Constance 68, 140
Bennett, Joan 143
Benny, Jack 128, 155, 156, 217, 218, 225
Bentley Avenue 162
Beradino, John 104, 105
Bergen, Candice 84
Bergen, Edgar 103
Bergen, Polly 103
Bergman, Ingrid 48, 58, 112, 132, 151

Berkeley, Busby 190, 251
Berle, Milton 161
Berle, Ruth 161
Berlin, Irving 42
Berman, Pandro 99
Bermuda Dunes Apartments 44
Bern, Paul 15, 109, 110, 121, 160
Bernhiemer Mansion 36, 37
Berry, Jan 138, 153
Besser, Joe 204, 205
Best, Edna 68
The Best Man (1954) 189
The Best Man (1960) 230
Beverly Crest Drive 86, 87
Beverly Drive 90, 91, 92, 93, 128, 129
Beverly Estates Drive 106
Beverly Farms, Massachusetts 2
The Beverly Hillbillies (television series) 93, 112
Beverly Hills Cop (1984) 148
Beverly Hills fire, 1961 148, 149, 152
Beverly Hills Hotel 2, 95, 96
Beverly Hills 90210 61, 89
Bewitched (television series) 47, 57, 105
Bianchi, Kenneth 25, 26, 240, 243
The Big Combo (1955) 205
The Big House (1930) 101
The Big Parade (1925) 10, 68, 249
The Big Street (1942) 39
The Big Trail (234) 234
A Bill of Divorcement (1932) 60, 168
A Bill of Divorcement (1940) 68
Billionaire Boys Club 25, 143, 166, 167
Billy Jack (1971) 172
Biloxi Avenue 204, 205
Bioff, Willie 137, 138
Biograph Studios 1, 66
The Birdman of Alcatraz (1962) 152
The Birds (1961) 151
The Birth of a Nation (1915) 18
Bixby, Bill 160, 161
Black Dahlia murder 12
Black Maria 2
Black Widow Murders: The Blanche Taylor Moore Story 105
The Blackbird (1926) 172
The Blackboard Jungle (1955) 99
blacklisting 183, 221
Blackouts 37
Blanc, Mel 9, 153, 154, 192
Blandick, Clara 17
The Blob (1958) 207
Bloch, Robert 52
Blond Venus (1932) 68
Blondeau Tavern 2
Blondell, Joan 237
Blonds at Work (1938) 185
Blood and Sand (1922) 111
Blood and Sand (1941) 17, 149
Bloomingdale, Alfred 61, 107, 207

The Blue Angel (1930) 137
The Blues Brothers (1981) 56
Boardman, Eleanor 17
The Boat (1921) 97
Boca de Canyon Drive 183
Boesky, Ivan 96
Bogart, Humphrey 9, 41, 58, 60, 80, 86, 104, 115, 155, 157, 171, 208, 217, 236
Bogdanovich, Peter 161
Bohana, Donald 231
Boland, Mary 129
Boles, John 163
Bolger, Ray 93, 230
Bolton, Michael 166
bombings 22, 23, 225
Bonanza (television series) 2, 191, 225
Bond, Carrie Jacobs 36, 238
Bondi, Beulah 14, 15
Bonsal Drive 191, 192
Boobs in Arms (1920) 11
Booke, Sorrell 212
Boomerang (1947) 221
Border Patrol (1943) 53
Born Yesterday (1950) 38, 184
Boston Avenue 247
Boston Blackie (serial, 1940s) 127, 128
Bosworth, Hobart 79
Bow, Clara 79, 118, 119, 135, 136, 153, 206, 213, 224, 234, 238
Bowling Green Way 171, 172
Bowmont Drive 69, 84, 85
Boy Meets Girl (1938) 37
Boyer, Charles 88, 89, 226
Boyer, Elisa 254
Boyer, Michael 88, 89, 226
Boys Town (1938) 60
Brabin, Charles 126, 172
Brady, Scott 230
The Brady Bunch (television series) 243
Brando, Cheyenne 89
Brando, Christian 89
Brando, Marlon 89
Bravo Apartments 27
Breakfast at Tiffany's (1961) 119
Brennan, Walter 226
Brent, Evelyn 119
Brent, George 217
Brewster's Millions (1926) 99
Briarcliff Road 24
Brice, Fanny 82, 157, 158
The Bride of Frankenstein (1935) 186
The Bride of the Monster (1955) 247
The Bride Walks Out (1936) 189
The Bride Wore Red (1937) 168
Bridges, Beau 157
Bridges, Jeff 157
Bridges, Lloyd 157
The Bridges at Toko-Ri (1955) 151
The Bridges of Madison County (1995) 233

The Brief Moment (1933) 189
Brigadoon (1954) 127
Brigham Young (1940) 149
Bringing Up Baby (1938) 214
Brisson, Freddie 129
Bristol Drive 178, 179, 180
Britton, Pamela 241
Broadus, Calvin "Snoop Doggy Dogg" 250
Broadway After Dark (1924) 133
The Broadway Melody (1926) 51
The Broadway Melody of 1935 (1935) 142, 156
The Broadway Melody of 1938 (1938) 185
Broccoli, Albert "Cubby" 79, 80
Brosnan, Pierce 80
brothels 51, 57
The Brothers Karamazov (1958) 221
Brown, Clarence 238
Brown, David 235
Brown, Joe E. 149, 153, 154, 180
Brown, Lansing 77
Brown of Harvard (1926) 173
Browne, Jackson 196
Browning, Tod 92, 172, 173
Bruce, Honey 54
Bruce, Lenny 54
Bruce, Virginia 185
Bruckheimer, Jerry 148
Bruckman, Clyde 201
Bryson, Winifred 99
Buckland, Vida 36
Buckland, Wilfred 36
Buckley, William F. 146
The Buddy Holly Story (1978) 191
Bugliosi, Vincent 246
A Bullet for Joey (1955) 90
The Bullfighter and the Lady (1951) 136
Bundy, Carol 243
Bundy Drive 171, 172, 174
bungalows, Beverly Hills Hotel 96
Buono, Angelo 25, 240, 243
Burke, Billie 168
Burnett, Lester Smiley 242
Burning Sands (1922) 152
Burns, George 26, 38, 123, 124, 238
Burns and Allen 38, 123, 124
Burnside Avenue 26, 38, 123, 124, 238
Burroughs, Edgar Rice 36, 149, 219, 220
Burton, Richard 96
Bus Stop 67
Busey, Gary 191
Bushman, Francis X. 15, 187, 238
The Butcher Boy (1917) 97
Butterfield 8 (1960) 99
Buttons, Red 148
Buzzell, Eddie 79
Byington, Spring 33

Caan, James 167
Cabot, Bruce 145
Cabot, Sebastian 163
Cabrillo Drive 85
The Caddy (1956) 57
Cagney, Jimmy 45, 217
Cagney and Lacey (television series) 208
Cahn, Sammy 163
Cahuenga Boulevard 76, 205
The Caine Mutiny (1949) 127
Calhern, Louis 10, 116
Call Northside 777 (1948) 100, 205
The Call of the Wild (1935) 176, 232
Call Out the Marines (1942) 30
Cambridge, Godfrey 242
Camden Drive 132
Cameraman (1928) 201
Cameron, David 98
Camille (1927) 136
Camino Palmiero Drive 39
Campbell, Alan 68, 69
Can-Can (1960) 80, 156
cancer: brain, death by 84, 91, 169, 235; breast, death by 38, 91; colon, death by 69, 208; larynx, death by 91, 173; liver, death by 39, 40, 86; lung, death by 20, 58, 61, 75, 84, 155, 165, 183, 186, 213, 222; pancreas, death by 105, 156; prostate, death by 47, 114, 161, 202; skin, death by 91; stomach, death by 191, 192, 234; throat, death by 104, 160, 205; unspecified, death by 34, 38, 46, 58, 61, 70, 84, 86, 90, 91, 97, 98, 99, 100, 102, 105, 119, 126, 129, 132, 136, 143, 167, 171, 173, 212, 214, 221, 247; uterine, death by 91
Candy, John 183
Cannon 210
Cannonball Run II (1984) 123
Canon Drive 127, 128
Canova, Judy 237
Cantor, Eddie 79, 157, 225
Cantor, Ida 79
Canyon Drive 25
Capital News 157
Capone, Al 137
Capote, Truman 153, 163
Capra, Frank 83, 137, 180, 183, 248
Capri Drive 185
Captain Kidd (1945) 136
Captain Midnight (television serial, 1950s) 209
"Captain Spaulding" (drug dealer) 3
Captains Courageous (1937) 60
Carbon Beach 88
Carbon Canyon Drive 235
Carey, Macdonald 108, 225
Carla Ridge Drive 86

Carlton Way 20
Carmen, Jewel 189, 190
Carmen (1918) 147
Carolwood Drive 117
Caron, Leslie 196
Carousel (1956) 192
Carpenter, Karen 235, 236
Carpenter, Richard 235, 236
The Carpetbaggers (1964) 176
Carradine, John 176
Carrillo, Leo 192
Carroll, Earl 236
Carson, Jack 214, 217, 240
Carson, Joanna 153
Carson, Johnny 153
Carter, Dixie 70, 71
Cartwright Avenue 206
Caruso, Enrico 168
Carver, Louise 223
Casablanca (1942) 9, 41, 58, 236
Casalotti, Adriana 70
Cassavetes, John 48, 163
Cassidy, David 65
Cassidy, Jack 65
Cassidy, Shaun 65
Cassini, Oleg 170
Castillian Apartments 246
Castillo del Lago 34
Cat Ballou (1964) 163
Cat on a Hot Tin Roof (1958) 99, 214
CBS 38
Cedarbrook Drive 89, 104
Centaur Film Company 2
Centinella Drive 224
Century Park Drive 160
cerebral hemorrhage, death by 18, 19, 44, 66, 92, 140, 158, 218
Chalon Road 150, 151
The Champ (1931) 101
Chandler, Jeff 225
Chandler, Raymond 209
Chaney, Lon 139, 172, 238, 253
Chaney, Lon, Jr. 17, 209
Channel Drive 192, 193
Chaplin, Charles 7, 8, 11, 21, 25, 43, 44, 51, 65, 99, 103, 106, 117, 127, 128, 133, 197, 222, 243, 253
Chaplin, Charles, Jr. 11, 43, 44, 128
Chaplin, Hannah 7, 8
Chaplin, Lita Grey 44, 128
Charade 119
Charing Cross Road 155, 156
Charleson, Kate 39
Charleson, Leslie 39
Charlie Chan (movie serial) 54
Charlie Chan at the Wax Museum (1940) 54
Charlie Chan in the City of Darkness (1941) 54
Charlie Chan in Treasure Island (1939) 54
Charlie Chan's Murder Cruise (1940) 54

Charlie's Angels 46
Chase, Charlie 20
The Chaser (1928) 46
Chateau Elysee Apartments 26
Chateau Marmont Hotel 56, 78
Cheaper by the Dozen (1949) 91
The Cheat (1931) 40
Cheers (television series) 87, 208
Cheremoya Drive 30, 31
Cherokee Hotel 14
Cherokee Street 14
Cherrill, Virginia 25
Chessman, Carl 47, 244, 245
Chevalier, Maurice 147
The Chickens Come Home (1930) 189
Chico and the Man 58, 157
The Chief (1933) 167
A Child Is Waiting (1962) 48
Children of Divorce (1927) 118, 135, 153
children, illegitimate 128, 129
The China Clipper (1937) 37
China Seas (1935) 71, 121, 129
Chinatown (1974) 5
Chitty Chitty Bang Bang (1968) 80
Christi, Frank 46
Christian, Marc 87
Christian Science 121, 122
Christopher Bean (1933) 126, 131
Cielo Drive 112, 113
The Circus (1914) 133
The Circus Clown (1934) 180
Cisco Kid (movie serial) 192
Citizen Kane (1941) 12, 40, 183, 201
City Lights (1921) 25, 134
City Streets (1933) 192
Civilization (1916) 105
Clark, David 12
Clark, Doug 243
Clark, Marcia 62
Clarkson Avenue 161
Clift, Montgomery 35, 106
Clinton, Clifford 22, 23
The Clock (1945) 186
Close Encounters of the Third Kind (1977) 140
Cloudy with Showers (1934) 102
Club House Drive 232
Club View Drive 159, 160
Clyde, Andy 238
Coastline Drive 191
Cobb, Lee J. 221
The Cocoanuts (1929) 74, 82
Cohen, Mickey 49, 59, 60, 99, 133, 177
Cohn, Harry 9, 64, 77, 148
Colasanto, Nicholas 208
Colbert, Claudette 68, 182
Coldwater Canyon Drive 88, 89, 90, 91
Cole, Cornelius 12
Cole, Nat King 73, 74, 238

Colfax Avenue 206, 207
The College Holiday (1936) 156
Collins, Jackie 84
Collins, Joan 84, 85
Collins, Ray Bidwell 241, 242
Colman, Ronald 59, 68, 103
Colorado Boulevard 243, 245
Colton, John 182, 199, 200
Columbia Pictures 60, 140, 204
Columbo, Ross 76, 77, 238
Columbus Avenue 248
Combs, Roy 244
Come and Get It (1936) 218
Come Back, Little Sheba (1952) 152
The Command Decision (1948) 218
The Commish (television series) 44
Comstock Apartments 158
Comstock Avenue 157, 158
Conklin, Chester 222
Conner, Mike 217
Connery, Sean 80
The Conquerer (1956) 91, 165
Conrad, William 210
Convy, Bert 169
Coogan, Jackie 17, 128, 226
The Cook (1918) 97
Cooke, Sam 238, 254
Cooper, Gary 28, 53, 54, 76, 115, 118, 119, 129, 135, 137, 151, 157, 213, 217, 234
Cooper, Jackie 101
Copacabana (1947) 135
Corday, Jo Rich 163
Cordell Drive 60
Cornell, Kathryn 182
The Corpse Had a Familiar Face 105
Corsaut, Aneta 207
Cortez, Ricardo 70
Cosby, Bill 84
The Cosby Show (television series) 87
Costello, Louis 210, 221
Costello, Louis, Jr. 210
The Cotton Club (1982) 210
Cotten, Joseph 167
"The Count" (drug dealer) 3
The Country Doctor (1936) 131
The Country Girl (1954) 151, 194
The Court Martial of Billy Mitchell (1957) 105
Courtney Terrace 42
The Courtship of Andy Hardy (1942) 71
The Courtship of Eddie's Father 160
Cousins (1989) 157
Cousteau, Jacques 84
The Cowboy from Brooklyn (1938) 165
Cowlings, Al 181, 215
Cox, Wally 152
Crane, Cheryl 99, 133

Crane, Norma 163
Crash, Darby 75
Crawford, Charles 12
Crawford, Christina 178
Crawford, Joan 5, 12, 42, 68, 73, 83, 92, 117, 134, 173, 178, 179, 206
Creighton, Cleva 253
Crescenda Street 169
Crescent Drive 96, 104, 127
Crime and Punishment (1935) 41
The Crime Doctor (television series) 99
The Crimson Tide (1994) 148
Crocker, Harry 133, 134
Cromwell, Mary Louise 184
Crosby, Bing 45, 77, 80, 151, 152, 156, 209, 226, 227
Crosby, Dixie Lee 156
Crosby, Kathryn 226
Crothers, Benjamin "Scatman" 242
The Crowd Roars (1937) 206
Cruze, James 10
Cuban Love Song (1932) 172
Cuban Rebel Girls (1960) 38
Cudahy, Elizabeth 26, 42
Cudahy, John 26, 42
Cukor, George 60, 234
Curson Avenue 40
Curtis, Tony 118, 146, 151, 154, 180
Cute Eyes (1942) 205
Cybill (television series) 43
Cynthia Street 69

Dagwood 7
Daily Mirror (newspaper) 176
Damone, Vic 142
Dandridge, Dorothy 3, 66 238
Dane, Karl 68, 74
Dangerous Minds (1995) 148
Danielson, Romina 85
The Danny Thomas Show (television series) 84, 241
Dano, Royal 200
Danziger, Daisy 23, 24
Dark Waters (1944) 102
Darnell, Linda 149, 206
Darrin, Bobby 77
Darwell, Jane 238
Dastinger, Sabu 242
Dastinger, Sheik 242
David Copperfield (1935) 60, 71
Davies, Marion 3, 7, 8, 14, 15, 26, 90, 91, 93, 94, 98, 103, 106, 199
Davis, Bette 15, 17, 18, 68, 71, 73, 88, 99, 149, 171, 182, 189, 207, 208, 240
Davis, Joan 149, 230
Davis, Marvin 96
Davis, Sammy, Jr. 9, 103, 104, 107, 123, 148
Dawson, Richard 244
Day, Doris 24, 240

A Day at the Races (1937) 66, 74, 82, 189
Days of Our Lives (television series) 108
Days of Thunder (1990) 148
The Daytime Wife (1939) 149
de Acosta, Mercedes 182, 184, 185, 199, 200
The Dead and Buried (1981) 58
Deadline for Murder (1946) 30
Dean, James 37, 47, 56, 142, 213
The Dean Martin Show 123
Death of a Salesman (1951) 192, 221
de Corsia, Ted 91
de Frasso, Countess Dorothy Taylor 119
de Havilland, Olivia 89, 217
Dekker, Albert 20, 21
Dekker, John 170, 171, 176
Delfern Drive 119, 120
Delon, Alain 177
DeMille, Beatrice 27, 28
DeMille, Cecil B. 2, 6, 10, 12, 21, 27, 28, 35, 95, 96, 101, 117
DeMille, Kathryn 22
DeMille Drive 21, 22, 117
DeMille, Manor 27, 28
The Dentist (1932) 22
Depp, Johnny 59, 248
Designing Women (television series) 70
Desire (1936) 118
The Desperate Hours (1955) 171
D'Este Drive 184
Destry Rides Again (1939) 100
The Devil and Miss Jones (1941) 33
The Devil and the Deep (1932) 40
The Devil Is a Woman (1935) 184
The Devil Makes Three (1952) 142
The Devil's Brigade (1968) 247
Devine, Andy 192
Devotion (1931) 192
Dial M for Murder (1954) 151
The Diamond (1935) 218
Diamonds Are Forever (1971) 80
The Diary of a Chambermaid (1946) 105
The Diary of Anne Frank (1959) 167
The Dick Powell Show (television series) 165
The Dick Van Dyke Show (television series) 82, 84
Dickinson, Angie 86
Die Hard (1988) 59, 191
Dietrich, Marlene 5, 32, 68, 83, 90, 96, 107, 137, 146, 184, 199, 200
Dillinger, John 192
DiMaggio, Joe 3, 64, 122, 163
The Dinah Shore Show (television series) 97
Dines, Courtland 253

Dinner at Eight (1934) 60, 101, 121, 126, 131, 168
The Dirty Dozen (1967) 48
Disney, Roy 23
Disney, Walt 70, 117, 149, 237
Disney Studios 23
Distant Drums (1952) 118
District Attorney's office, L.A. 12, 22; corruption in 12, 22
Divine 41
divorce 15, 20, 25, 42, 63, 84, 85, 88, 89, 98, 99, 101, 104, 121, 122, 128, 136, 142, 146, 152, 161, 162, 174, 179, 180, 184, 186, 187, 200, 210, 211, 215, 216, 217, 219, 222, 224, 231, 232, 241, 244, 247, 249
Dix Street 28
Dr. Cyclops (1941) 20
Dr. Jekyll and Mr. Hyde (1941) 133
Dr. Kildare (1935) 137, 160, 176
Dr. No (1962) 169
Dr. Strangelove (1963) 169
Dr. X (1932) 184
Dodge City (1939) 217
Dodsworth (1936) 96
Doheny, E.L. 81
Doheny, Ned 81
Doheny Drive 61
Doheny Mansion 81
Doherty, Shannen 61, 89, 108, 109
Dolly, Jenny 17
Dolly, Rosie 17
The Donna Reed Show (television series) 160
Dopey Dicks 12
Dorn, Philip 165
Dorsey, Tommy 80
Dosti, Arben 143
Double Indemnity (1944) 30
The Double Wedding (1937) 54
Dough and Dynamite (1919) 222
Dougherty, Jack 247
Douglas, Diandra 144
Douglas, Michael 107, 144
Douglas, Paul 38
Douras, Marion *see* Davies, Marion
Dove, Billie 72, 149
Down Argentina Way (1940) 134
Dracula (1931) 19, 172, 226
Dragna, Jack 49, 177
Dragnet 242
Dressler, Marie 126, 127, 240
Drieser, Theodore 65, 238
Drollet, Dag 89
drowning, death by 22, 48, 58, 59, 180, 186, 210, 231, 232
Dru, Joanne 86
drug overdose, death by 3, 4, 12, 17, 37, 46, 48, 55, 56, 59, 66, 70, 75, 77, 78, 86, 117, 129, 130, 142, 146, 148, 152, 153, 156, 173, 177, 183, 185, 186, 198, 199, 247
Drums of the Desert (1927) 99

Duck Soup (1933) 74
Duel, Peter 32
Duel in the Sun (1947) 68
Duffy's Tavern (1951) 205
Duke, Doris 112
Duke, James Buchanan 112
The Dukes of Hazard (television series) 212
Dull, Judy 64
Dumont, Margaret 74, 75
Duncan, Isadora 182
Duncan, Rosetta 238
Dunne, Dominic 66, 67
Dunne, Dominique 66, 67, 163, 216
Dunne, Ellen Griffin 66
Dunne, Griffin 66
Durand Drive 34
Durant, Ariel 24, 163
Durant, Will 24, 163
Durante, Jimmy 152, 225, 226
Durbin, Deanna 45
Durston, Edward 59
Dwan, Alan 126
Dynasty (television series) 87

Eagels, Jeanne 68
earthquake(s) 101
East of Eden (1954) 47, 213
East Side/West Side (1948) 210
Easton Drive 109
Eastwood, Clint 65, 200
Easy Aces (television series) 38
Easy Rider (1969) 150
Eaton, Dr. Hubert 236, 238
Ecstasy (1992) 46
Ed Wood (1994) 248
Ed Wynn's Carnival 167
Eddington, Nora 146
Eddy, Nelson 9, 147, 168, 171, 189
The Edge of Darkness (1943) 217
Edison, Thomas 1
Edmunds, Larry 31, 32
Edward Scissorhands (1991) 61
The Eiger Sanction (1977) 65
El Cerrito Place 39
El Dorado (1967) 234
Eldridge, Florence 116
The Electric House (1923) 97
The Elephant Boy (1937) 242
Elliott, Cass 48
Ellis Island (1935) 206
Elm Drive 124, 144
Elmer Gantry (1960) 152
El Roble Lane 85, 86
El Royale Apartments 18, 77
Elysian Park 26
Emma (1932) 126
emphysema, death by 214, 222, 223
Encino Drive 218, 219
"End of the Perfect Day" 36
The Enemy Below (1945) 213
The Englishman Who Went Up a Hill... (1995) 43

Entwhistle, Peg 31, 32
Eslaminia, Reza 143
Esmond, Jill 104
Essanay Studios 101, 127, 218
estates 2, 15, 16, 17, 20, 21, 22, 36, 37, 42, 50, 58, 60, 67, 81, 89, 90, 91, 93, 97, 98, 101, 103, 104, 105, 106, 109, 110, 111, 112, 114, 115, 121, 145, 146, 147, 150, 155, 170, 179, 180, 181, 184, 185, 187, 199, 210, 216, 217, 219, 220, 234, 250, 251, 252, 253
Ettig, Ruth 45
Evans, Linda 86
Evans, Robert 138
Evanston Street 177, 178
Evanview Drive 57, 58
Evelyn Prentiss (1934) 129
Evening Shade (television series) 70
"Everybody Loves Somebody" 121
Everybody Sing (1938) 157
executions, legal 23, 64, 188, 245, 246
Ex-Lady (1933) 189
Exodus (1960) 221
The Exorcist (1973) 221
extortion 72, 88

F Troop (television series) 238
Faces (1968) 48
Factor, Dean 108, 109
Fairbanks, Douglas, Jr. 179
Fairbanks, Douglas, Sr. 2, 3, 9, 10, 15, 35, 95, 98, 103, 104, 133, 180, 195, 196, 199
Fairfax Avenue 62, 63
Fairford 194
"Faith" 127
Faith, Percy 225
The Falcon (serial, 1930's) 152
Falcon's Lair 111, 112, 114, 115
Fallen Angel (1946) 150
Family Feud (television series) 244
Family Ties (television series) 222
Famous Players Studio 2
Fantasy Island 202
Far from the Maddening Crowd (1967) 96
A Farewell to Arms (1932) 133
Farmdale Street 206
Farmer, Francis 18
The Farmer's Daughter (1947) 48, 167
The Farmer's Daughter (television series) 48
Farnsworth, Arthur 18
Farnum, Franklyn 70
Farrow, Mia 81, 119
The Fatal Glass of Beer (1933) 22, 201
The Father of the Bride (1950) 99, 127, 168

Faulkner, William 14
Fay, Frank 179
FBI Story (1959) 100
The Fearless Vampire Killers (1967) 113
Fein, Art 75
Feldman, Charlie 122
Feldman, Marty 242
Female Jungle (1954) 118
Ferrar, Geraldine 26
Ferrigno, Lou 161
Fibber McGee and Molly (movie serial, 1935–1956) 226
Fiddler on the Roof 163
Field of Dreams (1989) 152
Fields, W.C. 21, 22, 31, 74, 77, 79, 127, 157, 171, 176, 201
Fighting Seabees (1944) 234
Figueroa Street 254
Finch, Peter 9, 95, 96, 104
Fine, Larry 60, 61, 165, 204, 238
fire, death by 65, 66, 130, 145, 150
Fire Over England (1936) 104
Fisher, Eddy 96
Fit for a King (1937) 180
Fitzgerald, Ella 117, 118
Fitzgerald, F. Scott 44
Fitzgerald, Zelda 58
Five Pennies (1959) 240
fixers (studio public relations departments) 4, 26, 47, 54, 58, 60, 83, 108, 109, 110, 121, 128, 129, 130, 133, 134, 137, 139, 148, 156, 160, 172, 173, 178, 179, 187, 192
Flame of the Desert (1919) 26
Flame, Ditra 7
Flamingo Hotel 88
Flashdance (1983) 148
The Flats of Beverly Hills 68
Fleiss, Heidi 61, 107, 148
Fleming, Rhonda 156
Fleming, Victor 10
Flesh and Fantasy (1943) 102
The Flight of the Phoenix (1966) 100
Flippen, Jay C. 163
Flower Drum Song (1961) 84
Floyd Terrace 45
The Flying Tigers (1942) 30, 42
Flynn, Errol 26, 27, 39, 57, 59, 79, 89, 90, 99, 141, 145, 146, 171, 176, 217, 237
Flynt, Althea 146
Flynt, Larry 146
Folger, Abigail 112, 113
Follies of 1914 (1914) 167
Fonda, Bridget 150
Fonda, Henry 100, 120, 150
Fonda, Jane 150
Fonda, Peter 150
Fontaine, Joan 151
A Fool There Was (1916) 126
Foothill Drive 68, 81
For Me and My Gal (1942) 130

For Your Eyes Only (1981) 80
Ford, Glenn 99
Ford, John 86, 209, 230, 233
Forest Lawn Memorial
  Park–Glendale 236, 237, 238,
  239, 240
Forest Lawn Memorial
  Park–Hollywood Hills 240,
  241, 242
Forest Lawn Memorial Parks 5,
  24, 121, 123, 132, 187
Forever Amber (1947) 150
Forrest, Sally 110
Fort Utah (1961) 214
42nd Street (1933) 99
Fountain, Rex 149
Fountain Avenue 66
Four for Texas (1963) 123
*The Four Horsemen of the Apoca-
  lypse* (1923) 111, 131
Four Weddings and a Funeral
  (1994) 43
Fowler, Gene 176, 230
Fox Studios 234
Foxworth, Robert 105
FPO Studios 130
Francis, Lee 57
Frank, Milo 110
Frankenstein (1931) 19, 186
Franklin Avenue 36
Fraser Avenue 198, 199
Frawley, William 18, 77
Freaks (1932) 172
Frederick, Pauline 123
A Free Soul (1931) 137
Freed, Burt 171, 172
Freeman, Mona 156
The Freshman (1925) 201
The Friends of Eddie Coyle (1973)
  235
Frohman, Charles 168
From Here to Eternity (1953) 80,
  108, 152, 246
From Russia with Love (1963) 80
The Front Page (1931) 5, 133
Frontier Gal (1945) 17
Frontieri, Georgia 149
Frykowski, Woytek 112
The Fugitive (1993) 235
The Fugitive (television series)
  210, 225
Fuller, Bobby 35
Fuller Avenue 39
Fulton Street 75, 209, 210
Funny Face (1957) 92
The Fury (1936) 60
The Fury (1978) 48

Gable, Clark 28, 28, 33, 79, 80,
  115, 121, 151, 160, 172, 178, 189,
  216, 218, 232, 233, 238, 239
Gabor, Eva 119, 120, 163
Gabor, Magda 120, 152
Gabor, Zsa Zsa 120, 149, 152
Gambino, Carlo 81

Garbo, Greta 5, 17, 54, 68, 70, 71,
  93, 103, 107, 115, 126, 133, 134,
  140, 146, 147, 153, 176, 179, 182,
  185, 186
The Garden of Allah (1936) 226
Gardner, Ava 72, 73, 81, 149
Gardner, Reginald 241
Gardner Avenue 43
Garfield, John 208
Garland, Judy 57, 118, 127, 130, 140
Garner, James 89
Garrison, Michael 241
The Gay Divorcee (1930) 99
Gaye, Marvin 251, 252
Gaye, Marvin, Sr. 251, 252
Gaynor, Janet 5, 14, 36
Geffen, David 115
The General (1926) 97, 201
General Hospital (television series)
  39
Genesee Street 44
George, Christopher 165
*The George Burns–Gracie Allen
  Show* 123
The George Burns Show 123
George Washington Slept Here
  (1942) 217
George White's 1935 Scandals 142
Gere, Richard 13, 144
Gershwin, George 86, 92, 102,
  103, 115, 118
Gershwin, Ira 86, 92, 102, 103,
  115, 118
Getty, George 150
Getty, J. Paul 150
Getty, Jean Paul, II 150
Getty, Jean Paul, III 150
Getty, Jean Ronald 150
Gettysburg (1993) 235
Ghostbusters (1988) 48, 178
G.I. Blues (1960) 156
Giancana, Sam 81, 138
The Giant (1955) 213
Gibb, Andy 241
Gibbons, Irene 18
Gidget 32
Giesler, Jerry 45, 99 133, 190,
  244, 253
Gigi (1958) 127
Gilbert, John 51, 57, 93, 107, 136,
  173, 182
Gill, William 249
Gillespie, Haven 240
Gilligan's Island (television series)
  151
The Girl from Montmartre (1925)
  247
The Girl from Paris (1936) 189
A Girl in Every Port (1951) 38
The Girl of the Golden West (1938)
  147
The Girl on the Red Velvet Swing
  (1955) 201
The Girl Philippa (1917) 117
Girl Trouble (1940) 168

The Gladiator (1938) 180
The Glass Alibi (1946) 30
Glatman, Harvey 64
Gleason, Jackie 84
Glen Green Drive 32
Glen or Glenda (1953) 247
Glendon Avenue 162, 165
The Glenn Miller Story (1954) 100
Gless, Sharon 208, 209
The Gnome-Mobile (1967) 167
Goddard, Mark 65
Goddard, Paulette 32, 103
The Goddess (1918) 117
The Godfather (1972) 46, 138, 167
Godunov, Alexander 59
Goetz, Edie Mayer 120
Goetz, William 119, 120
Going Places (1939) 120
The Gold Rush (1924) 128
The Golden Boy (1939) 193, 221
Goldeneye (1995) 80
Goldfinger (1964) 80
Goldman, Ron 173, 714, 175, 181,
  182
Goldwyn, Samuel 84
Goldwyn Girls 79
Goldwyn Studios 91
Gomer Pyle (television series) 84
Gomez, Thomas 91
Gone with the Wind (1939) 10, 89,
  91, 102, 104, 108, 132, 194
Good Fellows (1943) 205
Good Night Nurse (1918) 97
Goodland Avenue 209
gossip columns 42, 106, 134
Gould, Elliott 29
Gower Street 11, 30
Grable, Betty 90
Grace Drive 15
Graham, Barbara 91, 245, 246;
  curse of 245, 246
Graham, Sheilah 44
Gramercy Park 251
The Grand Duchess and the Waiter
  (1926) 133
Grand Hotel (1932) 71, 101, 131,
  194
Grant, Cary 24, 25, 26, 36, 86,
  217
Grant, Hugh 42, 43
Granville, Bonita 225
Grauman, Sid 142, 240
Grauman's Chinese Theatre 142,
  143, 172, 240
Gray, Colleen 152
The Great Caruso (1951) 11, 95
The Great Dictator (1940) 222
The Great Gatsby (1949) 108, 212
The Great Train Robbery (1903) 1
The Great Ziegfeld (1936) 157
The Greatest Show on Earth (1952)
  100, 209
The Greatest Story Ever Told
  (1965) 56
Greed (1924) 131, 222

Green, Burton 2, 95
Green Acres (television series) 120
Greenbaum, Gus 138
Greenberg, Harry 29, 119
Greenberger, Laney Jacobs 211, 212
Greene, Lorne 225
Greenson, Ralph 176, 177
Gretna Green Way 175
Greystoke: The Legend of Tarzan (1987) 81
Griffin, Merv 120
Griffith, D.W. 1, 18, 66, 171
Griffith, Griffith J. 5
Griffith, Melanie 152
Griffith Park 5
Grim Game (1919) 50
Grismer Avenue 246
Groundhog Day (1994) 178
The Groundlings 218
Growing Pains (television series) 222
Guess Who's Coming to Dinner (1967) 60
Guestward Ho 86
A Guide for the Married Man (1967) 48, 156
Gung Ho (1986) 53
The Guns of Navarone (1961) 48
Gunsmoke (television series) 210
Guys and Dolls 84
Guzik, Jake Greasy Thumb 137
Gypsy (1962) 129

Habe, Hans 69
Habe, Marina 69
Hacienda Motel 254
Hackett, Buddy 138
Hackett, Joan 11
Haines, William 49, 173, 179, 201, 234, 235
Hairspray (1983) 41, 42
Hal Roach Studios 2, 180, 198, 203, 248
Haley, Jack 93, 94, 226, 228
The Half Breed (1916) 70
Half Wits Holiday (1948) 210
Hall, Arsenio 47
Halloway Drive 56
Hamden Place 187, 188
Hamill, Dorothy 123
Hamilton, Alana 89
Hamilton, Ashley 89
Hamilton, George 89
Hammer, Armand 163
Hammett, Dashiell 147
Hampton, John 62, 63
Hancock Park 70, 71, 72, 73, 74, 75, 76, 77, 78, 251, 252
Hang 'Em High (1968) 48
hanging, death by 39, 244
Hangover Square (1945) 150
Hannah, Darryl 196
Hanover Drive 116, 117
Hanson, Betty 145

Hanson, Einer 153
Happy Days (television series) 76, 163
Harburg, Yip 92, 153
Hardin, Tim 77, 78
Harding, Ann 47
Hardy, Oliver 197, 198, 203, 204
Hardy Boys (series) 71
Hargitay, Mickey 118
Harlow, Jean 14, 15, 71, 72, 73, 92, 96, 109, 110, 121, 122, 159, 160, 189, 236, 240
Harlow, Mama Jean 121, 122, 159, 240
Harold Way 19
Harper Avenue 64
Harrelson, Woody 146
Harris, John 1
Harris, Mildred 128
Harrison, Rachel Roberts 110, 111
Harrison, Rex 110, 111, 170, 185, 237
Hart to Hart (television series) 183, 184
Hartman, Brynn 218, 219
Hartman, Phil 218, 219
Hartzell Street 187
Harvey (1950) 100
Hatari! (1962) 119
Hatley, T. Marvin 240
hauntings 11, 18, 20, 28, 33, 35, 36, 37, 39, 40, 41, 42, 48, 50, 51, 59, 83, 85, 91, 92, 98, 101, 102, 103, 108, 110, 112, 114, 115, 118, 137, 139, 159, 160, 179, 183, 190, 191, 213, 233, 245, 252
Haver, June 168
Hawkes, Howard 86
Hawn, Goldie 186
Hawthorne Avenue 12, 42
Hawthorne Hotel 42
Hayden, Tom 166
Hayes, Helen 163
Haymes, Dick 86
Havenhurst Drive 25
Hayward, Leland 168
Hayward, Susan 91, 149, 206, 211
Hayworth, Rita 80, 225, 226
Hayworth Avenue 44
Hayworth Chateau Apartments 44
Healy, Ted 60, 165, 204
Hearst, Millicent 90
Hearst, William Randolph 3, 7, 8, 14, 15, 26, 90, 91, 93, 94, 98, 106, 134, 176, 199
heart attack, death by 12, 15, 18, 20, 22, 24, 27, 28, 31, 33, 38, 41, 42, 44, 45, 46, 48, 52, 56, 57, 60, 67, 68, 69, 71, 74, 79, 80, 81, 82, 83, 84, 93, 95, 96, 98, 99, 100, 101, 122, 123, 126, 127, 128, 134, 135, 141, 142, 144, 147, 148, 150, 152, 153, 168, 169, 172, 183, 192, 195, 200, 203, 204, 205,

206, 207, 208, 209, 210, 212, 216, 220, 221, 224, 230, 248
Heart of a Siren (1925) 247
Heat of the Night (television series) 188
Heather Court 88, 89
Heather Road 88
Heaven Can Wait (1943) 147
Heaven's Gate (1982) 167
Hecht, Harold 163
Hedren, Tippi 151, 152
Heflin, Van 56
Hefner, Hugh 163
Heidi (1937) 131
Heidt, Horace 242
Helena Street 176, 177
Hell on Frisco Bay (1956) 118
The Hell with Heroes (1968) 32
Hello Dolly (1969) 130
Hell's Angels (1931) 121
Hellzapoppin' (1941) 152
Hemingway, Ernest 86, 199
Hemingway, Margaux 198, 199
Hemingway, Mariel 161
Hendrix, Wanda 241
Hendry, Whitey 109, 110
hepatitis, death by 133
Hepburn, Katharine 33, 54, 56, 60, 68, 72, 73, 85, 88, 99, 100, 114, 120, 155, 168, 186, 214
Her First Bisquits (1909) 103
Herbie Goes Bananas (1970) 45
Here Comes Mr. Jordan (1941) 157
Here Comes the Groom (1934) 54
Herman, Pee Wee 219
Herman, Woody 9
Hersholt, Jean 131, 132
Hesby Street 207, 208
Hey, Rookie! (1944) 204
Hi Good Lookin' (1944) 39
Hickman, Edward 252
The High and Dry (1944) 38
The High and Mighty (1954) 234
High Chaparral (television series) 192
High Noon (1952) 102, 151
High Sierra (1941) 208
High Society (1956) 80
High Valley Place 214
Higher and Higher (1935) 80
Highland Avenue 20, 75
Hijazi, Tonya Anne 49
Hill, Virginia 88, 90, 138
Hill Street Blues (television series) 66, 87
Hillcrest Road 79, 81, 82
Hilliard, Harriet 39, 40, 41
Hillside Strangler murders 25, 26, 240, 243
Hilton, Nicky 217
Hinmen, Gary 191, 192
His Butler's Sister (1943) 45
His Girl Friday (1940) 129
His New Job (1915) 66
His Wedding Night (1917) 97

Hit the Hay (1945) 237
Hitchcock, Alfred 47, 52, 151, 152
Hodgkin's disease, death by 87
Hoffa, Jimmy 138
Hoffman, Abbie 166
Holbrook, Hal 70
Hold That Lion (1947) 210
Holden, Fay 238
Holden, William 151, 193, 194
Holland Brothers Kinetascope
  Parlor 3
Holly Mont Drive 28, 29
Hollywood Athletic Club 12
Hollywood Boulevard 18, 26, 41,
  54, 58
The Hollywood Canteen (1944)
  154, 156
Hollywood Citizen News 232
Hollywood Confidential (magazine)
  178
Hollywood Hills 45, 46, 47, 48,
  49, 50, 51, 52, 53, 54, 55
Hollywood Memorial Park 5, 6,
  7, 8, 9, 10, 11, 68, 247
Hollywood or Bust (1956) 123
Hollywood Reporter 25, 132, 141,
  185
Hollywood Roosevelt Hotel 35
Hollywood sign 31, 32
Hollywood Squares 122, 152
Hollywoodland 31, 32, 33
Holm, Peter 84, 85
Holmes, John 52, 53
Holy Cross Cemetary 201
Home Before Dark (1958) 119
homosexuality 14, 15, 23, 24, 25,
  27, 31, 32, 47, 49, 54, 56, 60, 81,
  83, 86, 87, 104, 111, 118, 119, 127,
  139, 140, 173, 179, 182, 186, 199,
  200, 234, 235, 240
Honeymoon in Vegas (1992) 167
The Honeymooners (television se-
  ries) 84
Honolulu (1939) 142
Honor's Altar (1915) 71
Hood, Darla 10
The Hooded Falcon 111
Hoogstratten, Dorothy 161, 162,
  163, 164
Hoogstratten, Louise 161
Hope Diamond 128; curse of 128
Hope, Bob 45, 209
Hopkins, Miriam 59, 107
Hopper, Hedda 105
Hoppy Serves a Writ (1942) 53
Horn Avenue 58
Horse Feathers (1932) 74, 82, 189
Horton, Edward Everett 238
Hoskins, Robert 34
Hot Shots (1991) 157
Hot Shots Part Deux (1994) 157
Hotel Elysee 106
Hotel for Women (1939) 149
Houdini, Harry 18, 50
House Calls 186

The House of Alex 61, 107
The House of Dracula (1946) 184
The House of Francis 57
The House of Frankenstein (1946)
  184
The House of Wax (1953) 61
The House of Westmore 206
House Un-American Activities
  Committee 133, 183, 221
How the West Was Won (1962)
  100, 221, 247
Howard, Helen 61
Howard, Jerome "Curly" 61, 204,
  209, 210
Howard, Leslie 132
Howard, Moe 60, 61, 160, 204
Howard, Shemp 60, 61, 160, 204,
  205, 210
Howard, Thelma 117
Howard, Willie 157
Hudnut, Winifred 111, 112
Hudson, Phyllis 106
Hudson, Rock 86, 87, 106
Hudson Street 20
Hughes, Howard 72, 73, 79, 81,
  88, 89, 96, 118, 121, 138, 139, 149,
  151
Humperdinck, Engelbert 118
The Hunchback of Notre Dame
  (1939) 40, 102
Hunt, Joe 143, 166, 167
The Hunt for Red October (1990)
  234
Hunter, Ross 84
Husbands (1970) 48
Hush, Hush Sweet Charlotte (1965)
  167
Hustler (magazine) 146
Huston, John 5, 96
Huston, Walter 95, 96
Hutton, Barbara 96, 103
Hutton Drive 110
Huxley, Aldous 46
Hyde, Johnny 122

"I Fought the Law"" 35
I Led Three Lives (television se-
  ries) 105
I Love Lucy (television series) 18,
  101
"I Love You Truly" 36
I Married an Angel (1942) 147,
  172
"I Only Have Eyes For You" 163
I Spy (television series) 84
I Want to Live (1956) 143, 245,
  246
I Was a Teenage Werewolf (1957)
  191
"If I Were a Carpenter" 77
I'll Cry Tomorrow (1955) 91
IMP Studios 66
In Old Arizona (1929) 99
Ince, Elinor 26, 106
Ince, Thomas 2, 3, 26, 105, 106, 131

The Incredible Hulk (television series) 161
Indecent Exposure 140
Indiana Jones and the Last Crusade
  (1988) 59
infidelity 3, 7, 9, 15, 25, 26, 30,
  40, 42, 43, 58, 60, 61, 72, 85,
  89, 90, 96, 104, 107, 111, 112, 122,
  123, 130, 136, 137, 143, 144, 147,
  149, 151, 159, 161, 176, 177, 180,
  184, 185, 189, 196, 206, 207, 210,
  211, 212, 217, 230, 232, 233, 237
ingestion of gasoline, death by 35
ingestion of poison, death by 66
Ingram, Rex 33, 242
Inherit the Wind (1960) 247
Interiors (1978) 235
Intermezzo (1939) 132
Internal Revenue Service 73, 104,
  210
Intolerance (1916) 18, 172
The Invisible Man (1933) 186
Ireland, John 86
Irene (1940) 168
Irvine Avenue 206
Isherwood, Christopher 193
It (1927) 135
It Could Happen to You (1996) 150
It Happens Every Spring (1949)
  38
It's a Wonderful Life (1948) 15, 84,
  100, 137
Iturbi, Jose 128, 230
Ivar Street 17

Jack Armstrong, All American Boy
  38
The Jack Benny Show 38
Jack Benny's Farewell 156
Jack Benny's Second Farewell 156
Jackson, Arthur 44
Jackson, Delores 231
Jackson, Tito 231
Jacobs-Bond, Carrie 36
Jagger, Mick 145
Jailbait (1954) 247
Jake and the Fatman (television
  series) 210
James, Rick 49
James Bond (movie serial) 79, 80
The James Mason Show (television
  series) 98
Jannings, Emil 42
Janssen, David 225
Jardine, Al 57
Jarmyn, Jil 206
Jaws: The Revenge (1987) 222
The Jazz Singer 224
Jeopardy (1953) 212
Jesse James (movie serial,
  1935–1950) 176, 206
Jesse L. Lasky Picture Company
  21, 35, 66, 95, 151
Jessel, George 79, 225
Jigsaw (1949) 42

The Jimmy Durante Show (television series) 135
Joan of Arc (1914) 101
Joe Forester 157
The Joey Bishop Show (television series) 160, 204
John, Elton 107
Johnny Angel (1945) 90
Johnny Apollo (1940) 209
Johnny Belinda (1948) 176
Johnny Eager (1940) 56
Johnny O'Clock (1944) 165, 221
Johnny Trouble (1957) 141
Johnny Yuma (television series) 85, 86
Johnson, Ben 86
Johnson, Nunnally 163
Johnson, Tor 19, 247
Jolson, Al 39, 217, 224, 225
Jones, Carolyn 69
Jones, Jennifer 68, 107, 170, 186
Jones, Lindley Spike 230
Jones, Quincy 118
Jones, Shirley 65
The Jonesy Pictures (1909–1912) 66
Joplin, Janis 37, 38
Jordan, James 226
Jordan, Marian 226
Jordan, Richard 235
Journey Into Fear (1942) 167, 183
Journey's End (1926) 186
The Joy Girl (1927) 126
Joyce, Frank 238
Judge Hardy's Children (1938) 71
Judgement at Nuremberg (1961) 152
Judith of Bethulia (1914) 137
jumping, death by 18, 31, 32, 59
The Jungle Book (1942) 242
The Jungle Princess (1936) 209
Just Like Heaven (1930) 119

Kanin, Garson 38
The Kansas Raiders (1941) 214
Kardashian, Robert 215
Karno, Fred 197
Kath, Terry 237
Kay, Herbie 209
Kaye, Danny 104, 240
Keaton, Buster 20, 51, 97, 98, 201, 222, 223, 241
Keeler, Ruby 39, 217
The Keeper of the Flame (1935) 14
Keith, Brian 150
Kelley, David 182
Kelley, Tom 64
Kelly, Gene 80, 99, 130, 131
Kelly, Grace 48, 151, 152, 156
Kelly, Paul 30, 31
Kennedy, Edgar L. 229
Kennedy, John F. 46, 81, 122, 176, 196, 212
Kennedy, John F., Jr. 196
Kennedy, Joseph, Sr. 26, 130, 131

Kennedy, Robert 176, 196
Kenton, Stan 165
Kerr, Joanne 152
Keystone Cops 20, 75, 222, 223
Keystone Studios 20, 75, 101
Khashoggi, Adnan 96
The Kid (1920) 128, 226
Kid Boots (1926) 79, 135
The Kid from Spain (1933) 79
Kid Millions (1935) 79
Kidnapped (1938) 99
kidnapping 45, 47, 137, 143, 150
Kiesler, Hedwig 4
Kilbride, Percy 14
Kilkea Drive 63
The Killers (1946) 152
Killian, Victor 17, 165
Killion Drive 202
Kimmel, John 244
Kinetascope 1
King, Alan 138
The King of Chinatown (1939) 54
Kings Road 65
The Kiss (1929) 176
Kiss Me Again (1925) 12, 135
Knickerbocker Hotel 18, 27
Knight, Ted 237
Korshak, Marshall 138
Korshak, Sidney 137, 138
Kotz, Florence 63
Kovacs, Ernie 158, 241
Kovacs, Mia 158, 161, 241
Krakower, Whitey 29
Kramer vs. Kramer (1979) 140
Krassner, Paul 166
Kupcinet, Irv 64
Kupcinet, Karen 64, 65

L.A. Law (television series) 49, 87
La Bohème (1926) 107
LaBianca, Leno 23, 187, 192, 224, 232, 246
LaBianca, Rosemary 23, 187, 192, 224, 232, 246
Ladd, Alan 80, 156, 205, 238
Ladd, Sue Carol 238
Lady Be Good (1941) 92, 142
The Lady from Shanghai (1948) 183
The Lady in Black 9
Lady in the Dark (1944) 162
Laemmle, Carl 2, 66, 106
Laemmle, Carlotta 163
Lafferty, Bernard 112
Lake, Arthur 7, 8
Lake, Patricia 7, 8, 90
Lake Hollywood Drive 45
LaMarr, Barbara 3, 9, 14, 15, 16, 189, 247
LaMarr, Hedy 115
Lamour, Dorothy 209
Lancaster, Burt 149, 152
Lanchester, Elsa 40
Landis, Carole 111, 152, 185

Landis, John 87, 248, 249
Landmark Hotel 37, 38
Landon, Michael 192, 225
Lane, Lola 176
Lang, Fritz 242
Lang, Jennings 143
Langdon, Harry 45, 46
Lansky, Meyer 81
Lantz, Walter 86
Lanza, Mario 230
La Peer Drive 67
La Presa Drive 37
Larchmont Avenue 70
Larga Street 244, 245
La Ronda Apartments 25
Las Palmas Boulevard 12
Las Palmas Hotel 12
Lasky, Jesse 10, 21, 66, 95
Lassie (television serial) 229
The Last Gangster (1937) 183
Last Train from Madrid (1937) 136
Laughlin Park Estates 21, 22
Laughton, Charles 40, 240
Laura (1944) 91
Laurel, Ida K. 197, 241
Laurel, Stan 197, 198, 203, 204, 241
Laurel and Hardy 11, 20, 45, 121, 128, 180, 189, 197, 201, 203, 204, 223, 240
Laurel Canyon 49, 50, 51, 52, 53, 54, 76
Laurel Canyon Drive 23, 49, 50, 53, 54, 76, 247, 248
Laurel Canyon Park 49
Laurel Drive 90, 91
Laurel Lane 91
Laurel Way 91
Lawford, Peter 104, 122, 123, 162, 163, 199
Lawler, Andy 119
The Lawman (1970) 235
Lawrence, Florence 66
Lawrence, Martin 107
lawsuit(s) 87, 110, 140, 142
Lazar, Irving "Swifty" 86, 163
Leary, Dr. Timothy 113, 114
Leave 'Em Laughing (1928) 201
Lee, Bruce 152
Lee, Leila 79
Leeds, Andrea 147
Leeds, Lila 53
The Legend of Lizzie Borden (1975) 105
Lehrmann, Henry "Pathé" 7
Leigh, Vivien 89, 104, 132, 151
Lemmon, Jack 154, 180
Lemmon, Lenore 108
The Lemon Drop Kid (1944) 18
Lennon, John 75, 96
Lennon, William 224
Lennon Sisters 224
Leona Drive 105
Leonard, Sheldon 83, 84

LeRoy, Baby 22
Les Misérables (1935) 40
Les Misérables (1952) 192
lesbianism 39, 40, 41, 49, 63, 83, 93, 126, 139, 140, 179, 182, 199, 209
Lethal Weapon (1988) 191
Let's Get a Divorce (1917) 168
Let's Make Love (1960) 96
The Letter (1929) 68
The Letter (1940) 68
Letter of Introduction (1938) 217
A Letter to Three Wives (1948) 38, 150
Letty Lynton (1932) 5
Levant, Oscar 163
Levin, Ron 25, 143
Lewis, David 186
Lewis, Jerry 38, 123
Lexington Drive 93, 94
Lexington House 93, 94, 199
Libelled Lady (1935) 121
Liberace 240
License to Kill 80
Lido Apartments 14, 17
Liesen, Marshall 35
The Life of the Party (1937) 74
Life with Father (1947) 12, 17
Life with Riley (television series) 180
Lillian Way 76
Linda Flora Drive 152
Lindacrest Drive 87, 88
Lindbergh kidnapping 137
Linden Drive 119, 137, 138, 139, 140, 141
Linkletter, Art 59, 242
Linkletter, Diane 59, 242
Lipstick (1976) 198
Lipton, Peggy 149
The Little Giant (1946) 74
Little Miss Marker (1934) 133
The Little Rascals (movie serial) 10, 248
Little Women (1933) 33, 238
Little Women (1935) 60
The Living Daylights 80
Livingston, Mary 225
Lloyd, Harold 127, 180, 201, 223
The Lloyd Bridges Show (television series) 157
Lockhart, Gene 229
Lockhart, June 229
Logan, Joshua 100
Logan, Margaret 187, 188
Loggins, Kenny 103
Lombard, Carole 26, 33, 77, 90, 151, 173, 189, 216, 218, 236, 237, 238, 239
London After Midnight (1927) 172
The Lone Wolf Takes a Holiday (1941) 157
The Loner (television serial) 157
The Long March (1925) 107

Long Pants (1927) 46
The Long Trail (1917) 26
Longdon, Patrick 34
Longridge Avenue 210, 211
Lookout Mountain Drive 50, 51
Loos, Anita 27, 135
Loring Drive 156, 157
Lorna Lane 173
Lorraine Boulevard 70
Lorre, Catherine 26
Lorre, Peter 9, 26, 58
Los Angeles Examiner (newspaper) 201
Los Angeles Times (newspaper) 134, 143, 146
Los Feliz Boulevard 22
The Lost Harem (1944) 67
Lost Horizon (1937) 84, 102
The Lost World (1925) 71
Louis, Joe E. 152
Louis Pasteur (1934) 120
Louise, Anita 119, 120, 163
Love, Bessie 50, 51
Love, Courtney 146
Love, Mike 57, 232
Love, Shawn 232
The Love Bug (1968) 45
Love Finds Andy Hardy (1938) 71, 225
Love Happy (1949) 82
Love Is a Many-Splendored Thing (1955) 194
Love Laughs at Andy Hardy (1946) 71, 225
Love Me or Leave Me (1955) 45
Love Me Tonight (1932) 147
Love on the Run (1936) 172
The Love Parade (1929) 127, 147
Love That Brute (1950) 38
Love Thy Neighbor (1940) 156
Lovejoy, Frank 230
The Lovers (1958) 84
"Love's Made a Fool of You" 35
The Loves of Pharaoh (1922) 42
"Lovin' You Is Easy" 163
Lowe, Edmund 139, 140
Lubin Film Company 203
Lubitsch, Ernst 12, 127, 147
Lucerne Boulevard 70
Luciano, Lucky 81, 90, 189, 190
Lugosi, Bela 19, 135, 172, 226, 228, 247
Lundigan, William 229
Lupino, Ida 207, 208
Lupino, Stanley 208
Lynde, Paul 122
Lyon, Bebe Daniels 11
Lyon, Ben 11
Lytess, Natasha 64

M (1931) 41
Ma and Pa Kettle (movie serial) 14
Ma and Pa Kettle in Waikiki (1955) 14

McAvoy, Freddie 145
McCadden Drive 73, 74
McCarthy, Joseph 133, 183, 221
McCarthy, Kevin 106
McCarty Drive 142
McClure, Doug 213
McClure, Suzette 88
MacDonald, Jeanette 147, 172, 189
McGrew, Charles 121
Mack, Charles 238
MacKay, Elsie 184
MacKaye, Dorothy 30
McKay, Scott 217
McLaglen, Victor 236, 237
MacLain, Shirley 123
MacLean, Edward 128
McLean, Evelyn Walsh 128
McMahon, Ed 103, 219
MacMurray, Fred 168
McQueen, Steve 207
Mad Love (1934) 41
Madame Du Barry (1918) 147
Madame X (1929) 54, 71
Made for Each Other (1939) 100
Made in Heaven (1921) 249
Madison, Guy 162
Madonna 34
Magic Castle 36, 37
The Magnificent Ambersons (1942) 167, 183
The Make Believe Wife (1918) 168
Malibu 2000 (television series) 43
Malle, Louis 84
Mallory, Patricia 68
Malotte, Albert Hay 240
The Maltese Falcon (1941) 5, 9, 41
The Man About Town (1939) 156
The Man Behind the Door (1915) 133
The Man from U.N.C.L.E. 112, 113
The Man in the Gray Flannel Suit (1956) 229
The Man on a Flying Trapeze (1934) 201
The Man on a Tightrope (1953) 133
The Man on the Eiffel Tower (1950) 42
Man Trouble (1930) 153
The Man Who Came to Dinner (1942) 217
The Man Who Loved Cat Dancing (1973) 221
The Man Who Shot Liberty Valance (1962) 234
The Man with the Golden Gun 80
Mancini, Henry 119
Mandalay Drive 214, 215, 216
Manhandled (1924) 139
Manhattan Cocktail (1928) 213, 214
Manhattan Melodrama (1935) 172, 192

Manhattan Place 70
Mann, Abbe 196
Mann, William J. 25
Manners, Margaret 103
Mannix (television series) 120
Mannix, Eddie 108
Mannix, Toni 108
Manpower (1941) 90
Mansfield, Jayne 7, 118
Mansfield Street 74
Manson, Charles 23, 112, 113, 187, 192, 232, 235
Manson Family 23, 112, 113, 187, 192, 232, 235
Mantrap (1926) 135
The Many Lives of Dobie Gillis 160
Maple Drive 123
Mapleton Drive 155, 156
Marbury, Elizabeth 182
March, Eve 85
March, Fredric 116, 120
Marie Antoinette (1938) 120
Marie Antoinette Apartments 165
Marion, Frances 114, 115
The Mark of the Vampire (1932) 172
The Mark of Zorro (1940) 9
Marley, Pev 150
Marlowe, Don 13
Marquesas Way 232
Marquette, Ron 43
marriage, studio arranged 23, 24, 47, 83, 139, 140, 234
The Marriage Circle (1924) 12, 133
Married ... with Children (television series) 25, 249
Marshall, Herbert 68
Marshall, Peter 86
Martin, Betty 178
Martin, Dean 38, 81, 123, 149, 163, 178
Martin, Dino 123
Martin, Mary 147
Martin, Steve 36
Martin, Strother 241
Martin, Tony 241
Marx, Chico 123, 144, 238
Marx, Groucho 74, 82, 144, 189
Marx, Gummo 144, 238
Marx, Harpo 123, 144, 218
Marx, Zeppo 132, 144
Marx Brothers 74, 75, 82, 144
Mary Hartman, Mary Hartman (television series) 17
Mary Poppins (1964) 167
The Mask of Fu Manchu (1932) 131
Mason, James 97, 98
Mason, Pamela 97, 98
Massey, Edith 165
Mata Hari (1931) 71
Mathis, June 9

The Mating Game (1959) 38
Matthau, Walter 192
Matuszak, John 46
Maxwell, Marilyn 67
Mayer, Louis B. 4, 48, 57, 70, 91, 93, 98, 117, 120, 121, 139, 149, 153, 159, 160, 172, 173, 182, 194, 196, 234
Mayer, Margaret 98
MCA Corporation 143
Me and My Gal (1932) 60
Meadows, Audrey 84
Meadows, Jayne 84
A Medal for Benny (1945) 209
Meet Me in St. Louis (1944) 127
Meet the Stewarts (1942) 194
Melcher, Marty 240
"Memories Are Made of This" 121
The Men from Shiloh 213
Men of Annapolis (television serial) 213
Menendez, Eric 124, 125
Menendez, Jose 59, 124, 125
Menendez, Kitty 124, 125
Menendez, Lyle 124, 125
Menjou, Adolphe 5, 133
mental illness 98, 104, 110
Mercury Theater 11, 167
Merrill, Gary 171
The Merry Widow (1924) 107
The Merry Widow (1934) 147
Methot, Mayo 58
Metro Studios 98
The Mexican Spitfire (1939) 76, 129
The Mexican Spitfire at Sea (1942) 129
The Mexican Spitfire in Mexico (1941) 129
The Mexican Spitfire Sees a Ghost (1943) 129
Mezzaluna Restaurant 173, 174
MGM Studios 38, 54, 60, 68, 109, 110, 127, 141, 142, 179, 195, 217
Michael, George 127
Michale Avenue 222, 223
Micheltorena Drive 23, 24
A Midsummer Night's Dream (1935) 120, 229
The Mighty Barnum (1935) 116, 133
Mildred Pierce (1945) 214
Milken, Michael 96, 216
Milland, Ray 151, 210
Millbrook Drive 212
Miller, Ann 98
Miller, Glenn 119
Miller, Marvin 165
Millete, Dorothy 110
The Million Dollar Legs (1932) 127
Mills, Harry 241
Milocevic, Milos 177

Milstead, Harris Glenn 41, 42
Min and Bill (1930) 101, 126
Mineo, Sal 56
Minnelli, Liza 96, 127
Minnelli, Vincente 57, 118, 127
Minor, Charlie 88
Minter, Mary Miles 3, 192, 193, 238, 252, 253
The Miracle of Morgan's Creek (1944) 116, 229
The Miracle on 34th Street (1947) 18, 58
Miranda, Carmen 134, 135
Misery (1990) 167
Missing in Action (1961) 32
Mr. Belvedere (1941) 11, 91
Mr. Belvedere Rings a Bell (1943) 86
Mr. Deeds Goes to Town (1937) 183
"Mr. Fix-it" (drug dealer) 3
Mr. Hobbs Takes a Vacation (1962) 38
Mr. Magoo (cartoon serial) 183
Mr. Moto (1935) 41
Mr. Peepers (television series) 152
Mr. Roberts (1954) 85, 186
Mr. Smith Goes to Washington (1941) 100, 102, 214, 218
Mitchell, Cameron 192
Mitchell, Thomas 102
Mitchelson, Marvin 98
Mitchum, Robert 52, 53, 147
Mix, Tom 127, 238
mob hit(s), death by 28, 29, 46, 49, 59
The Mod Squad (television serial) 120
Mogambo (1953) 151
Monaco Drive 185
The Money Pit (1984) 59
Monkey Business (1931) 82
Monohan, Mabel 245, 246
Monroe, Marilyn 4, 35, 63, 64, 82, 96, 118, 122, 154, 162, 163, 164, 176, 177, 179, 180, 196, 212
Montalban, Ricardo 120, 202
Montand, Yves 96
Monte Carlo (1930) 147
Monte Leon Drive 79
Montgomery, Elizabeth 105
Montgomery, Robert 105, 149
Monti, Carlotta 22
Moonraker (1979) 80
Moonstone Court 234, 235
Moore, Colleen 145
Moore, Grace 91, 170
Moore, Terry 96, 118
Moore, Tim 249
Moorehead, Agnes 91, 103, 166
Moreno, Antonio 23, 49
Moreno Drive 177
The Morey Amsterdam Show (television series) 82
Morgan, Frank 115, 116, 121
Morgan, Michele 80

Morgan, Ralph 116
Morgan, Vickie 61, 107, 206, 207
Morning Glory (1933) 99
Morris, Chester 127, 128
Morrison, Jim 78
Morrow, Vic 87, 225, 248, 249
Morton, Gary 101
Motion Picture (magazine) 135
Motion Picture Country Home
  and Hospital 122, 131
Motion Picture Relief Fund 131
Moulin Rouge (1920) 77
Mouse, Mickey 117
Movie Weekly (magazine) 178
Movin' On (television series) 247
Mrs. Parkington (1944) 218
Muir, Florabelle 60
Muirfield Drive 72, 73
Mulholland Drive 23, 47, 69, 88,
  89, 90
Mulholland House 89, 90
Mulholland Terrace 49
Mull, Martin 178
Multiview Drive 45
Munchkins 5
Muni, Paul 9, 120
murder, death by 9, 12, 13, 17, 22,
  23, 25, 26, 28, 29, 30, 35, 36,
  39, 46, 48, 49, 51, 52, 56, 62, 63,
  64, 65, 66, 67, 69, 81, 86, 88, 89,
  99, 108, 109, 112, 113, 119, 121,
  124, 133, 138, 143, 160, 166, 167,
  187, 188, 192, 193, 200, 206, 207,
  211, 212, 215, 216, 219, 222, 223,
  224, 232, 235, 243, 244, 246,
  249, 250, 251, 252, 253, 254
The Murder Man (1935) 100
Murder, Inc. 28
Murders in the Rue Morgue (1932)
  19
Murdoch, Rupert 114
Murphy, Audie 241
Murray, Bill 178
Murray, Charlie 20, 75
Murray, Eunice 177
Murray, Ken 37
Muscle Beach Party (1964) 41
The Musketeers of Pig Alley (1912)
  137
Mutiny on the Bounty (1935) 33,
  40, 194, 214
My Dear Secretary (1952) 205
My Favorite Martian (television
  series) 160
My Friend Flicka 120
My Friend Irma (1948) 38, 123
My Little Chickadee (1940) 22
My Man (1916) 157
My Man (1928) 157
My Sister Sam (television series)
  62
My World and Welcome to It (tele-
  vision series) 57, 84
The Mystery of the Wax Museum
  (1933) 184

The Naked Jungle (1954) 210
Napoli Drive 186
National Velvet (1944) 99, 238
natural gas, death by 32
Naturalist Church murders 48
Natwick, Mildred 100
Naughty Marietta (1935) 147
NBC 38, 45
Neal, Patricia 119
Neal, Tom 42
Neff, Wallace 103, 114
Negri, Pola 133, 147, 153, 182, 234
Neighbors (1977) 56
Nelson, David 39
Nelson, Harriet (Hilliard) 39, 40,
  242
Nelson, Oscar "Ham" 88
Nelson, Ozzie 39, 40, 242
Nelson, Rick 90, 242
Nestor Film Company 1
Network (1976) 9, 96
Never Give a Sucker an Even Break
  (1921) 74
Never Wave at a WAC (1953) 38
New Wave Hookers (1993) 46
Newley, Anthony 179
Newman, Paul 140
Newman, Valerie 210
NewsRadio (television series) 219
Niblo, Fred 114
Nichols, Ernest Loring Red 240
Nicholson, Jack 89, 107
nickelodeon 1, 2
A Night at Casablanca (1946) 82
A Night at the Opera (1937) 74,
  82
The Night Has a Thousand Eyes
  (1948) 162
Night Stalker Murders 249, 250
A Nightmare on Elm Street (1984)
  44
Nimoy, Leonard 149
Nine Months (1995) 43
Ninotchka (1939) 147
Niven, David 120, 141, 170, 185
Niven, Primula Rollo 170
No, No, Nanette (1930) 139
Nolan, Lloyd 163
None but the Lonely Heart (1944)
  141
Norma Place 68, 69
Norma Rae (1979) 172
Normand, Mabel 20, 75, 192, 253
Norris, Edward 217
Norris, Eleanor 222
North by Northwest (1959) 151
The Northern Trail (1921) 71
The Notorious (1947) 151
Novak, Kim 9, 104, 148, 149
Novarro, Ramon 12, 49
Now Vayager (1941) 15
Nurmi, Maila "Vampira" 247

Oak Glen Drive 45
Oakhurst Drive 68

Oakie, Jack 238
Oakmont Drive 180
Oberon, Merle 68, 237
O'Brian, Hugh 206
O'Brien, Edmund 226
O'Brien, Pat 60, 226
Ocean Avenue 193, 194, 197
Ocean House 199
O'Connor, Carroll 188, 189
O'Connor, Donald 179
O'Connor, Hugh 188, 189
Octopussy (1983) 80
The Odd Couple (1960) 45
Of Human Bondage (1934) 99, 132
Ogden Avenue 43
Oh, God! (1977) 212
Okinawa (1946) 192
Oland, Warner 54
The Old Dark House (1932) 186
Oldfield, Barney 226, 229
Oliver Twist (1921) 226
Olivier, Sir Laurence 86, 104
On Golden Pond (1981) 150
On Her Majesty's Secret Service
  (1969) 80
On the Town (1950) 130
On the Waterfront (1954) 221
One Million B.C. (1940) 185
One Night in the Tropics (1940)
  192
Ono, Yoko 96
Opposite Sex (1956) 217
Orange Drive 12, 77
Orbison, Roy 163
O'Rourke, Heather 199
Orry-Kelly, Jack 24
Our Gang (movie serial) 5, 104,
  180
Our Town (1940) 102
Out of the Fog (1941) 208
The Outlaw Josey Wales (1976)
  200
Outside the Law (1920) 172
Outward Bound (1930) 132
Overland Trail 213
Owlwood 118
Oxford Way 96, 97
Ozcot 14

Pacific Coast Highway 190, 191
Pacino, Al 138
Pal Joey (1957) 80
The Paleface (1922) 97
Palisades Avenue 196, 197
Palisades Beach Road 194, 195,
  196, 199
Palliko, Alan 246
Palliko, Judy Davis 246
Palliko, Kathryn 246
Palm Drive 121, 122
Palmer, Lilli 170, 185, 237
Palo Vista Drive 47
Pamela Drive 97, 98
The Pamela Mason Show (televi-
  sion series) 98

Pancoast, Marvin 207
Pandelios, Kim 25
The Panic 98
Pantages, Alexander 240, 253
Pantages Theater 240, 253
The Paper Dolls 157
Paramount Studios 87, 95, 99, 138, 212
Parent, Ronald 112, 113
Parker, Dorothy 68, 69
Parker, Marion 252
Parsaigian, Harry 188, 189
Parsons, Louella 42, 106, 229
Password (television series) 67
Pasternak, Joseph 149
Pat and Mike (1952) 60
Paterson, Pat 88, 89, 226
Pathé Film Company 203
Paths of Glory (1957) 171
The Patriot (1929) 71
The Patsy (1964) 41
The Pawns of Destiny (1915) 66
The Pawnshop (1915) 133
Payton, Barbara 42
Peck Drive 143
Peete, Louise 187, 188
Peggy (1916) 168
Penn, Joni Leigh 209
People Are Funny (1946) 39
The People vs. Larry Flynt (1996) 146
Peppard, George 87
The Perfect Fool 167
The Perils of Paulene (1947) 222
Perkins, Anthony 47
Perkins, Emmett 245
Perkins, Osgood 47
Perugia Way 186
Pete Kelly's Blues (1955) 118
Peter the Great (1923) 42
Peters, Elizabeth 238
Peters, Jean 96
Petersen, Paul 160
Petrified Forest (1936) 155
Petticoat Junction (television series) 113
Peyton Place (1957) 133, 160
Pfeiffer, Dee Dee 43
Pfeiffer, Michelle 43, 182
Pfeiffer, Virginia 46
The Pharmacist (1933) 22
The Philadelphia Story (1940) 100, 238
Phillips, John 145, 147
Phillips, Michelle 145, 147
Phoenix, River 59
Pickfair 2, 27, 103, 104, 195
Pickfair Way 104
Pickford, Charlotte (Smith) 98
Pickford, Jack 3, 98, 237, 238
Pickford, Lottie 98, 237
Pickford, Mary 2, 3, 35, 95, 98, 103, 104, 134, 147, 180, 192, 195, 237
The Picnic (1956) 148

The Picture of Dorian Gray (1945) 152
The Pillow of Death (1945) 17
Pillow Talk (1959) 84
Pinehurst Drive 35
Pink Panther (movie series) 107
The Pirate (1948) 127
The Pit and the Pendulum (1961) 61
Pittman, Jim 143
Pitts, Zasu 182, 189, 226
Plan 9 from Outer Space (1956) 19, 247, 248
Planes, Trains and Automobiles (1990) 183
Planet of the Apes (1972) 56
The Platinum Blonde (1931) 121
Playboy (magazine) 161, 162, 164
Plaza Suites Apartments 42
Pleshette, Suzanne 141
Plunkett, Ned 81
pnuemonia, death by 151, 184, 189, 195
Pocketful of Miracles (1961) 84, 102
Poitier, Sidney 99
Polanski, Roman 89
Polo Lounge 96
Poltergeist (1982) 66, 163
The Pool Shark (1915) 22
Porgy and Bess (1959) 66, 92, 238
pornography 46
Porter, Cole 118
Porter, Edwin S. 1
The Poseidon Adventure (1972) 58
Posetano Road 189, 190
Possessed (1947) 56
The Postman Always Rings Twice (1946) 133, 160
Powder River (1953) 192
Powell, Dick 91, 165, 214
Powell, Eleanor 9, 142, 143
Powell, Frank 124
Powell, William 79, 121, 240
Power, Tyrone, Jr. 7, 8, 12, 17, 149, 170
Power, Tyrone, Sr. 12
The Power and the Glory (1945) 96
Preminger, Otto 147
Prentiss, Ed 192
Presenting Lilli Mars (1943) 67
The President Vanishes (1934) 129
Presley, Elvis 156
Pretty Baby (1978) 84
Pretty Woman (1992) 13, 14, 144
Prevost, Marie 12
Price, Vincent 41, 61, 171, 176
The Price of Fear (1956) 48
The Pride of St. Louis (1952) 86
The Pride of the Yankees (1942) 118
Princeton, New Jersey 1
Prine, Andrew 65
Pringle, Eunice 253
Prinze, Freddie 58, 158, 161, 241
The Prison Warden (1949) 99

Prisoner of War (1954) 47
The Prisoner of Zenda (1922) 15, 49, 247
The Private Life of Henry VIII (1933) 40
Proffer, Sydney 110
prostitution 42, 43, 51, 57, 61, 107, 108, 148
The Proud and the Profane (1956) 194
Prowse, Juliet 81, 156
Pruter, Paula 184
Psycho (1960) 47, 52, 151
Public Enemy (1931) 121
Public Menace (1935) 17
publicity stunt(s) 66, 124, 125
Purviance, Edna 253
Pygmalion (1938) 132

Quebec Drive 30
Queen Elizabeth (liner) 233
Queen Florence Lane 221
The Queen of the Nightclubs (1929) 90
Quine, Richard 238
Quinn, Anthony 22, 120, 171, 176
Quinn, Christopher 22

racism 73
Radin, Roy 211, 212
Raft, George 28, 88, 90, 101, 208, 240, 241
Raging Bull (1981) 44
Rains, Claude 120
The Rake's Progress (1945) 237
Rally 'Round the Flag, Boys! (1942) 214
Ramanos, Nicco 213
Rambova, Natacha 14, 111, 112
Ramirez, Richard 249, 250
Ramis, Harold 178
Ramond, Harald 129
Rancho Street 217, 218
Rangely Drive 66
rape 2, 3, 7, 9, 51, 52, 89, 145, 146, 244, 253
Raphael, Stephen 145
Rappaport, David 49
Rappe, Virginia 7
Rasputin and the Empress (1933) 141
The Rat Pack 81, 104, 123, 148
The Rat Patrol 165
Rathbone, Basil 23
Rathbone, Ouida 23
Rathbun, Charles 25
The Raven (1915) 172
The Raven (1933) 19
The Raven (1962) 61
Ravenswood Apartments 77
Rawls, Lou 254
Raye, Martha 152, 179
Raymond, Gene 147, 189
Raymond, Ray 30, 31
The Razor's Edge (1946) 68, 91

Reagan, Ronald 47, 82, 107, 217, 226
Reap the Wild Wind (1942) 17, 91
Rear Window (1954) 100, 151
"Reason to Believe" 77
Rebecca (1940) 151, 152
The Rebel (television series) 85
Rebel Without a Cause (1955) 56, 85, 151, 213
Reckless (1935) 129
The Red Badge of Courage (1951) 5
The Red Beret (1953) 80
Red Dust (1932) 121, 189
Red Headed Woman (1932) 71, 121
The Red Lantern (1918) 101
Red Light Bandit 47, 244, 245
Red River (1948) 86, 240
The Red Shoe Diaries (television series) 43
The Red Skelton Show (television series) 67
Redford, Robert 150
Redgrave sisters 74
Redwing Street 221
Reed, Donna 126, 163
Reed, Robert 242, 243
The Reel Virginian (1924) 127
Reeves, George 108
The Reformer and the Redhead (1940) 165
Reid, Wallace 3
Reinhardt, Max 147
Reles, Abe "Kid Twist" 29
Relph, Phyllis 184
Remick, Lee 171
Renoir, Auguste 105
Renoir, Jean 66, 105
Requiem for a Heavyweight (1958) 169
respiratory failure, death by 123
Restless Souls (1918) 70
Rexford Drive 91, 92
Rhapsody in Blue (1945) 11, 79, 95
"Rhapsody in Blue" 92
Rhythm on the Range (1936) 152
Ricca, Paul 137
Rich, Buddy 163
Rich Man, Poor Man (television series) 161
Richardson, Helen 65, 238
Riddell, Robert A. 73
Riddle, Nelson 11
The Riders of Destiny (1933) 234
Ridgedale Drive 115, 116
Ridgeley, Andrew 127
Ridpath Drive 52
The Right Cross (1943) 165
Riklis, Meshulam 103–104
Rin-Tin-Tin 160
Rio Bravo (1958) 234, 247
Rio Lobo (1970) 206
Ripperton, Minnie 163, 164
Riptide (1934) 68
RKO Studios 31, 72, 182, 199

Roach, Hal 2, 180, 190, 197, 198, 203, 223, 248
Road to Hong Kong (1962) 209
Road to Mandalay (1927) 172
Road to Rio (1948) 209
Road to Singapore (1940) 209
Road to Utopia (1945) 209
Road to Zanzibar (1941) 45, 209
Robards, Jason 241
Robards, Jason Nilson 241
Robert Montgomery Presents (television series) 105
Roberts, Bobby 166
Roberts, Brooke 166
Roberts, Julia 13, 144
Roberts, Theodore 9
Robertson, Cliff 140
Robin and the Seven Hoods (1964) 123
Robinson, Dar Allen 242
Robinson, Edward G. 11, 26, 45, 90, 195
Robinson, Edward G., Jr. 11
The Rock (1996) 148
The Rockford Files (television series) 46
Rockingham Drive 100, 180, 181, 182
Rocky and Bullwinkle Presents (cartoon serial) 238
Rod Serling's Night Gallery (television series) 185
Rodeo Drive 129, 130, 131
Roeder, Ervin 85, 86
Rogers, Charles "Buddy" 67, 103, 104, 213
Rogers, Ginger 26, 99, 176
Rogers, Millicent 112
Rogers, Virginia 197
Rogers, Will 79, 82, 157, 187, 238
Roland, Gilbert 135, 136
Roland, Ruth 136
Roll, Ernest 246
Roman, Ruth 205
Roman Scandals (1934) 79
The Romance (1930) 17
Romeo and Juliet (1909) 66
Romeo and Juliet (1936) 131
Romero, Cesar 170
Rookies on Parade (1941) 37
Room Service (1938) 82
Rooney, Barbara Ann Thomason 177
Rooney, Mickey 71, 149, 177, 206
Roosevelt, Eleanor 182
Rosalie (1937) 142
Roscomare Road 152
Rose, Billy 158
Rose Marie (1936) 147
Rose o' the Sea (1922) 117
The Rose Tattoo (1951) 56
Roselli, Johnny 81, 138
Rosemarie 82
Rossellini, Roberto 112
Rossmore Avenue 77

Rosson, Harold 121
Round Valley Road 212
Rowlands, Gena 48
Roxbury Drive 99, 100, 101, 102, 136, 137, 142, 143
Royal Sherman Apartments 167
Rubens, Alma 70, 71
Rubin, Jerry 166
Rudolph, Lillian 241
Rudolph, Minnie Ripperton *see* Ripperton, Minnie
Ruggles, Charlie 236
Ruggles, Wesley 236
Rummel, Sam 49
Rummell Park 89
"Runaway" 249
Running on Empty (1988) 59
Russell, Gail 162
Russell, Jane 149
Russell, Lee 68
Russell, Rosalind 129, 229, 230
The Russians Are Coming, the Russians Are Coming (1964) 177

Sabrina (1954) 194
Sagal, Boris 249
Sagal, Katey 249
Sahara (1943) 157
Sailor Beware (1955) 57
The Saint (serial, 1939–1945) 152
St. Cloud Road 146
St. Elmo (1922) 99
St. Elsewhere (television series) 87, 222
St. Ives Drive 60
St. Johns, Adela Rogers 15
St. Pierre Road 145, 146
Saldana, Theresa 44
Saltair Drive 169, 170, 171, 186
Saltzman, Harry 80
Salute to the Marines (1943) 67
Sampson, Teddy 20
Sanders, George 152
The Sandpipers (1965) 113
Sands, Cinnamon 235
The Sands of Iwo Jima (1949) 234
San Francisco International Airport (television series) 157
San Simeon 93, 199
"Santa Claus Is Coming to Town" 240
The Santa Fe Trail (1940) 56
Santa Monica Boulevard 5, 161
Santo, Jack 245
San Vicente Boulevard 173, 174
San Ysidro Drive 104
Saps at Sea (1940) 127
Sarah Street 208
Saratoga (1937) 121
Sargent, Dick 47
Satterly, Peggy Lee 145, 146
Saturday Night and Sunday Morning (1960) 110

Saturday Night Live (television series) 56, 219
Savage (1921) 153
Savannah 46
Say It Again (1926) 222
Scala, Gia 48, 229
Scaramouche (1927) 71
Scared Stiff (1953) 57, 135
Scarface (1932) 9, 90, 121
The Scarlet Pimpernel (1934) 132
Schaeffer, Rebecca 62, 63
Schenck, Joseph 15, 42, 118, 136, 230, 251
Schroeder, Rick 101
Schwab's Drugstore 92
Schwartz, Mark 167
Scott, Randolph 24, 25, 26
Scott, Zachary 217
Sea Hunt (television series) 157
Seale, Bobby 166
Seattle Drive 47
Sebring, Jay 110, 112, 113
Secrets (1932) 103
See Here Private Hargrove (1944) 186
Seinfeld, Jake 152
Selby Avenue 166
Selfridge, Gordon 17
Sellers, Peter 107
Sellers, Victoria 107
Selznick, David O. 91, 98, 103, 107, 186, 238
Selznick, Irene Mayer 139
Selznick, Mary Jennifer 166
Semi-Tough (1980) 169
Senalda Drive 38
Sennett, Mack 7, 12, 20, 45, 75, 101, 126, 222, 223, 230
Sergeant Madden (1939) 101
Sergeant York (1941) 11, 95, 118
Sergeants Three (1962) 123
Serling, Rod 185
711 Ocean Drive (1950) 86
Seventh Heaven (1927) 5
Seventh Heaven (1937) 100
Shadow of a Doubt (1943) 108, 167
The Shadows (1959) 48
The Shaggy Dog (1958) 58
"Shall We Dance" 99
Shampoo (1975) 140
Shane (1953) 56
Shannon, Del 249
Shannon, Peg 206
Shaw, Artie 149
Shaw, Frank 22
Shawn, Dick 225
She Done Him Wrong (1933) 136
She Wore a Yellow Ribbon (1949) 86, 234
Shearer, Douglas 232
Shearer, Norma 68, 90, 160, 195, 232, 240
Sheen, Martin 107
The Sheik (1921) 66, 111, 133
Shelby, Charlotte 192, 193, 238, 253

Shelton Hotel 17
The Shemp Howard Show 204
Shenandoah (1966) 213
Sheridan, Ann 217
Sherlock, Jr. (1924) 97
Sherwood Place 211, 212
Shields, Jimmy 173, 201
Ship Ahoy (1942) 142
shooting, death by 12, 26, 29, 32, 35, 39, 42, 43, 46, 47, 48, 49, 52, 62, 63, 68, 77, 81, 88, 89, 91, 106, 108, 109, 112, 113, 127, 138, 140, 141, 143, 158, 161, 177, 188, 189, 192, 193, 200, 201, 202, 206, 209, 211, 212, 217, 218, 219, 222, 223, 224, 232, 235, 244, 246, 248, 249, 250, 251, 253, 254
The Shootist (1976) 100, 234
Shore, Dinah 81, 96, 97, 205
Shore, Pauly 46
Shorecliff Condominiums 194
Shoreham Drive 59
Shoreham Towers Apartments 58, 59
Shoreham Towers Condominiums 58, 59
Short, Beth 12, 14
The Show Off (1946) 67
The Shriek of Araby (1923) 127
Siegel, Benjamin "Bugsy" 4, 9, 28, 34, 45, 59, 88, 90, 92, 99, 119, 138, 139
Siegel, Esther 29
Sienna Way 149, 150
Sierra Towers Apartments 61
Silent Movie Theater 62, 63
The Silent World (1956) 84
Sills, Milton 153, 154
Simon, Neil 150
Simon, Simone 103
"Simple Song of Freedom" 77
Simpson, Don 148
Simpson, Marguerite 174, 180, 216
Simpson, Nicole Brown 170, 173, 174, 175, 180, 181, 215, 216
Simpson, O.J. 4, 62, 166, 173, 174, 175, 180, 181, 182, 215, 216
Sinatra, Frank 63, 64, 80, 81, 104, 120, 123, 148, 149, 156, 219
Sinatra, Nancy 81
Sing, Baby, Sing (1936) 133
Singin' in the Corn (1946) 237
Singin' in the Rain (1954) 130
The Singing Marine (1939) 165
Single Wives (1924) 26
The Sins of the Father (1929) 42
Skelton, Red 149
Slatzer, Robert 177
Slausen Avenue 225
Slide, Kelly, Slide (1927) 173
Sloan, Everett 183
The Small Town Girl (1936) 66
Smiley, Al 138

Smith, Anna Nicole 177
Smith, Cathy 56
Sneakers (1987) 59
Sneeze (1893) 1
Snow White and the Seven Dwarfs (1936) 70
Snyder, Moe "The Gimp" 45
Snyder, Paul 161
So Proudly We Hail (1943) 108
So This Is Paris (1926) 139
Sobek, Linda 25
Solomon and Sheba (1959) 9
Some Like it Hot (1959) 154, 180
Somebody Up There Likes Me (1956) 142
The Son of Frankenstein (1939) 19
The Son of the Sheik (1926) 66, 68
The Song of Bernadette (1952) 61, 221
Song of India (1949) 242
Sonny and Cher 118, 146
Sonora Avenue 244
Sothern, Ann 147, 189
Spellbound (1946) 151
Spelling, Aaron 156
Spencer, Herbert 12
The Spiral Staircase (1946) 141
The Spirit of St. Louis (1957) 100
The Spitfire (1934) 54
The Spitfire (1943) 132
Splendor (1935) 168
The Spoilers (1930) 118
The Sporting Life (1963) 110
Spreckles, Kay 216
The Spy Who Loved Me (1977) 80
The Squaw Man (1913) 2
stabbing, death by 12, 13, 23, 26, 56, 99, 112, 113, 133, 174, 175, 192, 243, 246, 250
Stack, Robert 120, 146
Stage Door Canteen (1943) 131, 167
Stagecoach (1939) 102
Stalag 17 (1953) 194
stalking 25, 26, 34, 44, 45, 63, 88
Stanciu, Bobby 39
Stand by for Action (1942) 67
Stand by Me (1986) 59
Stander, Lionel 183
Stanley Avenue 40
Stanton, Harry Dean 89
Stanwyck, Barbara 30, 68, 83, 179, 180, 183, 214, 218
Star 80 161, 164
Star Dust (1940) 150
A Star Is Born (1937) 5, 133, 183, 214
star maps 2
Stark, Ray 155
State of the Union (1948) 133
Steamboat Bill, Jr. (1928) 97
Stein, Gertrude 182
Stella (1950) 217
Stella Dallas (1925) 131
Stengel, Casey 237

Sterling, Ford 20, 75
Sterling, Jan 38
Stevens, Inger 48
Stevenson, Parker 217
Stewart, Anita 116, 117
Stewart, Gloria 99, 100
Stewart, Jimmy 15, 56, 99, 100, 214, 219
Stewart, Peggy 206
Stewart, Rod 77
Stiller, Mauritz 153
Stockton, Henry 246
Stockton, Sandra 246
The Stolen Life (1946) 17
Stompanato, Johnny 99, 132–133
Stone, Lewis 71, 72
Stone, Sly 147
Stone Canyon Road 148, 149
Stoneridge Road 242
Stonesboro Place 213
Stop Me If You've Heard This One 82
The Story of Mankind (1957) 38
The Story of Three Loves (1953) 141
Strange Cargo (1940) 41
Strangers in the Night (1923) 247
Strangers on the Train (1955) 151
strangulation, death by 65, 66, 67, 69, 243
Stratten, Dorothy 161, 162, 163, 164; *see also* Hoogstratten, Dorothy
The Strawberry Blonde (1941) 214
Street Angel (1928) 5
A Streetcar Named Desire (1948)
Streisand, Barbra 140
Strickling, Howard 109, 110, 172, 178
Stripes (1981) 183
stroke, death by 41, 91, 119, 123, 152, 180, 198, 203, 204, 210
The Student Prince (1927) 131, 147
suicide 2, 11, 12, 15, 17, 18, 26, 35, 36, 39, 42, 43, 46, 47, 49, 54, 56, 57, 59, 60, 61, 64, 66, 68, 79, 81, 88, 89, 95, 111, 117, 118, 127, 129, 130, 140, 141, 142, 150, 151, 152, 153, 154, 156, 158, 160, 161, 172, 173, 177, 182, 183, 185, 186, 187, 188, 189, 198, 199, 200, 201, 202, 206, 109, 217, 219, 220, 224, 226, 232, 244, 245, 249
Sullavan, Margaret 100, 168
Sullivan, Barry 212
Sultan of Brunei 96
The Summer Storm (1944) 150
Summer Vacation (1984) 183
Summit Drive 103, 104
The Sun Also Rises (1957) 9
Sunbrook Drive 113, 114
Sunset Bermuda Apartments 44
Sunset Boulevard (1950) 14, 194
Sunset Crest Drive 52
Sunset Marquis Hotel 243

Sunset Murders 243
Sunset Plaza Drive 57, 58
Sunset Strip 56, 57, 58, 59, 60, 61
Super Password (television series) 169
Superman 105
Sutter's Gold (1936) 218
Sutton Drive 213
Swallow Drive 61
Swamp Water (1926) 105
"Swanee" 92
Swanson, Gloria 14, 26, 101, 114, 130, 131
Sweeney, John 66, 67
Sweet, Blanche 17
The Sweethearts (1938) 147
Sweetzer Avenue 62
Swing Time (1936) 99
Switzer, Carl "Alfalfa" 5, 6, 248
Sycamore Avenue 35, 64
Sylvan Street 222
syphilis 3

tabloid press 19, 47, 56
Take Me Out to the Ballgame (1949) 80, 130
Talent Scout (television series) 67
Talk About a Lady (1945) 204
The Talk of the Town (1942) 157
Talmadge, Connie 11
Talmadge, Natalie 11, 97, 98
Talmadge, Norma 11, 15, 42, 69, 136
Talman, William 242
Tamarind Apartments 25, 26
Tamarind Drive 25, 26
Tara Drive 216
The Tarnished Lady (1931) 40, 60
Tartikoff, Brandon 87
Tarzan (1930) 129
Tarzan (character, television series) 36, 129, 145, 219, 220, 242
Tarzan, the Ape Man (1932) 172
Tarzana Drive 219, 220
Tashman, Lilyan 139, 140
Tate, Sharon 110, 112, 113, 187, 192, 224, 226, 227, 232, 246
Tattletales (television series) 169
The Taxi (1953) 48
Taylor, Elizabeth 96, 99, 106, 147, 217
Taylor, Robert 67, 83, 183, 237
Taylor, William Desmond 3, 9, 192, 193, 238, 253
Teesdale Street 208, 209
Tell It to the Marines (1926) 173
Tell Them Willie Boy Is Here (1969) 212
Tellegen, Lou 26
Temple Hill Drive 182
Temple, Shirley 30
The Ten Commandments (1924) 28
The Ten Commandments (1956) 28

Terms of Endearment (1983) 39
Terror Island (1920) 50
Terry, Alice 33
Terry, Phillip 179
Tess of Storm Country (1922) 131
The Texan (1930) 118
Thalberg, Irving 5, 57, 92, 99, 109, 110, 160, 182, 186, 194, 195, 199, 240
That Darned Cat (1965) 167
That Lady in Ermine (1948) 147
That Night in Rio (1943) 135
"That's Amore" 121
That's Entertainment (1974) 130
Thaw, Evelyn Nesbit 176, 200, 201, 230
Thaw, Harry 200, 201, 230
These Glamour Girls (1939) 120
They All Laughed (1981) 161
"They Can't Take That Away From Me" 92
They Died with Their Boots On (1940) 141, 145
They Drive by Night (1940) 9, 208, 217
They Stooge to Conga (1942) 157
They Were Expendable (1945) 234
They Won't Forget (1937) 132
The Thin Man (1934) 79
The Third Day (1965) 68
The Third Man (1949) 167, 172
13 Washington Square (1928) 130
Thirteen Women (1932) 31
Thirty Seconds Over Tokyo (1944) 53, 186
This Could be the Night (1957) 38
This Is Your Life (television series) 35
This Land Is Mine (1943) 105
This Man's Navy (1945) 101
This Reckless Age (1932) 206
Thomas Lally Electric Theatre 1
Thomas, Danny 84
Thomas, Olive 3
Thomason, Barbara Ann *see* Rooney, Barbara Ann
Thompson, Stella Marie 42, 43
Thomson, Thomas 114, 115
Thoroughly Modern Millie (1967) 84
Thorson, Scott 240
Thrasher Drive 60
Three and a Half Weeks (1924) 127
Three Arabian Nuts 12
Three Cheers for the Irish (1940) 102
Three Coins in the Fountain (1954) 91
Three Jills and a Jeep (1946) 152
The Three Musketeers (1921) 5, 15, 133, 247
The Three Musketeers (1948) 133
The Three Stooges 12, 60, 61, 157, 201, 204, 205
Three Women (1924) 12
Three's a Crowd (1927) 46

throat infection, death by 160
Thunder Bay 86
The Thunder Rock (1942) 237
Thunderball (1965) 80
Thunderbolt (1929) 214
Thy Name Is Woman (1923) 15, 247
Tibbetts, Lawrence 92
Tierney, Gene 170
Tilden, Bill 27
Titanic (1953) 91
To Be or Not to Be (1942) 147, 156
Todd, Thelma 189, 190, 191, 208, 226
Toklas, Alice B. 182
Toler, Sidney 54
Tom Sawyer (1930) 17
Tomlin, Lilly 22
Tone, Franchot 42, 179
The Tonight Show (television series) 59, 157
Too Late for Blues (1961) 48
Top Gun 148
Topanga Canyon Park 222
Topper (1937) 168
Topper Returns (1941) 185
Topside 15, 17
The Torrent (1926) 70
Torreyson Drive 89
Tortilla Flats (1942) 116
Tortuoso Way 148, 149
Tower Grove Road 107
Tower Road 107
Tracy, Louise 60
Tracy, Spencer 27, 47, 57, 60, 155, 186, 226, 236, 237
Tramp, Tramp, Tramp (1926) 46
Traubel, Helen 163
Travolta, Helen 242
Treasure Island (1934) 71, 101
A Tree Grows in Brooklyn (1945) 237
Trousdale Place 84
True, John 245, 246
True Grit (1969) 234
Tugboat Annie (1933) 101, 126
Turner, Lana 81, 99, 132, 133, 160, 206
Turpin, Ben 127, 128, 130
Tuttle, Frank 165
Tuttle, Lurene 238
12 Angry Men (1957) 221
20th Century–Fox Studios 149, 237
The Twilight Zone (television series) 185
Twilight Zone—The Movie (1985) 87, 225, 248

Unaccustomed As We Are (1929) 189
Uncle Tom's Cabin (1919) 12
Under Capricorn (1950) 151
Under the Red Robe (1923) 70
The Unfaithful (1947) 217

Unfaithfully Yours (1948) 150
The Unholy Three (1925) 172
The Uninvited (1944) 162
United Artists Company 103
Universal City, California 2
The Unknown (1927) 172
Up in Arms (1944) 74
Up the River (1930) 60
uremic poisoning, death by 121, 123
Utter-McKinley Mortuary 59, 89, 90

Valentino, Alberto 112
Valentino, Rudolph 5, 7, 9, 14, 49, 68, 77, 90, 106, 111, 112, 114, 127, 133, 163, 187, 247
Vallee, Rudy 118
The Valley of the Dolls (1968) 113
Valley Vista Drive 212, 213, 214
Van Dyke, Dick 82
Van Dyke, Woody 147, 172
Van Nuys, Mary 86
Van Sickle, James 63
Van Zandt, Philip 11
Vann, Bruce 140
Vanowen Drive 223
Vargas, Alberto 3
Vargas Girl 3
Vasquez, Tiburico 51, 55
vaudeville 46, 68, 165
Velez, Lupe 53, 54, 76, 119, 129, 130, 172
The Velvet Touch (1948) 129
Venice Beach 232
Ventura Boulevard 216, 217
Verdugo Avenue 243
Verdugo Vista Drive 244
Vermont Avenue 253
Vertigo (1959) 148, 151
Victor/Victoria (1982) 119
Vidor, Charles 9
Vidor, King 10, 93
Viertel, Peter 31, 193
Viertel, Salka 31, 193
A View to a Kill (1985) 80
Vignola, Robert 14, 15
Villa Capri Restaurant 123, 213
The Village of the Damned (1960) 152
Villechaize, Herve 202, 203
Vine Street 26
The Violent Years (1957) 247
Viper Room 59
The Virginian (1927) 96, 221
The Virginian (television series) 221
The Virtuous Wives (1918) 117
Vista del Mar Avenue 28
Vitagraph Studios 30, 66, 68, 116, 117, 222
Vitascope 1
Viva Villa! (1934) 192
von Sternberg, Josef 137
von Stroheim, Eric 131

Vose Street 202
Voyage to the Bottom of the Sea (television series) 165
voyeurism 89, 103, 185

Wagenheim, Charles 17
Wagner, Robert 183
The Wagonmaster (1950) 86
Wagons Westward (1940) 120
Waikiki Wedding (1937) 152
Wake Island (1942) 108
Wake Up the Dream (1933) 77
A Walk in the Sun (1945) 157
Walker, Helen 205
Walker, Robert 170, 186
Wallace, Beryl 236
Walsh, Raoul 216, 251
Walston, Ray 160
Walther Way 175, 176
Wanger, Walter 143
The War of the Worlds (radio performance) 11, 40, 41, 183
Ward, Clara 238
The Warlock (1959) 214
Warner, Jack 19, 115
Warner Bros. Studios 37, 145, 206
Warren, Harry S. 163
Washington Post (newspaper) 128
The Waterloo Bridge (1931) 186
Watson, Tex 113
Watson, William 247
Watsonia Terrace 14, 15, 16
Waverly Drive 23
Way Down East (1935) 33
Way of the Flesh (1927) 42
Wayne, Bruce 242
Wayne, Carol 59
Wayne, David 186
Wayne, Esperanza "Chata" 210, 211, 217
Wayne, John 17, 86, 91, 100, 135, 162, 206, 210, 211, 217, 218, 233, 234
The Weaker Sex? (television series) 98
Weather Underground 113
Webb, Chick 117
Webb, Clifton 11, 83, 91
Webb, Jack 61, 242
Webb, Richard 209
Wedgewood Place 14
A Weekend in Havana (1941) 48
Weems, Ted 67
Weissmuller, Johnny 54, 129, 145
Welles, Orson 11, 40, 41, 167, 183, 200, 201
West, Eve Arden 162, 163
West, Mae 77
West, Roland 189, 190, 191
West of Zanzibar (1929) 99
West Side Story (1952) 56
Westbourne Avenue 66
Westgate Avenue 172, 173
Westholme Apartments 167

Westmore, Percival "Perc" 206
Westwood Memorial Park 162, 163, 164, 165
Weyburn Avenue 165
Whale, James 186
What a Way to Go! (1964) 74
What Next, Private Hargrove? (1957) 192
What Price Glory (1926) 236
Whatever Happened to Baby Jane? (1962) 73
Whatever Happened to Baby Jane? (1991) 74
The Wheeler Dealers (1963) 113
Where the Pavement Ends (1923) 49
White, Stanford 200, 201, 230
The White Alley (1916) 218
White Fang 176
White Flame Murders 244
The White Woman (1933) 14
Whitley, H.J. 14
Whitley Avenue 14, 15, 16, 17
Whitley Heights, California 14, 15, 16, 17, 187
Whitley Terrace 15, 16
Whittier Drive 117, 118
Wide Open Faces (1938) 180
Wilcox, Daieda 9
Wilcox, Horace 9
Wilcox Street 17
The Wild Bunch (1969) 20
The Wild Goose 234
The Wild Orchids (1929) 71
Wilde, Cornel 163
Wilder, Billy 30, 38, 161
Wilding, Michael 106
Wilkerson, William 132
Will Rogers Memorial Park 127
Willat, Irving 72
Willat Studios 72
William Morris Agency 122
Williams, Lionel R. 56, 57
Wilsey, Shannon 46
Wilshire Boulevard 165, 166, 167, 201

Wilshire Comstock Apartments 159
Wilshire Manning Apartment 166, 167
Wilson, Brian 57, 149
Wilson, Carl 57, 58
Wilson, Dennis 57, 58, 163, 187, 232
Wilson, Marie 37, 38, 240
Wilton Place 252
Win, Lose, or Draw (television series) 169
Winger, Debra 39
Wings (1927) 135, 249
The Winning of Barbara Worth (1927) 118
Winston, Al 204
Winwood, Estelle 165
witchcraft 160
With a Song in My Heart (1952) 91
Withers, Jane 154
The Witness (1985) 59
Witness for the Prosecution (1957) 9
The Wizard (television series) 49
The Wizard of Oz (1939) 5, 14, 17, 57, 92, 93, 115, 116, 121, 152, 168, 226, 230
Woldemarian, Phillip 250
Wolf, George 34
Wolf Song (1929) 54, 76, 77, 34
Wolf's Lair 34
Woman (1939) 129, 206
"The Woman in Black" 7, 9
The Woman in the Window (1945) 45
A Woman of Affairs (1929) 71
A Woman Rebels (1936) 56
Woman of the Year (1941) 60
A Woman Under the Influence (1974) 87
Wonderland Drive 52, 53
Wonderland Drive Murders 52
Wood, Ed, Jr. 19, 247, 248
Wood, Natalie 48, 163
Woodburn Avenue 168

Woodrow Wilson Drive 46, 47, 48
Woodstock Road 48
Woody Woodpecker (cartoon character) 86
Woolf, Edgar Allen 92
Wright, Evelyn 244
Wright, Paul 244
The Wrong Door Raid 63, 64
Wuthering Heights (1939) 237
Wynn, Ed 22, 167, 169
Wynn, Keenan 167, 169

Xanadu (1980) 130

Yanks (1980) 110
The Yearling (1946) 238
You Bet Your Life (television series) 74
You Can't Take It with You (1938) 33, 100
You Only Live Twice (1967) 80
"You'll Never Know How Much I Love You" 163
Young, Loretta 60, 232, 233
The Young at Heart (1937) 168
The Young at Heart (1947) 147
The Young Lions (1958) 121
Youth Runs Wild (1944) 225
Yucca Street 12, 17

Zadora, Pia 103, 104
Zakall, S.Z. 236
Zanuck, Darryl 165, 202
Zappa, Ahmet 202
Zappa, Diva 202
Zappa, Dweezil 202
Zappa, Frank 165, 202
Zappa, Moon Unit 202
Zero, Christopher 232
Ziegfeld, Florenz 13, 167, 168
Ziegfeld Follies 3, 13, 17, 45, 79, 139, 157, 167, 168, 206
The Ziegfeld Follies (1944) 67, 127, 157
Zimbalist, Efrem, Jr. 34
Zukor, Adolph 2